7/98

REBECCA GRATZ

AMERICAN JEWISH CIVILIZATION SERIES

Editors

MOSES RISCHIN
San Francisco State University

JONATHAN D. SARNA
Brandeis University

*A complete listing of the books in this series
can be found at the back of this volume.*

REBECCA GRATZ

Women and Judaism in Antebellum America

DIANNE ASHTON

Wayne State University Press   Detroit

Library of Congress Cataloging-in-Publication Data

Ashton, Dianne.
    Rebecca Gratz : women and Judaism in antebellum America / Dianne
Ashton.
        p. cm.—(American Jewish civilization series)
    Includes bibliographical references and index.
    ISBN 0-8143-2666-8 (alk. paper)
    1. Gratz, Rebecca, 1781–1869. 2. Jews—Pennsylvania—
Philadelphia—Biography. 3. Jewish women—Pennyslvania—
Philadelphia—Biography. 4. Jewish religious education of
children—Pennsylvania—Philadelphia—History—19th century.
    5. Philadelphia (Pa.)—Biography. I. Title II. Series.
    F158.9.J5A84   1997
    917.48'11004924'0092—dc21
                                                          97-24407

All photos are courtesy of the American Jewish Archives, Cincinnati Campus,
Hebrew Union College, Jewish Institute of Religion.

For RICHARD

CONTENTS

ACKNOWLEDGMENTS

Some say the author's job is a lonely one, but I have shared in the advice and support of extraordinary individuals. I am especially grateful to the late Jacob Rader Marcus, who first urged me to turn a story about antebellum Jewish acculturation into a story about Gratz, warning me that I would have to "worry over" every letter she wrote. His personal attention to my work and his mastery of the early period in American Jewish history were crucial at the early stages of my research.

Early on, I received an extended fellowship to the American Jewish Archives that allowed me access to archival records and to enter a world of scholarship where antebellum Jews are known so well that they are the topic of dinner table gossip. Jonathan Sarna's informed and wise discussions, real interest, and excellent suggestions over the years have proved invaluable. Abraham Peck suggested new sources, posed interesting questions, and introduced me to Faith Rogow and Lance Sussman, colleagues then working at the archives, researching American Jewish women and Isaac Leeser. We formed a group whose enthusiasm and exchange of ideas made the work a true pleasure.

Thanks also to the Religion Department at Temple University for financial support and encouragement for my early work, which became my doctoral dissertation. I am deeply grateful to Rowan University for awarding me the time to complete this book through both research grants and a sabbatical leave.

When I began the project, the historical study of American Jewish women was barely alive. Feminist scholarship dealt almost exclusively with Protestant women in the northeast. Several individuals generously shared their time and expertise to aid me in this work. I am especially grateful to Anne Boylan, Abraham Karp, Moses Rischin, Allen Davis, Morris Vogel, Murray Friedman, Sylvia Baer, and Mary Ann McLoughlin. I would not have

11

been able to succeed without the intellectual support of friends Colleen McDannell, Hasia Diner, Pamela Nadell, Diane Lichtenstein, Lynn Hankinson Nelson, Sue Elwell, Norbert Samuelson, Sara Horowitz, Yael Zerubavel, Ellen Umansky, and Karen Erdos. They offered wonderful suggestions and enthusiastic encouragement for what seemed an endless task.

Gratz remains a much beloved figure, and, especially in Philadelphia, tales and rumors about her life and character seem to float in the air. As a result, I felt that I could trust little secondhand information. I clung to archival records as if to a lifeboat and culled material from many institutions. Archivists Fanny Zelcer and Kevin Proffitt, along with their outstanding staff at the American Jewish Archives, made the long hours of research profitable, efficient, and fun. They are an extraordinarily fine group. Thanks, too, to Ida Selavan at the Hebrew Union College Library and to Bernard Wax, the late Nathan Kaganoff, and Michael Feldberg at the American Jewish Historical Society for sending me crucial documents. Lily Schwartz at the Philadelphia Jewish Archives and Leslie Morris at the Rosenbach Museum, who worked with me during the earliest stages of this project, were especially helpful. I am also grateful to the staffs of Philadelphia's Library Company and the Historical Society of Pennsylvania. The late Philadelphia historian John Francis Marion located a huge cache of Gratz family letters and arranged for them to be deposited at the American Philosophical Society. I am especially indebted to Beth Carroll-Horrocks at the institution for allowing me access to that collection of Gratz family papers, then unprocessed. Mrs. Florence Finkel, in charge of Mikveh Israel's archives, generously allowed me access to materials found only in their collection that shed light on Gratz's life. I am deeply grateful to Mikveh Israel for its kindness and its commitment to the study of Philadelphia's Jewish history. I am especially grateful to Arthur Evans and Jennifer Backer at Wayne State University Press, and Jonathan Lawrence. Their enthusiasm and suggestions vastly improved the book.

I dedicate this book to my husband, Richard Drucker, whose intellectual curiosity, expertise, patience, love, humor, and generosity of spirit made it possible for me to complete this volume. I can imagine neither a better partner nor a truer love.

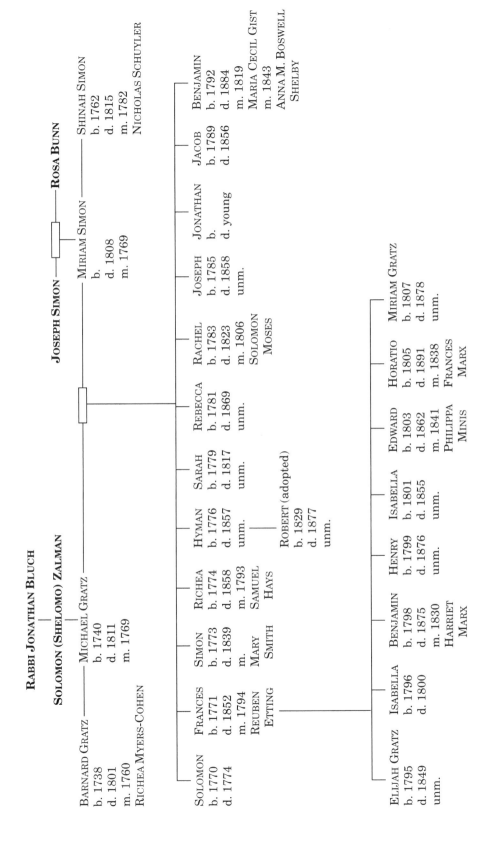

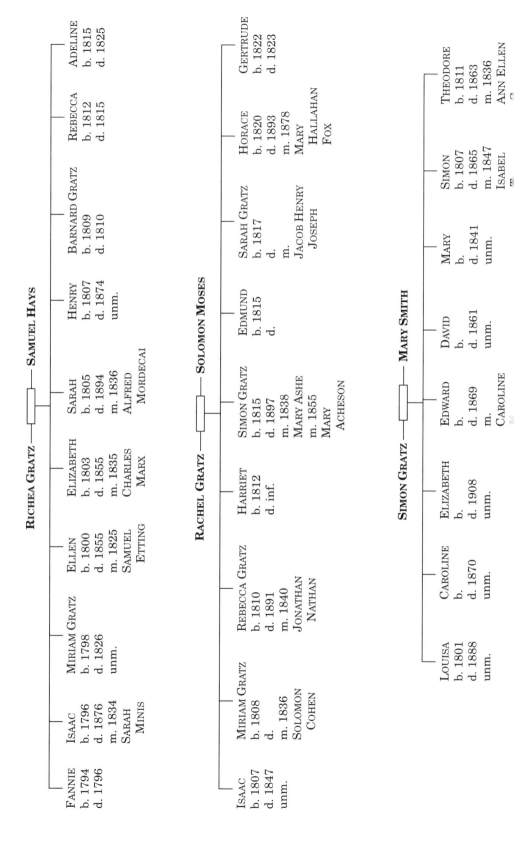

RICHEA GRATZ — SAMUEL HAYS

- FANNIE b. 1794 d. 1796
- ISAAC b. 1796 d. 1876 m. 1834 SARAH MINIS
- MIRIAM GRATZ b. 1798 d. 1826 unm.
- ELLEN b. 1800 d. 1855 m. 1825 SAMUEL ETTING
- ELIZABETH b. 1803 d. 1855 m. 1835 CHARLES MARX
- SARAH b. 1805 d. 1894 m. 1836 ALFRED MORDECAI
- HENRY b. 1807 d. 1874 unm.
- BARNARD GRATZ b. 1809 d. 1810
- REBECCA b. 1812 d. 1815
- ADELINE b. 1815 d. 1825

RACHEL GRATZ — SOLOMON MOSES

- ISAAC b. 1807 d. 1847 unm.
- MIRIAM GRATZ b. 1808 d. m. 1836 SOLOMON COHEN
- REBECCA GRATZ b. 1810 d. 1891 m. 1840 JONATHAN NATHAN
- HARRIET b. 1812 d. inf.
- SIMON GRATZ b. 1815 d. 1897 m. 1838 MARY ASHE m. 1855 MARY ACHESON
- EDMUND b. 1815 d.
- SARAH GRATZ b. 1817 d. m. JACOB HENRY JOSEPH
- HORACE b. 1820 d. 1893 m. 1878 MARY HALLAHAN FOX
- GERTRUDE b. 1822 d. 1823

SIMON GRATZ — MARY SMITH

- LOUISA b. 1801 d. 1888 unm.
- CAROLINE b. d. 1870 unm.
- ELIZABETH b. d. 1908 unm.
- EDWARD b. d. 1869 m. CAROLINE
- DAVID b. d. 1861 unm.
- MARY b. d. 1841 unm.
- SIMON b. 1807 d. 1865 m. 1847 ISABEL
- THEODORE b. 1811 d. 1863 m. 1836 ANN ELLEN

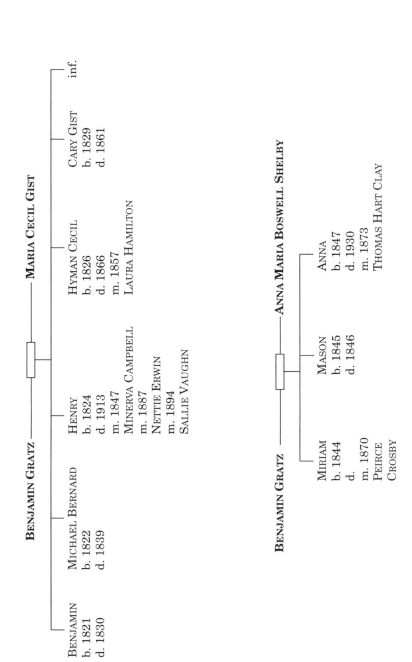

Benjamin Gratz ———— **Maria Cecil Gist**

Benjamin	Michael Bernard	Henry	Hyman Cecil	Cary Gist	inf.
b. 1821	b. 1822	b. 1824	b. 1826	b. 1829	
d. 1830	d. 1839	d. 1913	d. 1866	d. 1861	
		m. 1847	m. 1857		
		Minerva Campbell	Laura Hamilton		
		m. 1887			
		Nettie Erwin			
		m. 1894			
		Sallie Vaughn			

Benjamin Gratz ———— **Anna Maria Boswell Shelby**

Miriam	Mason	Anna
b. 1844	b. 1845	b. 1847
d.	d. 1846	d. 1930
m. 1870		m. 1873
Peirce		Thomas Hart Clay
Crosby		

INTRODUCTION

Rebecca Gratz, the foremost American Jewish woman of the nineteenth century, lived from the post-Revolutionary era through the close of the Civil War. Her life spanned a dynamic and crucial time in the nation's history.[1] Accustomed from youth to Philadelphia's highly charged political atmosphere, Gratz became and remained a fervent patriot throughout her life. The idealism, hope, energy, and commitment to the nation that swirled in the city's local culture captured Gratz's imagination from youth. Because of her family's unique position in Philadelphia's social structure, Gratz experienced a blend of Jewish ethical and American idealist values. These values, fueled by political rhetoric, secular literature, and Jewish religious worship traditions, along with the self-denial and Christianity-inspired piety touted in the women's literature of her time, became her own.

Born in Lancaster, Pennsylvania, on March 4, 1781, Gratz lived her long and influential life in Philadelphia, where she enjoyed the cultural and economic advantages her family's wealth afforded her.[2] Well educated for her day, Gratz attended women's academies and read in her father's extensive library stocked with works of literature, history, and popular science. As an adult she added Judaica, seeking original new works in English and works recently translated into English, as well as requesting new books and early readings of works-in-progress from knowledgeable American Jews such as hazan Isaac Leeser and educator Jacob Mordecai.

Both a voracious reader and an energetic writer, Gratz was an unusually articulate and expressive woman and conducted an extensive correspondence with family and friends. While a young woman, Gratz was part of a circle of writers who contributed to the *Port Folio,* which was published in Philadelphia and was considered the finest literary magazine in the country.[3] Gratz herself never published literary works; after abandoning early attempts at poetry, she confined her literary talent to an extensive correspondence and to the many annual reports she composed for the organizations which she served as secretary. By age nineteen Gratz had already become a dedicated correspondent who eagerly sought occasions to write letters. These letters, preserved by her friends and family, as well as their descendants, offer us a window into Gratz's life and world.

Because of her social class and education, Gratz counted among her closest friends educated gentile men and women who shared her interests in literature, the arts, and religion. The children of Alexander Hamilton, publisher John Fenno, and Rev. John Ewing, provost of the University of Pennsylvania, also were among her companions. Gratz's deep friendship with Maria Fenno (later Hoffman), forged in their late teens, remained strong until Maria's death almost forty years later, despite Hoffman's relocation to New York City in 1800. Samuel Ewing, an attorney with literary pretensions and son of Reverend Ewing, accompanied Gratz to an Assembly Ball, and a good deal of gossip spread about their somewhat stormy relationship. Gertrude Meredith, whose husband invested in business ventures with Gratz's older brothers and whose home served as Philadelphia's literary salon, became one of Gratz's most intimate friends. Gratz was so well placed in elite Philadelphia circles that Washington Irving asked her to introduce Thomas Sully to Philadelphia patrons when the artist moved there. The collected Gratz family portraits include many by Sully as well as by Edward Malbone, Anna Claypoole Peale, and Gilbert Stuart.

Despite her intimacies with these Christians, Gratz insisted that they respect her Jewish faith. She argued strenuously with her Christian friends for Judaism's equality with Christianity, and argued equally for Jewish and Christian social integration.[4] Later in her life she disputed her own synagogue president's authority to withdraw privileges customarily extended to non-Jewish relations of its members. Her stubborn insistence that these non-Jews receive equal treatment by the synagogue illustrates her dedication to American ideals of religious equality.

Informed by her American and Jewish ideas, values, and attitudes, Gratz created and managed a variety of municipal and Jewish institutions for charity and education. As the first person to create independent Jewish women's organizations in America,

Gratz extended her family's existing commitment to building Jewish and civic institutions. Her mother, who died when Gratz was only twenty-seven, encouraged her in women's charities. Gratz's male relatives enthusiastically created many new organizations and improved old ones. Although her father, Michael, and uncle Barnard were orphans, their older brother Hayim, who remained in Europe, accepted the civic leadership of the Jewish community of the small town of Tworog, in Silesia, leadership engendered by his financial success.[5] As Michael and Barnard earned their own wealth through merchant shipping ventures in Philadelphia, they supported the American Revolution, signed several Non-Importation Agreements, and assumed leadership of the city's sole Jewish congregation, Mikveh Israel, placing that loose organization on a more sound legal and financial footing.[6] Rebecca's eldest brothers, Simon and Hyman, continued their father's commitment to their synagogue, and the Gratz siblings remained the largest contributors to the congregation for many decades. Four of Rebecca's brothers—Simon, Hyman, Joseph, and Jacob—served on the synagogue's board of directors, or junta, and Hyman served as its treasurer for thirty years.[7] Rebecca's youngest brother, Benjamin, who moved to Lexington, Kentucky, while still a young man, joined the board of trustees of Transylvania University and continued to serve as a trustee for sixty years.[8] The Gratz family also was deeply committed to establishing new cultural institutions in the growing city of Philadelphia. Together or singly, they founded, helped to establish, or were longtime contributors to the Pennsylvania Academy of Fine Arts, three libraries, and a short-lived school for the "deaf and dumb."[9] To this list, Gratz added her own institutions and charities.

A woman of unusual influence,[10] Gratz was herself influenced by her sisters' devotion to their own families. Her three sisters who married bore a total of twenty-seven children, many of whom Gratz helped to deliver.[11] Among Gratz and her sisters, letters and conversations centered around domesticity and child rearing. She learned much from all of her female relatives and consequently established institutions to benefit women and children. Although Gratz built institutions to strengthen families, she thought few marriages happy and few men likely to be an "agreeable domestic companion" for herself.[12] She remained unmarried and lived with her unmarried siblings—Hyman, Joseph, Jacob, and Sarah—throughout her life. Despite her skepticism about marriage, Gratz adored children. Rachel Gratz Moses, Gratz's youngest sister, often looked to Gratz for companionship, advice, and aid. When Rachel died in 1823 leaving six children, Gratz brought the children home with her and raised them.[13]

With her mother, Miriam, and older sister Richea, Gratz at twenty helped to found a charitable society for women, the Female Association for the Relief of Women and Children in Reduced Circumstances. Early on Gratz became the organization's executive secretary, an office she grew to love and sought in most of the organizations she established. Fourteen years later in 1815 she worked with other Philadelphia women in establishing the city's first orphan asylum, remaining its executive secretary for forty years. As the rate of Jewish immigration to Philadelphia increased in the second decade of the nineteenth century, Gratz established America's first independent Jewish women's charitable society (1819), the first Jewish Sunday school (1838), and the first American Jewish foster home (1855), shaping a Jewish arm of what has been called America's "benevolent empire."[14] Gratz's influence was not confined to her own city. Soon after she opened the Sunday school in Philadelphia, she advised another woman on establishing a similar institution in Baltimore. In 1830, Gratz advised her sister-in-law Maria Gist Gratz on creating and running the first orphan asylum in Lexington, Kentucky.

The Gratz family's philanthropy rested on its financial success. As early as 1813, Simon Gratz, Rebecca's oldest brother, opened the Schuylkill Bank in partnership with Philadelphia businessman and civic leader William Meredith. Simon entered that business partnership while also leading the Gratz family business, which he inherited from his father and ran in partnership with his younger brother Hyman. Hyman himself became director of the Pennyslvania Company for Insurance on Lives and Granting Annuities, later the First Pennsylvania Bank, five years later.[15] After 1826, when Simon and Hyman Gratz suffered bankruptcy of their joint ventures—which sustained the family business of land speculating, coastal shipping, and dry goods supplies—their financial interests further diverged. Hyman remained a banker for the rest of his life, while still investing in coastal shipping and dry goods sales with his younger brothers Joseph and Jacob, who, by 1820, individually opened dry goods warehouses near Seventh and Market Streets in Philadelphia. Conversations among the men in the Gratz home were filled with talk of distant places, new transactions, and the establishment of new organizations.

The Gratz family's far-flung enterprises required a constant flow of letters to maintain communication, and in the Gratz home letter writing was a serious and almost constant activity. Family matters often mixed with business concerns. Michael Gratz's daughters, as well as his sons, embraced correspondence. Rebecca's letters to her brothers Joseph and Benjamin reveal her deep affection for these men. Joseph's lively wit, taste for adventure, and social ease made him a favorite companion for Gratz, and the pair shared a friendship with literary humorist Washington Irving. Four years younger than Rebecca, Joseph often accompanied her on trips to vacation spots like the hot springs in Saratoga, New York, to New York City, where they visited old friends, and to the New Jersey shore. As a young woman, Gratz often traveled with her younger sister, Rachel, along with a brother or two. To Benjamin, the youngest sibling, Gratz was an older adviser rather than companion. Benjamin settled in Lexington, Kentucky, in 1819 and married Maria Gist, the niece of Henry Clay, the following year.

Raised in a decidedly exuberant family known for its patriotism, civic activism, and artistic taste, Rebecca Gratz refused to accept the unflattering and marginalizing depictions of Jews popular in romantic fiction in the early nineteenth century.[16] Around 1822, shortly after British author and educator Maria Edgeworth published *Harrington*, Gratz wrote to Edgeworth protesting the book's depiction of a marriage between a Jewish woman and a Christian man in which the woman ultimately embraces Christianity. She knew that many Christians considered intermarriage a legitimate method for bringing Jews to Christianity. In her own family, however, as well as in the case of many such marriages in early America, intermarried spouses retained their separate religious commitments.[17] Moreover, in much of the nineteenth century's popular culture, the piety that had become a sign of women's respectability was nearly always depicted as Christian piety. Gratz fought all her life for Judaism to be acknowledged as having the same capacity for instilling female piety as did Christianity. Gratz preferred Sir Walter Scott's *Ivanhoe*, in which a Jewish woman refuses to wed the Christian hero of the tale out of loyalty to her faith and her father, to Edgeworth's story.

Catherine Sedgwick, an American writer of Christian children's books, admired Gratz and sought a more intimate relationship with her. Gratz, however, disliked what she saw as Sedgwick's prejudice against non-Christians and her New England snobbery. But Gratz's disappointment in Christian literary women such as Edgeworth and Sedgwick deepened her appreciation of Jewish British author Grace Aguilar, whose books asserted that Jewish spirituality equaled or surpassed that of Christianity and who addressed a primarily female reading public. Aguilar's didactic theologies inspired and legitimated both Gratz's personal relationships with Christian women and her public endeavors in Jewish religious education.

Gratz's religious beliefs reflected her participation in Mikveh Israel as well as her own diverse readings and lively discussions with Christian friends. Although Gratz, like most Jewish women and some men, knew no Hebrew, her congregation's early use of prayer books imported from England, with English translations on facing pages, allowed her a satisfying synagogue experience throughout her life. Gratz also found religious insight in Shakespeare's dramas and sonnets and gleaned moral guidance from writers such as Thomas Carlyle. Yet she insisted that her Christian friends respect her own understandings of biblical texts and frequently argued Judaism's truth to them. She also insisted on Jews' right to be treated as equals, both as citizens and as pious individuals, under the Constitution. These lifelong religious discussions shaped her religious ideas and deepened her convictions. While Gratz believed that American religious freedom presaged a new epoch in Jewish history, she also believed that if Jews were to be respected by the Christian majority they must become religiously knowledgeable and observant and must demonstrate a high regard for their religious heritage. Consequently, she was appalled by Judaism's nascent Reform movement, which diminished ritual and renounced Judaism's nationalist claims.[18]

Gratz's commitment to furthering charitable resources for women, promoting Judaism in a Christian society, and advancing women's roles in Jewish life provided the foundation for her communal activities. Although she shared art, literature, and theater interests with friends and family throughout her life, her deeper commitments lay in leading charitable and religious institutions. As the executive secretary of her organizations, Gratz not only maintained organizational records but also annually addressed the managing boards on policy in each year-end secretary's report. During these early years of the nation's life, while it still imported most of its reading material from England, public speech held extraordinary power and individuals deemed eloquent wielded that power.[19] Gratz's institutions regularly published her reports as pamphlets or in the popular press in order to raise public support for their work. Thus her role as secretary enhanced Gratz's prestige and provided her a public forum from which to advance her own ideas about how to foster both women's roles and Judaism in America. Her Jewish institutions especially reflected her own strong idealism, leadership, and activism.

Gratz's communal efforts were part of a burgeoning of women's charitable associations throughout America, most of which touted quasi-religious goals. Women's participation in the nationwide Protestant revival called the Second Great Awakening tended to increase their self-confidence, but women's secular literature, too, helped women to imagine new possibilities for themselves.[20] Benevolent societies, unlike temperance, antislavery, or women's rights organizations, found nearly universal approval and public favor for their work.[21] Women's piety and charitable activities became emblems of civility in the antebellum era, a period of economic booms and panics in which few families could sustain their financial security. As a Victorian ethos took hold after the 1830s, piety and charity became the hallmark of "respectable" women.[22] The upswing in religious and charitable activities among antebellum Christian women,[23] the general approval for such activity,[24] and her family's wealth all encouraged Gratz to devote her life to philanthropy and religious education rather than to marriage and more traditional domestic pursuits.[25] Her efforts led Gratz's Christian contemporaries to see in her the same virtues they believed were best taught by Christianity. Jews admired her strong and innovative leadership of new organizations that benefited American Jews. By middle age, Gratz was renowned in Jewish circles around the country.

A religious woman, Gratz grew more devout as the years went by. After her sister Sarah's death in 1817, Gratz went into a period of mourning. During that time she intensified her study of Judaism and sought the company of her sister congregants at Mikveh Israel. Within a year she launched a small religious school for the benefit of her many nieces and nephews, instructed by a young rabbi hoping for employment at her synagogue.[26] At the same time that Judaism grew increasingly important to her, the intensifying evangelism of Christian women spurred her to defend Judaism and Jews in concrete ways. Noting that Christian charitable women evangelized while aiding the poor, Gratz became convinced that Philadelphia's Jewish women and children needed their own charitable institution to see Jewish families through financial difficulties. In 1819 she gathered women of her congregation to found the country's first nonsynagogal Jewish charity, the Female Hebrew Benevolent Society (FHBS).[27] The FHBS provided food, fuel, shelter, and later an employment bureau and traveler's aid service. Serving only Jewish women and their children, the FHBS later coordinated its efforts with those of sewing and fuel societies serving needy local Jews. Gratz offered significant advice and aid to these societies as well. Grounded in many years of her strong leadership, the FHBS remained an independent society throughout the nineteenth and twentieth centuries.[28]

The founding of Gratz's first two institutions for Jews, the Female Hebrew Benevolent Society and the Hebrew Sunday School, coincided with national economic depressions.[29] To Gratz's mind, however, neither of these organizations served solely charitable purposes but advanced Judaism as well. Influenced by the religious and political transformations taking place nationally and locally, Gratz matured into a social visionary whose dreams for American Jewish life far surpassed the realities she saw around her. She was the first to apply the Sunday school format to Jewish education. The FHBS women hoped to provide religious education soon after the organization's founding, but they were unable to do so until 1838, when Gratz established the Hebrew Sunday School (HSS), a coeducational institution, with herself as superintendent. She also served as secretary of the managing society (the Hebrew Sunday School Society) and held both offices until she was in her eighties. Her sister congregants Simha Peixotto and Rachel Peixotto Pyke, who ran a private school in their home, joined her as teachers and wrote many of the textbooks initially used by the school. With students ranging in age from early childhood to early teens, the school flourished, opened several branches, and served more than four thousand students by the end of the nineteenth century. It remained an independent, citywide institution until 1993, when it merged with another citywide Jewish school.[30] Especially through the HSS, Gratz reconciled and expressed both her profound American patriotism and her even more profound faith in the God of Israel.

Under Gratz's leadership, the HSS offered Jewish women their first public role in teaching religion and determining curriculum in a Jewish school. Only female graduates were invited to join the faculty, and the HSS teacher training program furthered the women's religious education. Gratz advised Jewish women in Charleston, Savannah, and Baltimore on establishing similar schools there.[31] Their efforts prompted the country's leading Jewish educators—especially Isaac Leeser, who wrote and translated Jewish catechisms for the school—to provide materials for their use. Leeser publicized the HSS in his monthly magazine, *The Occident and American Jewish Advocate*, and encouraged Jewish women around the country to take similar action.[32] As American culture came to view women's piety as a mark of civility, Gratz hoped the school would demonstrate that Jewish women's piety equaled that of Christian women.

During the 1850s, the plight of an increasing number of Jewish immigrants convinced Gratz of the need for a Jewish Foster Home (JFH). Jewish orphan associations in New York and New Orleans, which relied on foster families, grew inadequate as immigration increased. The first residential homes in those cities were not exclusively for the use of Jewish children. The elderly Gratz, who had served for forty years on the board of the Philadelphia Orphan Asylum, became vice president of the JFH managing society soon after its founding in 1855. Already in her seventies, she at first preferred to limit her activities to committee work, and helped select and supervise the matron, helped purchase the building, and regularly visited the home. She guided her niece Louisa Gratz, along with another unmarried young woman of her congregation, to assume formal leadership. Gratz herself served as overall advisor to the young institution. But soon after its founding, the board pressed Gratz to assume a more formal role, and she agreed to the vice presidency. By then, Gratz had earned a considerable reputation both locally and around the country, and her presence on its board gave the new institution prestige and visibility.[33] The JFH remained an important institution in Jewish Philadelphia and, long after Gratz's death, merged with several other institutions to form Philadelphia's Association for Jewish Children. Probably due to Gratz's influence, her older brother Hyman bequeathed the funds that established the first independent college of Jewish studies in America, Gratz College.[34]

Many historians have noted the rapid rise of nineteenth-century German-Jewish immigrants from poverty to wealth.[35] They have told the story of Jewish men who often began peddling with packs on their backs, speaking little English, but who rapidly became shopkeepers and businessmen. As many immigrants learned, however, wealth alone did not bring respectability. It was up to the women of the family to display those characteristics that would confirm the family's status.[36] Standing at the pinnacle of American Jewish female respectability, Rebecca Gratz defined it for others and provided them with the means and rationale for attaining it. Gratz's devotion to Judaism and her promotion of religious piety among younger Jewish women earned her the respect of nearly every Jewish male religious leader. Moreover, Gratz's organizations, especially the HSS, worked with a broadly inclusive definition of Jewishness that encompassed all of Philadelphia's Jews at a time when differences in national origin, worship style, and religious philosophy were splintering the unity that had characterized the city's colonial Jewish life.[37] Histories of American Judaism largely have explained the growth and effect of these differences; they have failed to explain women's efforts to unite Jews under female leadership. Gratz's success in surmounting differences and, to a degree, unifying the city's Jews offers a new gender analysis of nineteenth-century American Judaism.

Through her organizations, her own willingness to become a model of female Jewish piety and respectability, and her endless advice freely given to Jewish women around the country, Gratz helped to mold American Judaism as it took shape in the earliest days of the Republic. Her work, and the work of women who labored with her and like her in other towns around the country, can be thought of as a "domestication" of American Judaism. Domestication here carries a threefold meaning. In one sense, a domestication of Judaism means adapting those institutional forms invented and proven successful by other American religions and applying them to strengthen American Jewish life. The HSS is the most striking example of this sort of domestication, but the FHBS and the JFH also used institutional forms first established by non-Jews.

Domestication also means the focus on home life and relationships that the term implies. Each of the institutions Gratz founded sought to enhance Jewish home life. Finally, domestication also indicates that Gratz and the many women who worked alongside her participated in the phenomenon women's historians have identified as "domestic feminism," whereby women used a rhetoric of domesticity to justify their work outside of their own homes. By these criteria, Gratz successfully shaped a process that can usefully be called the domestication of American Judaism. By developing institutions for Jewish women that mirrored those of Christian women, Gratz eased Jewish women's acculturation into American life and brought the values sustaining those institutions—such as the importance of female piety, women's religious leadership, and religious education for women—into Jewish lives. Together, these changes countered an Americanization of Judaism already transforming synagogue worship. While those synagogue changes have been well documented elsewhere, Gratz's story teaches us that domestic feminism was an emergent and dynamic process affecting Jewish life in the antebellum period. Thus, synagogue changes were part of a larger, gender-differentiated transformation of antebellum Judaism.

Gratz outlived all but her youngest sibling, Benjamin, most of her friends, and many of her nieces and nephews. Despite her bereavement in her last years, she was relieved that what she believed to be the American experiment in freedom had not ended with the Civil War. She was sure that her lasting monument would be the Hebrew Sunday School, the institution that most reflected her own unique blend of Judaism and American culture and the most successful of her endeavors.

Although Gratz was born in the eighteenth century, she faced many of the same dilemmas now posed to American Jews. Because she was personally challenged to confront and resolve the challenges to her identity as a Jew, hers is a modern story. Today, most American Jews are positioned in society in a manner similar to American-born Jews in Gratz's time—they are participants in American culture who often are not very well educated in Judaism. However, most scholarship about the ways in which Jews accommodated American ideas and manners to Jewish tradition has focused on immigrants, suggesting that the dialogue between Jewish and American culture follows a trajectory from strangeness to assimilation, a trajectory marked by a growing ease in American society experienced by immigrants' descendants. Gratz's story suggests that accommodation and adaptation are ongoing processes that offer Jews challenges with distinctive features in each generation; these challenges are basic conditions of American Jewish life.

For Gratz, her very acceptance in Philadelphia's elite society and participation in American culture challenged her to articulate her Jewish faith and identity and to advance women's position in both Jewish and American life. A devout Jew, Gratz translated her religious devotion and personal commitment to enhancing Jewish life in the United States into innovative and important new institutions for Jewish charity and religious education. In an era when women had little, if any, route to rewarding labor, Gratz founded and led five different women's organizations, thereby creating a full-time career, albeit one that offered no financial reward. Reflecting her concern for the well-being of both general American and Jewish societies, two of her organizations served a largely non-Jewish population. All of her organizations focused especially on the needs of women. Gratz used her stature to benefit others, especially poorer Jews struggling to make their way in America.

Rebecca Gratz remains something of an enigma. Despite her reputed beauty, wealth, and love for children, she never married, contrary to Jewish religious and cultural traditions that expect everyone to marry. Legend has it that Gratz was the prototype for Rebecca of York, the Jewish heroine in Sir Walter Scott's popular novel *Ivanhoe*. Rebecca of York loved the Christian Ivanhoe, but refused to marry him and chose instead to care for her father, who depended on her. Scott's portrayal of the familial affection among Jews beset by the prejudices of medieval England has been called the first positive depiction of Jews in modern fiction.[38] Some who knew Gratz, and many who learned about her since, have thought that she was indeed Scott's model. The legend that grew up about Gratz utilizes a historical fact, Gratz's unmarried life, and imaginatively constructs a special significance for it. The Gratz legend, as it was related through reminiscences, popular histories, newspaper articles, essays, and plays, suggests that its creators desired to clothe Gratz's real life in sentimental dress. Thus draped in sentimentality, her life served the cultural and psychological needs of both its originators and its potential audience.

Gratz was a romantic and glamorous figure for many American Jews, most especially for the women in her congregation, the members of the institutions that she founded, and many generations of Jewish women since then. Though she was born in Philadelphia when it was the capital of a new democracy, her image became enmeshed in the hopes and dreams of those Jewish immigrants who came to America hoping for real acceptance and prosperity in the new land. Through her leadership, Gratz showed other American Jewish women, most of whom were immigrants, how to join the respectable middle class and, at the same time, to advance the meager resources of nineteenth-century American Jewish communities. With the "unsubdued spirit" that she believed would enable her to overcome any of life's difficulties, Gratz entered history books as well as popular folklore.

1

The Gratz Family
in Early Philadelphia

"Becky is the same kind body she always was."
MIRIAM SIMON GRATZ, 1790[1]

Rebecca Gratz lived at the center of the American universe, growing to maturity in post-Revolutionary Philadelphia when it was the nation's capital. There she developed her deeply rooted optimism and the confidence that she could shape the world. While her mother delivered Rebecca, her seventh child, among her own family in Lancaster, Pennsylvania, on March 4, 1781, her father remained in Philadelphia, building ships, running the British blockades, and privateering for the new country, often in partnership with men who had signed the Declaration of Independence only a few years earlier.[2] As the nation developed into maturity, so did Gratz.

Philadelphia's Early Growth and Diversity

Philadelphia's thriving port, its religious tolerance, and its easy access to the western Pennsylvanian frontier combined to fuel the city's exuberant growth. By 1690, its 22 shopkeepers and 119 craftsmen plied 35 different trades.[3] Thirty years later, Philadelphia passed Charleston in annual volume of trade, and more than eight hundred important merchants resided there. Jews, like Quakers, established mercantile partnerships largely with co-religionists along the Atlantic ports. Members of the Jewish

Levy and Franks merchant families were based in Philadelphia, New York, and England.[4] Three stage lines soon ran south to Baltimore and beyond, as well as north to New York. Voting rights were limited to men owning more than £50 worth of personal property. Because only about fifty of the city's male inhabitants qualified, voting rights actually exacerbated growing class and gender divisions. Many of these men lived in the five hundred brick homes that helped to frame dirty, unpaved streets.[5]

Philadelphia's comparative religious tolerance and economic growth attracted adventurous people from widely diverse backgrounds. By 1700, Quakers, who had established the colony of Pennsylvania, comprised the largest single religious group although they made up only 40 percent of the population. Anglican Thomas Bray donated two hundred volumes to the tiny Anglican congregation in 1698, forming the city's first library.[6] Roman Catholics soon built the first Catholic chapel, on Willing's Alley. By mid-century Germans became the largest single ethnic group, practicing Reformed Church, Lutheran, Roman Catholic, and Moravian varieties of Christianity. By then Presbyterians had outdistanced Quakers, becoming the largest denomination. Presbyterians such as William Allen, the city's wealthiest man, were, like Quakers and Jews, engaged in merchant shipping. By 1750, only about a dozen Jewish men lived in the city but they had already formed a congregation that met regularly for worship in a house on Sterling Alley near Race Street between Third and Fourth Streets.[7] Rebecca Gratz's family later joined that congregation. By 1779, the board of trustees at the College of Philadelphia overturned its historic Anglican dominance, renamed the school the University of Pennsylvania, and appointed John Ewing, a Presbyterian minister with some scientific attainments, provost.[8] Gratz later counted Ewing's children among her close friends.

Church membership also marked class and privilege in eighteenth-century Philadelphia. Only wealthy Protestant males enjoyed full legal rights. Catholics were barred from serving in the local militia, although they paid the militia tax.[9] Although Jews fascinated many eighteenth-century Protestants as people of the 'Old Testament,' and Hebraists were found among leading Puritans and Quakers, a deeper mistrust of non-Christians led early Quakers to limit Pennsylvania's public offices to those who "Professed faith in Jesus Christ."[10] Nonetheless, tolerance was the everyday rule, and by the mid-eighteenth century, Philadelphia joined New York and Charleston as a major center of Jewish colonial life. David Franks joined the city's social elite, married an Episcopalian woman, and became a charter member of the prestigious Dancing Assembly when it organized in 1748. The Assemblies, which Quakers avoided due to religious scruples against both dancing and extravagant dress, were designed to promote marriages among the tight circle of wealthy Philadelphians who effectively ran the city.

As Philadelphia's population grew, its civic and literary culture emerged. In 1729, Benjamin Franklin made the *Pennsylvania Gazette* into the first weekly newspaper in the colonies. Later he published Samuel Richardson's *Pamela,* the first novel published in America. As postmaster, Franklin instituted regular mail deliveries between Philadelphia and New York and Boston, with more sporadic deliveries to towns west and south. One Jewish man played "a very good violine" at the city's music club.[11] Philadelphia's material culture illustrated its frontier sophistication. Many merchants set cobblestones or paving blocks in streets in front of their stores.[12] By mid-century, the city boasted both public and private wells and 120 taverns.[13] Most streets were bordered with brick or flagstone sidewalks, some with sideposts that protected pedestrians from street traffic. Eager to display their gentility, Philadelphians in mid-eighteenth century maintained public gardens from Front Street to the Delaware River, as well as small plots of land near the western outskirts of the city as campgrounds for visiting Native Americans.[14]

Gratz's uncle and father, Barnard and Michael Gratz, orphaned in Europe, were among thousands of newcomers who came to Philadelphia at mid-century with hopes of success. While immigrants from overseas arrived at the port, artisans and entrepreneurs from other cities in the colonies arrived by stagecoach, and refugees from Indian wars in the western part of the state arrived via the wagon road from Lancaster, the "most frequently used highway in America."[15] Ships arriving at the city's booming port carried immigrants as well as goods. In 1749 twenty-two ships brought seven thousand persons. Philadelphia built more ships on its waterfront than any other American port city, and leadership in shipbuilding soon passed from Boston to Philadelphia. The city's shipbuilders capitalized on their easy access to ash and cedar in Pennsylvania and New Jersey, paid less for materials, and so built their ships 10 to 15 percent more cheaply than did shipbuilders in England.[16] The Gratz brothers later joined the ranks of Philadelphia's merchant-shippers.

The Gratzes

Raised in Langendorf, Silesia, the Gratz brothers had lived with their oldest brother, Hayim, after their father's early death. There, under Frederick the Great, taxes on Jews grew more severe, Jewish marriages were restricted, and Jewish entry into trades was largely prohibited.[17] To escape these circumstances, Barnard Gratz moved in his early teens to his cousin Solomon Henry's in London. Successful in shipping and exporting, Henry taught Barnard to be a merchant. Henry's business contacts included David Franks in Philadelphia, and by 1754 Barnard Gratz had settled there, working for Franks at twenty-one pounds per year.[18] These men were merchant venturers—buying, selling, and shipping cargoes on their "own account and risk." Franks encouraged Barnard to venture with his own savings, and during the French and Indian Wars, when many merchants lost everything, Barnard made some gains. In 1758 he wrote to his London cousin inviting his younger brother Michael, then living with Henry, to join him in Philadelphia. Twenty-one-year-old Barnard was planning to leave Franks and felt that eighteen-year-old Michael could step into his position there.[19]

Michael Gratz had been a "rolling stone" until then, failing in business ventures with firms in Berlin and Amsterdam before moving on to cousin Henry.[20] The same year that Barnard arrived in Philadelphia, Michael had boarded a ship bound for the East Indies, but he lost his investment only a few years later.[21] Barnard thought that the unsettled style of the American colonies would suit his brother's temperament and might enable Michael to become a trustworthy business partner—for Barnard. Michael set off for Philadelphia soon after learning of Barnard's letter.[22]

The Gratz brothers came to America in a pattern typical of many immigrant groups whose single men traveled along routes established by townsmen in search of economic opportunities.[23] Their immigration also extended an old pattern used by Jews during crises. Family ties linking people in distant areas enabled those in trouble to ask for help from relatives currently enjoying good times. Long after Michael had settled in Philadelphia, he answered requests for aid from his brothers and sisters still in Europe.[24]

By 1760, Michael and Barnard Gratz were both settled in Philadelphia.[25] They arrived twenty years before Emperor Joseph II's 1782 Patent of Tolerance launched Jewish entry into German economic and intellectual society.[26] In Philadelphia the Gratz brothers adjusted to a religiously integrated and tolerant world as they Americanized. The Gratzes merged easily with the cluster of Jews they found in Philadelphia, despite the fact that a Sephardic style of worship, reflecting the traditions of those Jews who originally fled to the West from Iberia in 1492, was in standard use.[27] The first Jews to arrive in North America were Sephardic, and by the late eighteenth century their style of worship had become the American Jewish tradition. The folk traditions of Sephardic Jews, developed among Jews living in Moslem countries, maintained traditional synagogue and home religious observances while entering into associations with non-Jews in matters outside of religion.[28] That approach to Judaism suited America's Jews, who enjoyed widespread tolerance and integration.

America did suit Michael. Early on both Barnard and Michael lived at 107 Sassafras Street, and from 1759 to 1763 they made financial ventures together and independently.[29] By 1765, Michael had left Franks and, exploring markets along the western rim of the Atlantic, independently shipped kosher meat to Jewish communities in the Caribbean on a regular basis. With a variety of partners, the Gratz brothers also bought land in the western sections of Pennsylvania and in Ohio, Kentucky, and Indiana. Through their firm, B. & M. Gratz, they maintained a warehouse in Philadelphia and sold supplies to merchants engaged in outfitting settlers to the new lands.[30] They exported agricultural produce from Pennsylvania's farms and imported finished British goods, such as teapots and china, as well as rum and sugar from the Caribbean. Wars with Native Americans, the French, and later the British, as well as successive economic panics, booms, and embargoes, posed frequent obstacles to their success.[31]

As the Gratz brothers' wealth increased, they began traveling in Philadelphia's elite social circles, comprised largely of a powerful Anglican and Presbyterian upper class.[32] Its members, whose activities included Assembly Balls and shared military experience in the First City Troop, were also part of a national elite. Although in 1774 the top 10 percent of Philadelphia's taxpaying households owned 89 percent of the taxable property, rich and poor lived "jumbled together in a narrow compass of the town" and relative calm prevailed. City government was led by committees of commissioners, and a "remarkably inclusive network of business and economic relationships," supplemented daily by "trade and sociability," sustained the city.[33]

Most Jewish traders and merchants who settled in various outlying early towns in Pennsylvania were associated with either Lancaster or Philadelphia at various times in their lives, often for worship on important holidays or in order to associate with other Jews in Jewish communal activities after their children were born. Among the Gratz brothers' business associates was Joseph Simon of Lancaster, Pennsylvania, who would become Rebecca Gratz's grandfather. Simon was an old business partner of David Franks and looked forward to new associations with Franks's protégés. Simon's partnerships with merchant shippers enabled him to trade goods with settlers and Native Americans on the frontier. So extensive were his trading activities that for many years he supported a Lancaster silversmith who produced silver objects for trade with Indians at Fort Pittsburgh.[34]

Settled in Lancaster by 1747, Simon maintained a shop there in addition to partnerships with traders and peddlers who would travel throughout small towns and frontier areas. He also speculated in land on the frontier. Simon's sons-in-law became important business partners, and a fortunate handful of young Jewish men learned their business by clerking for Simon, writing his letters, and keeping his financial records.[35] A religious man, Simon also sought Jewish business contacts because he had eligible daughters at home. An observant Jew, he paid a *shokhet* (ritual butcher) to kill his family's meat according to Jewish law—and no doubt also to serve Jews nearby. Simon also kept a Torah scroll in his home, where local Jews met for religious worship.[36]

Michael and Barnard Gratz both married according to the marriage values in premodern European Jewish culture, which expected devotion between husbands and wives to grow from their religious duties, their extensive interfamilial ties, and their economic interdependence. Men exercised religious leadership both in the synagogue and at home. Husbands owed wives sexual satisfaction, children, and material welfare. Wives owed husbands children and observance of the rules for domestic purity that affected their sexual relations and their diet. Wives could enter into contracts and own property, rights denied to married women in America and England until the late nineteenth century. An ideal match combined wealth and religious education, literacy, and piety. This arrangement, based on *yichus,* or status determined by a combination of piety, education, and wealth, provided financial support for religious leaders and put a voice for religious ethics in the homes of the wealthy. The custom of arranged marriages enabled Jews in premodern Europe and Asia to create a reciprocal system of exchange that helped maintain both the economy and the religious leadership of Jewish communities.[37]

Although Barnard and Michael acted as their own match-makers, they at least followed the traditional standards of yichus.[38] As an American-born woman and the daughter of the most influential and pious Jewish merchant in Pennsylvania, Miriam Simon had yichus. (Her father, Joseph Simon, disliked Michael Gratz initially.) Barnard and Michael could, on their side, claim noted rabbis as grandfather, great-grandfather, and uncle.[39] June 20, 1769, Michael and Miriam's wedding day, was a major social event among Jews in Philadelphia, and Barnard brought young Gershom Seixas, hazan (reader) at New York's Shearith Israel, from New York to perform the ceremony.[40] Barnard's wife, New Yorker Richea Myers-Cohen, had died five years earlier, shortly after the birth of their daughter, Rachel, and Michael and Miriam soon became surrogate parents for their niece.[41]

At the time of Michael and Miriam's marriage, about one hundred Jewish men lived in Philadelphia. Their tiny congregation owned a small building for worship on Sterling Alley, but two years later they dedicated larger rented quarters on Cherry Alley, north of High Street (now Market). In 1771, Barnard Gratz wrote to London's Bevis Marks congregation about replacing their loaned Torah scroll with a permanent one.[42] In London on business that year, Barnard purchased a Torah scroll and prayer books to be shipped to the Philadelphia congregation.[43] Bevis Marks was the leading Jewish congregation in England and, like Shearith Israel, followed a Sephardic ritual style. Both congregations provided guidance and some supplies when the Philadelphia congregation, with the financial support of Barnard and Michael Gratz, took more formal shape in 1782. As a result, the congregation continued the Sephardic ritual style shared by the New York and London congregations.[44]

Barnard and Michael Gratz and other Jews in North America valued the tolerance shown them and hoped to share the full equality promised in the documents of the Revolution—the Declaration of Independence and the Constitution and Bill of Rights.[45] One historian has argued that the Gratz brothers' reputations as reliable, patriotic businessmen, along with their wealth, opened their way to local leadership. Their participation in the Revolutionary War "raised Jews status as Americans while simultaneously heightening their expectations and self-assuredness."[46] After signing the Non-Importation Agreement of 1769, the Gratz brothers were known to be on the side of independence.[47] They supplied blankets and leggings to American troops.[48] When the British occupied Philadelphia in 1777, the Gratzes moved temporarily to Lancaster.[49]

By the time of the Revolution, Philadelphia was the second-largest city in the British Empire. During the war, Jews from Newport, Charleston, Savannah, and New York came to Philadelphia, and Gershom Mendes Seixas took over as hazan there. In 1782, with an expanded congregation, Philadelphia's Jews formally constituted their congregation, and Barnard Gratz was one of five members of the board.[50] They named it Kahal Kadosh Mikveh Israel (Holy Community Hope of Israel) because this synagogue was the center for all Jewish community life in Philadelphia. From this synagogue, Philadelphia's Jews received charity, religious education, ritual sanction of life-cycle events, kosher meat, matzo on Passover, the companionship of coreligionists, and burial in consecrated ground.

Although Philadelphia's Jews experienced greater freedom than did Jews in Europe, they were sometimes the object of social hostility. In 1782, when Mikveh Israel planned to build a larger synagogue on Sterling Alley, the German Reformed Church next to the desired lot objected strenuously. Negotiations broke down and, in an effort to restore peace, Mikveh Israel changed its plans despite losing a significant investment in land and labor. They built their synagogue on a less suitable lot on Cherry Street and laid the cornerstone with funds contributed by Jews from both Philadelphia and Lancaster.[51] Displaying their patriotism and gratitude to their new country, members of the congregation invited the president, vice president, and executive council of the Commonwealth of Pennsylvania to the dedication of the new synagogue.[52] Barnard Gratz had the honor of carrying the Torah scroll into the new sanctuary.[53]

The congregation may have invited Pennsylvania's leaders to their synagogue dedication with the hope of overturning limitations on Jewish rights in the state. The Pennsylvania General Assembly's oath of office limited legislative participation to Christians. Barnard Gratz, as one of five members of the synagogue board, signed a petition protesting the matter sent to the state legislature in 1783.[54] Five years later, Mikveh Israel president Jonas Phillips petitioned the Pennsylvania Constitutional Convention to repeal the test oath that required avowal of faith in both the Old and New Testaments, asking that Jews be allowed to swear oaths of allegiance only on the Old Testament. Phillips's language reflected both European legal traditions identifying Jews as a separate nation and the American individualism that he believed would regard Jews as members of a free society.[55] Moreover, the variation among Christian denominations, which grew more diverse in the next century, enabled Jews to argue equality for their own biblical religion.

Although the synagogue board and several non-Jews argued support for Jews' rights in petitions and local newspapers, the Pennsylvania assembly did not change its oath until after the Bill of Rights was ratified, in 1790. The new oath limited participation to any man who believed in God and in an afterlife of rewards and punishments—thus excluding atheists and, of course, women.[56]

Philadelphia's Jewish men soon won their argument that federal standards for religious freedom could override local restrictions and gained their right to hold office in Pennsylvania. By 1790 Jews had also learned that they had friends among non-Jews. In 1782, most of the New Yorkers returned home, reorganized their congregation, and sent a formal offer to Seixas to return north as hazan, which he did the following January.[57] In 1788, with the New Yorkers gone, Mikveh Israel was completely out of funds and appealed to the city's non-Jews for donations. Benjamin Franklin contributed five pounds.[58] Mikveh Israel finally raised the needed funds by running a public lottery.

Women's Responsibilities

As Philadelphia's growing economy exacerbated class divisions, women's education became one indicator of a family's status. Working-class women needed an education in the family trades and housekeeping skills appropriate to their daily needs. Middle-class women often attended the proliferating women's schools that taught map reading, grammar, and ciphering so that they could participate in their family businesses and be true "helpmeets" to their husbands, in addition to learning housekeeping and nursing skills. Many upper-class women, like Michael Gratz's daughters, attended women's academies where they learned French, embroidery, literature, and science, in addition to map reading and ciphering. Newspaper advertisements for women's academies and for women's labor illustrate these class differences among women.[59]

Schools offering instruction in needlework, drawing, music, reading, grammar, and morals continued to thrive during the nineteenth century. But those offering arithmetic, English grammar, and globe reading, a curriculum appropriate for a trade center, also grew. As the frontier moved west, opportunities for city women to run their own businesses diminished. Therefore, urban women who worked usually did so for wages or in businesses run by men, often their family members.[60]

Magazines carried articles advising women about their true nature. In January 1793, *Ladies Magazine,* written for women by men, carried an article titled "On Female Authorship" that praised women's literary success but insisted that their education should be limited to poetry and novels and exclude the classics.[61] Classical literature is tough and intellectual, according to the author, while novels and poetry are soft and emotional, and thus suitable for women. This bias parallels the traditional rabbinic view that held its religious texts beyond the ken of women. But ironically, the realm that rabbinic opinion found appropriate for women's reading included the classics of Western culture and literature.

Like many parents in the days before public educational institutions, Miriam and Michael Gratz kept a stock of books to help them educate their children at home. As a child, Rebecca Gratz read teacher's assistants, histories, and literary classics. Teacher's assistants were books specially designed to help parents instruct their children and were extremely popular in the days before public schools. Each teacher's assistant in the Gratz home included a preface citing reasons for educating daughters. Some said that because women may become widows they must be educated to take care of themselves. Others suggested that a mother must be able to educate her children because husbands are rarely, if ever, at home.[62] One English author, J. Hamilton Moore, gave a more complex and less instrumental argument. Learning is necessary to women of quality or fortune, she wrote, because they have more time on their hands and lead a sedentary life, while the employments of "the other sex . . . are often inconsistent with study and contemplation."[63]

According to Moore, women have "that natural gift of speech in greater perfection" than do men, and since men of fortune are generally "strangers" to the world of letters, a young heir ought not to be a "dunce both by father and mother's side." Asserting intellectual equality between men and women, she concluded, "Learning and knowledge are perfections in women . . . as we are reasonable creatures . . . on the same level with the male."[64] Moore's book provided the basis for many of Rebecca Gratz's attitudes about education.

Michael Gratz's own library challenged his children and enriched their education. His collection reflected his Jewish concerns, his cosmopolitan outlook, and his family's needs and interests. Michael owned David Levi's translations of the Pentateuch, which, with Hebrew on the facing page, include notes explaining the relationship of Bible stories to contemporary Jewish practice.[65] The family also owned Levi's account of Jewish rites and ceremonies, which included a discussion of beliefs and a refutation of Christianity's assertion that it alone introduced the world to the ideas of resurrection and heaven. Meant for practical use by Jews, the book offered a brief guide to home worship services and an introduction to Talmud.[66] Barnard Gratz owned Levi's English-Hebrew prayer books for home worship, Sabbath, festivals, and holy days.[67] Levi's works, like most volumes on Judaism in America during those years, were published in England, as were most books owned by North Americans, although some were published in Philadelphia. Some books, like a French grammar and a tour of London, enabled the family to thrive in an international environment.[68] But many volumes in the Gratz library were more philosophical, such as the translations of Marie de Condorcet's *Outlines of an Historical View of the Progress of the Human Mind* and François de Le Vayer's *Notitia historicorum selectorum, or Animadversion upon the Ancient and Famous Greek and Latin Historians.*[69] The Gratzes shared a strong interest in the sort of philosophical history popular in the early part of the last century. They were great fans of Napoleon, whose conquest of Germanic lands ended Jewish confinement to ghettos there, and owned a copy of his memoirs.[70] The family's library included David

Hume's *History of England,* Milton's *Paradise Lost* and *Paradise Regained, The Poetical Works of Peter Pindar,* Shakespeare's collected works, and several collections of plays adapted from those performed at Covent Garden, London.[71]

In addition to their home library, Michael and Miriam also provided at least three of their children with more formal educations. Hyman and Richea, Rebecca's older brother and sister, lived in Lancaster for a time, where they attended Franklin College (later Franklin and Marshall College) in its first class, and Richea was the first Jewish woman so educated.[72] The extent of Rebecca's own formal education is uncertain; some records suggest that she attended a finishing school, but other evidence suggests she also attended the Young Ladies Academy.[73] This academy, begun in Philadelphia in 1787 by John Poor, a Harvard graduate and native of Massachusetts, was the first chartered institution for higher education for young women in America. Benjamin Rush, the city's famous physician and amateur philosopher, was probably its most vocal supporter.[74] Rush taught chemistry for women, and thought that his course, along with one on natural philosophy, would "prevent superstition by explaining the causes . . . of natural evil . . . such as are capable of being applied to domestic and culinary purposes."[75]

The academy also taught religious principles that were popular in the new republic. "Better Confucian or Mohammedan principles than no . . . principles at all," said Rush.[76] Catechism classes were taught by the major Protestant denominations represented by the students and trustees, with prizes awarded in each. Piety was thought to be a lady's best "safeguard and security,"[77] as well as her responsibility. Soon students from the Caribbean to Nova Scotia enrolled in the academy, believed to be the best women's school in the country.

Gratz's greater literary ease when compared to her sisters, her close familiarity with the deistic rhetoric of the day, and her conviction that women had a crucial role to play in national life, though from the private sphere, strongly indicate her formal education in a women's academy.[78] Perhaps more telling, Jacob Cohen, minister of her synagogue, was one of the academy's seventeen trustees, of whom ten were ministers. With the trustees, Cohen attended quarterly exams and voted on matters of school policy. The Gratz family led the synagogue during these years, and Cohen could hardly have taken on that outside responsibility without their approval. But it was just that kind of community involvement that Jews wanted from their clergy in early America. Jewish ministers were to represent Judaism intelligently to the community at large to ease Jewish integration. Cohen's involvement with the academy was most likely triggered by synagogue families who wanted their daughters to attend the academy.[79]

Although she was born in Lancaster, Pennsylvania, Rebecca Gratz was a lifelong Philadelphian.[80] Her basic values took shape during the Federalist era, when Philadelphia was the capital of the new country, and she watched those around her create history as the new country invented a new social contract. Ubiquitous political speeches and articles talked of civic responsibility and often claimed that even women shouldered public duties. This ideology, usually called "republican motherhood," posited a patriotic obligation that women owed their country beyond any duties to their husbands or fathers—the country's future depended in part upon women who educated their sons to be well informed about political matters and to accept civic responsibilities; women of all classes should learn republican and patriotic values.[81]

For Gratz and other women of her generation, patriotism was a social responsibility they could claim alongside men. Even if a woman only contributed to the patriotic education of other women's children, she performed a service to her country. Republican motherhood extended civic virtue—the configuration of emotions and attitudes that resulted in behavior congruent with harmonious public life and the survival of the society—to women. These values were taught at the Young Ladies Academy, which thrived in the political energy that infused everyday life in Philadelphia.

Though many Americans believed that some sort of religion was crucial to harmonious public life, religion's role in Pennsylvania remained unsettled. Despite constitutional promises of religious freedom, most Americans expected widespread fear of God and divine judgment to keep social order. Christian assertions about the nature of God and the role of Jesus in securing eternal life appeared in many new state constitutions. Attempting to control corrupt politicians, most states included statements about an afterlife of rewards and punishments in their oaths of office.[82]

The Gratz family shared the popular belief in God and his divine power of judgment but grounded those beliefs in Judaism rather than Christianity. Michael continued the traditional role of religious leader at home to whatever extent he could. Because he traveled extensively for business purposes, Miriam occasionally took daily responsibility for home religion. It is likely that she maintained a kosher kitchen, since kosher meat was important to her father. When the older Gratz children visited family, friends, and resorts in New York, New Jersey, and Maryland, Michael and Miriam sought assurances that their children were avoiding foods forbidden by Jewish dietary laws.[83] However, the limited resources for Jewish life in Philadelphia shaped and constrained domestic Judaism. Although Mikveh Israel opened a mikvah in 1786 for married women to use each month, it fell to disrepair. Until 1814, when it was refurbished after Philadelphia installed water pipes throughout the city, Jews used the Delaware River for ritual immersion.[84]

Although Rebecca's father sometimes used Yiddish in his business correspondence, her mother understood no Yiddish and spoke English only.[85] The Gratz home language was English, and the home culture was American. Despite these differences from most observant European Jews, the Gratz women unquestionably considered themselves loyal to Judaism and its traditions. Miriam and Rebecca attended synagogue regularly, although they understood little or no Hebrew. Happily for them, after 1792 their synagogue used prayer books shipped from England with English translations on the facing pages.[86]

Michael Gratz maintained many Jewish religious practices, quickly closing letters before sundown on Friday evening, sending a pair of tefillin (phylacteries) to a friend who needed them, sending money to a group of poor Jews in Hebron in 1763, and working with Barnard to get Philadelphia's quorum of Jewish worshipers established in a properly appointed synagogue and cemetery.[87] The Gratzes remained leaders of Mikveh Israel for many years. Considering the service that Michael's sons gave to the congregation, we can safely assume that Michael also put considerable effort into his role in home worship.[88]

The Bonding of the Generations

Michael and Barnard arranged their own marriages on the traditional basis of yichus, but new marriage values emphasizing the importance of affection and compatibility influenced Michael's children.[89] The freedom to choose a spouse for companionship carried with it the freedom to avoid marriage altogether, and half of Michael and Miriam's children remained unmarried. As adults, their children found three styles of family life: marriage to Jews, marriage to non-Jews but retaining Jewish identity, and the single life marked by extensive municipal and Jewish communal service. Of the ten Gratz children who lived to adulthood—Frances, Simon, Richea, Hyman, Sarah, Rebecca, Rachel, Joseph, Jacob, and Benjamin—five married and produced forty-three children, thirty-one of whom lived to adulthood.[90] Although American colonial fertility rates were well above those of European countries, by the second half of the eighteenth century they had begun to decline. For women of Miriam's generation, births dropped from more than 6.7 births per woman to approximately 5.0 births per woman. While one historian suggests that this drop reflects the use of some form of birth control, the Gratz family appears to have used none.[91]

Of all Michael and Miriam's children, only Frances, Richea, and Rachel married Jews; two sons—Benjamin and Simon—married Christian women. Richea married Samuel Hays, a man ten years older than she, in December 1793. Frances waited another year before marrying Reuben Etting, eleven years her senior, and moving to Baltimore.[92] Benjamin settled in Lexington, Kentucky, and eventually married twice, both times to Christian women who raised the children in a mix of Judaism and Christianity. Simon's wife was also a non-Jew, and his children and Ben's were raised similarly.[93] Of the Gratz grandchildren who lived to adulthood, twelve never married, ten married Jews, and nine married non-Jews.

Familial links permeated the Gratzes' business, religious, and social lives. Rebecca's friend Arabella Solomon of Lancaster married Philadelphia's Zalegman Phillips, the first professing Jewish lawyer in the city, in 1805. Arabella was the granddaughter of Joseph Solomon, a shopkeeper and merchant born in London who was in Lancaster before Joseph Simon. The Zalegmans, like the Gratzes, took an active role in Mikveh Israel, and Rebecca and Arabella were lifelong friends. Arabella's daughters Emily and Ellen later became two of Gratz's most reliable associates. Arabella's sister married Elijah Etting, the only Jew in York, Pennsylvania, and their son Solomon married another sister of Miriam Simon Gratz.[94]

Family ties also provided education and business training for the Gratz children. Hyman and Simon, Rebecca's oldest brothers, served as apprentices to their grandfather Joseph Simon between 1790 and 1795. In 1798 they opened S & H Gratz, sometimes

known as Simon Gratz & Brother, a partnership that continued
the family business. After working in Lancaster, the brothers increased land speculation and outfitting of settlers traveling west,
turning the family business emphasis inland. A middle brother,
Joseph, the most cosmopolitan of the brothers, occasionally traveled to Hamburg, Germany, to Leipzig, and to Gibraltar to conduct family business. Joseph and Jacob, Gratz brothers near in
age, both ran their own businesses in addition to participating
in family partnerships. Both Jacob and the youngest brother,
Benjamin, graduated from the University of Pennsylvania, and
eventually studied law to protect family interests. After 1780,
Michael, Barnard, and Joseph Simon, along with nearly a dozen
partners, became joint owners of immense tracts of cheap land
west of the Susquehanna and as far as Illinois.[95] Because of legal
disputes over state boundaries and federal jurisdictions, these
land ventures embroiled the Gratz family in court battles for the
next forty years.[96]

The Bonding of Correspondence

Frequent and lengthy correspondence held together the
diverse Gratz business, social, and familial relationships. Most
Gratz family members were prolific letter writers. In the late
eighteenth century, well-written letters marked an individual's education and refinement, but they carried practical importance as
well. Through letters, parents assessed their children's emotional
maturity and educational attainments. Children strove to display
their mastery of appropriate conventions of social relations, terms
of deference and endearment, on appropriate occasions.[97] Parents
encouraged correspondence among children and between children
and their own friends. Miriam Gratz, whose writing ability was
minimal at the time of her marriage, learned to write the sort of
letter expected of an urban woman of her class. While nursing her
sister's family in Baltimore in 1797, she wrote a lengthy, flowery
letter to her daughter Rebecca thanking her for sending news
about the family in Philadelphia.[98] Her children knew the letter
cost their mother some effort.

For the Gratzes, letters also maintained their financial,
familial, and religious ties. By mail, they planned family gatherings, holiday celebrations, business ventures, and travels. They
exchanged recipes, philosophies, ideas, gossip, and news of life

around the Atlantic rim, in Lancaster, Charleston, Baltimore, Philadelphia, New York, and London. They balanced Jewish observance with American customs, and with friendships, business partnerships, and marriages with non-Jews. Like their new nation, they sought universals for human rights that would allow them their particular freedoms. For them, as for all Jews, such freedom was an entirely new experience. Their letters kept them linked to a significant, if far-flung, network of Jews supplementing the local small, though growing, Jewish community.

More than others in her family, Rebecca Gratz loved to write letters. From them we can gain some sense of the intensity of the emotional life of these Jewish Atlantic rim families whose ties were cemented on so many levels. Communication across distances was their lifeblood, and letters among relations were nearly as important as a clerk's records for the smooth running of their economies. Rebecca's letters show that her friendships included whole families, as well as selected individuals. Among her closest friends was Maria Fenno, three years her senior and daughter of publisher John Fenno. She was equally friendly with Maria's sisters Harriet and Mary Elizabeth, as well as her parents. The Fennos came to Philadelphia from New York in 1790, after John Fenno, who published the pro-Federalist *Gazette of the United States,* was awarded government contracts.[99]

As teenagers, Rebecca Gratz and Maria Fenno established a strong and lifelong friendship. Their early letters reflect their primary interests: friendship, love, and the opposite sex. During one of Rebecca's many visits to Baltimore to visit her cousin Rachel and her sister Fanny, Maria urged Gratz not to miss seeing the Grenadier Brothers on the Fourth of July—the "handsomest young men in the city are in that corps."[100] When Maria spent an entire winter visiting New York City, their friendship barely suffered. Letters were often delivered by intermediaries, and hand-delivering a letter was a good way for a friend to gain an introduction. James Caldwell, visiting New York at the same time as Fenno, renewed an acquaintanceship with Gratz by asking Fenno to write a letter which Caldwell delivered.

The young women circulated and quashed gossip about romances in these letters. In 1795 Maria assured fourteen-year-old Rebecca that she "care[d] for no one in particular . . . [and] will be all the same a hundred years hence."[101] The two young women compared the social customs prevailing in the two cities, and Maria wrote with surprise that in New York "young ladies often have parties of themselves and young fellows from twenty to thirty in number in which the utmost sociability reigns." Maria told Rebecca of her new "best friend" in New York and through Rebecca sent regards to James Caldwell and his sisters.[102] Again visiting New York two years later, Maria Fenno complained of too few interesting men. Staying near the southern tip of Manhattan, she nonetheless went "whortleberrying in a large swamp 2½ miles" from where she lived, and the only man she had seen went on the boat with her.[103]

Despite their shared delight in teenage gossip, Gratz's friendship with Fenno soon turned grim. The yellow fever epidemic of 1793 had killed a tenth of Philadelphia's population and panicked the residents, and returned with even greater devastation in 1798. Most of the Gratzes went to either Baltimore or Lancaster during the epidemic, but Simon Gratz stayed in Philadelphia, despite his family's worries. Rebecca wrote to her sister Sarah about two families who had lost their wealth in the chaotic time, perhaps reflecting her own feelings about Simon's determination to continue business as usual, asserting that "easy mediocrity" is preferable to riches, for the former brings contentment, and the latter only "a multiplicity of desires."[104]

During that epidemic, Fenno's parents died within months of each other.[105] Gratz had known that Maria's father was ill, but she learned about Mrs. Fenno's death from women visiting Miriam. "Calamity fills our city," Rebecca wrote to her sister Rachel. Surrounded by family relationships as Gratz was, she found it hard to comprehend Maria's life without parents. "Poor Maria and poor Harriet!" she exclaimed. "Left orphans at a period of life when the . . . care of a watchful, tender parent was most necessary . . . to confirm in their . . . hearts the love of virtue." Maria and her sister Harriet were now left with only one older brother to care for them, a situation that Rebecca thought bordered on serious neglect. John Ward Fenno, Maria's older brother still in New York, rescued his father's paper, which he sold in 1800, and brought Maria and his younger siblings into his home. Gratz reflected, "Who can guide [them] through the many difficulties which . . . often obstruct a female's passage through this world of care?"[106]

Growing up in a family for which emotional and social ties carried material consequences, Rebecca Gratz approached social obligations with profound seriousness. When only seventeen, and one of three beautiful, wealthy, teenage sisters, Gratz was kept under the watchful eyes of her parents and older siblings. Her critiques of other women's morals reveal a teenager learning to adapt to the intricacies of social expectations for upper-class women and learning the language of social approbation. She lamented the life of a woman who, "left in [an] uncultivated state which precludes knowledge of right and wrong," had "bartered . . . prospects of comfort for wretchedness and self reproach."[107] A woman's ability to "regulate" her emotions, as Rebecca phrased it, and to adjust her mind and behavior so that she became "an ornament to society" were, for a woman of Gratz's class, as crucial to her future as a man's ability to learn a trade or business. Philadelphia was a mercantile city, and wealth brought the entire Gratz family into the city's elite circles. Rebecca Gratz attended balls and teas where she met visiting French nobility, the Bonapartes and the Murats. Michael Gratz hired a French tutor, either for himself or his children.[108]

When the Gratzes moved to a new house at 232 High Street in December 1798, fifteen-year-old Rachel, who had not yet learned to be as philosophical about life as the more mature, seventeen-year-old Rebecca, complained to her older sister. Rebecca couched an imperious dismissal of her younger sister's anxiety in a formidable command of letter conventions. Advising her sister to "have no regret" at leaving the house she had grown up in, Rebecca wrote, "It matters not from whence we set out . . . change of habitation is one of those trifling occurrences in life as scarcely deserves serious consideration." On the chance that Rachel worried a new house would be unlucky, Gratz embarrassed her out of such an idea by remarking that she "trust[ed] that no one [is] so very weak as to imagine in any other [house] they would have been exempt . . . from fate."[109]

Rebecca often advised her sister Rachel against giving in to her emotions, telling the younger girl that it was weak to do so. Weakness and strength were played out in the realm of emotions for Gratz, and strength was always her goal. Her attitudes reflect the emotional world in which she was raised, one that taught women a variety of means for controlling their emotions, bending them to accomplishing life's tasks. Skills for emotional control enabled women to thrive in a world of familial relationships dense with obligation. Emotional control also might enable a woman to traverse the social terrain of the federalist city.

Yet, Rebecca's advice to Rachel about regulating emotions reveals an underlying anxiety about her own emotional life. Her explanations of how precisely emotions could be tamed rested on a personal knowledge of the sentiments she discussed. She watched others cope, hoping to learn by example. Stunned by the grief Maria endured at the loss of her parents, she appreciated what Maria's own letters taught her about how both "severity of mind" and a natural "thoughtlessness" enabled her friend to withstand the loss.[110] Living in a family with layers of emotional, religious, and financial alliances, Rebecca knew that the most personal experiences could carry a wide range of consequences.

While Rebecca freely advised her younger sister, she looked to her older sister Sarah for guidance. In July 1800, Sarah visited the Ettings in Baltimore while Rebecca, Rachel, and others stayed in Philadelphia. The sisters in Philadelphia missed Sarah's expertise—they were making shirts out of three lengths of linen, and absent Sarah was "the most industrious" of the sisters. Rebecca, the most avid letter writer, begged Sarah to write more often, explaining that her "chief pleasure is derived from receiving letters." While Sarah preferred household tasks, Rebecca grasped any excuse to sit down with her pen, explaining to her sister that she was "conscious that [my letters] afford you no amusement, but they prevent anxiety—and give me the pleasure of conversing with you—therefore I write."

That July, only a few days after Maria Fenno and her siblings left for New York, Rebecca complained to Sarah that Mary Caldwell, James Caldwell's sister, was acting strangely. "We have seen nothing of her but in the street," she complained. "A friendly nod or 'Good Evening, Becky,' [is] all that passes—her voice and manner is that of a friend [and] I am convinced she still loves us—but cannot solve the mystery . . . of this estrangement. It has caused me the bitterest moments of pain in my existence." This secret she shared only with Sarah. "To you I acknowledge that many hours have been spent in the agony a heart can feel for the loss of a friend. I cannot see her without agitation—and her passing me in the street causes a palpitation that destroys the pleasure of whatever company I may be with." Searching for an explanation, she told Sarah that an acquaintance of theirs, Mr. Lysle, a "man of uncommon sense and penetration . . . tells me [close friendships among women] are rarely found to exist after marriage." Horrified by the idea, Rebecca rejected it completely. "I must differ from him," she argued as much to herself as to Sarah, "tho' alas too many examples corroborate the idea."[111]

Although Rebecca freely admitted to Sarah her own anguish at losing Mary's friendship, to Rachel, who mourned Maria's company, she advised only a determined optimism. Gratz's command of the language of emotions blossomed under her sister's distress. Convinced that health and success were linked to a positive frame of mind, Rebecca advised Rachel to use her mental powers to lift her spirits. "Do not my sister suffer the energy of your soul to be wasted in vain regret," she advised. "Trust me, my dear girl." But Rachel was inconsolable. Rebecca used several arguments to change her sister's mind. The Fennos were happy to be returning to New York, and Gratz was not about to show more distress about the separation than they did. If Maria preferred New York to the intimacy of their friendship, Rebecca would not let her own distress show. "Our friends are satisfied and happy," she pointed out. "We mourn the loss of their society . . . [but] the benediction of Heaven will follow them to New York—we may yet again be united," Rebecca argued. But she hoped to effect a deeper change on Rachel's basic mental attitude, to make her an optimist. Amazed at her sister's capacity for grief, she asked her, "Why torment [yourself] with supposed misfortune? 'Tis impious to distrust providence."

By her late teens, Rebecca wielded an impressive command of language both to communicate her thoughts and to direct her own emotional life. She achieved emotional discipline by naming and redirecting sentiments. Determined to convince Rachel that there was a positive way to look at their mutual loss, she continued, "I cannot think with you that the prospect is dark, that the future promises no pleasure. . . . [W]e may be happy, Rachel, if we are not determined to prevent blessings by imaginary sorrows." She advised Rachel to think about their mother, "who sees you a victim to uncontrolled feeling. . . . [Y]ou destroy the peace of your family." She urged Rachel to learn to direct her love and sensitivity toward others so that she was not injured by her own emotions. "That sensibility which properly directed is the noblest quality of mind," Rebecca explained, "you suffer to prey on your health to silence the voice of reason—and degenerate into weakness. Rouse yourself, my dear girl." From the lofty view offered by her eighteen years, Rebecca patiently explained to sixteen-year-old Rachel that the complexities of personal relationships required more than simply

giving or withholding love. Girlhood was supposed to be a time
of delight, she was convinced, and Rachel's despair was ruining
her young life. "At an age you are most fitted for every enjoyment,
let the benevolence of your heart teach you another lesson, that
when the happiness of our friends requires it, it becomes our duty
to banish a favorite passion."

Maria and her sister Harriet were optimistic about returning
to New York and living with their brother Ward there, and Rebecca
urged Rachel to think of them as models of how to face life's difficulties. "Tell me whether you think [their positive attitudes] the
result of virtue, strength of mind, piety, and every noble principle
that exalts human nature, or a want of sensibility and feeling. . . .
If it was not the first, neither you nor I would love them as we
do. To be worthy of such friends then my dear sister, prove you
are not so weak, at least strive to imitate their example, and the
success will amply repay your exertions." Losing patience, she
added, "Rachel, if you have not the fortitude for the trials you have
encountered, how will you survive . . . life?" Promising Rachel that
her attempts to alter her feelings would bring their own rewards,
she went on, "Your heart will be gratified. . . . Sensibility, instead
of being expressed in sighs and tears, will shine forth in smiles . . .
reflect in the [faces] of your friends . . . and carry back to your bosom . . . pleasure." Rebecca apologized for sermonizing, flattering
her sister's "powers of . . . mind" and saying that she "only wanted
to awaken them."

After advising Rachel on her relationships with Maria and
Harriet, Rebecca aired her own concerns about a young writer
named Andrew who sent her verses and a letter. She judged the
verses "very fine" but was more pleased by his "friendly letter."
But the man appeared unhappy when they met last. In another
mystery, two men who recently courted the sisters no longer visited them. A third man hinted he knew the reason, which Rebecca
insisted must be a rational one, but offered no further information. "It would be humiliating to appear anxious," Rebecca said
to her sister.[112] To navigate the mysteries of social protocol, Gratz
believed a woman's best allies were self-respect, optimism, and a
rational mind.

Sensitive perception, self-respect, optimism, and rational-
ity, qualities already apparent in her teen years, underlay all
of Rebecca's various accomplishments throughout her life. Her
linguistic skills enabled her to identify, express, and reshape her

experiences and, to a degree, influence those of her loved ones. Her parents' immigrant and small-town origins placed special burdens on their children to reflect the manners, abilities, and attitudes shared among Philadelphia's elite citizens. Rebecca seemed to accept readily the emotional demands of self-discipline and leadership of others. These abilities and attitudes, which Gratz developed in her teens, served her well throughout her life.

2

A Personality Transformed: 1800–1815

"Do not get too fond of oysters."
REBECCA GRATZ, 1802

"There are many kinds of trials in this life, but an unsubdued spirit may overcome them all."
REBECCA GRATZ, 1813

Rebecca Gratz delighted in the company of sophisticated and witty literary people who gathered in Philadelphia. From her late teen years into middle age, she attended the prestigious Assembly Balls as well as private teas, cotillions, and informal gatherings at the homes of the well educated among the social aristocracy. Although she missed Maria Fenno's company, she soon developed close friendships among the men and women she met at these gatherings, many of whom also knew the Fennos. Her family's wealth and patriotism, along with her own charm and erudition, soon made her an accepted insider in this elite, non-Jewish group.

It was a heady time for a young woman to socialize at the height of Philadelphia's society. Still in the glow of national eminence, city of the Revolution and capital during the Federalist era, Philadelphia's name almost defined American prestige. Moreover, its commercial growth surpassed that of nearly every other port city. By 1800, Philadelphia was America's first major industrial city and, with nearly sixty-eight thousand people, also the country's largest city. When Baltimore actually exported more than Philadelphia during the last two years of the eighteenth century, Philadelphians responded by paving the nation's first highway, the old road to Lancaster. With an unequaled link to inland markets, Philadelphia's port reclaimed its lead. In 1800 forty ships exclusively engaged in China trade were based at its port.

Although the city lost prestige and the financial advantages associated with the nation's capital when the federal government moved to the Potomac in 1800, Philadelphia's port and its link to the western frontier ensured that the city would continue to be an important trade center, and rapid growth continued. More than four hundred new homes, most of red brick, were built each year during the first quarter of the nineteenth century. Statuary and fountains appeared in city parks; new large white marble public buildings, often Greek or Roman revival style, were built; and a variety of cultural and educational institutions were established. Gilbert Stuart, Charles Willson Peale, Rembrandt Peale, Anna Claypoole Peale, and Thomas Sully, some of the country's best portraitists and artists, lived in Philadelphia. Book publishers produced more than five hundred thousand volumes by 1810, and several theaters thrived. It is not so surprising that when the Bonaparte families were exiled from France during the Napoleonic Wars, they came to what one historian has called the "Athens of America"—Philadelphia.[1]

Yet while Rebecca enjoyed a social life of glamour and intellectual stimulation, she endured tragedy at home, as if mirroring the city's experiences of both prosperity and loss. After her four-year-old niece Isabella died on January 6, 1800, Rebecca descended into a year of grief, struggle, and familial demands. A grim year persuaded her that personal sanity, physical health, and family intimacy all could shatter. The year's sadness lingered with Maria Fenno's move to New York and persisted through Michael Gratz's immobilizing depression that summer.[2] It echoed throughout her twenties, as she balanced society's delights with personal sorrows. Through that crucible she developed her own religious ideas and personal priorities and found an arena in which she thrived, the world of benevolent societies.

Benevolent societies seemed to offer Rebecca her only chance for a rewarding life outside the confines of a narrow domesticity. While her brothers, father, and uncle had focused most of their attention on business activities, neither Rebecca nor her mother and sisters had any part to play in the family's financial affairs. Although eastern European Jewish women frequently participated in or presided over business ventures, the Gratz family business—shipping goods to the Caribbean and selling land and supplies to settlers on America's western frontier—involved only men.[3] Jewish law gave women the right to own property and to enter into contracts even after marriage. As long as Jews were not emancipated, that law prevailed in their daily affairs. But in Pennsylvania, married women did not achieve full property rights until 1848, long after the death of Rebecca's mother.[4] Before then, Jewish women, who were fully integrated into American society, shared the economic disabilities of non-Jewish women.

Nor did Michael's or Barnard's sons-in-law share in the family business. Only Michael's five sons, the brothers' only male offspring, were invited into the family firm.[5] Like her mother and sisters, Gratz watched the kaleidoscope of transactions, travels, financial booms, and recessions absorb her male kin. Shut out of the family business by American law and circumscribed in her religious activities by Jewish tradition, she adopted the lifestyle of other American women of her class, Jewish and non-Jewish.[6]

Family, Friends, and Sickbeds

The letters Rebecca received from Maria Fenno trace the difference between her best friend's carefree socializing and Gratz's own nineteenth year. In February 1800, a young Maria described the spontaneity and eroticism of the New York singles scene to Rebecca. One Friday afternoon, a simple visit for tea turned into a party when the hostess called a fiddler and her husband brought several men home with him. About nine couples formed, who, after a late supper, enjoyed "the cushion dance," in which men and women took turns dropping a cushion at the feet of the person from whom they desired a kiss. Sophisticated twenty-two-year-old Maria dubbed the evening "charming."[7] New York's social life, as Maria described it, was far more freewheeling than Philadelphia's.

By contrast, Gratz's world that summer was defined and limited by family tragedies and burdens. By the time Richea's daughter Ellen was born in Baltimore on June 18, a stroke coupled with acute depression had left Michael Gratz bedridden and speechless. Rebecca's brothers Simon and Hyman, in their twenties, had taken over the family finances in 1799, so Michael's illness did not mean financial disaster for his family.[8] Nonetheless, he could offer little advice that year as the brothers focused more on inland trade than on shipping, entering into an array of partnerships with

Joseph Simon and other speculators and merchants in eastern Pennsylvania.

Rebecca helped her mother care for Michael, but other sisters were sent elsewhere. Rachel visited Maria in New York, and new friendships formed between Fenno and that city's Jewish families who also befriended Rachel—the Seixas, Moses, Levy, and Cohen families.[9] Sarah, two years older than Rebecca, went to Baltimore to help Frances and Richea with their young families and took Benjamin, only eight years old, with her. Jacob, age eleven, and Joseph, age fifteen, remained at home with Rebecca and their mother.

Miriam Simon Gratz had trained Sarah and Rebecca in home nursing skills and responsibilities. Colonial and antebellum women commonly cared for the sick at home and prepared medicines as they preserved foods. Almanacs written by physicians advised readers that exercise, fresh air, a simple diet, and cleanliness would help them avoid disease. Once ill, however, bloodletting, blistering, purging, and plastering the sick became the rule.[10] Physicians would be called for those heroic measures, but women provided day-to-day nursing care. Sarah and Rebecca, who remained single, along with their mother, cared for their three married sisters through twenty-seven childbirths.[11]

Nursing did not come easily to Gratz, but she wanted to be useful to her family and so strove to perform the tasks they demanded of her. Tending to her father and watching her mother struggle and suffer through his care, Rebecca experienced deep emotional distress and confided only in her older sister. "Oh Sally! each morning that I enter his chamber to take his breakfast I am tortured with ten thousand pangs," she admitted. While fearing for her father, Rebecca also worried about her mother. "As often as possible I entreat [mother] to repeat her visit [to Bloomfield]. Some relaxation from her painful task of attending our dear father is necessary—agonizing as it is to view his situation." Anxious about both parents as she was, it took some inner strength for Gratz to urge her mother to leave. With Miriam gone, Rebecca would be left alone to care for her father. And, as she admitted to Sarah, tending Michael was agonizing. She tried to steel herself for the work, to force her own behavior to match that of her mother.

Guilt-ridden by her own revulsion at nursing her father, Rebecca could not forgive herself for her emotions. At nineteen, she believed that she ought to be able to cope in as disciplined a manner as did her mother, who, at fifty-eight, had the benefit of decades of nursing experience. Gratz explained to Sarah that if Miriam could act "with fortitude . . . should not a daughter stand the trial?" Gratz struggled to interpret Michael's endless silence optimistically and grasped at religion for comfort. "Tonight his face looked composed," she wrote hopefully to her sister. "I think even in his present state he is not destitute of happiness—he is melancholy from retirement—his thoughts are no doubt gloomy— and yet I sometimes think he by reflection strives to reconcile his mind to his situation." Hard as that was to substantiate, she explained her reasoning to Sarah. "Though a mental disease . . . preys upon him, I have seen his eyes raised to Heaven—then bow his head—[as if to say] I submit."[12] For Gratz, a faith in God that brought courage in the face of misfortune was the key to maintaining one's sanity. If her father could do that, despite an illness that left him unable to leave his room or to speak, he could still be counted among the sane. Desperately worried about both her parents, Rebecca begged Sarah to write often, explaining that her "greatest pleasure derived from receiving letters."[13]

The next month Michael's condition improved, and Rebecca and her mother indulged in a vacation at a nearby resort called "The Cottage." Peggy Ewing, a friend from Philadelphia, visited Rebecca there. Gratz told Sarah how much she liked Ewing, a "very amiable girl [whom] I really love . . . very much."[14] Peggy's younger brother Samuel, a lawyer and essayist, frequently visited Rebecca and her brothers. Samuel was two years younger than Gratz, and his closest friendship among the Gratzes was with Joseph, who was near to Sam's age and, according to Miriam, "the handsomest of the flock."[15] Never far from a book, Rebecca was reading *St. Leon* by William Godwin and had just finished *The Mysteries of Udolpho.*[16]

As if coming from another world, Maria Fenno's letters to Rebecca recounted New York's social excitement, considering the charms of various beaus and posing questions about what love must feel like. "[You and I] have often talked of such things, Becky, [and] I wish we could now. You will be astonished to see such a subject in a letter." Because letters could be picked up and read by anyone, the two women thought it safer to confine some topics to conversations, but Maria was so curious about love that she risked gossip and tried to draw Rebecca out on the subject. "I can safely say I have never been in love," she began. Fenno was not sure exactly what Gratz's experiences were, alternately claiming that "our experiences on the subject of love is [sic] nearly equal" and "I suppose you are more experienced in this important subject, can't you give me some information?" Despite her inexperience, Maria was convinced that a woman could only love in response to a man's first loving her.[17]

But Rebecca was too absorbed by family crises for such musings. Sarah remained in Baltimore with Frances, where a yellow fever epidemic hit during the national elections. To calm her sister's worries, Sarah wrote to Rebecca about politics instead of the epidemic. The family's political commitments were solidly Federalist, though Sarah admitted to Gratz that she was "sorry to say that I seldom meet with a good Federalist." The Gratzes had three reasons for their political preferences. First, the federal Constitution guaranteed religious freedom, a right that local governments sometimes did not truly honor. Second, Alexander Hamilton, director of the Treasury and proponent of Federalism, seemed to them to have the best plan for ensuring the financial soundness of the new government. And third, until Hamilton agreed to Jefferson's demand that the federal government move nearer to Virginia, the Federalist party was associated with Philadelphia.[18]

By November 1800, Rebecca was desperate for Sarah to return home. Although she understood her sister's desire to stay with Frances, she admitted plaintively, "I cannot bear the idea of a long dreary winter without your company—I will say no more—the day is overcast and unpleasant [and] my mind bears a great resemblance to the weather."[19] When Sarah did not respond with a return date, Rebecca tried again to pry her sister out of Baltimore. Sarah's last letter had sounded gloomy, and her father's illness left Rebecca worried about anyone's gloom. Afraid that Sarah too might be incapacitated by depression, which would force Rebecca to nurse another family member on whom she customarily depended, Gratz responded angrily. Obliged to abandon both adolescence and freedom, Rebecca feared seeing her own weaknesses in her older sister, who no doubt shared many of Gratz's own feelings. Rebecca's attempt to cheer her sister was bathed in the guilt she had been feeling all year. Gratz could not help but see her sister's gloom as weakness. "I am sorry you . . . give way to lowness of spirits. There are few pleasures enough in this life. We ought not lessen the number by encouraging discontent." Rebecca's solution to Sarah's sadness—returning home. "I think you would be happy at home. The arms of your affectionate Parents and Sisters are extended to fold you in their fond embrace. It would give me joy . . . to have the society of [my] companion and friend." Not only was Sarah her "companion and friend," but the older sister could take over some of Gratz's nursing duties. As the years passed, Gratz often blended encouragement with guilt. But that day she felt guilty for sending her sister a thoroughly self-serving letter. Gratz sent another one that afternoon, advising her to try to lift her spirits with a good book and "cultivate an intimacy with Mrs. Barney," a woman whom Rebecca knew in Baltimore.[20]

Lonely for her sisters, a letter from Rachel restored Rebecca's spirits. "I wept and laughed by turns, my feelings were too powerful for control," she began. "Peter [a servant] brought me to my senses by a loud laugh which I suppose the extraordinary appearance I made excited." Knowing that Rachel was thoroughly enjoying herself in New York, Rebecca sketched Philadelphia's attractions for her. She tried a more subtle approach to bring Rachel home than the straightforward begging that had failed to move Sarah. To Sarah, Gratz wrote about women friends, but she wrote about men to Rachel and Maria.

One beau, James Caldwell, visited Rebecca, urging her to write to Rachel about his affection for the younger sister. Caldwell "spent Monday evening here. He says he watched two hours on Wed. for you at Bristol—he wished to say farewell and exchange promises to drink to each other's health. He bids me bid love to you all and god bless you for him." Caldwell seemed unable to decide between Rachel and Rebecca. Hoping to stir Rachel's nostalgia for home, Rebecca painted the evening's scene: "I am writing at the card table. Brothers Simon and Hyman . . . have their ledger book on it and keep repeating aloud the figures they are setting down. . . . Ben stands at my right hand, spelling every word I write." Gratz wrestled with her own need for letters from Rachel and her growing tendency to think like a nurse. The next week she told Rachel, "Go to bed early—don't stay up writing letters to me."[21] For her part, Sarah soon assured Rebecca that the family would be reunited when Frances visited during Passover in the spring, and added that Benjamin had "gone to church with his nurse."[22] While the Gratzes' own religious observance remained steadfastly Jewish, they were not complete strangers to churches.

Rebecca, Sarah, and Rachel, three unmarried sisters, entertained each other in their letters with conversations about

romances and men. They often discussed the men who visited
them, and each sister had her favorite. Rebecca's closest friends
were not Jews, and her friendship with Sam Ewing was warm but
stormy. Sam had been in Easton that fall, and when he returned
in November they "quarreled a bit" but solved the disagreement.[23]
Sarah preferred James Caldwell, who had recently passed through
Baltimore on his way to Washington and visited her there. "I
hope to have the happiness of seeing him [when he returns] and
every attention in my power shall be paid him . . . you know he
was ever a particular favorite of mine." Lest such an outburst
of emotion put Sarah in an embarrassing position, she qualified
her interest as that of "an attached Sister" and professed love
for "every individual of that amiable family." But she added, "He
is really a worthy young man."[24] Indeed, the three sisters doted
on Caldwell, who had just joined the navy. Rebecca told Rachel
that she "wept for hours at the idea of the dangers to which he
will be exposed," as neither stagecoaches nor oceangoing ships
provided secure passage. But that year, as she nursed her father,
Rebecca denied any emotions that might interfere with her ability
to function as she must. No sooner was her worry for Caldwell on
paper than she subdued it with the consolation that "heaven is
ever mindful of the good and our friend merits that."[25]

Rachel, removed from her family's crises, worried about Rebecca's state of mind during that difficult year. She tried to lift
Gratz's spirits by urging her to let others see her original unpublished poetry, but Rebecca rejected the idea. "You know I have long
since given up all attempts at poetry. It used to amuse me before I
had read any well written verse, but now I cannot bear . . . to read
[that] poor nonsensical stuff and would not certainly be so ridicu-
lous as to give it to others."[26] Rather than risk embarrassment,
Rebecca confined her literary creativity to a more conventional
and less challenging form—letters. Like her father and brothers,
whose extensive business correspondence was crucial to their success, Rebecca approached letters seriously.

In a family that relied on correspondence, Rebecca's outflow
surpassed everyone's except the business correspondence, demonstrating the central role letters played in her life. In 1800 letters
linked her to the world of normal teenage fun enjoyed by Rachel
and Maria in New York, and Rebecca could imagine herself still
part of that world. Letters also linked her to Sarah, the sister
who understood her best. On a deeper level, the letters allowed

Rebecca to imaginatively escape her home, to give expression to emotions otherwise suppressed while she carried out her nursing duties and consoled her mother. As she constructed her sentences she shaped the self she wanted to be and created the Rebecca Gratz she believed she must become. Although poetry might have enabled her to express her emotions more honestly, it would not have afforded her the same opportunities for both linking her to loved ones and creating the adult persona she had determined to wear.[27]

For Gratz, letters to Rachel and Maria in New York helped her explain the frustrations of her life. Detailing for Rachel her "painful sensations" as "our dear James Caldwell" said good-bye before another journey, she wished that "fate had painted . . . a different path for him."[28] Maria Fenno soon convinced Rebecca to make a serious effort at verse once again by promising to pay more attention to her own letters to Gratz. One night, after Maria attended a terrible production of *Othello,* she left a room "full of beaus" to write to Gratz.[29] Rebecca replied that though she had been "a good deal occupied in writing [poems]," the work did not "speed much."[30] If Rachel and Maria hoped to divert Gratz's gloom by getting her involved in poetry, it did not work. When Maria's older brother visited Philadelphia and the Gratzes one evening, he reminded Rebecca of the "melancholy expectation of seeing for the last time, for fifteen months, my favorite, James." Grasping for some way to link herself with Caldwell again, she thought to "get . . . some ribbon to make [him] a watch chain, but I don't know how he will get it for I shall not see him again. . . . Ah me!"[31]

Other responsibilities also prevented Gratz from writing poetry. By the end of 1800, she shouldered more nursing duties normally performed by her mother. After helping her mother care for her father, she had some training and a deeper appreciation for her mother's burdens.[32] Most women of her era nursed their families to one degree or another, and Gratz continued her mother's practice of tending the family's pregnancies, births, illnesses, and deaths.[33] This was a grim era for such a role. Typhoid, cholera, and yellow fever epidemics recurred frequently during warm seasons in the cities from New York to New Orleans.[34] Sewage and water dispersal systems were inefficient. Philadelphia did not bring water to poorer homes scattered in the alleys and shadows of the rich, yet poorer neighbors served as domestic servants, cooks, wet nurses, laundresses, seamstresses, and tailors to the wealthy.[35]

Many Philadelphians tried to avoid contagion by moving to the countryside, and the Gratzes often relocated to Lansdowne, Germantown, or Lancaster. Newspapers reported on epidemics and notified escapees when it was safe to return home.[36]

During this era most people spoke of individual constitutional states that needed particular routines to protect and maintain health.[37] People were thought delicate or hardy, nervous or phlegmatic, and expected these different types to require special balances of excitement or rest, spicy or bland food, and more or less exercise, sleep, or alcohol. Gratz's own recipe for health included bran bread and plenty of exercise.

At nineteen Gratz had already learned to suppress her own desires to meet her obligations to those she loved, but at twenty she watched her siblings develop new attachments of their own. Her brother Simon, who had moved with his bride Mary Smith to Willington, his estate just two miles away on north Broad Street, welcomed his first child, Louisa, in March 1801, Gratz's own birthday month.[38] Although others around her married, Gratz distrusted romance. Perhaps thinking again of her feelings for James Caldwell, Gratz warned Maria Fenno against trusting her heart too easily, for hearts were "unaccountable and self-directed [and] often prove cheats." Even worse, they "gain mastery over judgment, reason and all . . . advisors . . . which inhabit the head." With aging parents, Gratz saw marriage's trials more clearly than its delights. She warned Maria, "Your heart [can] give you the slip . . . [and] when it has once found a resting place in another bosom it will not return to yours tho you plead with sighs and tears." The solution? "Gain another [heart] before you part with your own," but "don't put too much confidence in its present security."[39]

Despite Rebecca's admonitions, Maria sought romance. Her sister Harriet had married a few months earlier, and Maria missed the parade of suitors coming to their house.[40] Rebecca chided her for being concerned about a lack of beaus. She remarked that Maria was old enough to know that "a handsome woman has . . . more admirers than friends," and Gratz did not value mere admirers. "Those who seek only a face will be but transient acquaintances." Perhaps to quiet her friend's fears, perhaps revealing her own true feelings, she offered Maria the comfort of her own friendship. "If fate does not . . . lead us to [marriage] . . . we will be happy still, and in a faithful tender friendship find a substitute for Love—or a consolation for its tricks, should we either of us at the age of sixty have reason to complain of its treachery."[41] Gratz probably had good reason to doubt her ability to distinguish between admirers and lovers. Portraits painted of her in youth and middle age show a beautiful, fashionable, elegant, and sensuous woman. She often asked that Maria not contribute to her vanity with too much praise.

But within a month Maria had married Judge Josiah Ogden Hoffman, attorney general of New York state, a widower fourteen years her senior with four children. Rebecca was shocked, but unwilling to lose Maria's friendship. "The Husband of Maria will be dear to the heart of her Becky," she wrote to her newly married friend, curtailing her criticisms of marriage and romance.[42] Sarah, then visiting their grandfather in Lancaster, reassured Gratz, writing that Hoffman "is a worthy and respectable man [who] will render [Maria] perfectly happy and strew her path with roses. Aunt Shinah says he is a man of sense and talents."[43] Resigned, Gratz cultivated close relationships with Maria's stepchildren and children. She determined to bring Maria's new family into her own and often invited her mother and siblings to add postscripts to her letters to Maria.[44]

Maria continued to encourage her Philadelphia friend's more literary efforts. Her own letters were terse and, compared with Gratz's, dull. She sighed, "How I wish for that easy stile [*sic*] you possess."[45] Raised with newspapermen, Maria appreciated her friend's gift for language even though she lacked it herself. That year, Maria and Rebecca began life journeys down very different paths.

The Female Association

One Philadelphia evening in 1801, Miriam, Rebecca, and Rachel met twenty other women at a home on Front Street to formally establish a new women's organization designed to aid elite women whose families had lost their wealth. In this, the first nonsectarian women's charitable organization in the city, eight of the twenty-three original members were Jews, and many were mothers and their daughters. They called their group the Female Association for the Relief of Women and Children in Reduced Circumstances. Although most of the city's women's organizations were formed by and for coreligionists, this organization formed an alliance among women of the same economic and social class. The women of the Female Association (FA) aided "gentlewomen" new to poverty through no fault of their own; "honest and industrious suffering under sickness and misfortune."[46]

Like all benevolent societies of the era, the FA had very specific ideas about its target population and its criteria for aid. The women of the middle and upper classes who formed benevolent societies believed that the purpose of charity was to help eradicate poverty by easing the suffering that inhibited self-discipline and an individual's ability to work. Nearly all charitable groups thought of themselves as dispersing funds donated by compassionate citizens, and therefore holding a "sacred trust." Donors had to be assured that the organization would not give its funds to any but the "worthy poor," people who were industrious, frugal, clean, and pious, but poor through no real fault of their own.

Generally, the FA considered legitimate causes of poverty to be sickness or death of the family's main provider, business reversals through fires or other catastrophes, or dependence on a man in a respectable but financially unrewarding profession such as the ministry. A woman might also be legitimately poor if she depended on an intemperate, irresponsible, ill, or unsuccessful man or if she had been widowed or abandoned. Women also had to prove their own worth by displaying virtues associated with "decency" and by being ashamed of their poverty. Many wealthier people believed that individuals became poor through alcoholism, laziness, and general irresponsibility, so benevolent societies had to assure their donors repeatedly that they scrutinized their petitioners to ensure that they did not promote "pauperism." Benevolent societies' concern for their funds matched the attitude toward money that they expected from their clients, an attitude that they knew was shared by their donors.[47]

The FA focused its attention primarily on women who had "known better days." They were not seeking help "for the needy indiscriminately, but for those who . . . [were] REDUCED." But it was also a mutual aid society for upper-class women, and petitioners' names were never mentioned in written reports so that the women receiving aid would not suffer "exposure." The FA's constitution made plain this perspective. "How hard . . . it is to have the tastes, the habits, the longings and recollections, if not of affluence, at least of comfort, and yet to be poor." Women with these memories, they believed, were "the real sufferers." The FA also hoped to provide education for poor children and insisted that mothers who received aid from them educate their children in a manner approved by the FA.[48]

To ensure that the FA would be able to maintain control of its funds, the constitution stated explicitly that the treasurer "must be chosen from among the UNMARRIED LADIES" and that the treasurer's term in office was to "stop at her marriage." Because Pennsylvania's Married Women's Property Act was still almost fifty years away, this stipulation protected the charity's funds from becoming the property of the treasurer's husband. The treasurer signed all checks, banked, and paid the accounts—single adult women were crucial to the group's viability. Although most nineteenth-century women's groups placed financial leadership and control in the hands of a trusted man, the FA women were not only confident of their own ability to handle money, they insisted on it. Women in wealthy families managed complex household finances and participated in frequent conversations about financial management. Moreover, incorporating as a charitable society enabled women to overcome the legal limitations on their rights to own, hold, and convey property and funds. By forming such societies, women could engage in financial investments and disbursements, activities otherwise the province of men.[49] Gratz would later insist that all of her organizations hold onto their own, independent finances.

Organizations like the FA reflected the changing situation of women's economy during the early nineteenth century. Colonial inheritance laws enabled daughters to inherit realty and to retain it after marriage. The same was not true of personal property, which became the property of a woman's husband at marriage and so was often bequeathed to sons. As fewer people lived on land they owned, fewer women had any independent source of wealth.[50] Reflecting on some of the things she heard at these meetings, Rebecca wrote to Maria in 1801, "I think every other distress supportable, but what a woman must experience who loves her husband—yet must acknowledge him a villain."[51]

Difficult as life may have been for women who were no longer wealthy, working women faced even greater difficulties during the antebellum period. Despite Philadelphia's steadily growing industrial base, many poor women who sought wage labor found none. Although the city had taken its first steps in providing a central water supply to promote manufacturing,[52] custom dictated that men and women not work side-by-side, and industries gave

the best-paying work to men.[53] Unemployed men often went west,
but poor women usually entered almshouses,[54] and frequently
women comprised more than half of Philadelphia's poorhouse population.[55] Although the city established a tax to fund the education
of poor children, most of them spent their days working.[56] Inside
poorhouses, women residents knitted, spun, sewed, and manu-
factured linen.[57] During the War of 1812, looms were installed
and poorhouse women supplied troops with blankets, uniforms,
and bandages.[58] Reflecting the common middle-class belief that
the poor lacked the discipline that fear of God might inspire,
Presbyterian ministers commonly lectured in poorhouses on Sunday mornings as early as 1811. Eventually, other ministers were
allowed to talk with the poorhouse residents on Sunday afternoons.[59]

In this uncertain economic climate, Rebecca's own sense of
class differences had less to do with wealth than with what Americans were calling "refinement." Visiting her grandfather's poorer
neighbors in Lancaster, she wrote to her sister Rachel that the "old
man and his wife are lively—good humored people. I told the latter
she must come and see me—oh no she reply'd I can't do that— . . .
how can I go to see quality. I told her I should be very glad to see
her that we are all equals—yes but everybody don't think so, she
reply'd. And so we are Rachel—her heart is pure and uncorrupted.
She feels happy in her retirement and says she would not go into
the wicked world where every word is accompanied by an oath."[60]
For Gratz, a woman's religious faith and personal piety lifted her
above her economic class.

Culture and Anti-Semitism

The second standard by which to measure personal worth,
a standard encompassing refined manners and intellectual pursuits, appealed to Gratz. Although her family's wealth placed
her in Philadelphia's upper class, she felt the precariousness of
their business ventures and, seeking another basis for her status,
gravitated to the literary circle of the city's society. Her education,
love of reading, and respect for the written word made her welcome there. Philadelphians often considered themselves at the
pinnacle of the nation's refined society. The *Port Folio,* a local
weekly magazine edited by Harvard graduate and Episcopal lay
preacher Joseph Dennie, was thought the best literary journal

in the country. Josiah Quincy called it "very far superior to any magazine ever attempted in [America]."[61]

On arriving in Philadelphia from Massachusetts, Dennie organized a literary "Tuesday Club" in 1801, a group that included the cultural elite of what was recently the capital of the country, including men of the Cadwalader, Hamilton, Wharton, Ewing, Rush, and Peters families. The magazine made Dennie a leader in literary and cultural circles and a favorite of Gertrude Gouverneur Meredith, whose home was the center of local literary culture and where Dennie stayed when he first arrived in the city.[62] Meredith was the niece of Gouverneur Morris, delegate to the Constitutional Convention and U.S. senator from 1800 to 1803. Michael Gratz and Joseph Simon enjoyed business partnerships with Meredith's husband, William.[63] Rebecca and her brother Joseph subscribed to the *Port Folio,* and Rebecca read it avidly. "Submitted to men of affluence . . . liberality and . . . letters" from 1801 to 1827, the magazine flourished long after Dennie died from alcohol-related causes in 1812.[64] In 1809 Dennie switched from a weekly to a monthly format, and during his illness Nicholas Biddle, later president of the United States Bank, ran the magazine.

Refinement in Philadelphia did not preclude anti-Semitism. Even sophisticated publications seldom questioned their bigotry regarding Jews, and Rebecca paid a price for her association with the *Port Folio* crowd. Impressed and intimidated as she was by the literary men, she faced their contempt for Jews in silence. The first issue of the *Port Folio* opened with a journal of a tour through Silesia, her father's birthplace, which described Berlin as "an old town . . . [with] about twelve thousand inhabitants, of which a quarter part are . . . FILTH[Y] . . . Jews."[65] Written by John Quincy Adams, excerpts from this journal opened every issue from January to October. The editor's column, titled "Morals," often exhorted readers to avoid the lure of "irreligion," by which Dennie meant any ideas other than those of Christianity, including works by those famous non-Christians Plato and Socrates.[66] Yet Dennie loved satire, and the first issue devoted three of the first *Port Folio*'s eight pages to a translation of the thirteenth satire of Juvenal, alongside the Latin original.

From John Fenno's *Gazette,* Dennie had learned that political invective could promote a journal's success. Dennie attacked American patriotism, which he called a blend of pride, ignorance, jealousy, rivalry, and hatred. After remarking that each nation finds a reason to justify ill feeling toward another, he labeled Jews "the pattern of ill-temper."[67] Almost anti-democratic, Dennie bewailed the loss of English culture and maligned Noah Webster for including many Americanisms in his dictionary. An Anglophile, Dennie happily published a letter by Gratz urging theatrical reviewers to be more critical, especially of performances of Shakespeare's plays, and demanding that reviewers look beyond the actors' physical attractions. After Rebecca saw the *Othello* troupe Maria had disliked, she too was appalled by the performance. Advising actors to reread Shakespeare's plays until they understood them, she argued that Americans should continue bringing actors from England until American actors improved. Rebecca signed with the letter "R."[68] Faced with anti-Jewish prejudice in her favorite magazine, Gratz determined to prove, with the example of her own life, that Jews could be sophisticated and refined.

Although the Gratzes were well integrated into Philadelphia society, local culture was thoroughly infused with the heritage of Christianity. The easy use of anti-Semitic stereotypes and remarks, even among the intellectual elite, reflected their use in the theater, where variations on Shylock abounded. Ubiquitous references to Christian books for sale, meetings and worship services to be held, and allusions to Christian ideas, texts, and holidays appeared in the daily newspapers. Although American Jews never suffered the violence encountered by other American racial, religious, and ethnic groups, Jews worried about slander in the press. America was among the first countries in the world to offer citizenship rights to Jews on the same basis that it offered rights to others, and Jews fervently hoped religious freedom would spread to other countries. If anti-Jewish comments in the press were convincing, then the American experiment in religious freedom might fail.[69]

Most worrisome to Jewish readers were the articles that blamed Jews for a variety of social ills. Jews usually responded with letters to the press defending themselves. The first such print confrontation erupted over the problem of national debts after the Revolution when articles appeared blaming "Jew brokers" for the general economic malaise. Magazine caricatures of Jews draped with jewelry continued this theme throughout the nineteenth century.[70]

Despite the openly anti-Jewish remarks Rebecca encountered, she never retreated from gentile American society. Her closest friends were non-Jews and she associated with gentile

men only. In February 1801, Gratz accompanied Sam Ewing to
a Dancing Assembly at Oeller's Hotel. Dancing typically began
at 7:00 P.M. and continued, with a light supper, until midnight.[71]
The next year, Maria confided to her that Sam, visiting New York,
"insisted on" a letter ready for him to deliver to Rebecca when he
returned home. Calling his infatuation with Gratz "another fit of
his old complaint," Maria teased Rebecca that Sam still loved her.
The next month Ewing sent Rachel an essay that he had written a
year earlier praising Rebecca. Describing her "mind discriminat-
ing and correct, expanded by observation and by books—with a disposition formed to cheer and charm . . . she will . . . as a wife . . .
render anyone happy whose . . . disposition is not at war with
happiness."[72] Yet if he intended to marry Gratz, no engagement
was ever announced. Moreover, Gratz continued to tell Ewing's
sister Peggy and other friends that she was a stranger to love
and that she had her doubts about the happiness of most marriages. Peggy Ewing, who herself harbored strong doubts about
marriage, was incredulous that Gratz knew even "one pair . . .
[who had] discovered . . . happiness . . . in the garden of wedlock.
I look upon [that] as . . . a miracle."[73] Despite Gratz's reluctance
to discuss love or her own emotions in a letter, she would not
have disparaged marriage to Ewing's sister if she secretly hoped
to marry him.

Letters, Wills, and More Friends

As Gratz denied herself her own poetry writing, letters took
on an enormous importance. They became her voice and symbolized her friends, providing imaginary contact with loved ones until
she could be with them. She saved Maria's letters and admitted to
her that "when my spirits are uncommonly depressed I fly to my
desk, and [re]read [your letters]." She saved them in chronological
order and sorted them when she was bored. "Yesterday . . . [they]
wanted arranging . . . [and] in looking for dates I could not refold
them unread and thus, when evening came I was obliged to leave
them in greater confusion than before. . . . I shall cheat another
gloomy day by putting them in order."[74] Gratz and Rachel visited
New York and Maria in June 1802, soon after Harriet Fenno
Rodman and her new husband returned from their trip to New
Orleans.[75]

However, other duties soon returned Gratz's attention to
family matters. In August, when Sarah fell ill and a doctor visited

the house to bleed her, Rebecca left Rachel in New York and returned to Philadelphia to care for her sister. Upon leaving, she cautioned Rachel not to get "too fond of oysters," a food forbidden by Jewish dietary law, because she would have to give them up when she returned home.[76] The comment reveals Gratz's attitude toward her own life. Oysters symbolized the worldly pleasures enjoyed by their non-Jewish friend, Maria Fenno, that must eventually be given up for family responsibilities. Rebecca, who had taken up those duties, reminded Rachel that her home, too, was elsewhere. In her typically oblique way, Gratz expressed her fear of losing people she loved. Maria Fenno had became almost a surrogate older sister to young Rachel, and Gratz's remark reveals her fear of losing her special place in Rachel's affections. It also betrays Rebecca's resentment that Rachel enjoyed a carefree adolescence while Gratz assumed difficult family duties.

The following May, Gratz answered another call for help. This time she relocated to Frances's home in Baltimore to await the birth of another Etting child. Rebecca pronounced Frances's children "lovely, interesting, and engaging, but not so handsome as Richea's."[77] Waiting for Frances to deliver, Rebecca went to the races and the theater, where she sat in General Ridgley's box and met his daughter. Edward Coale, sitting in the box next to them, struck up a conversation and brought her a copy of the *Port Folio* the next day. Gratz decided he was the most "genteel" man she had seen in Baltimore, but sent love to James Caldwell via Peggy Ewing. She hoped to see another man, an Andrew N., soon.[78] She mused about a Mr. Bayley whom she left back in Philadelphia, and asked Rachel to "make minute observations on his conduct and manner and give me your opinion—I regret that I did not see him before I left home."[79] Charles N. flattered her with his attentions, and Edward Coale visited her whenever he could bring a *Port Folio* issue. Another Baltimore man offered Gratz the use of his library.[80] Sam Ewing, who frequently published verse in the *Port Folio* under the pseudonym "Jaques," was in Baltimore at the same time, visiting his sister Sarah Ewing Hall.

Rebecca and Sam shared a lively interest in literature and letters. In 1803 he sent Gratz an essay satirizing the local women in a rather tortured style, concluding that he longed to find a silent one—hardly a reassuring thought for an intelligent woman like Gratz.[81] Nonetheless, their friendship survived. Rebecca ordinarily held strong opinions, but she revised her own thoughts to match

Sam's on the essays of Isaac D'Israeli. After Rebecca told Rachel that she found D'Israeli's essays "far more entertaining than the Romances—but I was much pleased with the latter, I never read language so splendid," Sam convinced her that D'Israeli's writing only appeared to be excellent, but in fact, was not very good. It was "too splendid."

Rebecca explained to Rachel, "So much as to destroy the interest of his tales . . . I read them with great pleasure and admired the ingenuity with which he introduced the birth of the arts—in the history of his lovers in arcadia. . . . But I never read a book of which I did not retain a more distinct recollection of the different tales it contained—which I attribute to that brilliant stile [sic] which dazzles and confuses the senses—and tho I was not sensible of the justice of Mr. E's observation . . . [I] am now willing to think he was right." Gratz enjoyed Sam Ewing's wit and company. He was known for his kindness and what others called his "conversational powers."[82]

Whatever Rebecca's relationship with Sam Ewing, it did not preclude meeting other men. In fact, Sam advised Edward Coale that the *Port Folio* was "a passport to favor" with Gratz, and because Coale only visited her when he could bring an issue of the magazine, he only saw her once each week—a situation Gratz would have changed. Sam Ewing soon returned to Philadelphia, and Rebecca admitted that "he did not part with me in very great friendship, tho nothing occurred that was intended to give offense."[83] Coale continued to visit Gratz and to bring her issues of the *Port Folio*. "Every time I see him he is more agreeable. We talked of the Philadelphia Literary Club."[84]

Rebecca Gratz was unquestionably an intellectual woman of her era. She philosophized about all her experiences, including her dreams, and quickly adapted new ideas and images to her own thoughts. "What an unaccountable mimickry of real life is the delusion of a dream—but it is a proof of the mind's activity," she wrote to Richea. Like most people of her day, she looked to religion and literature for metaphors by which to understand her inner life. "I sometimes . . . think dreams . . . resemble the transmigration of souls," she wrote. Echoing Shakespeare, she continued, "Perhaps life is but a dream of immortal spirits—and the term of man's existence is no more than a night in the proportion of eternity."[85] Family events probably provoked Gratz's thoughts about souls coming into the world. Richea's daughter Elizabeth Rosa had been born a month before, and Frances's new son, Edward, would arrive in two days. Rebecca spent her free time reading Mrs. Montagu's essays on Shakespeare and hoped to write to Richea about them in moments she could steal between social events and caring for Frances and her new baby.[86]

When Gratz returned to Philadelphia that fall, she resumed her work with the Female Association. By 1803 the group had opened a soup kitchen and was dispensing aid to individual women on a regular basis. Among its original founders were several sets of mothers and daughters, and its close, intergenerational network put into action the sentiments expressed in the family letters Gratz had contributed to throughout her youth. Like those early letters, the FA forged links between families and strengthened ties among family members through shared activities.

In Philadelphia, Rebecca spent many evenings at home, sometimes playing checkers with Hyman and enjoying the company of her new neighbor Peggy Ewing, who, like Gratz, nursed her family and friends.[87] In fact, the two women met while spending twenty-four hours in a sickroom. "We might have met at every party given that whole season . . . and not have known each other so well," Gratz remarked.[88]

The death of Gratz's grandfather Joseph Simon on January 24, 1804, deepened her growing sense of the precariousness of life and strengthened her resolve to keep ties of friendship and family strong and clear. That resolve was reinforced with the reading of Simon's will. Michael Gratz and Simon jointly had owned vast tracts of land west of the Susquehanna River for almost twenty years, but Simon bought and sold them in his own name. He was supposed to turn over to Michael his share of the sales or rentals after each transaction, but by the time Simon died the two men had long-standing disagreements over Michael's shares. Court judgments during Simon's lifetime were in Michael's favor. As a result, Simon left his daughter Miriam only one hundred pounds specie, in effect completely writing her out of his will, with the proviso that if her husband Michael forgave the balance of Simon's debt, that is, Michael's shares of land transactions, Miriam would share equally in her siblings' inheritance.

During Simon's last years he made new partnerships with sons-in-law Solomon Myers-Cohen, Solomon Etting, and Levy Phillips, men who had married his daughters Belah, Rachel, and

Leah. Phillips was the executor of Simon's will, and Simon left the bulk of his estate to Leah Phillips and Belah Myers-Cohen, both of whom had large families. Smaller amounts were left for the care of his two retarded sons and his unmarried daughter, and four hundred pounds went to Shinah Simon Schuyler, who had no children. Whatever misgivings Simon may have felt about Shinah's marriage to a non-Jew, his will did not reflect animosity— Shinah's inheritance was to go to her husband if she predeceased him. Only Miriam Gratz's family was cut out of the will, which fostered anger among the Gratz men.

With Simon's death a good deal of family unity broke apart, and Jewish life in Lancaster faded. Joseph Simon's was the last interment in that town's Jewish cemetery until a second wave of settlers moved there and performed a burial in 1855. Simon's death was in effect the end of the first Jewish community of Lancaster.[89]

The adversarial relationships with Joseph Simon and his heirs that engrossed Michael and Simon Gratz had little effect on the lives of Rebecca and her sisters, which remained focused on domestic and cultural matters. In May 1804, Rachel Gratz and Gertrude Meredith happened to be in Baltimore at the same time. Rachel was visiting Frances, and she insisted to Rebecca that neither of these two gifted women, Frances or Gertrude, could compare, in her judgment, with Rebecca. Gratz thought her sister's idea absurd, and worried about Rachel's ability to see her as she was. "Your love . . . is . . . invaluable to me . . . [but] how can you think so highly of me when you have Mrs. Meredith's wisdom and Fanny's wit with you?"[90] That summer, Rebecca traveled to New York. While Simon Gratz divided land left to him by Aaron Levy to create the borough of Gratz in Dauphin County, Pennsylvania, Rebecca and Sarah visited their friends and Richea in New York, lodging in Princeton along the way.[91] The visit to New York cemented Gratz's friendship with Judge Hoffman, and when his daughter Matilda enrolled in Madam Greland's Boarding School in Philadelphia that October, he asked both Gratz and Gertrude Meredith to keep an eye on the girl. He asked Gratz to learn the rate at which linens would be supplied and sought her advice on whether Matilda ought to manage her laundry. Hoffman thought the girl too immature for such responsibilities; Maria thought otherwise, but they agreed to let Gratz's opinion decide the matter.

Hoffman hoped the friendship he formed with Gratz would "possess all the fervor of youth and the strength of time." They were both, as he said, "sensible people."[92]

Gertrude Meredith and Gratz were themselves developing a close friendship. In September 1805, Gertrude and her children went to Newark to escape Philadelphia's end-of-summer heat and epidemic, while her husband, William Meredith, stayed in the city. Gertrude adored her husband and wrote letters with original love poems to him almost daily. When she learned he had been invited to the Gratz house, she urged him to accept the invitation. Detailing for him her high regard for Rebecca, Gertrude said she "possesses great powers of pleasing . . . especially in the epistolary."[93] Although Meredith was a deeply religious woman who undertook formal though private theological studies, she often arrived at conclusions different from most Protestant ministers of her day. Gratz's loyalty to Judaism appealed to Meredith's piety.

Like Judge Hoffman, Gertrude thought Rebecca, a "sensible and amiable woman." She wrote that, as such, Gratz might, "like the few righteous persons [who] saved the city of Nineveh from destruction . . . save her family from that scorn and contempt which we *liberal* Christians generally attach to Jews." One night, while comforting a sick infant, Gertrude Meredith read a play and wrote a long letter to Rebecca as she rocked the cradle. She "so beguiled the night that I was really astonished when the day dawned" and told her husband to send word to Rebecca that she planned to visit her as soon as she returned to the city.[94]

The two women continued to correspond, sometimes writing about Mr. Meredith, who, much to his wife's regret, traveled extensively on business and while serving as a member of the Pennsylvania State Legislature. Although Gertrude often told her husband that she was less interested in riches than in his companionship, she hesitated to advise him on what she saw as his rightful sphere, business. But through her correspondence with Gratz she strengthened her resolve. Fearful that William endangered his health by remaining in the city, she prefaced her plea to her husband with Gratz's own advice to her: "I think it is high time that you lay your commands on your husband to join you, or at least to abscond from the city. Yesterday there was considerable alarm in your neighborhood, and . . . Mr. Meredith is almost the only person remaining there."[95]

Gratz understood Meredith's anxiety over the danger the city posed to her husband. Gratz's own worries for her family, especially for her traveling brothers, caused her enormous anguish. Health's demands, both mental and physical, superseded those of the marketplace, she believed. Those priorities, she thought, legitimized her desire to "command" the more powerful and respectable male world. It was the sort of emotion that would later flower into the domestic feminism that historians have noted common among reform and benevolent society women in Victorian America.[96]

Enjoying the satisfactions of an eminent circle of literary friends, Rebecca tried to inspire Mary Elizabeth Fenno, Maria's younger sister, to improve her own literary skills. Harriet, Maria's older sister, had already published in the *Port Folio*.[97] Mary replied, "If you want me to improve . . . write to me soon . . . [as] there is nothing like emulation and no letters are so well calculated to excite as yours." Mary's view of the literary world was more realistic than Gratz's. She knew that talent often went unrewarded. In an effort to convince Gratz of this, Mary pointed out that their mutual friend, author James Paulding, a friend of Washington Irving, was thoroughly unappreciated in 1805 New York society. He "frequently stalks by in the street," Mary wrote, "sometimes with a salutation and sometimes without . . . my heart bleeds for him, how well and how true he writes."[98]

Although Gratz's activities in literary and social worlds were often constrained and interrupted by her family's needs, she found time to write long letters when, for example, Sarah's superior skills released her from familial demands. In July 1805, Rebecca and Rachel visited Saratoga Springs, New York, while Sarah and Richea, whose daughter Sarah Ann was due to be born in September, vacationed at the New Jersey shore. Rebecca's letters to her sisters were full of advice, questions, and gossip, but her letters to her mother were travelogues capturing the world as she experienced it in lively prose. One Sunday morning, Gratz wrote to her mother from a riverboat on the Hudson River. Rebecca and Rachel were traveling to Saratoga Springs with Hyman and Solomon Moses, the latter Rachel's beau.

Assuring her mother that her "wandering daughters" were well, Gratz detailed a river storm and its effects on their ship. "Before we had time to lower the sails the sloop was almost on her beam's end. Several hogsheads that were on deck were rolled completely across the sloop and one quarter cask of wine overboard.

Trunks dancing over the cabin floor and plates and dishes crash-
ing in the most unharmonious concert. Our crew are chiefly female so you may imagine the storm was not altogether [outside]."
Nonetheless, Gratz was having a wonderful time. "We have a
delightful sloop, almost new, with every convenience and good
provisions so the only disadvantage we can complain of arrives
from the winds and a very timid Captain. We are now aground
on the flats and shall continue at anchor until the tide rises at
midnight."

　　Rebecca found even the obnoxious passengers entertaining.
"We have an intelligent man on board but he is a clergyman
[from] Staten Island, who spends every evening Psalm singing
which as his voice is as musical as his zeal is great does not
encourage our happiness as sufficiently as it may advance his
interest with Heaven." Rebecca assured her mother that their
rooms were satisfactory, that friends had supplied them kosher
meat, and that they ate well. But Rachel, who still suffered from
a cold she had when they left home, was eating only "chicken
water today." The next day was *Tishah-b'Av*, a day of fasting
commemorating the destruction of the temple in Jerusalem. Gratz
explained to her mother that although she ate dinner at 2:30 in
the afternoon, it was "the first time I ever broke my fast on this
anniversary but it was only on the condition that I could induce
Rachel to eat and did not think she was strong enough to go
through the day." Reassuring her parents of her religious loyalty,
she told them of her prayers and her respect for them. "Having
passed the morning at my devotion on board sloop I consented to
break my fast at dinner—would to God I knew how you and my
dearest Father are! . . . [W]e have smoked beef and a tongue and
Mr. Gumpert is at the [Saratoga] springs in a private house where
he provides meat for his own table so my affectionate parents need
feel no apprehensions respecting our diet."[99]

　　By now in her mid-twenties, Rebecca also began occasionally
caring for the children of family and friends. At the end of the
year, Judge Hoffman, Maria's husband, wrote to Gratz asking
her to keep an eye on their daughter Ann, who, at fifteen, had
convinced her parents to let her join Matilda at Madam Greland's
Boarding School in Philadelphia. Hoffman had misgivings about
letting Ann—brilliant, beautiful, and immature—leave the family
home and hoped Gratz would watch over her. "I commit her to your
protection—she loves and respects you," he wrote.[100] Rebecca also

took care of her own nieces and nephews. That fall, Richea left her children with Gratz and her aging parents while she visited Bloomfield with Rachel. Gratz loved the experience. "Rosa is the soul of the house," she wrote delightedly to her sisters. "We have all found her so entertaining that we shall not know how to part with her." Lest Richea think that they were having too much fun indulging her children, Gratz added, "Every attention [you] require is paid to their diet."[101]

Hoffman's fears about Ann's immaturity soon were fulfilled. The girl was walking around the city barefoot, because Madam Greland would not supply her with the shoes that Maria was sure her husband had paid for. Although Hoffman sent money to Ann, the girl spent it to hire people to work for her and was deeply in debt. Instead of sending more money to the girl, Maria sent a twenty-pound note to Gratz, asking her to "relieve [Ann] from her distress."[102] Maria was grateful to her friend, and on her own twenty-sixth birthday, on March 17, wrote, "The first action of the twentysixth year of my life is writing a letter to you." Maria was happy and contented in her marriage, and when March 4, Rebecca's birthday, passed she had thought of her friend. "I . . . wished that another [year] might see you happy as I feel myself and possessed of the greatest blessing in this life—a good husband."[103]

Although Gratz did not marry, her sister Rachel soon did. Rachel Gratz fell in love with New Yorker Solomon Moses, a man whom Sarah Gratz did not like. When Rachel broke the news to her family, Rebecca, who was with Rachel in New York, wrote to Sarah urging her to accept Rachel's choice for the sake of peace in the family. Appealing both to Sarah's "goodness of heart" and "reason," she begged, "for God's sake, be careful that you suffer not your feelings to wound the heart of our Rachel—she loves Sol Moses." Rachel, afraid to confront Sarah, asked Rebecca to intervene. Hoping to maintain peace between her sisters, Rebecca appealed to Sarah's love for Rachel: "the whole of [Solomon Moses's] life will be to promote her happiness . . . cheer her heart and be . . . a comfort. I hope our parents won't be unhappy . . . they shouldn't . . . Sol is universally esteemed here . . . and he really appears . . . affectionate, kind, attentive, and watchful." What more could she say to cool Sarah's fears?

Yet Rebecca harbored her own misgivings over Rachel's marriage. She could not stand to lose this sister and confided in Sarah:

"My foolish head will not cease palpitating when I think of our Rachel . . . Rachel! Our Beloved Sister!" She despaired of losing Rachel's company, and feared Rachel's possible unhappiness. She appealed to Sarah. "You my sister! . . . say you are pleased—say our parents sanction her choice—say you are all happy—and bid me be so—or tell me your sorrows and I will weep—this state of anxiety and suspense is insupportable. Rachel's [situation] cannot be more poignant—but a word from some of you may calm my heart to peace."[104] Rachel married Solomon Moses on June 24, 1806.

Rebecca stayed in New York throughout the summer, helped Rachel get settled in her new home, and met artist Edward Malbone, who painted miniature portraits of both sisters.[105] That August, Rachel accompanied Rebecca to the Sans Souci Hotel in Saratoga Springs. To Sarah, Gratz admitted that Rachel "complained a good deal, if she were not married I should feel uneasy about her . . . no appetite . . . [won't] drink the water and having no curiosity to satisfy grows tired—as for society . . . she has collected it all in one object—her husband." Rebecca had never seen behavior like Rachel's. If this was love, she did not find it appealing. But Rachel's discomfort was more likely pregnancy than lovesickness, as her son Isaac was born about seven months later.

Despite Rachel's complaints, Gratz enjoyed Sans Souci. "The females, as is frequently the case at such places—are the most numerous and in all respects superior," she wrote to Sarah. "Among them however we have instances on whom the pen of satire might justly be employed . . . some I have found to admire, some to esteem, and a few to love, among my own sex—but there is not an interesting man . . . altho in truth we are not destitute of wisdom, of talents, or of entertaining companions. There are examples here too of no ordinary cast masculine and feminine."

Rebecca reveled in describing the Saratoga resort to Sarah, who was herself on a holiday in Long Beach, New Jersey. "Anyone inclined to while away a summer might pass it here and at its close, wake himself as from a dream," she wrote. "And as the flitting vision passes in review over his imagination, he would in the crude mass of indistinct events distinguish nothing—nightly dancing and long, the ringing of bells and laughing, loud talking, tricks of legerdemain, the evening promenade, the music of the flute—raising of ghosts—Malbone and dancing men . . . and mineral water facilities . . . [in] this busy scene of idleness that while

I am summoning them up for your information—they alternately echo through my ears and I can scarcely realize that I am really in my chamber."[106]

Literary Circles and Friendships

Gratz's greatest delight was socializing with interesting, intelligent people at resorts in New York and Baltimore and at home. Well read, educated, and wealthy, Gratz was among the first generation of American women in the North to form a leisure class. She thought *"gaietie de coeur* essential to family life."[107] While socializing with Philadelphia's elites, Rebecca met other distinguished people, among them Joseph Bonaparte and his daughter. She was flattered that at one ball, "the King . . . conduct[ed] himself like a well bred gentleman among his peers."[108] At twenty-six, in a year during which Frances, Richea, and Rachel each bore children, Rebecca enjoyed Philadelphia's parties, teas, cotillions, assemblies, balls, and theater, and noted that "the fashionable world is unmarred by political troubles."[109]

While Gratz was at the center of the city's social elite, Washington Irving sent Thomas Sully, then an aspiring young artist, to visit her, trusting that she would introduce him to the people most likely to ensure his success in Philadelphia. In June 1807, Thomas Sully painted what he called a "fancy picture" of Gratz from the portrait of her done by Edward Malbone for the actor Thomas Cooper. Sully eventually produced more than twenty-six hundred paintings, including a few of Gratz, and was known for a "freshness and sensuality" different from other portraitists of his day.[110] The Gratz family supported many local artists. Simon, Hyman, and Joseph were among the Academy of Fine Arts' first subscribers, and Simon Gratz donated a block of black jet for the center stone of the school's new lobby in 1807.[111]

During 1806 and 1807, Gratz secretly returned to writing poetry. Writing four poems on birchbark sheets and tying them together with a pink ribbon, she created a fascicle. The first poem traced the emotional turmoil experienced by her and an unnamed man whose religion prohibited their marriage. She expressed anguish at being unable to soothe his distress. The latter three poems voiced and shaped her own emotions to help her gain, as she phrased it, "a heart of ease."[112] Forming a repeated refrain, a heart of ease epitomized Rebecca's goal for her own emotional state.

Gratz had often used letters to clarify her ideas and shape her feelings, hoping to restore relationships to their smooth sequence by a persuasive line of text; her poems, however, enabled her to overcome a breach in a relationship that would not be restored. The poems name no names, but they may have referred to Sam Ewing, whose Presbyterian faith would have demanded Gratz's conversion before marriage. Moreover, Sam was two years her junior, and two of the poems refer to the anguish of a "youth."[113] Three of the poems are rather clichéd, sentimental ditties of the sort often written by women in the last century, but the fourth has a very different tone, similar in attitude to Wordsworth and the British romantics: "The world has deceived me and I will in my truth deceive it," she wrote. This poem expresses her frustration and anger that at only twenty-seven, before she had experienced much of the world, it had already rejected her.[114]

However deep the wound she suffered at the "stern hand of religion," she neither stopped cultivating relationships with non-Jewish men nor began associating with Jewish men. On the contrary, over the next few years her general socializing among the gentile elite increased, offering her an escape from her relentless responsibilities at home. About that time she also wrote a eulogy to friendship, a poem in which a late-autumn flower garden illustrated the point that "Love—Friendship—all must die." Though the world separated friends, "memory shall rescue them with pride," she wrote.[115] By her late twenties, Gratz had lost her innocence about the degree to which Jews were accepted in a Christian world.

Rebecca's preference for educated, literary men arose no doubt from both the pleasant companionship they offered and the fact that they, unlike the men in her family, spent a good deal of time at home. Gratz's family experience taught her that business fortunes were unpredictable. She reveals in dozens of letters her anxiety for her brothers' safety each time they traveled inland or abroad on business, and she no doubt wanted to avoid adding a traveling husband to her worries. Perhaps she remembered the old standards of yichus, by which daughters of wealthy, observant families could hope to marry the best-educated and most literate men, who were thought to make the best husbands. So valued were these unions that one Jewish proverb claimed, "Marrying your daughter to an ignorant man is like tying her to a lion."[116]

But education alone would not satisfy Gratz. Couples must be matched in temperament because a wife was expected to submit to her husband's ways. "No one . . . thinks . . . [the Kuhn] marriage of great promise," she gossiped. "He . . . has always lived a solitary life . . . and unless Ellen can influence the graces into him, they will be obliged to study the dead languages, and read classics together." She assured Maria that the bride was simply "captivated by his intellect," something Rebecca could understand, but she did not expect them to be happy. Reflecting her own feelings, Gratz was sure that the bride had "lived too much in the world to retire at twenty from its pleasures." On the other hand, she felt "there is such a charm in the wit and easy conversation of . . . men of letters, that they seem the best society in the world."[117] There was one such man who seemed better than others. "I think so highly of James [Paulding] that [I] . . . believe he would make an excellent husband and agreeable domestic companion."[118] Unfortunately for Gratz, within two years Paulding would marry Washington Irving's sister.

Gratz's friendships with gentile men grew naturally from lifelong friendships with gentile women. For most of her women friends, religion was a favorite topic of conversation. After the disestablishment of religion, a wide assortment of religious and political groups strove to Christianize the country.[119] Evangelists and missionaries often sought out poor Jews, but sometimes evangelizing was—as in the case of Gratz and her brother Joseph, a member of the prestigious First City Troop—an invitation to an already accepted person to join the majority. Indeed, even her beloved Hoffmans never gave up hope of converting Gratz to Christianity.[120]

Gratz discussed religion most often with Gertrude Meredith, who was considered a "towering intellect" and who, like Gratz's mother, bore twelve children. Meredith's mansion was a center of Philadelphia's literary culture, but not of fashionable society.[121] Meredith and Gratz exchanged and critiqued books and interpreted the events of each other's lives. Later in the century, women often formed literary clubs for this purpose, but Gratz selected friends with whom she could expand her intellectual life.

Gratz felt more confident when expressing her thoughts to women than to men. Rather than retreating from or ignoring the anti-Semitism she encountered among gentile women, she attacked their prejudices directly, hoping to eliminate them. In

1807 she asked Gertrude Meredith about the origin and continu-
ance of anti-Semitism among Christians, and received a lengthy
response. Meredith did not believe it her duty to convert Jews
to Christianity, and even encouraged her Jewish friends to remain steadfast in their faith. When she invited the Gratzes to
dinner, she assured them that "the feast shall be according to law
and none shall compel you to eat of that which is forbidden."[122]
Meredith explained that she thought the Bible taught that virtue
and faith are the most important aspects of any religion, and that
they outweighed religious doctrine in earning God's forgiveness.
After making it clear that she had "never felt . . . prejudice against
Jews," Meredith located the origin of anti-Semitism in the "malig-
nity of the primitive Christians who were not sufficiently enlightened to enjoy at once the privileges which their divine Master
yielded them." If they had been so enlightened, instead of "malice
against the Jews who condemned and crucified our blessed Jesus,
they would have felt . . . compassion and pity for an unfortunate
nation." A Christian's task is to learn from Jesus, Meredith wrote,
accepting that Jews, not Romans, had crucified Jesus, but because
Jesus said, "Father, forgive them for they know not what they do,"
a Christian should likewise forgive Jews.

Meredith went on to express her affection for the Gratz family. She saw the Gratzes like herself—as sinners "walking humbly
in the sight of heaven," not "left in the dark without hope of salvation," while the "proud fanatick [is] like the Pharisee of old. Tis
virtue exalts the human mind and virtue is the same whether . . .
in the bosoms of Christians or . . . the patriarchal breast." Meredith admitted the fanaticism and self-righteousness among some
Christian evangelists. She called Presbyterians "a sect . . . more
malignant than any others against your nation" and recalled an
incident in which she had publicly defended "a virtuous Jew" and
his expectation of reaching heaven.

"It absolutely gives me the spleen when I hear violent assen-
tations [*sic*] against the wickedness of the Jews," Meredith wrote.
She went on to give Gratz her ideas on the state and future of
Judaism in America. She wished that "your establishment was on
a better footing in our land and that the inferior classes in your
society would begin to . . . support their faith by . . . attention to
their religious duties and by a steady and uniform course of virtuous conduct." Such a change would, she thought, free the "temple"
from "unjust domination by a den of thieves." This was hardly a

compliment to Gratz, whose brothers held leadership responsibilities in the synagogue, but because Gratz knew Meredith's insults sprang from ignorance and not prejudice, she remained her friend and educated her about Jews and Judaism.

Meredith's position was similar to that of Christians who believed that Jews must return to Zion, rebuild the ancient temple in Jerusalem, and reinstate its rites in order for Jesus to return to earth. Many of these Christians believed that, like Meredith, they loved the Jews. Meredith believed Judaism was "that holy religion which . . . is undoubtedly the most ancient of which we have any knowledge, was certainly of divine origin, was practiced and supported by Jesus Christ, and . . . was the instrument in almightly hands of that redemption from sin to which we Christians cling as our rock of defense." Christians ought not to feel the "contempt and hatred of Jews which we too often find as overgrown weeds in the wisest heads."

Meredith asked the Gratzes to "continue to adhere to their faith . . . and though [Jews may] continue to suffer reproach among men, yet will [your] reward be greater in heaven where I hope to see you all established as the chosen flock of an almighty Father." She concluded her argument by asking Gratz's forgiveness if she had written "a single sentence hurtful to your sentiments or feelings. . . . If I am in error you . . . must correct me for my mind is always open . . . when a sensible and amiable friend leads the way."[123] Meredith's unwavering support for Judaism's legitimacy strengthened the women's friendship and encouraged Gratz to pursue religious conversations with other non-Jewish women friends. Religion shaped Gratz's friendships with women throughout her life.

Gratz enjoyed secular culture through her friendships with men. By 1807, Rebecca socialized among the *Port Folio*'s inner circle. John Ewing Hall, Sam's nephew in Baltimore, whose writing she encouraged, compiled an index to the magazine's first two years especially for Rebecca and Sarah. Perhaps reminded of her father's illness, Rebecca took time to write to this very melancholy man who hoped to succeed as an author. When Washington Irving visited Baltimore that year, Hall introduced the more famous writer to Baltimore society, ushering him among the literary women.

Hall had just published a lengthy poem titled *Anacreon* and asked Gratz what his Philadelphia friends thought of it. He planned to send a volume to Sam Ewing, and suggested that she borrow that copy. Hall was sending his latest work, "Sonnet to My Mistress' Eyebrow," to Joseph Dennie for the *Port Folio*. Despite his social obligations, Hall told Gratz that were it not for letters from a few friends, he would leave Baltimore and "hie to the woods of Tennessee."[124] But Hall stayed where he was and continued to write to Gratz. "How often do I wish that I had your friendly fireside within an hour's walk," he wrote the next winter. "Solitude is very agreeable, but yet one wants a friend to whom one can say 'solitude is very agreeable.'"[125]

Hall scolded Gratz for not writing to him more often and accused her of "dissipation" through too much dancing, music, and tea. He assured her that he could see the decay of the *Port Folio*.[126] Rather than look for Hall when she went to Baltimore that June to help Frances deliver a new baby, Gratz hoped to see more of a Mr. House, a man introduced to her by Peggy Ewing. "You must have cautioned him against me," she wrote to her friend, because "unless to accompany some lady, he has paid me but one visit since I came to Baltimore." Despite his disinterest, Gratz was sure that she could win him. "Expect to hear of our conquest in my next letter."[127] But no conquest occurred.

Sam Ewing visited the Baltimore family, but Gratz explained to his sister that "he has not got over his silent fit yet. All our friends are surprised at his taciturnicity [*sic*]." Despite his moodiness, he brought Gratz the first issue of a new journal.[128] Yet when the two went riding he neglected to show Gratz a particular tree in Baltimore that he had promised to point out. So stormy was their friendship that Gratz was sure that he neglected it solely because he had promised it to her.[129] No doubt Gratz's skepticism about romance contributed to their difficulties. Gratz explained to Peggy that she was "never one of the numerous train of worshippers [to] the Goddess of romance."[130]

Sam announced his engagement to another woman that year, and Gertrude Meredith wrote to Sam's sister, Sarah Hall, that it was the winter's favorite gossip topic. The Philadelphia women doubted Ewing's sincerity. "As his nuptial morn approaches he begins to look . . . as if he thought the season of love and poetry was fast declining," Meredith quipped. Many of Sam's poems in the *Port Folio* were titled "Reflections in Solitude," and Meredith remarked that if Sam wrote negative "Reflections on the Holy State of Wedlock," a "knot of wives among us . . . are determined to make him swallow every word."[131]

Death, Depression, and Travels

Seeking a vacation from family duties, Gratz visited New York again in May 1808. Her mother, who was quite ill, was anxious for her safety.[132] When Miriam Gratz died that September, Gertrude Meredith wrote a poetic condolence letter illustrating her belief that heaven is not denied to Jews. "If to the 'pure of heart' all bliss is given / Thy lot, my friends is surely fixed in heav'n." She asked Gratz not to believe that she had no comfort left. Indeed, her mother now "may mediate 'twixt her children and their God!" and "Her happy spirit still may cling to thee." Instead of mourning, Rebecca ought to "cheer and like thy pious parent be / In duty steadfast and from murmuring free" until "the dread mandate of death's awful call / in better Worlds unite us all."[133] Gratz's many other gentile friends also offered condolences. Caroline Ogden, a cousin of Gertrude Meredith's, urged Gratz to remember that "the dispensations of God are just, and it is our duty to [show] fortitude and patience, which I am confident . . . you will . . . do."[134]

Gratz visited her mother's portrait daily, feeling that her "only consolation was to gaze on it." She hoped to learn pious resignation from the expression on her mother's face. Such resignation, she believed, had been her mother's "most conspicuous virtue" and the one Gratz worked hardest to develop in herself. She was shaken by the effect of her mother's death on her father's "already depressed mind." One day, when Michael broke down after looking at his wife's portrait, Rebecca decided to close the room where it was kept. Her father's deep and long-lasting grief frightened her and no doubt convinced Gratz that her "first duty [was] to . . . cheer [his] gloomy despondency."[135] To honor their mother, Rachel named her daughter, born a month after her mother's death, Miriam Gratz Moses. Deep in her own grief and worrying about her father's depression, Rebecca again grew anxious about everyone's emotional health. She even advised Maria against spending so much time in the nursery that she lost the rejuvenating experience of socializing with her adult friends and family.[136]

To steady her own emotions, Gratz turned to religion. She read the Bible for guidance in developing the kind of virtuous character that she thought God wanted from her. Like Gertrude Meredith, she believed that virtue and faith were the essence of all religion. Gratz's view of God was the omnipotent, omniscient, merciful, and just creator and father she read about and on whom she depended daily. Like many other antebellum women, Gratz's spirituality sought active expression in worship and in community service, an approach to religious life also strongly endorsed by Judaism.

In March 1809, Maria's daughter Matilda contracted consumption, left boarding school, and returned to New York. Ann, who had also returned home to help her mother, wrote to Rebecca in April that Matilda had improved after mercurial ointment "removed the fever." Ann's relief at her sister's improvement was also relief for her stepmother, Maria, who was Matilda's "constant attendant."[137] But Matilda died a month later. Ann's letter to Gratz was more a lecture to herself, reciting the religious ideas about death that she had been taught. "[Matilda] has made a happy exchange . . . [she is] reunited with her mother . . . [in] a kingdom which will have no end," she wrote. Ann hoped that Rebecca had "humbly" accepted Matilda's "joyful escape" from this life. Ann also assured Rebecca that Maria, who had been ashen with weariness during Matilda's last weeks, had begun to recover. "Roses begin to appear in her cheeks and in a few days her health will be perfectly re-established," she promised.

Ann assured Gratz that her letters during Matilda's illness "afforded me the greatest consolation," and asked Gratz to continue writing to her, to be her friend as well as her stepmother's. As if to demonstrate that she could give as well as receive, as a friend ought, she continued, "I am not unmindful of your sorrows Becky. How is Mrs. Etting? dear Rachel and Sally? I love you all. After the loss I have sustained my soul clings closer to those I have left to me."[138] Nothing could have made Rebecca happier. In her relationship with Ann, Gratz began a pattern that she followed throughout her life, establishing close bonds with the children of her friends and relatives.

Gratz assumed that, because he was a man, Judge Hoffman would be less emotional over his daughter's death than would his wife, and Gratz wrote to him that the "consolation of having fulfilled every duty is sufficient, with your due reverence to the will of God to reconcile you." But to Maria she wrote that the "disappointment of a fond parent's heart . . . can only be mitigated by the reflection that the stroke was given by an unerring hand. . . . [Matilda's] heavenly soul . . . was prepared to reach the glory to which all our hopes point." Using a sentimental idea popular in women's literature, and a staple of the Protestant theology she had learned from Meredith, Caroline Ogden, and

Ann Hoffman, Gratz told her friend Maria that her stepdaughter had gone to a happier world where she would be cared for by a better Father. Gratz tried to minimize the loss by making it temporary.[139]

While Maria had tended Matilda in New York, Gratz continued to nurse her family in Philadelphia. By 1809 she was sure enough of her skills that she identified her most important nursing tools as an "appetite and a tolerable share of composure." Gratz worried about everyone's pregnancies, and about all of her nieces and nephews as they reached their teen years.[140] Medical wisdom held pregnancy and childbirth to be a true danger to women because they disrupted the flow of fluids. Although the Gratzes patronized the most prestigious doctors in Philadelphia— Rush, Chapman, and Kuhn—the family had a very high rate of worrisome pregnancies and childhood deaths. Doctors routinely bled women in the last month of pregnancy if they complained of too much discomfort.[141] Just as pregnancy posed one threat to health, so breast-feeding posed another. Gratz advised her friends against breast-feeding in summer and in southern climates.[142]

At twenty-eight, with her sisters having borne eighteen children among them, Gratz was beginning to have to account for her single state. While vacationing at the Cottage, she could reflect on the way her life was headed, and felt that she continued unmarried both because of her own choices and because of those made by the men she had known. Gratz accepted her state philosophically, rationalizing to Peggy that she believed it "better to wander alone, through the neglected path of single life—than with an ungenial companion traverse a Garden [of wedlock] where every fragrant flower blooms to the eye—but withers to the touch—where every bright prospect is obscured by the cloud of discontent—or lost in the whirlwind of contention."

Rebecca admitted that hers was not the general view of marriage, conceding that she saw the "extreme dark side" of the marriage union. But, she continued, "We can be moderately happy single and expect exquisite felicity when we marry." Lest her friend think her a hopeless romantic, she argued, "A married man told me last week there was no medium between happiness and misery in that state—he has been twice married—and . . . has experienced both." Marriage with neither an "amiable domestic companion" nor an overwhelming passion, Rebecca believed, was a poor life indeed. She would rather stay single.[143] One historian has called that attitude "single blessedness," and notes that it was common among many unmarried antebellum women. These women, much like Gratz, called their liberty a "better husband."[144]

In 1810, when Sam Ewing married Elizabeth Redman, Gratz congratulated Peggy on acquiring a sister-in-law. Revealing her own deepest emotional experience, she explained, "The happy combination of sister and friend appears to me as one of those extra blessings with which Heaven intended to counterbalance a thousand of life's sorrows and privations."[145] Sam sent a poem to Rebecca, calling her "best friend to the man who is to be married and to the woman who swears she never will be married!"[146]

While Sam married, Rebecca went to New York to help Rachel, whose daughter Miriam was ill and who was due to deliver another child, whom she named Rebecca Gratz Moses. In Gratz's absence, Sarah relayed messages between the board of the Female Association and her sister. Another woman fulfilled Gratz's FA duties while she was in New York, and Sarah conveyed requests for advice about what was to be done.

Now it was Sarah's turn to impatiently await Rebecca's return. "I cannot bear to think how much longer we shall yet be separated," she complained. "Had you gone on a pleasure trip . . . I should have participated in your enjoyments . . . but now I can only view you confined to a sick room, sacrificing your rest and perhaps your health." How would Sarah cope if the family's other nurse, Rebecca, herself became ill? An exhausted Sarah was soon nursing a niece in Baltimore; Frances's Isabella was sick. Richea's son Barnard had died in May. "I sometimes think you and I will be obliged to get M . . . d to get rid of *our* troubles," she complained to Gratz.[147] Sarah could not even bring herself to spell out the word "married."

Despite her own ambivalence about marriage, Gratz was convinced that her brothers had no legitimate reasons for staying single, so she and Sarah kept house for them and moralized at them as they saw fit. When Joseph left for Europe in 1810, Gratz advised him to associate with "refined" women, rather than another sort which he had preferred. "I hope . . . you will . . . cultivate a taste for the society of the refined among our sex," she admonished him. Such a woman would be the sort of sister-friend she would like. Reaching for a way to convince Joseph, she tried tying her idea to his interest in business contacts. "Besides the pleasure to be derived from their conversation, you will always be sure to meet the most polished men in their circles." Finally, she took a religious route. "There is no better safeguard to the morals, and consequently to the happiness of a young man than the friendship of amiable women."[148] She admitted to Maria that she frequently "upbraid[ed her] bachelor brothers for continuing in their single state. A bad example in the eldest seems to inflict them, and I fear we shall all grow old together in the family mansion."[149] Yet we cannot take seriously her unhappiness at that prospect, since it was largely this state of affairs that allowed her to remain single. Moreover, her letters to her brother Joseph, whom she thought the family wit and who often accompanied her on trips to Saratoga Springs, reveal her delight in his company.[150]

At the end of November 1810, Simon Gratz too was considering a journey, making arrangements to leave Philadelphia on business for at least a month. Michael Gratz was ill and depressed again, and Sarah panicked. "Come Home!" she wrote to Rebecca, still in New York. "Leave Rachel and her children there if you have to." Rebecca stayed with Rachel and Richea in New York, and Sarah's panic passed. Sarah simply did not tell Michael that Simon was preparing to leave. "As there is now a possibility of your returning before [Simon] goes, I do not mean to tell him til the last of the weekend. Simon starts on Sunday."[151]

Michael Gratz lived to see his youngest son, Benjamin, graduate from the University of Pennsylvania, but died in September 1811, ten years after the death of his brother Barnard. Her father's death exacerbated Gratz's anxiety about her brothers' travels. Enviously, Rebecca told Maria that she considered her lucky to be "free from [the] care [and] anxiety, which we, whose dearest interests are so often involved in dangers and hardships[,] must endure."[152] Although the Gratz men were wealthy, their financial success depended on good outcomes to repeated risks. They traveled extensively to locate good markets and assess lands. Rebecca found it all dizzying, and as family nurse she worried about their continual exposure to the health risks posed by frontier conditions, stagecoaches and ships, diseases in other towns, and poor heating. Gratz's worries grew even deeper when Benjamin and Joseph, members of the First City Troop, served as officers in the War of 1812.[153] Her brothers' obvious delight in their travels and adventures angered and bewildered Gratz. To her, their lives appeared as unstable as a "magic lantern." As she wrote to Maria in 1812, "Be thankful that your happiness . . . is not subject to the

ever varying scene which is so continually turning in the magic
lantern of a merchant's life."[154]

The year 1812 brought changes to the Gratz brothers' business dealings. New York City, whose port did not freeze, forged
ahead of Philadelphia in port trade, and Caribbean trade, which
had comprised a major portion of Gratz business, dropped dramatically because political uprisings there threatened travelers'
safety.[155] The Gratz brothers, who had been engaged in land speculation in the American West for decades, relied more and more
on inland trade. Hyman spent most of the year traveling west and
exploring family-owned lands in the Ohio valley and especially
eastern Kentucky. At Dripping Springs, Kentucky, near Mammoth
Cave, he wrote to Rebecca that he was having a difficult time
getting laborers to clear out the enormous cave, but no problem
finding interested scientists, specialists, and tourists who wanted
to examine the natural wonder. While Hyman was in Kentucky
he missed seeing "the amiable Miss Myers," a New Yorker who
visited Gratz. Rebecca had hoped for a marriage between the two,
but Hyman said, "The fates are against me and I must submit
with patience." His mind was on the cave, not on marriage.[156]

Her brothers' travels deepened Gratz's sense of loss following
her parents' deaths and the deaths of nieces and nephews. By 1812
her parents had died and Richea and Frances each had buried
two children. Sarah had become sickly, and Aunt Shinah was an
invalid. Nursing her family in its illness, Gratz told Maria that
her "trials and deprivations . . . might even shake the resolution
of a manly breast."[157]

The country's renewed warfare with England worried Gratz.
Though not a pacifist, she hated wars that brought families into
"alarming states of anxiety." Because her brothers were under
orders, she felt the War of 1812 required "some fortitude and a
great deal more patriotism than [it] inspired."[158] Her aunt Sloe
Hays was more direct in her political criticism: "Were the world
composed of women we should have no weapons . . . but eyes and
tongue—and if they kill it is only an individual that suffers, not
nations," she wrote.[159]

Back home and year-round, women who bore as many children as the Gratz women required a great deal of care, and Rebecca
made the rounds of each household to see to each patient's comfort.
In March 1813, she called health "a fugitive from our family [who]
only visits us at intervals and a few at a time." She counted off the

invalids: "Richea and her infant (Rebecca born September 13) are very ill . . . and Sally . . . has taken to her bed again." Blaming the weather, she said, "March . . . is very unfriendly to delicacy and other female qualifications."[160]

Gratz's health remained generally good, and in her letters she rarely complained of anything more than a headache or cold. When Maria Fenno Hoffman heard rumors that Rebecca looked unwell, Gratz blamed the demands of nursing and worry. "Perpetual care is certainly a mortal foe to good looks and good spirits so you will most likely have heard very sad accounts of me." But she assured her friend that her health was "not in the least impaired by the unusual calls that have been made upon me." Knowing Maria's concern for the family, she went on, "My present solicitude is for Rachel whose spirits have never recovered the shock they sustained at the . . . death of her infant."[161] Rachel's daughter Harriet, born in October, had died in infancy.

Celibacy, Religion, Children, and Correspondence

Considering her social milieu, it is not surprising that Gratz grew skittish about marriage. Benjamin Rush, family physician to the Gratzes, argued in 1812 that sex could injure health. Moralists in the late eighteenth and early nineteenth centuries suggested that women had fewer sexual desires and that, perhaps, their lusts would be awakened by their husbands. These ideas had circulated in America largely among Puritan evangelicals.[162] By the nineteenth century, illusions of female purity buttressed social prejudices, and sexual stereotypes portrayed uncontrolled sexuality among Native Americans, blacks, Mexicans, and the "lower classes," especially on the part of women.[163] The sharpest distinction in the ideology of sexual natures lay between the southern women of the planter class, who were expected to be nearly totally frigid, and slave women, who were required to be available to their master's sexual demands.[164] As a Jewish woman who saw American anti-Jewish feeling increasing, Gratz may have felt pressured to demonstrate that Jewish women could be sexually pure.[165]

In antebellum Philadelphia spinsters were not uncommon, especially among the middle and upper classes. The single life chosen by Rebecca, Sarah, and three of their brothers paralleled the high rate of celibacy among the influential Quakers in Philadelphia. Among other leading families of the early Philadelphia

Jewish community, the experience was similar.[166] One historian has argued that antebellum Protestant sects that advocated or required celibacy viewed it not only as a means of spiritual growth and self-discipline, but also as an aid in affecting the attitudes of the wider American society. Celibacy freed those sectarians from the narrower domestic concerns of nuclear families.[167] Celibacy functioned similarly for Gratz, for whom a perceived less passionate nature offered greater moral authority.

Single people in prosperous American Jewish families, whom statistics and yichus kept eligible nearly all their adult lives, must have deliberately chosen that course for themselves. Though the single men did not have statistics on their side, their yichus was even greater, yet the opportunities high status gave three out of five Gratz brothers did not induce them to marry. Ironically, sometimes prestige inhibited marriage. Sloe Hays, Gratz's aunt in Richmond, Virginia, was courted by an immigrant whom the family so ridiculed that the marriage never took place.[168] Also, when women died in childbirth, widowers sometimes sought older wives who could step in as mother to an established brood.

Regardless of her celibacy, Gratz cared deeply about children, especially their education. Occasionally she approached publishers with ideas for children's books. She tried to interest Maria Fenno Hoffman in "sketch[ing] a set of cuts for the story of Redriding Hood and the Wolf King which I shall send. . . . I have applied to a printer to publish it. . . . I propose sitting myself in my sleighing costume for the grandmum." Another friend of hers wrote a book for her own children which was printed by "one of the Episcopal charity schools. I believe it is intended as easy lessons on the Gospel."[169] Philadelphia women were creating new materials, usually religious, with which to educate their children and the children of their community.

Religion, legally a matter of private conscience, was being grasped seriously by more and more women, and women increasingly filled the pews of most Christian churches.[170] In 1812, when Gratz again visited New York, Mary Elizabeth Fenno, Maria's younger sister, attended worship services with her at Shearith Israel. It was not the first time Gratz had invited a Protestant friend to synagogue. However, she admitted that it was the "first time in my life I felt pride in explaining to a stranger the forms and ceremonies which by Mr. Seixas's illustration did not lose their solemnity."[171]

But Gratz's friends respected her religion, at least in principle, regardless of her embarrassment over the seeming lack of solemnity in the synagogue. Gertrude Meredith especially assured Gratz of her regard. That year Meredith's husband became a director of the bank organized at Simon Gratz's countinghouse, and friendships between the two families deepened.[172] When Gertrude invited young Benjamin to a dinner party at her house in 1813, she assured Rebecca that the other guests would "make no attempt to convert him." When the women debated whether or not a woman friend of theirs would likely get to heaven, Meredith archly pointed out that it had yet to be determined "what a woman would really consider a *Heaven*," suggesting that one's ultimate reward was more individually designed than the popular Christian vision of cherubs riding on clouds afforded. For Meredith, one sex's ultimate reward might well be the other's crushing disappointment.[173]

While Gratz's Christian friends debated the landscape and access roads to heaven, her own attitudes about religion reflected Judaism's focus on responsibilities in this world. For Gratz, the greatest gift of religion was its capacity to promote mental health. "Poor spirits" could be dangerous to one's health, she was sure, and so should be avoided at all costs. To Gratz, mental health was the single most important key to overcoming tragedy, surviving illness, and living a respectable life in which one could find joy despite adversity. "There are many kinds of trials in this life," she wrote in 1813, "but an unsubdued spirit may overcome them all."[174]

Religion could both raise one's spirits and provide a community of relationships. Condolence letters that passed between Gratz and her Christian friends often mentioned the need for women to learn to submit to their losses and accept them as God's will. Their letters illustrate the difficulty that the women experienced in accomplishing this psychological feat. But through her conviction that an "unsubdued spirit" enabled her to survive tragedy, Gratz explored the idea in a new way. For her, coming from a Jewish tradition that sees a religious obligation to improve the world and carry out communal responsibilities, faith in God meant accepting life in order to continue and expand one's good deeds.[175] Jewish women's religious traditions, which consisted of far fewer ritual obligations than men observed, found religious virtue in charitable and ethical action.[176]

Gratz preferred benevolent involvement with children. Spending more and more time in her sisters' large households,

Gratz discovered that she found children entertaining and fasci-
nating. By 1815 she had twenty-seven nieces and nephews, many
of whom she had helped deliver. She wrote to Maria, who was
then educating her own children, that the "occupation of school
mistress is excellent. If you are like me you will never tire of it."
She went on, "children are very good society. I am never more
entertained than in Rachel's nursery or when Sister [Richea] Hays'
little girls . . . pass weeks at our house. Their reading exercises are
quite as improving to me as to them."[177]

In 1815 Gratz joined several other Philadelphia women in
establishing the city's first orphan asylum. Both the Female Association and the Philadelphia Orphan Asylum (POA) were largely
the work of Presbyterian women, and although the FA had briefly
offered care for orphans, it shifted its work to educating young
women when the POA organized. Gratz remained on the board
of managers of both the FA and the POA, serving as secretary
for both—the POA for almost forty years. Despite their Christian
rhetoric, Gratz became one of their most important fund-raisers.[178]

Although she immersed herself in the day-to-day needs of
the POA, Gratz rather coyly described her days as passing in a
"very trifling manner." "Rachel's children are my favorite toys,"
she wrote to Maria. "I read a little and sew a little and write
a little and gossip a little for the sake of the poor—go about
lecturing or spoiling the children of the different families, and fall
pretty much into the habits of other old maids."[179] Although Gratz
trivialized her activities, it was only polite humility. She raised
money and material donations for orphans and the city's "reduced"
women and maintained two organizations' correspondence and
her scattered family's relationships.

In 1815 Gratz still refused to claim that her work was important, but she did find her work meaningful. Her leadership of
benevolent societies provided an arena in which she could display
expertise, sometimes earned through painful experience in her
own family. Just as important, charitable leadership gave her
a means for developing personal authority in Philadelphia comparable to the communal authority her brothers enjoyed. When
acting as a manager of the POA, she was not a younger sister
whose idiosyncracies were intimately known; she was a woman of
stature. In that capacity, she was treated with respect, not pitied
as an old maid. With each new organization she founded, Gratz
increased her power and stature.

3

The Founding of the Female Hebrew Benevolent Society: 1817–1830

"In that title ["sister"] I look for such love as has been the most fertile source of comfort to me thro my life."
REBECCA GRATZ, 1820

Rebecca Gratz soon faced a new challenge to her mental health, or, as she called it, her spiritual strength. In midwinter 1817, when Rebecca was thirty-six, her sister Sarah died after a long illness. The two sisters, closest in age in a large family, had grown up sharing their bed, clothing, and daily activities.[1] As the sisters who nursed other family members, they shared a unique perspective on domesticity. As their mother aged, Sarah took over the household management and became the home's stabilizing anchor.[2] With Sarah, Rebecca shared special responsibilities, traveling among family households to aid in illnesses and crises. Although sisters Frances, Richea, and Rachel all married and withdrew into their own domestic lives, as long as Sarah lived, Gratz had a partner in her worries. With Sarah's death, she lost the person who understood her best. Without Sarah, Rebecca was left alone in her role and was the only woman, apart from the servants, in the Philadelphia home she shared with Hyman, Joseph, Jacob, and Benjamin. It is hardly surprising that Gratz's "wounded feelings sought retirement."[3]

Jewish mourning rites and the deepening interest in religion she shared with her gentile women friends drew Gratz into religious debates that both eased her personal grief and strengthened her religious convictions. While Rebecca's many non-Jewish friends counseled her to adopt their religious attitudes toward grief, those ideas, based on biblical traditions, were not so far from Gratz's own beliefs, grounded in Judaism. Maria Hoffman and Gertrude Meredith judged religious ideas by two criteria. First, they determined whether an idea could be grounded in biblical sources. For Gratz, this meant the Hebrew Bible and the biblical interpretations she learned from Jewish prayer books and holiday celebrations. Second, they had to find the ideas capable of promoting increased levels of personal piety, to have a real effect on their own experience.

Rebecca assured Maria Hoffman that "tho [I am] far less happy than you have known me, [I] am still too sensible of the blessings I possess to mourn unduly." Nonetheless, she endured a painful daily struggle with grief. Each day was "freighted with fatal remembrances" and she admitted that she was "more than usually depressed," but she assured Hoffman that she did not "reject consolations—and am even cheerful sometimes and always resigned. . . . I exert all my reason and all the strength of my mind to resist depression. I . . . walk every day . . . [and] in our large family I am seldom alone." Yet, she admitted to Maria, "it is not so easy when the elasticity of youth is gone . . . [and] I do not believe I could have parted with the companion and darling of my infant years the sharer of every after scene of my life, and faithful sympathizer of all my cares with greater fortitude than I have done now."[4]

The Rise of Antebellum Evangelism

Gratz's deepened need for both religion and familial companionship following Sarah's death paralleled trends in American society, particularly among women. While some Philadelphians welcomed Shakespearean actor Edmund Kean in 1821[5] and called their city the "Athens of America," others strove to Christianize the city's soul. Historian Jon Butler has argued that at the time of the American Revolution no more than 10 percent of the American population belonged to a Christian church. Widespread interest in alchemy, magical cures, and natural and supernatural lore persisted well into the nineteenth century, and strict denominational allegiance was rare.[6] Spiritualism, efforts to contact the dead, and calculations about the second coming of Jesus drew widespread attention, and religious utopian communities flourished throughout the antebellum period.[7] Christian clergy fought what they saw as magical and utilitarian religion with evangelical societies and revivals, and attempted to use secular laws to fight against what they viewed as false beliefs.

Efforts to Christianize the nation intensified in the early decades of the nineteenth century. For example, in 1814 the Philadelphia Bible Society printed and distributed Christian Bibles and tracts, supplied missionaries nationally, and organized a Female Bible Society (FBS) to raise funds to increase book production. Bible societies were very popular among women, and one year later the FBS listed almost seven hundred contributors.[8] The majority of Philadelphia's religious citizens supported evangelical activities. Between 1780 and 1860, Christian denominations expanded their organizational superstructure, and the growth in number of Christian churches "outstripped the national population growth." The total number of Christian congregations expanded from about 2,500 in 1780 to 11,000 in 1820 and 52,000 in 1860.[9]

Women participated enthusiastically in evangelical work, which was available to all Christians and not confined to seminary-trained individuals.[10] Women evangelists commonly believed that the "primary goal of the church was to evangelize the world."[11] Propriety kept these women from entering male environments to spread Christianity, so they were more likely to approach Jewish women and children than Jewish men. However, antebellum Jews formed less than 1 percent of the country's population, and in 1825 there were no more than three thousand Jews in America.[12] Between 1800 and 1860, Philadelphia's Jewish population, second only to that of New York, grew from approximately 200 to 8,000, while the city's population grew from 41,000 to almost 670,000.[13]

Christian evangelists succeeded in converting only a handful of American Jews. In 1816 the *Niles' Weekly Register* ridiculed missionary groups for spending "$500,000 over five years for the conversion, real or supposed, of *five* Jews."[14] Nonetheless, in 1823, missionary-minded Christians established the Philadelphia chapter of the American Society for the Melioration of the Condition of the Jews.[15] Some Americans considered targeting Jews a hopeless waste of evangelical effort. Others were theologically or politically opposed to establishing a national American religious orthodoxy.

Some Americans thought evangelism smacked of illiberalism and intolerance. But, as historian Hasia Diner has noted, "conversionists far outnumbered their opponents."[16]

Because most missionaries targeted poor families, Gratz's wealth and status shielded her from many unwanted visits by strangers hoping to convert her, and her firsthand experience of Christian evangelism was limited to her dialogues with Christian women friends. Gratz and her friends spent most of their time discussing ideas on which they agreed, only probing gently into possible disagreements. Gratz's optimism and confidence that Jews could be fully accepted in America was, in part, confirmed by the largely polite and respectful manner in which these women treated her and conducted their discussions about religion.

When she took over the Gratz household after Sarah's death, Rebecca had yet to develop household skills and found it difficult to control her servants. She wrote to Maria about a project that she called an employment agency, actually a referral system for recording servants' employment histories. Gratz hoped it would assure that only applicants with good letters would be recommended for hire, but the high percentage of immigrants and migrants looking for domestic service positions made the project impossible.[17] Eventually, she mastered her servant difficulties, probably because she preferred sorting letters and visiting her sister Rachel to housework.

Gratz's grief sobered her interests, and she began spending more time doing charitable work and studying religion and less time with what she called "the fashionable world." In 1818 she wrote to Maria that she was "trying to be useful among the orphans," and that year saw her first steps toward running a Jewish school, studying Hebrew with the women and children of her extended family. Hyman Gratz was on the synagogue committee and knew Rebecca wanted a Hebrew teacher, so he brought Solomon I. Cohen, who was hoping to be hired for a position at Mikveh Israel, home to meet Rebecca. After a month of afternoon lessons at her house, Gratz enthusiastically reported to Maria that the school was a success: "Elkalah Cohen, Maria and Ellen Hays and [eleven] little ones . . . have been for the last month outlining pronouns and etc. with as much zeal as success!" she reported. "I expect we shall make out very well if [our teacher] continues here long enough to take us through the grammar."[18] Gratz so admired Cohen that she sent a copy of his book on Judaism to Maria in New York.[19]

Gratz created her informal religious school for the women and children of her family only two years after Joanna Graham Bethune established the first Protestant Sunday school in New York. By the end of the first year Bethune's school had grown to twenty-one schools, with 250 teachers and more than 3,000 pupils.[20] Through her correspondence with Maria Fenno Hoffman and her own visits to family and friends in New York, Gratz knew of Bethune's work. Smaller, congregation-based Sunday schools, usually led by men, first appeared in Philadelphia in the 1790s,[21] and in 1817 Philadelphia's Sunday and Adult School, forerunner to the powerful American Sunday School Union, was formed.[22] Although Gratz's home school never grew beyond her family, it was the only such effort for Jewish children in Philadelphia. Wealthy Jews often hired tutors for their children, but her effort was the first time a group of Jewish children had been brought together in Philadelphia for religious education outside the synagogue. Indeed, formal Jewish religious education in Philadelphia did not extend beyond bar mitzvah tutorials for twelve-year-old boys.

As the evangelical movement gathered momentum, the public use of religious rhetoric increased. By 1819, newspapers printed theological opinions expressed in poems like "To Whom Should We Go But To Thee."

> When rankling sorrows wound the soul,
> and cares invade the breast;
> When DISTANT seems the blissful goal,
> of peace, and lasting rest
> . . .
> Blessed SAVIOUR—'tis to thee alone.[23]

Poulson's American Daily Advertiser of January 1, 1819, included three Christmas poems that likened town watchmen to the angels who, in Christian folklore, announced the birth of Jesus. Framed by a pedestal, two Ionic columns, and an open-winged eagle, the poems asked Philadelphians to give cash gifts to the town watchmen.[24] A few weeks later, the paper described a home Christmas pageant in Pennsylvania. In a home prayer hall draped with evergreens, children played the piano, sang psalms, and questioned adults about the story of Christmas by referring to an oversized painting of the nativity scene. The article assured readers that it was an excellent way to teach children about Christmas, assuming that everyone would want to do so.[25]

These public assertions of Christianity in newspapers, along with Shylock-like images of Jews in theater and folklore, formed a boundary between Christians and Jews in American culture, a boundary that Gratz sought to erase by demonstrating her own usefulness, respectability, and piety and by insisting on her right to equal treatment under American law. If her Christian friends accepted her, she believed, she could influence them to accept all Jews. With this attitude she attended meetings of the Philadelphia Orphan Asylum (POA), which opened with a prayer, often delivered by a Presbyterian minister. The asylum itself required daily Bible readings and mealtime prayers.[26] Indeed, Gratz's interests can be seen as a measure of her thorough participation in American culture and its trends. About 1819, she wrote to Maria Hoffman that she was "much pleased" by a Mr. Everett, a minister she had heard speak, and urged Hoffman to attend his church in New York. Preachers who traveled a circuit of churches throughout the States developed reputations that sometimes attracted large, interreligious audiences. Gratz was often among the listeners. Everett had attracted "several clergymen and a large congregation of different sects of christians . . . and I believe all were gratified and none offended," she wrote. Everett was a Unitarian, yet Gratz thought "an episcopal bishop might have said amen to the whole." She found Everett's "eloquence so simple and touching that his taste as well as his understanding would have [been] approved" by the most conservative sect.[27] Rebecca liked the Unitarian approach, which combined a concept of God that was close to Judaism's principle of unity with lessons about virtue couched in popular language. She developed a close friendship with Unitarian Reverend and Mrs. Furness and attended Reverend Furness's church more than once, as did her nieces and other female relatives.[28] These charitable and religious activities provided friendship and a renewed sense of purpose for Gratz, now left nearly alone at home while her brothers took up new business travels.

Brothers' Business

In the large Gratz family, members diversified in their responsibilities. Simon and Hyman, the eldest sons, followed most closely in the pattern set by Michael and Barnard, entering into many of the same trading and land speculating partnerships begun by their father and uncle and forming many other similar limited partnerships as time went on. The youngest sons, Benjamin and Jacob, both studied trade and business law to protect new ventures begun by their brothers. Benjamin went west to oversee land trading in the Mississippi valley, while Jacob stayed in Philadelphia near the port. Middle brothers Joseph and Jacob also entered into their own trading partnerships, both with their brothers and independently, at times opening their own warehouses in Philadelphia.

While Gratz cultivated her religious life, her brothers traveled the countryside and explored new business ventures in an effort to keep the family's finances attuned to the expanding economy of the country. In November 1817, Jacob traveled around the Pennsylvania countryside examining landholdings.[29] The next year, while Hyman was elected a director of the Pennsylvania Company for Insurance on Lives and Granting Annuities, forerunner to the First Pennsylvania Bank, Benjamin went further west, to Ohio, Indiana, and Kentucky, to look at land his brothers were acquiring and to oversee the negotiations. A few months later, Rebecca lamented to Maria that "brother Hyman soon followed Ben to Kentucky and sister Etting has moved into the country. Her son Edward has gone to Baltimore . . . we have been scattering until only a small portion of the family are left."[30]

In July 1819 Joseph and William Meredith left for an extended tour on horseback, visiting lands in Pennsylvania and New York that the men owned or hoped to acquire. Joseph, the most loquacious of the brothers, understood that his sister longed to be included in her brothers' lives and wrote frequently to Rebecca back home, describing his travels to her in vivid detail.[31]

In August, Joseph found a comfortable tavern in Rochester, New York, after a visit to Niagara Falls, and wrote to Rebecca from there. Like most people, Joseph was astounded by the natural grandeur of the falls and wanted his sister to have the same experience. "You must see them, and it will go hard but you shall visit them next year," he promised. He also visited Painted Post, Chemung River, Lake Ontario, and Fort Erie, Canada, where he felt he was "treading on sacred ground." "[William Meredith] never expected to see such sights," Joseph told his sister. "Let his family know he is in good health."[32]

By the end of August, Joseph and Meredith were in Saratoga Springs on their way home. Joseph had been thrilled by the mountains in western New York and Pennsylvania. "I would not give one acre of improved mountain land for ten under the same kind of improvement in this level country," he asserted. From the springs they went on to the Genessee River, visiting the villages at the Finger Lakes, and then went a hundred miles beyond into hills. "I was busily employed among our tenants," he reported to his sister. "Many of them are doing pretty well—but the greatest part are poor, bad fellows—however the lands have improved, and I think as I always did that they are valuable, and really a fine estate."[33]

When Joseph returned home from his travels through upstate Pennsylvania and New York, he opened his own shops, first a counting house on South 8th Street and, later, a store on Front Street where he traded in India goods, gunpowder, yarns, and Madeira.[34] Jacob, who hated the countryside, opened a store around the corner from Simon and Hyman's place of business, S. & H. Gratz, selling dry goods, satin, damask, crepe, pongee, and brown Havana sugar.[35] That year, 1819, the Second Bank of the United States opened at 420 Chestnut Street in a white marble building modeled on the Parthenon.[36] But despite the financial confidence implied in its architecture, 1819 ushered in a terrible financial depression. Banknote circulation dropped from $110 million to $45 million.[37] Not surprisingly, the numbers and needs of the city's poor skyrocketed. To meet the needs of many families, Philadelphia's women developed dozens of new charitable societies.

The Female Hebrew Benevolent Society

Gratz and other women of Mikveh Israel believed that because evangelists targeted the poor, Jewish women needed their own charitable society and so established the nation's first non-synagogal Jewish charity, the Female Hebrew Benevolent Society (FHBS), in 1819. Initially, the FHBS provided food, fuel, clothing, and other necessities and hoped to promote Jewish education when funding increased. In later years the society also arranged for nurses, doctors, traveler's aid, and an employment bureau.[38] To be eligible for aid, a petitioner had to undergo a home visit by an FHBS manager and prove herself truly poor, clean, pious, and industrious.[39] Like most other benevolent societies of this era, the FHBS tried to protect the poor from want without encouraging pauperism.

The records of Philadelphia charitable societies and those of the FHBS give us a profile of poor Jewish women in Philadelphia. They were unmarried, sometimes immigrants, widowed, or dependent on men who could not support them.[40] Desertion posed difficulties for Jewish women at the end of the last century, and we have no reason to believe there were not similar problems earlier on, although organizational records were more circumspect in the antebellum era. The FHBS, for example, kept a special fund for needy women who came from formerly wealthy families holding membership in Mikveh Israel, and the details and names of these cases were never recorded in the minutes.[41] Other recipients were women peddlers who, according to the society's report, "returning with their baskets unemptied at the end of the day," could not feed their children.[42] Although it is impossible to tell who among the poor women defended in paternity suits by the city's Guardians of the Poor, an agency that oversaw the poorhouses, were Jews, at least one Jew, an S. Levy, was a Guardian who did bring suit.[43]

While some Americans believed that charitable societies exacerbated pauperism by encouraging idleness, others pointed out that women had unique, legitimate causes for their poverty.[44] In 1818, for example, the New York Committee on Pauperism admitted that women marshaled fewer resources than men, were more exposed to sudden reversals, and were more likely to require help in finding work.[45] Eleven years later, Philadelphia publisher Mathew Carey wrote that "females are obliged to earn half of what the most stupid of the other sex may earn," and plain seamstresses, who made clothing by hand, earned especially low wages, sometimes as little as eight and a half or fifteen cents per shirt. Ironically, charitable societies, which purchased the shirts to keep the women employed, offered so little for the garments that they drove prices down.[46]

Yet poor women were often suspected of being lazy and immoral. Pauperism was especially troublesome to the religious conscience because, as one minister said, "A virtuous people may expect peculiar interpolations of providence for their defense and prosperity."[47] Because of those assumptions, Philadelphia's poorest Jewish women and children often were subject to Christian preaching. Presbyterian ministers preached in the poorhouse on Sunday mornings, and those of other Christian denominations visited on Sunday afternoons. Private charitable societies dispensed similar Christian lessons with their material aid. In 1824,

Philadelphia abolished outdoor relief—welfare paid to people not confined to institutions—claiming that such funds were abused.[48]

Perhaps because it was a woman-led organization and women were not yet counted as synagogue members, the FHBS made no stipulation regarding synagogue attendance or membership for either their members or their clients. Nor did the FHBS, unlike the Female Association (FA), with which Gratz was still involved, require its treasurer to be an unmarried woman. Antebellum American women had no right to own property after marriage, and a treasurer legally could lose her organization's funds to her husband. Jewish law does allow married women to own property, and, whether or not Gratz knew of that law, organizational reports indicate that Jewish women expected their husbands to support their causes. Nonetheless, Gratz, who never married, was the FHBS secretary for its first four decades. Widow Esther Hart, granddaughter of Jacob Cohen, a former hazan at Mikveh Israel, and her unmarried daughter Louisa were among the managers, along with Ellen and Emily Phillips, both unmarried.[49]

Gratz's experience in municipal organizations such as the FA and the POA helped her to take the lead in organizing Jewish groups.[50] Experience made her proposals credible and specific, justified by the failures, as she knew them, of municipal groups to meet the needs of Jews. These organizations addressed different populations with different goals, however, and Gratz remained on the board of managers of each of them for most of her life. The FA served women in Philadelphia's formerly wealthy, but newly poor, families in a period of economic instability, while the POA served the city's orphans during a period of heavy immigration and intense social mobility, the latter often leading to desertion of families by men seeking better financial opportunities elsewhere.

The FHBS, in contrast, strove to care for poor Jewish women, protecting them from both poverty and evangelists. FA veteran Rebecca Phillips was elected "First Directress" and Gratz took her favorite role, secretary. As secretary, Gratz wrote the organization's constitution, kept the minutes of all meetings, and wrote all correspondence and annual reports. These two women's sisters, Arabella Phillips and Richea Gratz Hays, were among the managers, along with Esther Hart and other women of Mikveh Israel.

The FHBS women hoped to be "useful to their indigent sisters of the house of Israel." The managers' domestic and familial metaphors added to the legitimacy of this new endeavor that brought Jewish women into public charity.[51] Antebellum writers cloaked charitable work in romantic notions of women's nature by speaking of benevolence as an extension of home and women's sphere.[52] Like other women of her time, Gratz used rhetoric that linked women's public work to home life and made women's societies an extension of women's kin-work, while making it easier for poor Jewish women to receive charity.[53] By extending the rhetoric of home to the house of Israel, Gratz located the FHBS within both American culture and Jewish tradition. The rhetoric also reveals Gratz's hope that the organizations would replace her diminished family.[54] Instead of establishing her own family to compensate for her losses, Gratz, like her bachelor brothers, preferred communal endeavors to private domesticity. However, the only communal activities available to her were those that promoted domestic life.[55]

As an American Jewish organization, the FHBS drew on both American and traditionally Jewish organizational styles and approaches to charity. Most American women's charitable societies of the era, including the FHBS, framed a written constitution regarding rules about meetings, the uses of money, and the requirements for potential recipients of charity.[56] The preamble to the organization's first constitution reminded readers that *tzedakah* (charity seen as righteousness) is a religious obligation for Jews, but the statement of principles written later in the constitution answered the tenor of Philadelphians' anger over what they saw as misspent charity, promising not to give to the "idle and improvident though their poverty may excite pity." These principles legitimized the FHBS as a vehicle for inculcating middle-class notions of virtue among the poor.[57]

As in nearly every other American charitable society of its day, the FHBS managers circulated their printed constitutions among potential donors and plainly promised that donations would not be wasted. The constitution explained that the managers viewed their organization as a "sacred trust" whose funds would be distributed "only when the purposes of charity can be effected." The women of the FHBS promised to give only to petitioners who were "pining in obscurity" rather than to street beggars, and to the sick and infirm. They promised, too, to act "with delicacy" toward those "who had seen better days," and to offer "secret relief" to "reduced families in our congregation."[58]

Philadelphia's primary municipal charitable agency, the Guardians of the Poor, which divided the city into districts and supervised traffic at the house of refuge and workhouse, provided another model for Gratz's organizations. An organization run by men, it made recommendations to the city and state governments about poor laws and generated funds to cope with disasters. The practice of dividing the city into districts supervised by committees was adopted by later charitable agencies, including the FA and the FHBS.[59]

Although the FHBS women adapted many elements of American organizations in forming their society, they counted on Jewish traditions to ensure its success. In part because of the community ethic inherent in tzedakah, the women of the FHBS expected their menfolk to support their organization financially. Whatever their personal opinions about American individualism, the women of Gratz's Jewish organizations clearly expected all Jews to contribute to their cause, because they hoped to benefit all Jews, directly or indirectly. Jews who did not need the services of the FHBS were provided a means of carrying out a religious commandment, that is, offering charity. They also believed all Jews would benefit: that by caring for indigent Jews they would demonstrate to gentile Americans that Jews were not draining the nation's resources, but were both contributing to America and supporting their own brethren.

Reflecting the Gratz brothers' ideas about sound investments, the FHBS invested all donations "above $10" in municipal and United States bonds and railroad stock to form a permanent fund that would create an operating budget. A visiting committee called on petitioners to "inquire respecting their characters." Visiting committees became the standard way for women to participate in Jewish philanthropies, including those run by men, throughout the century. Like the FA, the FHBS charter assured donors that the society would assist the poor only with "necessaries, rather than money." Finally, the constitution announced the hope that someday the FHBS would be able to educate the children of indigent families, but they were unable to do so for almost twenty years.[60]

Barbara Welter has argued that women's entry into new fields usually followed a change in social conditions that reduced the need for female acquiescence to male leadership. She identified three circumstances that could precipitate this movement:

a need to place people in some area barred to men but where women could be admitted; by men's diminishing interest in one type of work when other fields offer greater rewards; or when a general desire to maintain an institution is not matched by an equal desire to fund its operations.[61] All three reasons appear to have been operating in Jewish Philadelphia at the time of the founding of the FHBS. The longevity of women's groups, however, depended on whether or not natural leaders emerged within their ranks.[62]

Before the FHBS was founded, the only other Jewish sources for charity were a synagogue's small alms fund and begging. Because, strictly speaking, only men were members of a synagogue, a widow had little leverage with which to provoke its generosity, despite the religious commandment to protect widows. A wife who wanted aid for her family usually had to convince her husband to ask for help, because synagogue presidents customarily sought to ensure that the funds would not be squandered by men who legally controlled their family's finances. Women hoped to avoid the embarrassment of being named in the synagogue's charity records. Minutes of the FHBS show that women often chose to avoid the synagogue out of concern for their reputations as good housewives.

Itinerant Jewish men were by far the easiest cases for synagogue presidents to deal with, because the accepted response was a donation sufficient to send the petitioner to another Jewish community in another town.[63] From 1820 to 1880 most immigrants were Dorfjuden from Bavaria and Posen—with minimal education in Europe and a smattering of exposure to German culture—who worked as peddlers and tailors.[64] Philadelphia lacked both an independent organization for Jewish welfare and authoritative rabbinic leadership, and Gratz easily stepped into that breach.

As with her early involvement in the FA, Gratz strengthened old ties and forged new ones through management of the FHBS. Most of the members and donors during its first year belonged to only seventeen families, many of whom were linked by marriage. Like synagogue membership, the FHBS was a family activity. The names Levy, Cohen, Nunes, Nones, Etting, Gratz, Hays, Hart, Moss, Marks, Nathan, Phillips, Pesoa, and Peixotto—all members of Mikveh Israel—appear repeatedly on the list of subscribers and members.

Late in 1819, Gratz gained a new sister and colleague when Benjamin married Maria Cecil Gist of Kentucky and settled in Lexington.[65] Maria was the sort of person who would have joined Gratz on the board of the POA, had she lived in Philadelphia. Rebecca immediately established a close relationship with Gist, even though she believed that marriage between people of different religions put too much pressure on both parties to compromise their beliefs and thought that child rearing required religious unity between the parents.[66] The traditional Jewish response to intermarriage, coming from days when there was no way for people to live in the same legal world if they lived in different religious worlds, was to mourn the loss of the Jewish child as if he or she had died. But that behavior was seldom the norm in America, and when Benjamin married Maria, Rebecca decided to do everything she could to make her tie to them as strong as possible. The fact that Maria Gist was just the sort of person whom Rebecca had always preferred in her close friends no doubt influenced her decision. Gist was an educated, genteel, intelligent woman with an active interest in religion that was nonetheless free of dogmatism. Moreover, Gist was the granddaughter of a governor of Kentucky and a niece of Henry Clay. As Gratz had once explained to Peggy Ewing, she expected her brothers' marriages to bring her more sisters. After Sarah's death, her need for close sisterhood was greater than ever.

Gratz told her new sister-in-law in no uncertain terms that she expected intimacy through letters. Telling Maria to "banish reserve now . . . for we are Sisters and with that loved title you have a claim to my warmest affection," she explained both what Maria could expect from her and what she expected from Maria. "In that title too I look for such love as has been the most fertile source of comfort and friends to me thro my life." But Maria did not initially respond with intimacy. Several months later Gratz tried again, using household imagery to convey to Maria exactly what she wanted. Offended that Maria did not "introduce me to your domestic repositories," Rebecca threatened to "in like manner treat you as a parlor visitor[,] but I am getting tired of ceremony."[67] She told Maria that she expected them to be "sincere friends as well as affectionate Sisters to the end of our lives."[68] Rebecca hoped their correspondence would not consist of general small talk, but rather the "minute" details of domestic life along with the emotions and thoughts arising from domesticity. She hoped that as they corresponded, they "may venture to linger on a corner sofa and feel perfectly at our ease."[69] Finally, Rebecca and Maria agreed to write every two weeks, without waiting for special news.[70]

Female Piety and Literary Heroes

America's rapidly growing population was increasingly literate, creating a large reading market for countless new periodicals and volumes.[71] Authorship became one of the few routes to an income available to "respectable women," as the ideology of separate spheres, consigning women to the private sphere, took hold in the 1830s. In Philadelphia, advertisements for books written by women favored historical romances and memoirs of aristocratic or religious women. Wild West tales, boys' adventure stories, mysteries, and textbooks also were often written by women, many under male pseudonyms.[72]

While the Gratz men helped advance secular culture in Philadelphia, Gratz's own activities were increasingly grounded in religious literature. Rebecca remarked to Maria Hoffman that "our ladies are becoming quite literary,"[73] as Sarah Ewing Hall prepared a manuscript called *Conversations on the Bible* in which "a concise and connected history comprising the . . . Pentateuch is contained." Gratz thought the volume "very interesting."[74] From 1820 to 1865, literary magazines addressing domestic and religious issues proliferated.[75] Technological changes transformed publishing into a leading industry, concentrated primarily in New York, but with important publishing houses in Philadelphia and Boston. Women and ministers alike took advantage of this publishing explosion to argue their convictions, demonstrate their talents, and supplement their often meager resources.[76]

By 1820, Gratz wrote her letters from the family's new home on Chestnut Avenue near Seventh Street, about five blocks west of their former home on High Street. An avid reader, she noted new literary activity by women, commented on their work, and promoted these writings among other women readers. In April of that year, Gratz wrote enthusiastically to her sister-in-law Maria about Sir Walter Scott's new book *Ivanhoe,* asking, "Tell me what you think of my namesake Rebecca."[77] Rebecca sent Maria a copy to be sure she read it. Its heroine, Rebecca of York, has been called the first favorable depiction of a Jew in English fiction, and Gratz eagerly sought her sister-in-law's opinion of the character. Most important, she hoped Maria would agree that the character was not only plausible but also "just such a representation of a good girl as . . . human nature can reach." Would her Christian friends and relatives find it believable that so virtuous a female could be, and remain, a Jew as Rebecca did in the tale? Maria responded as Rebecca hoped she would, admitting that she admired the character.[78]

For Gratz, Scott's Rebecca became a test of her friends' opinions about Jews, and Gratz contrasted that book with one published in England only three years earlier by Maria Edgeworth. Titled *Harrington,* the novel traced the cause of prejudice against Jews in Europe and depicted, as Gratz phrased it, "an Israelite without guile." But *Harrington's* fatal flaw, as Gratz perceived it, was that the Jewish heroine, Berenice, married Harrington, a Christian, at the close of the tale, and accepted conversion to her husband's faith. From Edgeworth's perspective, the marriage indicated the ease with which Jews, who did not yet enjoy full equal rights in England, could be integrated into British society.

Both Rachel Mordecai Lazarus of Virginia, daughter of Judaic scholar Jacob Mordecai, and Gratz, however, viewed the marriage as a symbolic assertion that offering equal rights would be an efficient way to convert Jews to Christianity. The book launched an extensive correspondence between Lazarus and Edgeworth, particularly after Scott's *Ivanhoe,* in which a Jewish woman chooses to remain a Jew rather than marry the novel's Christian hero, appeared in 1819. Could such a choice be realistic? In 1821, after *Ivanhoe* reached America, Lazarus wrote to Edgeworth that Gratz was the prototype for Rebecca in *Ivanhoe,* proving the book's authenticity.[79] Intermarriage was a tender issue for Lazarus, for her older sister Ellen had married an Episcopalian and joined that church.

Intrigued, Edgeworth also wrote to Gratz, sending her a signed copy of *Harrington.* In response, Gratz explained that she was indebted to the author for the "manner in which you traced the cause and growth of prejudice against Jews." However, Gratz insisted that Edgeworth's characterization of Berenice was implausible. Depicted as a deeply pious young woman, Berenice "might have died for her religion . . . but . . . she would not have become the wife of Harrington," Gratz argued. Explaining both Jewish piety and literary requirements, Gratz contrasted Scott's work with Edgeworth's. By setting his tale in medieval England, a period when chivalry and tolerance could be romanticized, Scott "placed his heroine in situations to try her faith at the risk of life," Gratz pointed out. Believing that Edgeworth sympathized with Jewish martyrdom in Europe, she asserted, "I . . . believe his picture true to nature." Appealing to Edgeworth's standards as a writer, Gratz argued that marrying Harrington was inconsistent with the character of Berenice, a "consistency of character which Miss Edgeworth never violates in any of her tales." Whatever her disagreement with Edgeworth over Berenice's portrayal, Gratz understood that *Harrington* opposed prejudice against Jews, and for that she was grateful, and she assured Edgeworth that *Harrington* would stand alongside *Ivanhoe* in her library as "heartfelt illustrations of Christian charity towards their elder spiritual brother."[80]

By referring to Judaism as Christianity's "elder spiritual brother," Gratz endowed Judaism with both greater wisdom and more profound spirituality than Christianity. Her letter to the well-known British writer gave her a valuable opportunity to argue for Judaism. After years of religious debate with her Christian women friends, Gratz was ready to seize her opportunity to argue Judaism to an influential Christian woman. Yet however grateful she was to the English writer, Gratz would not give an inch.[81]

Charitable and Religious Obligations

The Gratz family maintained traditional Jewish holidays and Rebecca encouraged her nieces and nephews to develop a sense of Jewish piety. In August 1821, Richea's daughter Ellen Hays wrote to her aunt Rebecca from Long Branch assuring her that they had not forgotten the Jewish mourning day of *Tishah B'Av* that had recently passed. Visiting her aunt Rachel Moses that day, Ellen "found all there as [Gratz] would wish. Isabella [Etting, Fanny's daughter] came in Sunday evening to stay a few days with me and is now in the parlor with Sarah [Hays] reading the Lamentations," an essential part of *Tishah B'Av* observance.[82]

For most antebellum Americans, religious obligations included charitable activities. By the 1820s, hundreds of specialized charitable societies sought to care for the poor among diverse religious, and racial groups. The Daughters of Africa mutual aid society was founded by black women in 1821.[83] In 1829 Mathew Carey counted thirty-three female religious, charitable, and moral reform societies in Philadelphia, and separate orphanages existed for Roman Catholic, African American, and white Protestant children. Quaker, Episcopalian, and Catholic women organized distinct associations for the welfare of their women and children.[84]

Several of the Gratz men involved themselves in community service. In 1820, Richea's son Isaac Hays, a newly graduated opthamologist, opened his office in Philadelphia and offered his services to the FHBS and to Bikur Holim (Visitors of the Sick), the two Jewish charitable organizations in city, and a few years later to the POA.[85] That year fifteen Jews subscribed to the Athenaeum, an arts library in Philadelphia, which Jacob led. In 1821, Jacob travelled to Harrisburg, Pennsylvania, to petition the state legislature to fund a new school for the "deaf and dumb" in Philadelphia.[86] Joseph Gratz was on the first board of managers of the newly formed Apprentices Library, whose holdings were geared to the interests and needs of tradesmen. Nephew Benjamin Etting, who had been associated with the Board of Education, was elected secretary of the Mercantile Library, which served businessmen.[87]

Gratz continued to be looked to for leadership and advice in the organizations in which she was involved. In 1821, the POA board, facing both increased requests for aid and fewer donations, decided to publish a history of their institution that would emphasize its importance to Philadelphia. The Board asked Gratz, its secretary, to work with Baltimore writer Sarah Ewing Hall in compiling the volume, but the collaboration did not go well. Hall thought that Gratz, as the organization's secretary, ought to write it, while Gratz thought the task should fall to Hall, an already published and known author. "My Dear Becky," Hall wrote to her, "the editor is ready for our history of the Orphan House. If you are determined, cross as you are—to throw this business on me, you can I suppose furnish me with the documents." Hall wanted Gratz to at least provide the data from the minute books, which Gratz, as secretary, kept.

Gratz argued that her letters to Hall over the years provided ample detail about the organization's growth, and preferred not to make public all the information in the minutes. Hall responded that she could not find the letters: "I have put away your letters so carefully that it will cost me more time to hunt [them] up than to write the particulars [they] contain. I want however several other particulars which I shall probably obtain from your annual reports." Hoping to convince Gratz to accept at least partial responsibility for the volume, Hall urged her to write about the asylum's founding, limiting Hall's work to discussions of its impact on Philadelphia's poor. "I heartily wish you would write the historical part at least, were it only because you have more time than I have—to say nothing of your ability to do it better than I can," she explained.

Hoping to soften Gratz's opposition, Hall complimented her on the character of Rebecca in *Ivanhoe,* whom Hall firmly believed to be inspired by Gratz herself. "Are you not delighted with your sublime namesake in *Ivanhoe?*" Hall's sister Peggy Ewing had told her about the correspondence between Gratz and Edgeworth, and Hall used that information now, she hoped, to her advantage, "If Miss Edgeworth failed in her good intentions towards you—Walter Scott has made you ample amends. *Ivanhoe* is a misnomer; the title should have been *The Jewess.* Rebecca is completely the heroine of the tale, the only beautiful, and by far the most interesting person in the book. So firm, yet so tender—so heroic, yet so feminine, her character alone would place a wreath of glory on the brow of its author." Hall closed by lamenting that she lived so far from Gratz and asserting her affection for the Philadelphian.[88] Gratz provided information, but Hall, despite her pleadings, wrote the history.

Hall's solicitous praise for *Ivanhoe* was blatantly manipulative, but a failure. After many years of managing organizations, Gratz had grown utterly confident in her own judgments about them. The organizations were her career and she approached them with the dedication and the no-nonsense attitude that historian Lori Ginzberg found common to benevolent society managers in this era.[89] At forty, Gratz had lost interest in balls and gala events. She described a New Year's Eve ball at Mrs. John Sargeant's as "stale, flat, and unprofitable to me—the companions of former days have either passed away or lost interest in my heart and the idea has so much melancholy in it to me, that a ballroom seems more like a memorial of lost pleasures than an incitement to new ones."[90] Those companions who now bored her had not turned their intellectual abilities toward religious and charitable endeavors, the milieu of the developing women's culture. For Gratz, such endeavors carried an urgency that surpassed fancy dress balls. She complained that even her own letters were less interesting to write. Perhaps, as she said, her "cares and dull realities . . . [clipped] the wings of imagination."[91]

Gratz's time was filled with the day-to-day needs of the orphan asylum. In 1822, a fire—begun when two boys filled a clothing trunk with hearth coals—killed twenty-three of the 106 children living in the building. The matron's illness forced Gratz to make daily visits to both the matron and the asylum. The city's newly improved water supply saved most of the children from the fire, but the home was badly burned.[92] Gratz detailed her work: "What with thanking great and small distant and present donors, providing for the [asylum] family and legislating about the new asylum, I have not been a very companionable character to anyone above the rank of the poor orphans."[93] A year later, after the Pennsylvania legislature granted $5,000 and private donors contributed $28,000 more, Gratz was one of four women who furnished the new asylum and moved the residents into it.[94] She worried about long-term financial problems the fire caused: "I do not know that we have anything to complain of more than might be expected by those acquainted with public institutions, [but] . . . misfortunes . . . lose us friends."[95] That winter she kept busy supplying the kitchen, purchasing clothing, and preparing the children for their annual public exam.[96] The board used the children's exams to demonstrate the institution's effectiveness to the public, their donors.

Soon after she put the orphan asylum back in order, Rebecca's own family suffered another severe loss. In the evening of September 29, 1823, Rachel Gratz Moses died. Her infant daughter Gertrude, just thirteen months old, one of nine children born to Rachel and Solomon Moses, died the next morning. Gertrude Meredith wrote an obituary for Rachel, describing her as "sleep[ing] with her fathers in humble trust of a joyful resurrection to the heavenly Jerusalem."[97] Gratz immediately resigned from the FA board and brought Rachel's six remaining children home to live with her.[98]

Thus began a new phase of life for Gratz, who eight years earlier had remarked that "Rachel's children are my favorite toys."[99] Two years after Rachel's death, their father, Solomon Moses, bought a house directly opposite the Gratz home and the older children moved in with him, but Gratz continued to help him raise his children. She not only supervised their education, but was the person most like a mother to them for the rest of their lives. She told Maria Gist Gratz that they were the "objects of my constant and tenderest concern" and that they gave her a "deep interest in life." More than that, Rebecca felt that Rachel's children cheered her own life, whose "many and severe trials . . . might otherwise have made a weary pilgrimmage [*sic*]."[100]

Gratz found special interest in the lives and accomplishments of her nieces and nephews. One of her older nephews, Richea's son Isaac was selected by city leaders in 1823 to be one of six physicians for Philadelphia's dispensary. Gratz also strove to develop a close relationship with Benjamin and Maria's children in distant Lexington, although she seldom visited them. When their third child, Henry Howard, was born in July 1824, she sought news about her new nephew, who was named for Henry Clay.

Gratz's increased involvement in philanthropic organizations paralleled similar activities on the part of her bachelor brothers. Hyman Gratz was especially involved in guiding their congregation. In 1824 Hyman was elected treasurer of Mikveh Israel, a post he held for more than thirty years.[101] Eager to be part of the city's new cultural face, Mikveh Israel commissioned William Strickland, one of the city's most popular architects, to design a new synagogue building for the congregation. By January 1825, the new building on Cherry Street was ready, largely due to the Gratz family's contributions. Joseph Gratz, treasurer of the building committee, accepted pledges from his siblings totalling two thousand dollars. Simon Gratz alone gave one thousand dollars, and his brothers and Rebecca matched his gift.[102]

The dedication of the new building on January 21, 1825, attracted a large interreligious audience, including a local Christian bishop. Gertrude Meredith had planned to go, but the day's bad weather stopped her, although three of her children attended the ceremony.[103] In the dedication service, nine Torah scrolls were brought from the previous place of worship and placed in the ark of the new building. Rebecca viewed the ceremony lovingly and described the service in detail to Benjamin. "I have never witnessed a more impressive or solemn ceremony or one more calculated to elevate the mind to religious exercises," she wrote. Although the new building was a small, high-ceilinged brick rectangle with Egyptian-inspired marble lintels over the doors and windows, to Gratz it was "one of the most beautiful specimens of ancient architecture in the city."

Beginning just before sundown on Friday evening, the service was performed by lamplight. Moses Peixotto, then hazan of Shearith Israel in New York, assisted Abraham Keys, Mikveh

Israel's hazan. Simon Gratz opened the doors and intoned the initial blessing, and "the processions entered with the two Reverends in their robes followed by [men carrying] nine sacred scrolls," Gratz told Benjamin.[104] A choir chanted psalms as the scrolls were carried seven times around the reading desk in the center of the room; then Hebrew prayers were pronounced. According to Gratz, even the Christian bishop agreed that there had never been such fine "church music" sung in Philadelphia. Choirmaster Jacob Seixas and his sister Miriam, who were visiting from New York, led a choir made up of Mikveh Israel members. After the scrolls were placed in the ark, Peixotto and Keys recited more Hebrew prayers. Four different accounts of the event, all remarking on its solemnity, were published in local newspapers. One Christian observer wondered if the chants could have been the same music that Jesus had heard.[105]

The new synagogue reflected other growth in Philadelphia. The 108-mile Schuylkill Canal now brought anthracite coal from Port Carbon, above Reading, to the city's port.[106] The Schuylkill River was lined with wharves and canals connecting it to the Chesapeake Bay and Delaware River. Over one hundred mills in the Manayunk section of Philadelphia would soon ship goods along these canals. Joseph Dennie and the *Port Folio* were forgotten largely because the city's literary output had surpassed Dennie's accomplishments. By 1820, over one hundred thousand dollars in book sales in Philadelphia included science, religion, and literature.[107] The flavor of the town had so changed since its colonial heyday that in 1825 city councillors agreed that Philadelphians needed a reminder of its founders and named the public squares Penn, Logan, Washington, Franklin, Rittenhouse, and Independence. Beginning to develop a sense of its own place in history and to memorialize its early days, in 1827 the city erected a monument in Kensington commemorating William Penn's 1682 treaty with Native Americans.[108] Wealth enabled Philadelphians to display their taste for fine architecture, and in the 1820s and 1830s public buildings as diverse as the new Unitarian church at 10th and Locust, the Arch Street Theater, the Almshouse west of the Schuylkill River and the Merchants' Exchange at Third and Dock Streets all were built of white marble.

Just as Jews from New York traveled to Philadelphia to help make the synagogue dedication a more memorable occasion, so Jews within Philadelphia worked together in new ways for their general benefit. As new charitable societies emerged among Jews in Philadelphia, cooperation between men's and women's societies grew commonplace. For example, in 1825 a Jewish widower left town, abandoning three children. The United Hebrew Beneficent Society (UHBS), a men's charity founded three years earlier, asked the FHBS women to help care for the children, which they did. The UHBS hoped to provide for "unfortunate and indigent brethren" but functioned in many ways as a mutual aid society rather than as a benevolent society. Only men who married according to Jewish ritual and circumcised their male children could be members of the UHBS.

Insisting that "charity . . . strengthens the bonds of society" and intending to "provide for the sick of our persuasion," men of the UHBS also promised to visit the sick and provide a decent burial and a quorum for prayers at the homes of mourners. Additionally, they promised to see that boys were apprenticed with masters who would allow them to observe the Jewish Sabbath and holy days. Like the FHBS women, they hoped to provide for Jewish education as soon as funding permitted. Their "female relatives," they said, would attend to any necessary sewing for the poor. Membership in the UHBS was at first limited to Jewish men in Philadelphia, but because many Jewish men traveled the outlying counties as peddlers, it was soon extended to Jewish men throughout the state.[109]

Although Gratz had argued heatedly that a pious Jewish woman would not marry a non Jew, she knew that since the days of the earliest Jewish settlers, marriages between Jews and non-Jews were a fact of life. Yet Judaism prohibited such marriages, requiring many home practices, prayers, blessings, and observances. Dietary restrictions and customs, blessings before and after meals, Sabbath, Passover, Sukkot, and Hanukkah celebrations and observances each included domestic responsibilities for both men and women. Additionally, married Jewish women were required to ritually immerse in water and recite blessings monthly and to confine their sexual activity with their husbands to those "purified" times of each month. Traditional Jewish husbands relied on their wives' observance of both sexual and dietary restrictions. Jewish wives relied on their husbands to lead home worship and to oversee the religious rites relating to their children's development.

But in North America, several circumstances worked against Jewish marriages. First, because most immigrants were men,

the ratio of men to women did not equalize until later in the
nineteenth century, and then only in areas of high Jewish settlement. In frontier areas, Jewish men heavily outnumbered Jewish
women.[110] Second, immigrants came from widely scattered areas
of Europe, making knowledge about their family backgrounds
uncertain. New immigrants held little status in America, and an
American-born individual might be unwilling to marry an immigrant. Finally, American cultural values, which lauded individualism and romantic love, held little regard for other marriage
values.

Jewish congregations struggled to pressure their members
to abide by Jewish marriage standards. In 1826, Philadelphia's
Rodeph Shalom ruled that no member (only male adults were
counted as members) who had married a non-Jew could vote on
synagogue governance or be called to read the Torah scroll at
worship services. Yet the practical needs of Philadelphia's small
synagogues, which were wholly dependent on their membership
for funds, blunted the force of rulings of this sort.[111] Torn between
the desire to promote a high level of Jewish religious observance
and the need to keep contributing members, congregations ex-
perimented with various postures. Expressing the membership's
wishes rather than rabbinic judgment, synagogue constitutions
shifted away from prohibitions against intermarriage to procedu-
ral rules for proselytes and marriage.[112] In 1829, Rodeph Shalom
withdrew rules disallowing full membership to Jewish men married to gentile women. All members were welcome if they raised
their children as Jews. Mikveh Israel, with fewer immigrant members pressing to have things done as they were in Europe, avoided
the issue altogether.

Synagogues struggled with intermarriage when American
expectations for women's lives were changing. Widespread Christian revivals in the 1820s brought a new attitude toward women's
piety and purpose, which was reflected in women's literature. In
1828, Sarah Josepha Hale edited the *Ladies Magazine* and Hale's
opinions about women's place in American society are evidenced
in her early work there. "Let the education of women differ ever
so much in DETAIL," she explained to her readers, "its END is
the same, to qualify them to become wives and mothers." In a
rapidly diversifying society, she insisted that linguistic, religious,
and ethnic differences counted little against those of sex and gender. Hale wrote that women's "similarity of purpose produces a

similarity of thought, feeling, action and consequently CHARAC-
TER, which no uniformity of training could otherwise bestow."[113]
For Hale, the lives of all American women were governed by
a common framework of events, tasks, crises, and rewards. All
women faced lifelong dependency on men for financial support
and/or political safety, and most faced repeated childbirths that
would leave them progressively weaker and with progressively
greater responsibilities. Each hoped to find an old age among
people who still cared for her, knowing that the degree of ease
she would find depended on the degree of compassion she could
arouse in her benefactors.

As Jewish immigration increased in the 1820s and 1830s,
Jews' religious standards were more and more influenced by
American ideals and attitudes. One was that women were naturally more religious than men. This idea had a number of sources.
The literature of romanticism, which drew on the new middle-
class fascination with tales of chivalric old aristocrats and virtuous
individual upstarts, insisted that religion was ultimately a feeling
of devotion of a sort that seemed unlikely to occur among men who
were mired in earthly power. A combative, irreligious personality
seemed more suited to government, business, and soldiering, all
men's tasks. Popular literature by nineteenth-century Protestants
portrayed religion as fundamentally emotional, resting on feelings
of reverence, awe, gratitude, and dependence on God, feelings that
were thought natural to women.

Economic realities also supported the idea that women were
more religious and emotional than men. As the production of
goods moved out of homes and into factories, women became more
financially dependent on men as household economies changed
from production to consumption, and as commercial clothing, food-
stuffs, candles, medicine, and liquor appeared. Over the course
of the century, as women's home nursing and educational responsibilities diminished with the proliferation of hospitals and
schools, women's central responsibilities revolved around nurtur-
ing the emotional and spiritual lives of their families. Middle-
class women increasingly took up activities in all forms of religious
life—except the ministry itself, which remained barred to them.[114]
While women's piety became a mark of middle-class status
throughout western Europe as well, American evangelism gave
women's piety an activist cast both at home and in charitable
societies.[115] Indeed, these activities and this rhetoric supporting

women's religious and charitable activities became the foundation for what Ann Douglas has called the matriarchal culture of nineteenth-century America.[116]

These changes modified republican motherhood into an ideology suitable to the Victorian age. The women of America, as mothers, sisters, wives, and daughters, would influence the character of boys and men toward social virtue by religious education and emotional direction. Through them, women would determine social order and mold the nation's character. Many magazines written for women during this era referred to women's triumph in becoming society's leaders. Their leadership was thought proof of the high degree of civilization America had achieved.[117]

Hale's series, "Sketches of American Character," offered images of women as leaders of civility. In an essay on the village schoolmistress, Hale argued women's suitability for public teaching. "Their influence on the manners is readily and willingly conceded by everyone," she insisted. "Might not their influence on the MIND be made quite as irresistible, and far more beneficial, and that too, without violating . . . the PROPRIETY which, to make their examples valuable, should ever mark their conduct?"[118] Hale's argument was hardly revolutionary, as women had been running private schools for decades. But her goal was to open teaching to women as a profession, not limited to individual women whose family resources supported their venture in academia.

By the third decade of the nineteenth century, two ideas about the nature and role of women began appearing in tandem. As the intensity and number of revivals increased, to women's civilizing and education function emphasized in republican motherhood was added the ability to save the nation. This was a direct result of women's role in teaching religion in the family and acting as the bearers of religion because regular church attendance was becoming an evermore female activity. Since God acts within history to reward good and punish evil, Hale reasoned, there could be nothing more important to the country than God and his power to affect the history of the nation. As religion moved fully into the private sphere, women were no longer just civilizing or refining America, as assumed in republican motherhood; they were also saving it.[119] Eventually, these arguments supported what has been called a domestic feminism, framing a vision of the public good based on women's experience.[120]

Gratz agreed with Hale that among women, differences of opinion, even of religious opinion, could not override women's commonalities, which enabled women to work together effectively. But as women's responsibilities grew more clearly defined as religious, Gratz's relationships with Christian friends and co-workers grew more complex. Although she shared with them a deep, biblically based faith, her belief in the truth of Judaism conflicted with their Christian convictions.

Gratz and other American Jewish women of her era found themselves faced with taking a role in Judaism for which they had not been trained. Typically, Jewish women received little formal religious education, yet in America it was their responsibility to keep Judaism in their homes and Christianity out. Gratz showed Jewish women how to accomplish this task. Through the FHBS, she provided Jewish philanthropic women who hesitated to work in Christian organizations a means to display the values of spirituality and compassion that they shared with their gentile peers. Beginning with the FHBS, Gratz's organizations were founded on ideas shared by educated American women like Hale, Maria Gist, and Gertrude Meredith. For the organization's leaders, such as Gratz, the FHBS proved their outstanding qualities as American leaders in charitable societies, the arena most respected by influential Christian women. For the needy Jewish women, both immigrant and American-born, who received its assistance, the FHBS provided an avenue for finding the necessities of life, advice on acculturating to America and withstanding evangelical assaults, and contacts within the local Jewish community.

By the late 1820s Philadelphia's economy was again declining. The city's status as the nation's premier location for moving goods from the port to America's western frontier suffered a severe challenge when the Erie Canal opened in 1825. With the new canal, New York merchants could bring goods from the port of New York, which never froze, up the Hudson River, along the canal, and across the Great Lakes, stopping at hundreds of towns along the way. In July 1826, one year after the Erie Canal opened, Simon and Hyman Gratz faced bankruptcy.

The Gratz brothers were not the only Philadelphia merchants to feel the economic blow from New York, and they were treated with sympathy and encountered many small acts of kindness. Simon retained his presidency of the Schuylkill Bank, which he had helped to found in 1811. The Pennsylvania Company for Insurance in Lives and Granting Annuities, an organization Hyman had been associated with since 1818, soon elected him president. Relieved, Rebecca was grateful that they had "shed more tears of gratitude than grief." Abraham Elkin, a younger member of Mikveh Israel, had loaned money to Simon and Hyman. After Simon wrote Elkin a letter promising to pay him as soon as the brothers could do so, Elkin told him the debt was of no consequence and offered to redeem Simon's estate from foreclosure. "Poor Simon wept like a child when he related this anecdote to me," Gratz told her sister-in-law Maria.[121]

In response to their new financial situation, Rebecca, Hyman, Jacob, and Joseph planned their move to a smaller house at 2 Boston Row, behind Richea's house on Chestnut Street. Gratz knew that bankruptcies had destroyed some of Philadelphia's wealthiest families, and she focused on adjusting the household and quieting battles. She soon began to "philosophize on the subject—and examine . . . whether poverty be so great an evil . . . I have implicit faith in Scripture . . . I do not fear."[122] She rolled up the carpets and moved the household to a less auspicious neighborhood than their former large home on High Street (now Market) near Seventh Street. The former home had been twenty-eight feet wide and fifty-six feet deep, with mahogany folding doors, marble mantles, and spacious rooms. Around it were a bathhouse, a cistern, a large stable, and a carriage house.[123] But the new home was far from a hovel. To her sister-in-law Maria she described its two parlours "nearly covered by the mat taken from the floor of the [former] back room," a small dining room, a library, and bedrooms.[124]

4

The Founding of the Hebrew Sunday School: 1830–1840

"By sharing . . . troubles I gain admittance into the affections of my friends."[1]
REBECCA GRATZ, 1832

In the 1830s, Gratz became convinced that Jewish children urgently needed an institution that would help them resist the intensifying evangelism they would encounter while growing up in the United States. The school Gratz envisioned would not prepare boys to perform the Hebrew readings to become *b'nai mitzvah* or to lead prayers in the synagogue, the minimal goals of traditional Jewish religious education. Gratz believed that the future of Jewish life in America depended on a different sort of school. American Jewish boys and girls, she thought, needed to learn how to defend their Jewish beliefs, which would enable them to refute evangelists and to be the religious equals of their Christian neighbors. Jewish women and girls, especially, needed instruction in Judaism in order to claim the same moral authority accorded to white middle-class Christian women.

Gratz believed Jewish women needed to take the lead in keeping Judaism alive in their families, much as Christian women did in theirs. Jewish men, like their non-Jewish peers, spent increasingly less time on religious activities and more time on economic and political pursuits. Jewish teens needed a shared culture and meeting ground to form new Jewish families. Rebecca, through her own experience raising her nieces and nephews, and through her conversations with non-Jewish women friends and associates, gradually developed a philosophy and a plan.

The 1830s saw Philadelphia rise to national prominence again, with impressive growth and prosperity. In 1832, a railroad connected Reading to Philadelphia. By the middle of the decade, 394 miles of state railroad and canal works connected Philadelphia's port to Pittsburgh and its nearby rivers leading westward to Ohio and Kentucky.[2] The newly expanded port once again fed the city's economic growth.

The city's financial success attracted thousands of immigrants and migrants, and the local Jewish population grew to over three hundred families living in different areas of the city.[3] By the end of the decade, more than 164,000 people lived in Philadelphia County, and 93,652 lived in the city proper. New neighborhoods were constructed north and west of Seventh Street, in Northern Liberties, Kensington, and Spring Garden.[4] An omnibus conducted hourly runs between Second Street and the Schuylkill River, and individually named and decorated buses soon appeared on all major roads connecting these new, more distant areas to the city's core.

Religion and Social Order

Immigration and migration diversified Philadelphia's population and fueled ethnic conflicts. Following slave uprisings in the South and the Caribbean in the 1830s, many Philadelphians considered the antislavery movement subversive and, in 1834 and 1837, a few Philadelphians physically attacked the city's African-American residents.[5] Gratz remarked that local hostility toward the integrated wedding party of abolitionist Angelina Grimke was so intense that she "would not be surprised at any threats they may meet."[6] The Pennsylvania Anti-Slavery Headquarters was burned in 1838.[7]

Government and religious groups tried to restore order. With a huge increase in the number of poor children, in 1834 the Pennsylvania assembly laid the foundation for a statewide system of tax-supported schools.[8] Evangelists believed that only by turning American citizens to Christianity could the nation earn the two blessings of God it coveted—peace and prosperity. To that end, they evangelized in almshouses and established charitable and mission societies for the poor. One arm of the effort to Christianize the country was the Sunday school movement, heavily supported by the energies of religious women.[9] Since 1825, the Protestant American Sunday School Union claimed that a third of the six-to fifteen-year-olds in Philadelphia attended their schools.[10] In response, Roman Catholics and Jews developed their own schools and orphanages.[11]

Increasingly, arguments about religious issues appeared in the press around the country. Newspapers often reprinted articles originally published elsewhere, giving a semblance of uniformity to grassroots firestorms of debate. Several American newspapers had reprinted an article disparaging Judaism that originally appeared in the *London Quarterly Review*. In 1828 Rebecca's aunt Sloe Hays, living in Richmond, Virginia, wrote to her niece about a bright "young German," as she called him, who wrote "zealous papers . . . which . . . had been reprinted in the North." The man, Isaac Leeser, was working in his uncle's printing shop in Richmond when the editor of the *Richmond Whig* invited him to respond to the London article. Over the objections of several Jewish friends in Richmond who feared that a defense of Judaism would stir anti-Semitism, Leeser published a series of articles presenting the Jewish point of view that were later reprinted by newspapers in New York.[12] Gratz's aunt was among Leeser's staunchest supporters. Hays wrote that she "admired [his] good sense . . . piety and learning—and felt some little pride that amid ignorance and obscurity a genius should arise." Hays felt personally wounded by the attacks on Judaism that appeared in newspapers and magazines. Even Christians who thought they were defending Jews' rights, she felt, usually ended by insisting on Judaism's inferiority to Christianity.[13] Feeling vulnerable to Christian attack as she did, Hays celebrated Leeser's work.

Impressed with Leeser's abilities, Mikveh Israel hired him as their hazan the following year. Mikveh Israel valued both his knowledge of Judaism and his ability to defend intelligently their faith to the non-Jewish American public. Although he was born in Westphalia and trained in the prayer style used by Jews in northern Europe, he had learned the Spanish-Portuguese style of Hebrew reading and ritual custom while living with his uncle in Richmond, where he also had mastered English. Although Leeser was only twenty-three years old, both Jacob Mordecai and Leeser's uncle urged him to accept the position.[14]

Soon after he arrived, Gratz and other women in her congregation asked Leeser to deliver sermons on the Sabbath, an
innovation in Jewish worship. Traditionally, learned rabbis would
occasionally deliver lessons about the passage of the Torah read
in the synagogue that day, but such lessons were informative
rather than edifying. The style of sermon requested by the women
of Mikveh Israel brought the informative lecture closer to the
edifying lecture style used by most Protestant ministers. Leeser
agreed to their request and began delivering sermons immediately
following the regular worship service on Saturday mornings.[15]

Rebecca believed that regular exposure to edifying sermons
would deepen Jews' religious devotion as well as their commitment
to teach their faith to their children. In her own family, many
of her nieces and nephews were raised without Judaism. The
year that Leeser arrived in Philadelphia, Benjamin and Maria
Gratz welcomed their fifth child, and fifth son, Cary Gist Gratz.
Their children learned a mix of Judaism and Christianity, leaning
heavily toward Christianity.

Although Gratz held strong opinions on most matters, she
felt most passionately about the difficulties Jews faced in adjusting their traditional religious culture to the American culture in
which they were immersed. As Jewish immigration increased and
local Jewish communities grew, American Jewish family mores
changed. Demographic pressure favoring intermarriage diminished. Before significant Jewish immigration in the 1830s many
Jewish men married non-Jewish women, whereas by 1830 Jewish
women outnumbered men in New York, Philadelphia, Baltimore,
and Richmond.[16]

Friendship vs. Love

Jewish communities throughout the world historically relied
on a system of arranged marriages to provide financial support
for gifted religious leaders, to provide a voice for religious ethics
in the homes of the wealthy, to enforce Jewish values by marrying
wealth to religious learning, and to ensure that the entire community would fulfill the religious commandment to be fruitful and
multiply. An intricate array of gender-defined roles, most based on
religious obligations, provided the scaffolding for Jewish marital
life. Until love could grow between husband and wife, stability
would at least be assured.

In early-nineteenth-century America, this system broke down with the advent of romanticism, individualism, and scarcity. The "romantic love complex," which asserts that an overwhelming emotional experience is an appropriate basis for marriage, has been an ideology especially prominent in the United States.[17] Since the early eighteenth century, the importance of affection in the choice of a marriage partner increased. Portraits of women, such as those done by Thomas Sully of Gratz and her sisters, portrayed "young, full-bosomed, small-waisted and raven-haired women"—not the sturdy helpmeet of early-eighteenth-century portraits.[18] Yet despite the place of sexual attraction in affection, for nineteenth-century American middle- and upper-class women, passionlessness "was the coin which paid for their admission to moral society."[19]

Gratz's most fulfilling relationships continued to be those she shared with women and the literary elite of her city. Nearing fifty, Rebecca again enjoyed a lively social life. She found 1830 Philadelphia's round of parties, dinners, teas, and balls "delightful" and regretted that her sister-in-law could not visit from Kentucky to share the fun. "Everybody was delighted to honor . . . [author] Miss [Catherine] Sedgwick for a few weeks . . . with such kind intellectual parties as they thought would suit her taste—the old beaux—literati-philosophers all turned out and to the great amusement of the young girls and men, they brought the high flown compliments and flattery of the last century."[20] Sedgwick, a New England writer who was visiting Philadelphia, carried a letter of introduction to Rebecca from Maria and Ogden Hoffman. Sedgwick's own life was much like Gratz's. Both were single women who devoted themselves to their brothers and the children of their extended families. But instead of founding and leading benevolent or educational associations, as Gratz did, Sedgwick wrote extensively about ways in which the home was a "moral repository." Her books voiced her ideas about the dangers of mismatched couples, the virtues of Christianity, and the appeal of the single life.[21]

Sedgwick had first heard about Gratz in 1826 when she visited Virginia. Rebecca's aunt in Richmond, Sloe Hays, wrote to Gratz about her own recent meeting with Sedgwick, whom Hays judged "a fine judicious woman." Hays preferred Sedgwick's books to those of Maria Edgeworth. "Miss Sedgwick is happily exempt from vanity or presumption and makes her way good—by speaking

kindly and unaffectedly to the feelings of all." Hays developed a
friendship with Sedgwick when the writer visited Richmond that
year, and Sloe bragged to Sedgwick about her niece whose "charm
to life is being useful to others."[22]

Sedgwick, the same age as Gratz, eventually wrote sixteen
novels expressing her belief that the safety of the Republic depended on the domestic virtues of its people.[23] Toward the end of
her life she wrote a volume disputing the idea that single women
are useless. Hearing about Rebecca from her adoring aunt, Sedgwick determined to strike up a correspondence with her. She no
doubt solicited Gratz's friendship because she saw her as one of a
handful of women she considered her equals, but the two women
never grew close. Sedgwick was shocked to find a Jewish woman
who equaled what she believed to be her own refined gentility.
After she returned to New England, Sedgwick wrote to Gratz
that she was amazed to have found the Philadelphia Jew "quite
exempt from the flippancy and vulgarity of the 'nouveau riches' of
New York." Gratz was slow to respond, so Sedgwick tried more of
what she thought were compliments, listing Gratz's attributes in
a manner that flattered herself. "You have the mental cultivation
of our Eastern society," she told Gratz, "without the rigidity—it
is not coldness—of our northern constitutions." Excusing her own
rudeness, she explained, "Grace does not belong to our ungenial
climate," and signed her letter, "your affectionate friend."[24] The
friendship remained cool for some time.

The year 1831 was expansive and happy for Rebecca. She
finally allowed Sully to paint her portrait and planned to send
it to Benjamin and Maria in Kentucky, but she did not like the
result. Sully erased it and began a second portrait of her the
next year, when he also painted portraits of Benjamin and Maria.
Gratz's portrait went to Kentucky; Benjamin's and Maria's came
to Philadelphia.[25] Gratz regularly sent books to Kentucky for her
family to enjoy. In 1831 she assured Maria that "We shall soon
have [Washington] Irving's and [James] Paulding's books to send
you . . . the *life of Governour Morris* (by Jared Sparks) is so expen-
sive . . . you might think the price more than it is worth."[26] "Sir
Walter's *Tales* have just issued from the press this morning and
are only waiting a conveyance to Lexington."[27]

Benjamin and Maria brought their children to Philadelphia
for a visit early that June. The house was again filled with the
noise of children, and Benjamin and Maria impressed Gratz's older

nieces with their obvious marital happiness.[28] During their visit Maria and her sons toured the Philadelphia Orphan Asylum with Gratz.[29] Soon after their visit Gratz learned of the death of her old friend Maria Fenno Hoffman. Gratz had cultivated friendships with Hoffman's daughters and stepdaughters, just as she had with her own nieces and nephews, and it was one of Hoffman's daughters who broke the news to her. Rebecca found it difficult to express her grief, but her reticence indicates how deeply she mourned the loss of her childhood friend. To her sister-in-law she wrote simply, "I received a letter yesterday from Julia Hoffman mentioning the sudden and distressing death of Ogden's wife."[30] Gratz knew that her sister-in-law would understand. The two women had "often exchanged thoughts without the aid of words when together," and Rebecca thought that "a hint even at this distance will like a masonic sign, communicate what is passing in my heart."[31]

Gratz and Maria Gist Gratz often exchanged advice on running schools and, later, orphan asylums. By July 1831 Gratz was "busy hunting teachers" for the orphan asylum because one of their instructors was planning to move to Lexington, Kentucky, to live with her brother. Rebecca wrote to Maria recommending the woman and asking her to "be of service to her . . . if she opens a school."[32] In 1833, Maria Gist Gratz established the first orphan asylum in Lexington, Kentucky, and Rebecca provided her with a good deal of advice. "Tell me dearest sister if I can give you any further useful information respecting your orphan society—I will collect as many of the early reports as I can find—which may shew [*sic*] how ours was governed in its infancy." She immediately cautioned Maria that the chief difficulty faced by such institutions was finding a qualified and conscientious matron. If Maria could find a good one, Rebecca assured her, "half the difficulty will be avoided."[33]

Rebecca and her sister-in-law Maria seemed to live in separate subcultures—one in a major eastern seaport, the other in a rural town; one Jewish, the other Christian; one unmarried, the other a wife and mother with five sons—yet they shared remarkably similar understandings of their responsibilities and abilities as women, of morality, of spirituality, and of literary culture.

Women's magazines provided a good deal of the glue that held women's culture together. For example, in the short period from 1828 to 1830, one magazine, Philadelphia's *Ladies Literary*

Portfolio, published specialized articles and fiction geared to women. In 1830, the most famous and successful of women's magazines, *Godey's Ladies Book,* appeared. Women also found items geared to them in the general press. In the *Pennsylvania Packet,* a daily paper in Philadelphia, women read employment ads, meeting announcements, product advertising, and news and entertainment. Ads by and for midwives, cooks, seamstresses, companions, boarders, wet nurses, and women's academies were common. Notices of meetings and events, like a sale at the Female Hospitable Society Store or a meeting of the Soup Kitchen Society, a women's charity, appeared regularly. The many ads for domestic goods, women's hats, and sewing supplies showed that businessmen knew that women read these papers.

Just as a women's culture emerged in these years, so did a culture of children. In 1828 a Philadelphia House of Refuge for Juveniles opened at Fairmont and 15th Streets, the first separate poorhouse for children in the city.[34] With urbanization and industrialization, new relationships among women, children, and society were emerging, and in some cases, care for children moved out from under parental guardianship. They were banned from almshouses and removed from their mothers there by the 1830s,[35] becoming the concern of government and of women like Gratz.

Responding to Evangelism

Evangelism's challenge to Jewish women did not abate with the advent of Victorian culture.[36] The measure of domestic morality was the spiritual, pious woman who inspired and promoted religious activities at home. Because such piety was linked to Christianity, it challenged the respectability of Jewish women and their households. Although a growing number of poor Jewish women needed charitable aid, charity from both municipal and private sources came with exhortations about Christianity.[37]

As the pace and fervor of Christian sermonizing picked up, Gratz found more occasions to hear ministers with reputations for delivering great speeches. But as evangelism grew increasingly important, Unitarians, like her friend Rev. William H. Furness, pastor of the Unitarian Church of Philadelphia, sometimes incurred criticism, and Gratz attended his lectures, partly to "see how the people appreciate him."[38] Unitarians often came under the same attacks as did Jews for incorrect belief. But the evangelical movement also drew criticism. Many people were repulsed by its fire-and-brimstone style and its condemnation of those who did not share its beliefs.

When Stephen Girard, the wealthiest man in country, died in 1831, he left his entire estate to the city of Philadelphia to establish a nonreligious boarding school for orphan boys, Girard College.[39] Because he hoped that a "pure morality" might be taught to its students, however, he stipulated that clergy were to be barred from the school. Gratz explained to Maria that "nobody objects to his excluding the clergy from its walls." On the contrary, she felt that without clergy "we may hope that religion purer than that of the Sunday School Union will grow up and flourish there."[40] Sunday schools conducted "sweeps" on Sunday mornings that ushered all children on the streets into their classrooms.[41] In 1825 the American Sunday School Union (ASSU) claimed that one-third of the six- to fifteen-year-olds in Philadelphia attended their school.[42] Gratz and others felt that the ASSU was more concerned with counting the number of people they could claim to have converted than with the quality of the religious life those people practiced.[43]

Some Christian theologians suggested that religion was essentially a feeling of gratitude and dependence, and Victorian culture concluded that women were by nature religious and pious. Religion, therefore, proved a source of acceptable and admirable activities for women, and consequently Christian women dramatically enhanced their role in religious education, both at home and in Sunday schools.[44] It was among the middle and upper classes, where women earned little and thus were more dependent on men, that Victorian sexism held the greatest sway. Whatever their compassion and ethical motivation, philanthropy offered wealthier Jewish women a way to implement their own views about managing society and eradicating poverty along with a means to display their status.[45]

Literature, Theater, and Moral Values

Charitable societies and religious education provided respectable communal activities in the emerging women's culture, while literature and advice books inculcated values that supported those endeavors. Gratz continued to delight in literature of all sorts and was deeply influenced by it. Yet, she believed literature ought to promote morality and thought some romantic novels were

"offensive to good morals."[46] Although she had not seen her old
friend James Paulding in many years, she remained fond of him
and bought all his books, regardless of what she, or the critics,
thought of them. She disliked his romance of the colonial era
in *The Dutchman's Fireside* and thought his characters "modern
enough in their caprice of feelings."[47] But, loyal to her old friend,
she sent her Kentucky sister-in-law a copy of Paulding's *Westward
Ho!* "before a critic has the chance to forestall your relish."[48]

In 1832, Mrs. Furness, wife of Unitarian minister William
Furness, sent Gratz a copy of *The Mothers Book* by Lydia Maria
Child of Boston. Rebecca commented to her sister-in-law that
"it is very good and practicable, but I dare say you can bring
up your children as well without it." Gratz thought Child's advice to mothers on coping with a child's death "the most difficult
lesson she would inculcate and . . . would require us to remodel
our human affections on a more sublime nature." She thought it
impossible for a mother to accept calmly the death of her child,
even if she believed the child's soul went straight to heaven. Such
behavior just did not square with Gratz's experience. Her sister-
in-law Maria was a pious woman who grieved terribly when her
children died. When her newborn died that year, Maria Gist Gratz
blamed herself for neglecting some element of the child's care.
Rebecca urged her to console herself with her faith that the child's
death was the will of God, and not to "exaggerate the trial by
imagining any other cause."[49] Because Gratz involved herself with
the torments many women faced in family life, she saw many
mothers bury their children: "I . . . recently [saw] a Mother resign
a little suffering child with as much composure as I should wish
or approve, and yet she [felt] more agony than Mrs. Child thinks
consistent with religion or reason."[50]

Rebecca also discussed this very popular book with Julia
Hoffman, her close friend and sometime companion in her later
years. A few months after Maria Fenno Hoffman died, Julia visited
Rebecca. Julia planned only a short visit, but when foul weather
delayed her return trip to New York, she agreed to spend the
entire winter with Gratz. Gratz was delighted that she would
stay "so that I am not alone." Sarah Moses was then fifteen, and
Gratz was even more pleased that Julia, a few years older than
Sarah, would become a friend in the house for her. "Sarah . . . is
now becoming more in want of rational companions than play
fellows, and Julia is well educated and sensible—Sarah is fond

of her," Gratz explained.[51] It was the first of many winters that Hoffman, who never married, would spend with Gratz. Hoffman's visits became a tradition that continued long after Sarah married and moved away from Philadelphia.[52]

Despite the influences of secular literature and Christian evangelism, Gratz's religious attitudes continued to be shaped by Judaism. Her view of God was the omnipotent, omniscient, merciful, and just Creator and Father she read about in the Bible and in Jewish prayer books. Judaism teaches that the natural world is a gift from God, that people are to tend that world in their relationship with God, and that they ought to appreciate the gifts of this world that are believed to come from God. Gratz felt that because both her life and the world were utterly dependent on God, she had a good deal for which to be grateful. She told her sister-in-law Maria that she could not understand why "some moralists . . . call this good world by such hard names": disliking God's creation seemed blasphemous. It was illogical to her to propose that God had "withdrawn his favor from the beautiful planet he created in love—and bestowed all His treasures on another State in which the beings he placed in this must center all their joys." Heaven was something to look forward to and to console oneself with, but it was not to replace our focus on this world "where God placed us." Happiness on earth prepares us for happiness in heaven, Gratz believed. "How can we mixed creatures of clay be fitted for celestial transports if in this our probationary sphere no glimpse of heaven can be made visible, no touch of happiness enter our hearts?" Gratz insisted that human souls could not be "imprisoned all our natural lives" in an evil world "and still be fitted . . . for heaven." The revivalists like Charles Grandison Finney, regardless of their denomination, who traveled the states exhorting people to admit their sinful nature and ask Christ's forgiveness in order to reach heaven and transform their lives on earth, seemed to Gratz to be unnecessarily bleak.

Rebecca and her sister-in-law Maria had ample exposure to evangelical activities, as both Philadelphia and Kentucky were popular sites for traveling revivalists. In Philadelphia, revivalists worked both within established churches and in open public parks. In Kentucky they were more likely to set up large tents in open spaces, and the ensuing revival could continue for weeks. Maria discussed the religious attitudes she encountered at the revivals with her sister-in-law in Philadelphia. Rebecca's close friendship with her sister-in-law enabled her to continue the kind of religious debates she had enjoyed earlier with Gertrude Meredith.

Gratz disagreed with evangelical religious assumptions. As a Jew, she hoped to attain heaven more through her gratitude and obedience to God than through confessing sins in order to avoid hell. To her niece Miriam she fumed that the prevalent evangelical "despondency because we are placed little lower than angels" was disputing God's wisdom and "downright presumption."[53] She was sure that it was "just as much a duty to enjoy [life's pleasures] as it is a necessity to submit to sorrow." She explained to Maria that she loved a "joyful attitude acknowledging the gracious gifts bestowed by providence . . . which make us capable of conceiving the end for which we are designed." Lest Maria think she lacked the capacity to be self-reflective, she admitted to her that she thought self-examinations were "very edifying" but gave "little credit to the recorded self-abasements of sanctified persons."[54]

Gratz's understanding of the link between spirituality and virtue came from her exposure to both Judaism and American nineteenth-century culture. She believed her religious duties disciplined the selfishness that kept her from hearing God's word and trained her in the virtues that would bring spiritual rewards. These rewards were inner strength, health, happiness, and eternal life, all of which appear in both European Jewish folklore and popular American literature. The congruence in these rewards expected by both popular Judaism and popular Protestantism, as expressed by her family, her friends, and in sermons, as well as their shared bibliocentrism, convinced Gratz that Jews and Protestants should live easily together.

By taking an active role in communal affairs, Gratz created a bridge between Jewish and American cultures. According to biblical Judaism, true piety is performing God's will. Rabbinic traditions noted that in order to be able to distinguish self-motivated action from God-motivated action, it is important to maintain some sense of self. In the eleventh century, Bahya Ibn Pakuda's *Duties of the Heart* explained that actions were the outward signs of one's spiritual development. Some of Ibn Pakuda's work was incorporated into the Jewish prayer book used especially in the Sephardic service Gratz attended at Mikveh Israel and became part of mainstream Judaism.[55] Gratz understood her spiritual rewards in terms of the piety of the "true woman," the communal responsibility of the "republican mother," and Jewish piety.[56]

Gratz read the Bible for knowledge of God and for guidance in developing the kind of virtuous character that she believed God wanted from her. Like her friend Gertrude Meredith and her sister-in-law Maria, Rebecca saw virtue and faith as the core of religion. She enjoyed the popular literature that used biblical settings and characters if the stories enhanced her religious understanding by making Bible stories seem "more touching." She suggested to her sister-in-law Maria that they coordinate their Bible reading schedule and share their "meditations." Gratz admired Maria's "ingenious interpretations of the prophecies" because they were "practically good," although probably "too free for theologians." She decided that because Maria's lessons were good, she could legitimately "draw authority from Scriptures." "If everyone would follow your example the reign of peace would indeed be universal," she wrote.[57]

Gratz believed that literature and the arts could strengthen and shape spirituality, and as she raised Rachel's children she taught them to appreciate literature. In 1832 she told her sister-in-law that Rachel's daughter Sarah was beginning to "delight in poetry—Byron has been her great favorite." Maria urged Rebecca to introduce Sarah to the classical poets, and Gratz responded by teaching the girl to read "selections from Pope, Milton, and others to chastise her taste and give her other standards of excellence."[58]

Two years later Rebecca recommended Harriet Martineau's *Illustrations of Political Economy* to Maria for educating her children because it made "a dry subject very easily understood." Both Rebecca and Maria admired Martineau's books for children and her adult fiction, but they especially admired Martineau's critiques about the place of both religion and women in contemporary society. In 1834, Gratz brought the two women together.[59] When Martineau toured the country she visited Philadelphia, where she met Gratz before heading west. Rebecca wrote a letter of introduction to Maria for Martineau, and then wrote to Kentucky. "I am sure you will be pleased with her . . . [she is] perfectly well bred and unaffected. Her conversation [is] full of interesting anecdotes. . . . [She is] quite unassuming and willing to talk of her own works with candor and in all respects such a woman as one rarely meets and cannot fail to admire. . . . I know I have told you how much [her tales] pleased me."[60]

Gratz also enjoyed live drama, as did her brothers. More than five theaters offered plays and reviews nightly in Philadelphia, and most of the Gratz brothers attended, although Jacob, the least sociable of the family, seldom did so.[61] Rebecca complained to Maria that "while (actress) Miss [Fanny] Kemble is in town I spend a great many lone evenings—Hyman and Jo go to the theater—she is really charming. I have seen her three times and more wonderful still, Jac went once."[62] Kemble had made her stage debut in 1829, when her father, who owned a theater in Covent Garden, England, begged her to take a role to save him from financial ruin. Although she insisted that she hated acting, she was an enormous success and enjoyed fame on both sides of the Atlantic. During an extended run in Philadelphia, she also became close friends with Thomas Sully's wife, and Sully painted at least thirteen portraits of the actress in various costumes.[63]

Personal Challenges from Christianity

As Jewish and Christian women found their religious com-mitments of increasing importance, Gratz's encounters with Christian women grew difficult. She often told her sister-in-law Maria about clashes between women of different faiths. In 1832, Rebecca wrote to Maria about an incident at a meeting of the Philadelphia Orphan Asylum (POA). Gratz's friend Mrs. Furness wanted to adopt a girl from the orphanage and had asked Gratz, secretary of the board of managers, to submit her application. The board rejected the application because the Furnesses were Uni-tarians. Women whom Gratz identified only as "a church woman [and] a Presbyterian" insisted that a Unitarian influence would harm the child. Shocked, Gratz initiated a lengthy discussion about the way her co-workers allowed their personal religious convictions to affect their decisions for the city's orphans. "Ladies," she said, "there are many children under my special direction— you all know my creed—suppose I should want to bring one up in my family?" The board agreed that Gratz could do so only because "Jews do not think it a duty to convert." After a lengthy argument Gratz forced the issue to a vote, but to no avail. A long dispute on religion between Gratz and one of her co-workers continued after the meeting ended. "Though we have been more than twenty years acquainted, I expect that she will look shy on me for the rest of our lives," Rebecca wrote to Maria. "I am ashamed of such an illiberal spirit . . . what a pity that the best and holiest gift of God . . . should be perverted into a subject of strife."[64]

The whole situation angered Gratz. To her, the unique importance of the United States lay in the freedom (religious and otherwise) it guaranteed its citizens. As the public debate about religion echoed in debates about laws forbidding behavior that ran counter to Christian living, like the Sunday Sabbath laws enacted in many states and municipalities, Rebecca became convinced that men like her brothers, Jewish and American-born, ought to involve themselves in politics. She complained to her sister-in-law that she wished "our brothers had a little more public spirit— or at least would take some of the burdens of public affairs on themselves—they have time enough to spare." Although Gratz never mentioned the budding women's rights movement in any of her letters, more than a dozen years before the meeting at Seneca Falls she felt frustrated that as a woman, she was shut out of political leadership. "If I were a man," she argued to Maria, "I would like to have some share in public concerns."[65]

Jewish Religious Education

Without political opportunities, Gratz had to fight evangelists through religious argument alone, so she sought out instruction in Judaism to strengthen her abilities and her case. In 1832 she established a personal correspondence with Jacob Mordecai, Hebraist and educator in Virginia, who occasionally visited Philadelphia, Mikveh Israel, and the Gratzes. Mordecai was considered one of the best authorities on Judaism in the country, and Gratz asked him to send her "the outpourings of a mind long devoted to important researches after truth."[66]

Born in Philadelphia about the time that Michael Gratz arrived in town, Mordecai later worked for David Franks, as had Michael and Barnard, and finally settled in Warrenton, Virginia, as a local merchant. But Mordecai, who had a scholarly turn of mind, studied at the best schools available to him in Philadelphia, amassed an important library in philosophy and religion, and in 1809 opened the Female Academy in Warrenton. His daughters Emma and Ellen taught in the school, as did most of his children.[67] Rebecca was thrilled that "since [Mordecai's] return south he has twice written to me and sent me valuable papers of his own writing which I consider quite a treasure." One was a discussion of the biblical David, titled "David King of Israel—The Man after God's Own Heart." Rebecca promised her sister-in-law Maria that she would save them and show them to her, pointing out that Mordecai had "the advantage of understanding the language in which the scriptures were written." Furthermore, Mordecai had a "large learned library, a liberal spirit . . . and has frequent applications from Christian divines on scriptural texts which leads him into . . . examinations . . . conducted with good feeling and good taste."[68] Mordecai had, until then, "never printed a book but desired to make his own children and grandchildren well acquainted with the religion they profess."[69]

Rebecca collected books on Judaism, and most such books in the family library belonged to her. She also sought out Leeser's ideas about Judaism. He gave Gratz manuscript chapters of his translation of Moses Mendelssohn's *Jerusalem* to read as he finished them. Knowing the young man's tendency to write long, Germanic sentences, Gratz read Leeser's translations "with pencil in hand."[70] Gratz and her brothers discussed Gotthold Salomon's *Twelve Sermons,* delivered by Salomon at the Hamburgh Temple in Germany, cradle of the German Reform movement.[71] She also read religious writings by gentile women to learn their ideas on both spirituality and Jews. She was "charmed" by *The Life of Mrs. Hannah More,* a biography of a British Christian who wrote Bible commentaries. "I love a joyful gratitude acknowledging the gracious gifts bestowed by providence," Gratz wrote.[72]

Gratz's clash over religion with her co-workers at the POA reflected an intensifying religious conflict around the country. Evangelism was proving a relentless force in Philadelphia, and in 1834 a Christian neighbor asked to borrow Gratz's Bible to see if it said the same thing as the one she read. On returning it, the neighbor urged Rebecca not to let the "light that was in me be darkness" and to daily "examine myself" and study the Scriptures. Gratz responded first to the attitude of the evangelist. "She is so earnest that I cannot help being obliged to her—tho she sent me more books than I can read," she wrote to Maria. But she did not hide her irritation from her sister-in-law. Rebecca saw clearly that the women was trying to "canonize herself by my conversion."[73]

These religious disputes never prompted Gratz to resign from the POA board. On the contrary, they compelled her to remain actively involved, although she began talking about the need for a Jewish orphan asylum soon afterward. Philadelphia's Jewish community was too small to maintain an institution like that, however, and Jews around the country typically cared for orphans and other needy children by placing them in local orphanages or in foster care with other Jewish families. The institution she sought, which would care exclusively for Jewish children, would not open its doors for another twenty years. In the meantime, Gratz busily tended to POA needs, particularly when, in October 1834, an outbreak of smallpox and varioloid at the asylum sickened more than thirty children and killed one.[74]

Rebecca gleaned spiritual lessons from literature as well as from religion. "Shakespeare has beautifully expressed the powers of meditation to find books in the running brooks, sermons in stones and good in everything," she commented. "Does not this encourage us to believe that nature has done greatly for us?"[75] Gratz enjoyed Carlyle's *Sartor Resartus* and quoted Cowper that "the earth was made thus various that the mind of man studious of change and fond of novelty might be indulged."[76] Along with Shakespeare, Gratz read tracts like *Woman's Mission*. Although several books appeared with that title, at least four were American reprints of a British book by Aime Martin originally titled *Education of Mothers*. The title page asserted that a nation's "moral tone . . . depends on . . . women" who influence society by rising early and caring for their families. Rebecca thought the tract was "beautifully written, and . . . highly moral, setting forth the importance of proper education [on] the influence which woman possesses in society."[77]

Women's Mission

Gratz applied the book's message to her own relationship with her unmarried brothers. Although she had never married, Gratz felt that she understood men's emotional dependence on women as well as any wife did. "The man who has no one to influence and console him, when vehement passions, painful diseases and disappointed pride cross his vexed spirits," she wrote to Maria, "is a sad spectacle of suffering and helplessness." She believed that she helped her brothers cope with such problems. "I should be frightened for my own single brothers when such a picture is presented to my mind—if it were not for the hope that I may be able to repay all their goodness to me by keeping up a domestic home with those charities alive, which may rescue them from the worst effects of bachelorship—a care-for-nobody independence."[78]

Literature on women's mission emphasized women's role in raising children, and Gratz's many nieces and nephews provided her the opportunity to practice the ideas and approaches she

read about. Rebecca delighted in children and "never tire[d] of
being a schoolmistress. Their own words expressing their own
thoughts go quick[ly] to my heart," she explained. Gratz savored
the opportunity for personal authority that teaching offered, but
she also felt that "children are very good society," and most of her
letters included anecdotes about various children in her extended
family.[79] She opposed the frightening Calvinist approach to child
rearing that was still popular in antebellum America and felt that
childhood's happiness prepares children to appreciate divine love;
for her, childish happiness was the beginning of a religious life.[80]

Although Rebecca told a friend that "nothing . . . interest[s
me like] the development of young minds," by 1835 her nieces and
nephews were leaving behind both childhood and their childish
need for their aunt.[81] Richea's son Isaac Hays had already begun
his twenty-year position as staff surgeon at Wills Eye Hospital in
Philadelphia, and her daughter Elizabeth Rosa married Charles
Marx in Philadelphia that June. Richea's daughter Sarah Ann
married Alfred Mordecai the next year, and in 1836, Rachel's
daughter Miriam Gratz Moses, who had lived with Gratz since
her mother's death more than a decade earlier, married publisher
Solomon Cohen of South Carolina. Although the couple married
in Philadelphia, they soon settled in Charleston. Gratz cultivated
a close relationship with Cohen, an observant Jew whom she admired and respected. Letters from Rebecca to Miriam and her husband show an almost obsequious attitude, something rare indeed
in Gratz, and indicating the depth of her fear about losing her close
relationship with Miriam.[82] Miriam soon began an extensive and
intensive correspondence with Rebecca, occasionally asking if the
POA or the FHBS could find a place for an orphan from the South.[83]

The losses Gratz endured during 1835 and 1836 made them
difficult years, and she found herself again withdrawing from society's delights. "My time for amusements has gone by," she wrote to
her sister-in-law Maria. Joseph remained the most sociable member of the household. Describing an evening at home, she reported
"Jo . . . recreating himself with friends at the whist table—he and
Jac abandon tea parties altogether—Hyman sometimes goes—I
more rarely still. . . . I have not been to . . . a play since Fanny
Kemble retired."[84]

Joseph often tried to prod Rebecca out of too familiar sur-
roundings. In 1837 he wrote to her describing his wonderful
vacation at Saratoga Springs. The Sedgwicks were there, and

Catherine was asking for Gratz. He urged his sister to bring niece Sarah Moses and come up right away. Joseph offered to meet them and sent detailed instructions about the stagecoaches, ferries, and boats they would need to reach the resort.[85] But instead of Saratoga Springs, Rebecca went to New York, where she, Sarah, and Joseph were met by her old friend James Paulding. Rebecca wrote that he seemed as "glad to see me . . . as he was twenty years ago—we talked a whole day together and renewed so many agreeable passages in our lives, that I would willingly go to New York annually for another conference. Washington Irving came in too—and they were as brilliant as in the days of their youth."[86]

Despite the happiness she felt with her old friends, when Gratz returned to Philadelphia her attention returned to the issue of evangelism that distressed her so deeply. Many Jews were angered by the actions of Joseph Wolfe, a Jew who had converted to Christianity and worked for the Society for the Melioration of the Condition of the Jews. Rebecca wrote to Maria about her feelings: "I have not much respect for pious Zealots—there is so much pride and uncharitableness mixed with their self righteousness that it seldom comes to good." She concluded, "Thank god I have the law and the prophets and am willing to hear them."[87]

Maria often heard Rebecca's arguments against the effort to Christianize the country. To Gratz, if America's promise of religious freedom was to be fulfilled, then her Christian friends were obligated to respect her religion as fully as she was obligated to respect theirs. She could not understand "why the worship of God should be so fertile of ill will," but concluded that "some good end is to be answered." Anti-Semitism would not shake her faith. For her part, Maria had some difficulty understanding why her sister-in-law remained a Jew. Gratz explained that she was "in principle as well as in practice a conformist to the law," meaning the Torah. Torah, the first five books of the Bible, provides the foundation for Judaism. The prophets' ethical explanations of the laws found in Torah, and the rabbinic commentaries and applications of those laws, comprise Judaism's core. In an allusion to Christian assertions that faith in Jesus makes obedience to Jewish law unnecessary, Gratz insisted, "Now even IF THIS MIGHT NOT BE NECESSARY—it cannot be wrong." That statement, written in 1837, concluded any discussion about her future as a Jew. It is the most strident defense of her decision to remain a Jew that she made in all her frequent letters to her sister-in-law.

Maria and Rebecca continued to discuss their reading, to invoke God, and to offer religious perspectives on the events of their lives. Gratz regularly sent information about upcoming holidays and their preparations to Maria to keep Benjamin abreast of the Jewish liturgical calendar and to help Maria understand any holidays that he might choose to celebrate.[88] Some, like Sukkoth (Feast of Tabernacles), were celebrated by Benjamin's family in autumn 1837. Rebecca was delighted and admitted to Maria that she was "only once under the shelter of its roof and [ate] . . . only a little food—a little bread and salt—tho I enjoyed the sight . . . and listened to a hymn of Thanksgiving."[89]

As the decade went on, violence in Philadelphia grew more intense and more frequent. Anti-black riots became chronic in the city, and election rioting was common. Gangs, muggers, and volunteer fire companies routinely battled in the streets.[90] An economic panic had hit, and in 1837, as Hyman was elected treasurer of the Pennsylvania Company, a local bank,[91] striking mechanics lost their fight for a ten-hour day.[92] The next year Pennsylvania Hall was burned when it held an antislavery Convention of American Women.[93] Located just over the Mason-Dixon Line, Philadelphia was one of the first "safe" stops on the Underground Railroad and attracted one of the largest black populations of any northern city, despite the fact that the city's primary trade routes were with the South and its strong business and social alliances there kept it hostile to free blacks and abolitionists.[94] When Rachel's son Simon Gratz Moses married Mary Porter Ashe in 1838, the couple moved to St. Louis—partly to escape an increasingly violent city. Simon's older brother Isaac Moses already had moved to Mobile, Alabama.

The Hebrew Sunday School

Jewish immigrants during this era were tradesmen or peddlers and their families, or unmarried women hoping to marry a new immigrant in the United States. Almost invariably poor, they arrived already well used to hardship. Immigration itself was a dangerous undertaking. Most Jews were steerage passengers on sailing vessels (steamships appeared more than twenty years later). According to one historian, among these Jews "education other than for basic Jewish literacy ranked fairly low in family and communal priorities." They plied their trades: dry goods peddlers, glaziers, cigar makers, tailors, furriers, hoopskirt makers, cap-makers, needleworkers, bakers, paperhangers, shoe- and boot-makers, gold lace weavers, gold- and silversmiths, bookbinders, diamond cutters, and printers. Jewish girls in orphanages were trained in needlework. Among most Jews, however, "self employment was *the* goal,"[95] as a non-Jewish employer would not be likely to allow a Jewish worker to refrain from work on Saturday and other Jewish holidays, and Jews worried about the effect of anti-Jewish prejudice on their job security. Jews, like most other Americans, believed that mastery of a trade or business led to financial independence.[96] Families often combined their efforts, and daughters usually worked, as did many wives. Widows often carried on a family business. The smaller the store, the greater the likelihood that the entire family, including wife and daughters, labored there.[97]

Many of Philadelphia's new Jewish immigrants joined the Rodeph Shalom congregation, which practiced a style of worship more familiar to northern European Jews than that practiced at Mikveh Israel. Despite its attractiveness to new immigrants, Rodeph Shalom remained unable to provide much of an education to its members' children. In 1822 a number of Rodeph Shalom men formed the Hebra Gemiluth Hassadim Ve-Hinuch Nearim, a free loan and Hebrew educational society. Its dual goals reveal the group's chief obstacle to establishing a successful school—poverty. Students were too poor to pay the teacher's fee, and teachers were too poor to volunteer their time. The congregation tried to raise the funds by taxing seat holders, but still lacked sufficient financial support. The shortage of teachers led to huge classes, often with sixty or eighty children of varying ages and abilities. Moreover, none of the teachers were professionally trained educators. Not surprisingly, Rodeph Shalom suffered a rapid turnover in staff, and men joined the faculty only to supplement their incomes. In the 1840s the school operated only sporadically, yet before 1850 it remained the sole congregation-based Jewish religious school in the city. In 1856 when Dr. Henry Vidaver was chosen rabbi and school superintendent, he divided 167 students into two classes taught by two teachers. When enrollment dropped to 80 students by 1860, he believed only one teacher was needed. When enrollment increased to 114 students in 1873, only three teachers served them. German remained the language of instruction until the 1860s. Rodeph Shalom's staff frequently used corporal punishment to maintain discipline. Two new congregational schools, at Beth Israel and at Keneseth Israel, served mostly the sons of their congregation members. Both schools offered classes in the Bible, Hebrew reading, prayers, and Hebrew-German translation.[98]

But Gratz understood America differently from the new Jewish immigrants and the men who ran congregational schools for boys. She believed that financial independence alone would not be enough to enable immigrants to live socially respected lives in the United States. Nor would the ability to recite traditional prayers in Hebrew enable a Jewish child to withstand evangelical arguments. Like the men of the state assembly who had passed the Pennsylvania Free School Law that led to the founding of Philadelphia's Central High School in 1836, Gratz believed the immigrants would need education.[99] But she knew that Jewish students at Philadelphia's Central High School would mingle with Christian students and teachers who had been taught to evangelize, many by the American Sunday School Union.

Gratz attempted to solve the dilemma by forming a Jewish version of the powerful ASSU. Although in 1838 she explained to a preacher visiting at Furness's church that she "claimed the privilege of not being inimical to any man's religion," she hoped to block the power of evangelists.[100] Undoubtedly impressed by Catherine Beecher's 1835 *Essay on the Education of Female Teachers,* Gratz applied its goals to the Hebrew Sunday School (HSS). Beecher suggested that the American West could be "civilized" by sending trained female teachers to the frontier, where they could stabilize communities, first through their roles as teachers and then, eventually, by marrying and raising their own families and influencing their towns. Beecher's philosophy replaced Christian emotionalism with moral energy as a means to salvation.[101] Gratz took much the same attitude toward the role her Sunday school teachers might play in the Jewish community. The challenge to Jews was to Americanize new and poor Jewish immigrants and their families while encouraging them to remain Jewish, and to separate Jewish religion from forms of Jewish culture distinctive to Europe but thought unworkable in America. The Sunday school movement was adapted by Jewish women to Americanize Jewish children while educating them in Judaism in a way that would protect them against evangelists.

As early as 1835, Gratz began urging the women of the FHBS to take some action to improve the deplorable state of Jewish education in Philadelphia. In her secretary's report that year she laid out three separate arguments. She began by reminding the members that their petitioners were "fellow sojourners in this world of many wants and many sufferings," thereby inviting them to bridge the gulf between donor and recipient that charitable societies often created. By reminding the women that they too had experienced sufferings and want at some time in their lives, she tapped their sympathies for her cause. She urged the FHBS managers to view Jewish children throughout the city, including children of immigrants, as their own concern. Pointing out that their past "feebl[e]" efforts had "relieve[d] [only] the cravings of nature," she suggested that the organization direct its efforts to *"that most pressing need*—the mental impoverishment of those who are rising to take their places among the thousands of Israel scattered throughout the families of the earth."

Prior to this 1835 report, Gratz had reminded her readers about their responsibilities toward the poor only. In this report, written when she was fifty-four, she began arguing the duties generations hold toward each other. First, she addressed the FHBS women as mothers who cared about the "rising generations." Next she asked the younger FHBS members to consider their debt to the founders. Gratz had not yet created the institution she hoped to be remembered for. "In a little while the remnant of those who first plead for the female poor of this congregation will have passed away," she pointed out. How would the FHBS founders be remembered? "Perhaps the sweetest memorial raised to their names will be the record that they laid the corner stone to this institution." Gratz prodded the women, particularly the younger and more energetic among them, to fulfill the society's early dreams for establishing an institution for Jewish education, dreams that had long languished. She begged that the founders' work not die with them: "It is not too much to hope—too much to expect from the daughters of a noble race that they will be foremost in the work of Charity—provided their young hearts are impressed with its sacred duties." By appealing to the FHBS women's self-image, Gratz urged them to consider that the future of their organization, and their own memorials, rested on their ability to bring in younger Jewish women. To reach young Jewish women, Gratz argued, the FHBS women would have to "train . . . them in the way they should go."

Establishing this point, she then moved to practical matters. Previously, when the FHBS women had discussed providing education they were stopped by one practical limitation—they had no appropriately trained teacher. Gratz pointed out that now, in 1835, "we have . . . a Teacher desirous of [sharing] his . . . knowledge for the improvement of the rising generation." It seems likely that she was referring to Isaac Leeser, and this was so obvious to her audience that she did not need to mention him by name. Leeser read and understood Hebrew, and his ability to "study in the original language of scripture gives him advantages few here possess," she explained. How could the FHBS women not take advantage of this opportunity? Here was an individual who could oversee the curriculum of a Jewish school in Philadelphia.

Throughout her report Gratz pressed her case. The benefits of a Jewish education, she explained, would yield both material and social benefits, goals that the FHBS had historically considered most urgent. "The want of education shuts the door of advancement in private or public stations which an Israelite might obtain in this country," she pointed out. Many Jewish children attended school only to learn to read and write, and many others learned those skills while apprenticed to a tradesman. Jewish children lacked the sort of education that Gratz thought essential.

Using a prophetic tone, Gratz argued that the women were "obligat[ed to] . . . wip[e] off . . . that stigma which rebellion and disobedience" placed upon the Jewish nation. From her own experience, she believed that could be accomplished "when enlightened Jews mingle with the inhabitants of the land respecting their own laws and practicing the virtues required of the chosen people of God." The result might be more than material ease and social respect for Jews. It would be so revolutionary an experience it might herald the coming of the messiah. Just as Christian postmillennialists argued that Jesus would return after an era in which humanity had strived to improve the world, so Gratz argued that the FHBS women's work to improve the condition of Jewish life and Jewish citizenship in America "must prepare the way for that "prophet like unto Moses unto whom the gathering of the people shall be." She believed she had seen signs of a new era of Jewish history in her own life, in her close friendships with pious Christians, and in the effect of religious instruction she had seen among her Jewish friends and relatives. "We need look for no greater miracle than the changed heart that an enlightened faith—piety, self-respect and charity will engender to make our wilderness bloom—and a light shine on the mountains of ruin," Gratz insisted.

After tantalizing her audience with possibility of the coming of the messiah, Gratz presented pastoral images of planting and reaping. None of the FHBS women had farm experience, but they all had read those images in the Bible. Her audience interpreted these domestic and rustic pastoral images as religious images, giving her speech some of the force and authority of the Bible. "The grain must be sown before the harvest can be reaped," Gratz explained, "and if we are only employed in the humblest occupation of preparing the soil for future seasons of prosperity—our labor will not be lost to that Allseeing Eye that searches out the smallest grain of good and quickeneth it to an allotted end." Although Gratz was only delivering the secretary's annual report, her years of listening to sermons prepared her to sermonize effectively to her associates.[102]

On February 4, 1838, Gratz called a meeting of the FHBS to push the issue of forming a school. After "a spirited meeting" with lots of lively discussion, the board of managers of the FHBS resolved to move ahead with the plan Gratz proposed and open a school for Jewish religious education under their own direction. It was the first attempt to make Jewish education the responsibility of the community as a whole, rather than the responsibility of the leadership of a particular congregation or of individual parents. Teachers were to be appointed by the board from among the young women of their congregations. The HSS began with six teachers who were respected for their moral character and intelligence, including Simha Peixotto and Rachel Peixotto (Mrs. Eleazar) Pyke, sisters who ran a women's academy in Philadelphia; Louisa B. Hart, whose grandfather Jacob R. Cohen had served as Mikveh Israel's hazan; and Gratz herself. The school opened a month later, on Gratz's fifty-seventh birthday, with fifty pupils. The teachers were expected to abstain from all conversation with each other during school hours and to conduct themselves in a manner kind but strict, to teach as much by example as by "precept." Weekly assignments were addressed to Gratz, who, as superintendent, personally graded them. Each assignment examined a portion of the Bible, and good penmanship counted nearly as much as a correct answer.[103]

In the fall of 1838, Gratz wrote to her niece Miriam that "we have opened a Sunday School . . . and have more than seventy scholars [who] appear . . . interested." Although sure that "much good [would] result from it," she admitted that "it will require some labor to organize" and hoped that Miriam's husband, Solomon Cohen, would advise her. She often enlisted family help for her causes, but as it turned out, rather than receiving Cohen's advice, she advised Miriam about organizing a Sunday school in Savannah, Georgia, a few years later.[104] The Peixotto sisters, also seat holders in the women's section at Mikveh Israel, probably provided the school's pedagogical expertise. The sisters' academy in the Peixotto home at Fourth and Walnut Streets became the first site of the HSS.[105]

Gratz and other managers of the HSS found several ways to meet their financial expenses. As the parent organization to the HSS, the FHBS paid the Peixottos forty dollars per year for the use of their home. Private donors subscribed, and parents who could afford tuition paid two dollars. Many students themselves contributed to a collection box to defray the costs for others. Mikveh Israel was also a major contributor to the school. The school's most successful fund-raising efforts, however, were the public annual examinations, held at Mikveh Israel in the school's early years, to which the whole community was invited. Parents and donors could see their contributions' effect as students answered questions based on their academic work. The public final exam, with an appeal for funds made at its close, remained one of the HSS's primary fund-raising techniques until late in the century, when the school grew too large to showcase the children's work despite the use of large halls and more formal and selected student performances.[106]

Gratz fulfilled her personal interests in education and religion through her dual responsibilities as superintendent and teacher. Children's reading exercises, which usually were moral lessons in simple verse, were "quite as improving to me as to [them]."[107] Her classroom preparations gave her the opportunity to systematize her religious studies. A few months after the school opened, Rebecca suggested to her sister-in-law Maria that they coordinate their "meditations" on the Bible. Gratz was then reading the life of Samuel and remarked on Hannah's "most touching . . . self-sacrifice and devotion."[108] Although she felt that "silence . . . was originally intended for devotional purposes," she was convinced that religious education must structure religious life.[109]

Working with the FHBS, the HSS educated poor Jewish children and allowed Jewish women to teach religion publicly for the first time in Jewish history. By teaching in the school, American Jewish women demonstrated their piety and concern for social order during a time of rising anti-Semitism and evangelism. To Jewish immigrants, the HSS conveyed the idea that Jewish Americans maintained Judaism and that in America Jewish women had a public role in religious life. Emphasizing the Jewish Sabbath and its sacred domesticity, the HSS echoed, in Jewish terms, women's central importance in creating the domestic utopia described in American women's sentimental literature. The HSS taught that Jewish immigrants need not abandon Judaism and its home rituals. The school enjoyed immediate and widespread support. Leeser, who lamented the poor quality of Jewish education in America, quickly became the school's most energetic and important ally.[110] Impressed with the Philadelphia school's success, the women of New York's Shearith Israel congregation met in October 1838 to form the Association for the Moral and Religious Instruction of Children of the Jewish Faith. The group quickly approved the HSS plan and voted Gratz and Leeser honorary board members. Just as the FHBS and HSS worked hand in hand to provide both charity and education, so the New York association also provided clothing and shoes to students in need.[111] That year Gratz also sent lesson plans used in the HSS to Sally Lopez in Charleston, who opened a similar school there with Gratz's help.[112]

Rebecca happily reported to Miriam that the school was influencing Philadelphia's Jewish children. Shortly after the school opened, a student told his father that "the Lady at the Sunday school" told him not to attend public school classes on Saturday, but to "honor the Sabbath." "His parent was not displeased at the reproof," Gratz explained to Miriam, "for the next week we had three more of his children." Gratz was sure that the school would help Jewish immigrant families materially; since God was the master of Providence, it seemed to her only logical that "if we can teach the hearts of the children to seek God, there is no doubt their lives will be improved." Moreover, she believed that "Jewish dignity and honor," so central to Jewish "national character," grew out of Jewish religious devotion.[113]

According to Gratz, female teachers would increase their own religious understanding in the course of classroom preparations and would then heighten the religious awareness of their students. Students, in turn, many of whom were children of immigrants, would bring classroom lessons in Judaism to their parents, assuring them that it need not be abandoned in their adjustment to America. The students, drawn from all the Jewish congregations and neighborhoods around the city, would meet and get to know each other, thereby forming the largest pool of future Jewish marriage partners in Philadelphia. Finally, new teachers would emerge from among graduating women, and male and female graduates would raise families of their own in which standards for Jewish life were more in line with the general approach to religion in American culture.

The formation and success of the HSS came at a time when Gratz needed something to lift and guide her spirit. From 1838 to 1841 the United States Bank failed, and the ensuing economic panic made Philadelphia a city of distress.[114] In the midst of that financial catastrophe, Rebecca's oldest brother, Simon, died. Gratz responded to losses in her immediate family by intensifying her involvement in communal activities, and at the time of Simon's death she was already leading three women's organizations—the Female Association, the Philadelphia Orphan Asylum, and the Female Hebrew Benevolent Society. But she gave even more of her time and energy to the HSS than to any other commitment, convinced that the school was vitally important to the future of Jewish life in America.

5

The Lessons of the Hebrew Sunday School

"The sweetest memorial raised to [those who first plead for the female poor of this congregation] will be . . . this institution."
REBECCA GRATZ, 1835

Throughout her life, Gratz blended ideas drawn from her own American milieu and her personal understanding of Judaism to resolve conflicts and capitalize on her talents. The Hebrew Sunday School (HSS) exemplified that process more successfully than any other institution she led. By the time she was in her fifties, Gratz knew that because her brothers' children did not practice Judaism, no Jew would carry the Gratz name to future generations. Her organizations provided her firmest reassurance of an American Jewish future. The school she had urged the Female Hebrew Benevolent Society (FHBS) women to found conveyed her own understanding of Judaism, an understanding shaped, as we have seen, by the events and literature in America's women's culture and by her own religious experiences.

Growth

From 1840 to 1855, Philadelphians experienced "unprecedented civic violence" as the population mushroomed with ever growing numbers of immigrants. Debarkations at the port quintupled, from a little over three thousand to more than nineteen thousand. By 1850 almost a third of the city's population was foreign-born, usually from Ireland, Germany, and England.

Although the city experienced an economic depression at this time, population pressures created a housing boom that added several new neighborhoods west and north of the city: Nicetown, Germantown, Mount Airy, Chestnut Hill, Mantua, and Powelton. By 1844 the only building on the south side of Chestnut Street below 8th Street that was still used as a dwelling was converting its first floor into a store. In 1854 the city and county of Philadelphia were consolidated into one political unit.[1] As part of the effort to maintain peace among an increasingly diverse citizenry, religious groups sought new ways to bring a self-discipline grounded in faith to the general populace. Previously unenforced laws restricting public activities on Sundays found new advocates and new teeth.

Amid these pressures from immigration, poverty, and geographic dispersion, the HSS blossomed. Between 1840 and 1870, when Pennsylvania's Sunday Sabbath laws successfully restricted public activities, the HSS, like local Christian Sunday schools, tried to keep poor children from creating a nuisance on Sundays.[2] Gratz adapted the school's style and structure from those used by the Protestant American Sunday School Union (ASSU). Although the union's schools were originally designed to serve the children of the many unaffiliated Christian families, children in families who attended church regularly often preferred to join their friends in Sunday school rather than accompany their parents to church, and Sunday school teachers quickly claimed that in their schools "rich and poor meet together."

As middle-class families increasingly joined churches, smaller schools serving individual congregations replaced large, central Sunday schools.[3] Like the ASSU, the HSS was a mission school intended to reach all Jewish children and was never affiliated with any one congregation. Few antebellum synagogues could sustain an effective teacher-student ratio, and usually could only be relied on for bar mitzvah preparation tutorials. The HSS, by contrast, boasted a large, dedicated staff, taught in English, and supplemented the education synagogues offered.[4]

Isaac Leeser was distressed by the abysmal state of Philadelphia's Jewish education and at first thought it impossible for a Sunday school to deliver a truly thorough Jewish education. By 1840, however, at the HSS's second year-end exam, Leeser enthusiastically supported the HSS, approving new textbooks written by the Peixotto sisters, visiting classes, and writing his own catechism for their use. He criticized Rodeph Shalom's use of German instead of English for school instruction because he believed it prevented "fusion of the new immigrant with the native and older residents of the community." If the Jews of Philadelphia continued to be divided by language as well as national origin and class, mutual understanding and cooperation would be nearly impossible.[5]

Leeser was delighted to see women take an active role in Jewish education and advance the religious education of Jewish girls. He believed that if girls were educated with "a proper view of the duties they must perform . . . as loving mothers, the happiness of society would be placed on a much surer foundation of love and kindness."[6] Leeser's attitudes toward education reflected his personal history. After his father died in 1820, he lived in the home of Abraham Sutro, rabbi and superintendent of Hebrew schools in Munster, Germany, and its environs, accompanying Sutro on many of his visits to the area schools. In 1823, after Leeser relocated to Richmond, Virginia, he assisted Rev. Isaac Seixas, minister of the Spanish-Portuguese congregation there.[7] His personal and professional experience in Europe and in America convinced him that the HSS was a valuable new approach to Jewish education.

By 1841, with over one hundred students—approximately 80 to 90 percent of the city's English-speaking Jewish children—the school outgrew the Peixotto home. Mikveh Israel offered rooms in the synagogue, but Gratz refused to make it the school's permanent home.[8] She dreamed of a school used by all Jewish children in the city, and the Mikveh Israel synagogue on Cherry Street was too far from the neighborhoods of poorer Jews living south of Walnut and north of Spring Garden Streets. Also, Mikveh Israel's members were the elite of Philadelphia Jewry, and poorer parents and children might have been uncomfortable attending. Thus, after a brief stint in Mikveh Israel, the school moved for a short time into the Phoenix Hose Company and, in 1854, into the new Touro Hall, which became known as the Hebrew Education Society (HES) Building at 7th and Wood.[9] Judah Touro, a New Orleans philanthropist, had bequeathed twenty thousand dollars to the HES to carry out its plan for a Jewish day school that would teach both religious and secular subjects. After purchasing and renovating what was formerly a Baptist church, the HES opened its doors.[10]

In sharp contrast to the conflicts that synagogues engaged in over worship customs, language, family seating, congregational

governance, and reform—subjects that divided many nineteenth-
century Jewish congregations—the HSS had a broadly inclusive
understanding of the nature of Judaism, and this fostered steady
growth. Sabato Morais, minister of Mikveh Israel after Leeser,
marveled that Gratz made the school "acceptable to hundreds of
her . . . coreligionists, irrespective of their extraction or mode of
worship."[11] HSS students earned prizes for synagogue attendance,
and no one synagogue received preferential treatment. The synagogues were acknowledged and respected, but the goals of the
Sunday school went beyond support for synagogues.[12]

The HSS offered a new, American style of Judaism. Although
the school's female teachers broke with the tradition of male religious leadership, few of Philadelphia's Jews objected. Established and supported by the local Jewish elite, the school offered
a blend of popular American culture and Jewish tradition. Like
the Protestant rhetoric that filled the public press and turned up
in many conversations, the school's curriculum was bibliocentric.
Its lessons focused on Jewish principles, the creed (the Sh'ma
prayer), and biblical authority.[13] The school merely continued in a
systematic, public, and authoritative way the historic tradition
in which stories from Scripture had been taught informally to
children by knowledgeable mothers. Like Victorian culture and
feminized religion, the school emphasized the importance of domestic piety, the heart's longing for and devotion to God, and God's
loving kindness—all ideas that were staples of Jewish private
meditations, prayers, and mystical traditions. The HSS presented
them as the core of mainstream Judaism itself, and in the school
curriculum they took on a public, standardized form. By emphasizing the more individualistic elements of Jewish devotion, the
school tailored Judaism to fit the common American belief that
religion was a matter of personal conscience.[14]

This curriculum grew out of Gratz's religious conviction and
from the fact that none of the school's founders were qualified
to teach more than the Bible. Indeed, Gratz's family prayer book
included a daily prayer asking God to mercifully "implant the holy
law in our hearts that we may not sin," a phrase that might serve
as the theme of the HSS early lessons.[15] Because no English-
language Jewish textbooks or primers existed in America, the
ASSU provided the HSS with copies of the *King James Bible* and a
catechism, *Child's Scriptural Questions,* both used in their Protestant schools. Gratz and her fellow teachers adapted these texts by

tearing out and pasting over passages referring to Jesus. Gratz herself composed a book of daily morning prayers that were likely taught at school.[16] Rachel Peixotto Pyke wrote a Jewish version of the catechism, and Simha wrote an *Elementary Introduction to the Hebrew Scriptures*. Watching this struggle for educational materials, Leeser set to work on a catechism and his own English translation of the Hebrew Scriptures.[17]

In the Philadelphia HSS, the school day began with an assembly during which the superintendent led the opening prayer and read the Bible portion for the day. The selection most likely corresponded to the week's Torah portion read in the synagogues the day before. After the assembly, students broke into classroom groups in which teachers conducted lessons based on the assembly readings and tested students on their catechism. Each grade had its own additional educational goals, and students demonstrated their mastery of their work at the annual public exams, which, until 1876, were held on Purim. The youngest students learned to recite the creed (Sh'ma), middle classes studied catechisms, and older classes mastered individual books of the Bible. In 1841, for example, students were tested on Exodus, Ruth, and Esther. That highly unusual selection of Bible readings indicates the HSS's commitment to inculcating an appreciation for the importance of women in Jewish religious history. While Exodus is a foundational book for all of Judaism, Ruth and Esther point to women's contribution to Jews' understanding of their relationship to God and to each other.[18]

The HSS rewarded students for academic achievement and good conduct with colored tickets that could be traded for books or for small items made by the teachers. Teachers wrote the Ten Commandments on colored silk or illustrated a neatly written psalm. As the number of available books on Jewish topics grew, the school bought them for their library and gave them, as well as popular children's fiction, as rewards for punctuality, good behavior, and academic excellence to their best and oldest students.[19]

The annual exam included a call to young women to join the society's "labor of Love" and teach in the Sunday school. By 1861 twenty-five teachers served 250 students, and in that year, Gratz asked for "every willing-minded among the daughters of Israel in the congregations of our people who desire to assist," promising that all who could "donate two to three hours punctually on Sunday mornings without sacrifice of their domestic duties"

would find a "blessed reward in the consciousness of doing good."
In addition, volunteers would "acquire while they impart a knowledge of the Laws and Customs and duties of our Holy religion as
taught to Moses and our forefathers." In this plea, Gratz asked
women to move their sense of duty beyond their families—not to
the detriment of family life, but to improve the Jewish community
and their own knowledge of their religion.

Jewish women's self-fulfillment, community service, and
domestic responsibility were fused in the HSS. Gratz and her
associates viewed it as an opportunity to extend their familial
responsibilities and power to serve the children of the entire
community. The national basis of Jewish life evident in the Bible
allowed Jewish women to blend the rhetoric of patriotism, used
to express the American ideal of republican motherhood, with the
expectations for spiritual development expressed in the Victorian
ideal of true womanhood. Because she grew up a Philadelphian
in the Revolutionary era, Gratz easily absorbed patriotic rhetoric
and saw that ideologies about women could serve the best interests
of both Jewish women and the Jewish community as a whole.
Through their work, the HSS women hoped to prompt a spiritual
renewal among Philadelphia's Jews.[20]

Political and Religious Boundaries

Many Jews believed that efforts to enforce Christian morality
with secular law would eventually curtail their freedom, regardless of their patriotism.[21] One way to combat Christian prejudice
was for Jews to welcome openly non-Jews when they arrived on
synagogue doorsteps asking to observe the proceedings. Rabbi
Simon Tuska, the first American college graduate to become a
rabbi, published *Stranger in the Synagogue,* providing "guidance
in Jewish worship for the non-Jew."[22] But by the 1850s, both Isaac
Leeser and Isaac Mayer Wise believed the evangelical tone of
American society posed a threat to American Jewish freedom.[23]

The Sunday Sabbath law cases, reported in the popular
press, demonstrated that Jews could lose their right to observe
Jewish religious customs.[24] Many states strictly enforced these
laws. In Pennsylvania, Seventh Day Adventists were routinely
fined or jailed for working on their farms on Sundays. In other
states Jews were arrested for working in their shops on Sunday.[25] In the *Occident* Leeser kept a close watch on the progress

of these cases and published case summaries, judges' decisions, and his own analyses. Two cases against Jews in Richmond and Charleston in 1846 were decided in favor of the defendants. Judges found that the offenses—working in their shops on Sunday—did not pose a threat to the order of the town and therefore the local police ordinances forbidding Sunday labor were in violation of citizens' rights to free labor and religion. In Richmond the ordinance was struck down in favor of increased security on Sunday to control any violence that might erupt between blacks and whites. But in Charleston, the city appealed to the state supreme court and won. In his decision, Judge O'Neal insisted that since shopkeeping on Sunday "shock[ed] the moral sense of Christians" it was "therefore an act of licentiousness." He ruled that the Sunday Sabbath should be enforced because it was basic to the Christian moral system, the only basis of good morals he knew. As such it was basic to the morals of the country. Leeser responded immediately saying that if O'Neal had read the Bible he would know that "Christianity has no moral order not already known to Jews"; consequently their morality must be as "pure as the dominant church."[26]

That year the *Occident* reprinted an article from the *Philadelphia Public Ledger* on the decision of Pennsylvania's Supreme Court in the case of *Specht* v. *the Commonwealth*. Specht, a farmer and Seventh Day Adventist, had been fined for "following his avocation on Sunday." The opinions of the court focused on two main points. Judge Bell explained first that the well-being of every society requires a day of rest, and since most of the inhabitants of the state already rested on Sunday, the state could reasonably require all its citizens to do so without interfering with their religious freedom, since it did not ask them to perform any religious rites. He found the law reasonable, and therefore constitutional. However, Judge Coulter of the same court wrote that the law was "constitutional because [it] guard[s] the Christian Sabbath from profanation."[27]

These decisions brought a new element into the legal battle over the Sunday Sabbath, for they allowed workers to be jailed for offending the customs of their neighbors. Leeser was outraged. As the Adventists went to jail for harvesting their wheat, he wrote: "There is tyranny in this,—and . . . galling as there is no redress, the majority not likely to be willing to repeal a law, which, though evidently against the spirit of the Constitution, has been sanctioned by the Supreme Bench in deference to popular clamour."[28]

This Pennsylvania decision, and others like it, diminished Leeser's respect for judges. In 1846, under the headline "Ohio: Liberty of Conscience Triumphant," he had hailed Ohio's Sunday Sabbath laws, which exempted those who conscientiously observed Saturday.[29] But twelve years later, when these laws were tested in *Rice* v. *Cincinnati,* he wrote that no government court should be deciding matters of religious law. The court found that Mr. Rice had not conscientiously observed any Sabbath, because although he had gone to synagogue, his sons continued to work in his business, and he profited from their labor. Remembering the uses found in Europe for government courts that had become tribunals on Judaism, Leeser now saw this former hallmark of liberty as unfair and unconstitutional. It would allow Christian judges to determine matters of Jewish law.

After the Specht decision in 1848, Leeser ran articles on the customary and nonbinding nature of the Sunday Sabbath and its laws. These included a variety of exemptions, such as federal mail transport and cases acquitting Sunday workers whose jobs were considered essential, like Schuylkill River lockkeepers and blast furnace tenders. In 1856, Philadelphia police ignored Sunday statutes and allowed citizens to hire horses, sleighs, and drivers to enjoy the first great snowfall of winter. If these cases could override the statutes, then clearly they were founded on custom, not on constitutional or divine law.[30]

As minister of Mikveh Israel, Leeser also was in a position to fight Sunday Sabbath laws on religious grounds. After years of reading arguments among Christians and after completing his own translation of the Hebrew Bible, he felt ready to argue that the Sunday Sabbath laws had always been politically motivated, not the result of divine command. In 1858 he ran an article from a Christian paper, the *Sabbath Recorder,* in the *Occident,* asserting that the earliest Christians did not keep Sabbath on Sunday, that the Lord's Day commemorating the Resurrection was in Europe a day of recreation. When Protestants began reading the Bible, the writer noted, they found the command for a Sabbath and made it Sunday simply through custom, a custom that had been established by the Catholic Church to differentiate Christian society from Jewish society. Leeser also quoted the Christian editor of the *Cincinnati Commercial:* "If a Sabbath is at all commanded, which it surely is, the day, no less than the institution itself, is fixed by the will of God; wherefore all attempts at investing Sunday with a religious sanction must be fruitless."[31]

Once the battle began to be fought on religious ground, Leeser was on home territory. By arguing for the legitimacy of the commands of the Hebrew Bible, he could address both the right of Jews to protect their religious liberty and what he believed was the appalling trend toward non-observance openly endorsed by some of the new reformists. He would not have to argue for absolute freedom of conscience—an argument also used by the reformists against the legitimacy of Talmudic law—but could reassert the absolute moral authority of the Bible, a position popular with both Christians and Jews. He found the greatest model for republican government in ancient Israel and so saw the ideas of American liberty rising from biblical revelation. Just as both Christianity and the reformists allowed local adherents to shirk their religious duties, so judges who allowed local custom to override constitutional liberties shirked their duty to maintain the commandment in Numbers 15:15–16: "There shall be one law for you and the stranger among you." In this way, Leeser insisted that Jews' rights were not based on tolerance by the majority but by right as citizens of the nation. Therefore Jews could never be legally required to abandon their rights as citizens in order to protect the sanctity of the majority's religion.[32]

Yet by arguing finally for unhampered liberty, Leeser knew he was also protecting the rights of Jewish reformers to continue to grow in strength, despite his conviction that they were "false prophets." But that, after all, was an in-house matter, a problem of Jewish faithfulness to be addressed by Jews. The far more pressing problem was to protect the rights of observant Jews so that they were not encouraged by sheer economic necessity to violate so basic a commandment as the preservation of the Jewish Sabbath. This had to be done without antagonizing the Christian populace. Leeser supported the Hebrew Sunday School in part because it used the enforced Sunday Sabbath, women's spirituality, and the bibliocentrism of American culture to advance knowledge of Judaism among Jewish children and women.

Theological Sources and Perspectives

Gratz's blend of American ideas about domesticity, women's roles, and piety, along with Jewish bibliocentric spirituality, continued to shape the HSS curriculum throughout the nineteenth century.[33] From 1838 to 1900, the curriculum focused on the unity of God, the Ten Commandments, and stories from Hebrew Scriptures in translation. Teachers discussed life after death, obedience, gratitude to and love for God, the thirteen principles of the faith (written by Maimonides in the twelfth century and included in Jewish prayer books), the importance of piety, and concern for the Jewish community.

A traditionally observant commitment to Judaism is evident in the superintendent's report read at the twenty-sixth annual exam, in May 1864. It may have been read by Gratz, although she had resigned the post the previous October. "No worldly condition exempts . . . [Jews] from the . . . Holy Law. . . . In every Jews' heart, in every Jews' house, the Holy Law abides. God has given it as an inheritance to everyone born in Israel and the proud distinction of possessing such a treasure animates every heart to the faithful performance of its requirements."[34] This was a prescription for Jewish life, not a description of real Jewish devotion in Philadelphia. Gratz and the other leaders of the HSS thought the haphazard faithfulness of many Jews posed a problem for their own souls and for the future of Jewish life in America. They believed that Jews who were not proud of Jewish identity and faithful to traditional observance left themselves vulnerable to Christian missionaries. They thought poor Jewish immigrants were at the greatest risk, because they might abandon Judaism in their confusion over adjustment to American life. Gratz was also worried about conversions through marriage of Jewish Americans of her own class. Thus, the superintendent's report asserted the HSS's importance to a Jewish community in which, as her audience knew, Jewish life had not attained its goals.

Gratz personally evaluated every student and assigned each one to the most suitable class. Each school day began and ended in the same manner. At 10:00 A.M., a bell was rung and students stood as Gratz recited a brief opening prayer she had composed. After the prayer, students sat down and sang a hymn along with their teachers. Students and teachers then divided up into their separate classes, where teachers registered students' attendance. Lessons then began, during which teachers were admonished to keep the noise level as low as possible. As in many ASSU schools, several different class groups often met in separate areas of a single large room. Students could not leave the room or their places without a teacher's permission. At 11:45 the bell was rung again and books were collected. Gratz, as superintendent, then questioned students on the previous week's portion of Scripture, read a new portion, and sang another hymn with the students. Students then rose and repeated after the superintendent a hymn and a prayer. Teachers meanwhile marked lessons and distributed reward tickets to those students who had performed perfectly. Students were to be dismissed "in an orderly manner." Offering highly disciplined small classes conducted in English, the HSS presented a Jewish education light years away from the chaos reigning in congregational schools like that of Rodeph Shalom.[35]

The opening prayer recited each Sunday focused on the virtues that contributed to social order. Its three-part message was, first, that reverence and gratitude are essential to religious life; second, that orderly behavior resulted from faith in God; and third, that students' faith in God would bring them food, clothing, and help in daily life.[36]

Rachel Peixotto Pyke's catechism, *Scriptural Questions for the Use of Sunday Schools for the Instruction of Israelites,* was especially devoted to this combination of faith and social order. It opened with a long poem titled "Rebekah Parting with Her Son Jacob." Its message was that a child's loyalty to the God of Abraham was crucial to a Jewish mother's happiness and honor. The poem left the students with the impression that children of Israel are also the children of Rebekah, and it reminded them of the familial foundation of Judaism. Pyke's Catechism's twenty pages were devoted to teaching young children to control emotions and behavior while developing an idea of God as a parent. Missionaries had been focusing their attention on Jews in Philadelphia since 1824, and by 1838 the number of Jewish immigrants and indigents had mushroomed and missionaries were more active than ever. More children were bound out to tradesmen or left without parental supervision, no doubt leaving the wealthier teachers with the impression that students needed an extra reminder of maternal concern for their fidelity to Judaism. The equation of loyalty to Judaism and loyalty to one's mother presented in "Rebekah Parting with Her Son Jacob" is the heart of a child's Jewish ethnic identity. Pyke's catechism taught rudimentary principles of belief and tried to instill a sense of loyalty to, and identification with, the Jewish people.[37]

Students also used Simha Peixotto's *Elementary Introduction to the Hebrew Scriptures for the Use of Younger Children.*

Peixotto adapted this from a text issued by the ASSU and gave Leeser final approval of her work. Because it was originally a Protestant book, its structure helped Jewish children respond to missionaries with some knowledge of what to expect. It began with a basic definition of English terms such as "Bible" and "Scriptures," explained English titles of biblical books, and took the students through the Hebrew Bible. The presentation was a simple question-and-answer format:

> Q. What is the first book of the Bible called?
> A. Genesis.
> Q. What is the meaning of the word Genesis?
> A. Creation.
> Q. Of what does the first book in the Bible give an account?
> A. Of the Creation.
> Q. Who created the heavens, the earth, and all that therein?
> A. God.[38]

Leeser also wrote a catechism, translated and adapted from Eduard Kley's *Catechismus der Mosaichen Religion.*[39] Leeser intended the book to be for eight- to fourteen-year-olds, but Gratz and her staff used the book with older children because because his rhetoric was too adult and long winded. Divided into ten chapters with two appendices, Leeser discussed "Religion in General, The Mosaic Religion in Particular, God and His Attributes, The Relation of Man to God, The Law Revealed through Moses, The Moral Law, The Ten Commandments, The Kingdom of the Messiah, The Life after Death, Repentance and Atonement, The Ceremonial Law, and The Jewish Creed." Leeser wanted to teach Judaism while explaining its place among the religions of the world. He also wanted Jews to understand their own place in a non-Jewish, but largely Bible-based, American culture.[40] The festivals of Hanukkah and Purim, theologically of little importance but certainly the most fun for children, were celebrated annually at the school.[41]

Morning prayers composed by Gratz emphasized the children's utter dependence on God, who was presented as loving and merciful but demanding obedience. These prayers explain that God knows both what is in the children's hearts as well as what is on their lips. They ask God to help the children control their tempers both at home and in public and to help them develop faith and wisdom. In all of these respects, the prayers conform to both traditional Judaism and much of Christianity and present an understanding of God that the children could share with many of their Christian neighbors. However, the prayers are distinctive in the ways in which God is identified. Traditional Jewish appellations such as Rock, Redeemer, Creator, Savior, and Father are repeated throughout the prayers, but none of the prayers refers to God by another very common Jewish metaphor, King. A child of the American Revolution, Gratz remembered early America's vehement renunciation of earthly kings and all they stood for. To acculturate immigrants and their children, she may have felt it was best not to use the King metaphor.[42]

Ironically, although the HSS was the first step in radically changing the role of Jewish women by giving them a public, institutionalized role in Jewish religious education, women of the society opposed religious reform and viewed themselves as traditionally observant Jews. Like Leeser, they believed they adapted only the outer form of Judaism to American needs without changing traditional Jewish beliefs and women's piety. Although the HSS gave a public teaching role to women, it in no way broke with Jewish tradition by offering Talmudic study to women. By teaching in the vernacular instead of the "sacred tongue" (Hebrew) and by limiting their lessons to Bible stories, moral lessons, and principles of the faith found in any prayer book, the women stayed well within the bounds of traditional Jewish women's culture and religion. Only their formal role in a public educational institution was new.

Catechisms stirred a conceptual revolution in Jewish teaching in both Europe and America. Previously, Jewish educators used the Hebrew Bible as a reading primer. When that was mastered, students began to study its interpretations and analyses through rabbinic literature. By doing so, the sacred literature set the categories of thought by which all else was measured and analyzed. Catechisms, on the other hand, inserted Jewish answers into questions arising from categories of thought outside Judaism, especially from the philosophy of religion as taught in nineteenth-century German universities. This philosophy saw religion as a general category with many particular varieties, each with components such as faith, morality, and worship.[43]

The rules for decorum, pedagogy, and lesson planning set by the school conveyed the serious regard for religion held by Gratz and the other faculty. Gratz impressed upon the faculty that they must teach as much by example as "by precept." Through their manner they would communicate to their students the importance of the principles of Judaism. In training her faculty, Gratz advised them to be "patient, forbearing and affectionate." She urged them to be zealous in their work, and not to become discouraged by "dullness, obstinacy, . . . ill temper" on the part of students or by "the unreasonableness of parents."[44]

Gratz organized the school time—two hours each week— to enable her to control each day's program while allowing individual teachers to tailor their lessons to the abilities of their own students. Students and faculty experienced both the unity of the school and the individual attention necessary for the sort of education Gratz hoped to provide. The low teacher-student ratio, usually fewer than ten students per teacher, led to the sort of bond between teacher and student, and among students, that Gratz believed would deepen each person's emotional tie to the school and to Judaism. "If but a tenth [of your students] be impressed with the importance of divine truth—then you will not have labored in vain," she told her staff.[45]

Ideas in Jewish Education: Aguilar and Leeser

The HSS emphasized aspects of Judaism that were easy for children to maintain in Protestant, English-language culture: bibliocentrism, piety, and faith. From 1838 to 1865, two figures— Grace Aguilar and Isaac Leeser—provided the theological justification for this curriculum. Aguilar, an Englishwoman, was an experienced teacher and, with her mother, taught languages and literature in a private school of their own in England. Her deepest hope for Jews lay not in classroom study but in guided Bible meditations and prayer. "We must read and reread" the Bible, she wrote, "trusting in faith and prayer; and the answer will be given; the blessing of the Lord will be upon us." The Bible's importance was driven home to her by its central role in her own Spanish-Portuguese Jewish tradition, by Christian friends and authors, and by historians, philosophers, and poets who referred to it for sources, inspiration, arguments, and literary devices. Aguilar, who lived from 1816 to only 1847, wanted Jewish education to be able to compete with Christian education. In treatises on Judaism, inspirational poetry, advice books for Jewish women, romantic novels, and other sentimental literature, she argued for women's

leadership in vernacular, Bible-centered, and faith-centered public education for Jewish youth.[46] Two of her books, *The Spirit of
Judaism* (1842) and *The Jewish Faith* (1846), were designed to
aid Jewish women in teaching Judaism to children. Leeser edited
The Spirit of Judaism and published it in Philadelphia, where
Gratz and the HSS women quickly put it to use.[47] Leeser's opinions
are scattered in footnotes throughout the text. Comparing the
text with the notes reveals the leading antebellum American and
English Jewish theologians' perspectives on the problems faced by
nineteenth-century Jewish communities.

By 1845, *The Spirit of Judaism* was the most popular book in
the school's library. Gratz thought so highly of it—one chapter told
mothers how to teach Judaism to their children—that she gave
copies away to friends. *The Spirit of Judaism* was designed as a
treatise on the meaning of Judaism's central prayer, the "shemang
Israel," as Aguilar called the Sh'ma, taken from Deuteronomy 6:4–
19. Aguilar was the only Jewish woman theologian of the nineteenth century, and her many books found their largest audience
in the United States. Indeed, Gratz thought Aguilar's early death
was a "national calamity" for Jews.[48]

Together, Aguilar and Leeser provided a foundation for the
activities of the HSS.[49] Both Aguilar and Leeser believed that a
broad-based religious education was the best solution to problems
faced by Jews living as an emancipated religious minority. In *The
Spirit of Judaism,* Aguilar discusses the profound spirituality she
found in Judaism and argues for a theologically grounded religious
education for England's Jewish children, male and female. She
paints a bleak picture of young Jews who know nothing about
Judaism and turn to Christianity because they hear Christians
assert that only their religion is true. Aguilar claimed that in her
community there was no formal education for children apart from
bar mitzvah tutorials. (Leeser was so shocked to hear this that it
is more likely that it was only for young girls that was no formal
education was provided.)[50] Synagogue discourses rarely spoke to
young Jews. Because Aguilar saw knowledge of the Bible thriving
among Christians and not among Jews, she noted the number
of young Jews converting to Christianity and warned, "We stand
defenseless, for our own weapons are turned against ourselves."

Leeser thought Aguilar overestimated the number who "have
left our church [in England]" and wrote that "in America the
number is very small."[51] As a bachelor minister of two synagogues

and founder of a Hebrew day school and a rabbinic school, Leeser's circle of associates included the most committed and knowledgeable Jews of his day, nearly all of them men. Aguilar's father was president of her synagogue, but as a woman she was on the fringes of Judaism because her education, although exceptional (her father was her primary teacher for both Jewish and secular studies and taught her Hebrew and Josephus),[52] never included the sort of theological issues that interested her. As Leeser read Aguilar's account of the problem in England, he thought English Jews ought to "arise in their might and [construct] a thorough system of religious education."[53]

Aguilar's yearnings were primarily spiritual. Everyone needed the comfort of religion, she believed, regardless of his or her economic class or abilities. The mind "creates a happiness for itself . . . and this is the answer to our prayer[s] . . . the proof that God hears us." Yet religious happiness ought not to be confused with the enthusiasm that leads to fanaticism and then despair, she wrote. Contrary to the popular Christian assertion that individuals require an overwhelming emotional experience of God to save their souls, Aguilar claimed that true religious spirituality was a constant, calm love for God. Love for God is the route to heaven, she assured her readers, because love does not end with death; death is simply a "dark passage ending in eternal light . . . leading to His throne."[54] Rather than relying on emotions to guide the religious life, the religious life should guide emotions. Never wait for the proper mood to pray, she wrote; pray, and the proper mood will arrive.[55]

Leeser thought Aguilar's ideas about the dangers of too much enthusiasm were generally true, but that "an entire surrender to God . . . should not be called misguided." On the contrary, it should be "the guiding star of our lives." For Leeser, the "deep-seated conviction of . . . dependence on the Lord . . . enable[s] us to . . . sacrifice everything to our Maker's will." He believed the problem among Jews was apathy, not overzealousness. "Indifference or carelessness in prayer is . . . more frequent than the opposite extreme." But he agreed with Aguilar that people ought not to trust too much to the mood of the moment for their religious life. It was fortunate, he thought, that Jews are required to pray at specific times. "Even if we commence to pray without being properly prepared, we [may], as we proceed, become fired with . . . ardour, and pour fourth our spirit in real sincerity."[56]

Although Gratz believed that familial love was the first step toward love for God, the more philosophical Aguilar reversed that and believed love for God was the basis of earthly affection. Loving God, she felt, increased familial affection, and by clinging together people would keep each other close to God. Pointing to the stories of Ruth and Naomi, Hannah and Samuel, and Abraham and Isaac to substantiate her assertion, she turned those stories against Christianity's claim that it provides the sole route to heaven. "It is the weak-minded [person] who believes that only to himself is the grace of God vouchsafed. . . . [Those who] condemn the whole human race to perdition save the few who can be forced to think the same" are unloving and therefore unable to really understand religion, Aguilar wrote.[57]

Aguilar suggested that if Jews practiced their religion earnestly, attempts to convert them would cease. Christians harassed Jews and held Judaism in contempt only because Jews appear dissatisfied. Whether Aguilar actually believed so outrageous a statement—coming, as it did in her text, following an account of the Inquisition—is uncertain. Most likely she was appealing to what she thought to be the better selves of her Protestant countrymen, whom she often called "enlightened Christians." At the same time, such an argument appealed to Jews still adjusting to emancipation. "Let the Hebrew . . . make more evident his love to his God, his reverence to His ordinances, the comfort he derives from this communion," she wrote, "and we will hear no more of attempted conversions." Leeser, however, took her at her word and defended Jews. In "America and Germany . . . we are [not so] careless of spiritual religion," he wrote. Although our "scattered state . . . presents obstacles to the accession of . . . spiritual guides among us, . . . [we are not] less awake to the love and goodness of God than are our gentile neighbors."[58]

Despite their differences, Aguilar and Leeser held remarkably similar ideas about religious virtue and the nature of piety. Aguilar described piety as religious submission, humility, patience, forgiveness, and self-control, combined with "cherishing . . . that holy gentleness which never fails to render us beloved."[59] Her ideas mirrored the Victorian ideal of "true womanhood." In his editorial notes to *The Spirit of Judaism,* Leeser added an extensive quote from the *Sayings of the Fathers,* a standard guide to Jewish life, illustrating that Jewish tradition had long endorsed these same values. Such pious virtues were achieved by studying Talmud from a "pure motive." He who does so, Leeser wrote, "is rejoicing God, rejoicing man, and he is clothed with meekness and fear of the Lord." Such a person will be "modestly retiring, long-suffering, willingly forgiving insults offered him, and be raised and exalted above all creatures." Leeser then challenged Aguilar's readers to follow this guide. Ironically, he wrote this comment in a book he knew to be directed toward women, who were barred from Talmud study. The clear implication is that Leeser viewed piety itself as fundamentally the same for both men and women, and that one need not study Talmud to achieve it.[60]

Crossing Gender Roles through Piety

Gratz and the HSS managers created a curriculum that emphasized women's importance in Judaism by drawing on many resources. Leeser preached that women must have a religious education to qualify them for the "holy . . . [and] noble task . . . [of] sooth[ing], calm[ing]) and . . . render[ing] happy the rugged career of a father, a brother, a husband, or a child."[61] His approval must have been crucial to winning the support of the many Ashkenazic (northern European) Jews, by far the majority, who were accustomed to a religious community that was, at least among its religious leadership, highly differentiated by gender, because among these Jews, female prayer leaders commonly led women in synagogue worship.[62] In addition to his theological supervision of the textbooks, his concern for promoting fledgling Jewish religious institutions and cultural resources, and the influence on him of strong women leaders such as Aguilar, Gratz, and the Peixotto sisters, Leeser also perceived Jewish standards for piety in a way that was nearly identical with those of Victorian culture.

Despite the HSS founders' personal objections to Reform, books by reformers of one stripe or another found their way into the school's library, probably because so few English-language materials existed, and the library grew into an eclectic mix of approaches to Judaism. Several nineteenth-century Reform leaders claimed a commitment to "securing perfect equality between woman and man before God," although women were not ordained until 1972.[63] Samuel Pike's 1801 *Hebrew Lexicon* was joined by Rev. Dr. Leo Merzbacher's 1855 prayer book, the first American Reform liturgy compiled by a rabbi and used in New York's Reform Temple Emanu El.[64] An 1838 travelogue describing life in Syria was joined by an 1860 anonymous work, *Thoughts Suggested by Bible Texts,* and later by British Rev. Abraham P. Mendes's 1870 catechism, *The Law of Moses.*[65] As late as the 1870s, the more traditional HSS used the *Hebrew Sabbath School Visitor,* a children's magazine published in Cincinnati by Reform rabbi Max Lilienthal, as a pedagogical aid. Although the Philadelphians' contract with Lilienthal originally stipulated that they would be able to return free of charge any issues they found offensive, they renewed their subscription yearly.[66]

One regular column in the *Visitor* was "Little Nellie's Catechism." It described the efforts of Nellie, a Jewish Sunday school student, to train her younger brother and sister in Judaism by repeating to them the lessons she had learned in school. Nellie's mother listened appreciatively to her children while wishing that she herself could have attended such a school. Nellie's father was usually out of town on business. Stories in which daughters led their families in religious worship and education appeared more and more in popular literature, both Christian and Jewish, in the second half of the century. Just as in the antebellum era a mother's religious leadership was made plausible through nursing and educating her own children, the Sunday school movement that swept across the country made it plausible that both male and female children might instruct their parents on religious matters.[67]

Victorian culture in England and the United States often pulled Jewish men and women in directions opposite to those expected by Jewish tradition. While nineteenth-century Jewish men often simplified synagogue service and their domestic religious leadership, Jewish women appear to have taken on more responsibility for communal and familial religious life. Although the descriptions of piety in Victorian and traditional Jewish culture were nearly identical, in Jewish tradition women often shouldered financial duties so that men might fulfill religious obligations of prayer and study. Victorian culture presumed men to be immersed in financial responsibilities while women led their families into piety.[68] By teaching a Victorian American Judaism, the HSS offered a way for American Jewish women, both rich and poor, to demonstrate that "true women" could be religious Jews.

In 1845 a new *Parent and Teachers Assistant* designed to aid "Jewish mothers and teachers [in] imparting . . . the first ideas of the Deity" to young Jewish children appeared. Its unknown author developed a basic theology out of images and experiences central to the lives of women. God is first explained as the Creator who, while able to create out of nothing, created "things in such a way that they can reproduce themselves."[69] While men, too, can create things, manmade things lack the power to reproduce. The author underscored the point by inviting students to consider that their own mothers were once the babies of their mothers, and so on for generations. Finally, after asserting that God can see the part of us that "thinks, feels sorry or glad, pleased or displeased," because God is "pure spirit that fills all space," the book concluded by inviting children to trust the "Holy Bible" as the source for "all that God has made known to men about himself."[70] Published in Philadelphia with an introduction by Isaac Leeser, the book was recommended to women in Jewish congregations and by teachers in the HSS.

The Women

The minutes of the Hebrew Sunday School Society show that the founders continued to direct the organization as it grew. Most were from Mikveh Israel, the city's oldest congregation, and from the educated, middle-class merchant and business families. By and large, their own education had been the "papa's study" sort, with some additional time at women's academies, but in these families home lessons included instruction to develop managerial skills.

The Gratzes, Phillipses, Peixottos, and Harts led synagogues and other community organizations, and encouraged their daughters to become involved, too. Miriam Gratz had brought her daughters with her into the Female Association at its founding in 1801. Other mothers from among these families acted similarly.[71] Gratz participated in and continued this tradition, bringing other young women of her class into the Philadelphia associations she began and guiding her niece Miriam Moses Cohen in establishing a Hebrew Sunday School in Georgia.

The founders participated in the mission that popular American culture gave them: to civilize a fledgling nation in disarray through their influence in education and religion. Gratz, Ellen Phillips, Louisa B. Hart, Simha Peixotto, and others gained self-respect and a sense of purpose from this task. It was not simply that community service gave these unmarried women an occupation they would not otherwise have had because they were not mothers. Motherhood was a rite of passage for nineteenth-century women, and this was a passage to adult status that Gratz and her unmarried cohorts did not make. The school gave single women something to do, but success such as the HSS enjoyed did not emerge from mere busywork, and these single women did not lightly choose service over motherhood. In fact, the HSS resolved conflicts in the women's own religious identities.

Victorian American culture dictated that to be respected, women must be chaste and spiritual domestic guides, and this ideology was used by white Protestants to justify their superiority over both immigrants and nonwhites.[72] But Jewish culture claimed that God commanded Jewish women to be mothers and Jewish men to lead their families' lives. The HSS merged selected American ideas with those of Judaism and developed a structure that combined both worlds, using the Bible to both guide and instruct. In its bibliocentric curriculum, the HSS was an early expression of a genuinely American Judaism.

Gratz and her cohorts prized their independence and were proud of their accomplishments. Their association with each other involved much more than just class-time meetings; it gave them enormous satisfaction. Gratz called her work in the school "the crowning happiness of my days." Ellen Phillips and Louisa B. Hart both served as officers and board members until the end of their lives. Simha Peixotto was so attached to her work that she fought against resigning her board membership at seventy-eight, saying, "I am not a dead head and can serve in the holy cause."[73] Each of these women sat in the women's gallery at Mikveh Israel. Friendships nurtured in worship matured into the HSS.

Rebecca Gratz, by Thomas Sully

Rebecca Gratz,
by Edward Greene Malbone

Miriam Simon Gratz,
by Gilbert Stuart

Michael Gratz,
by William Edward West

Rebecca Gratz,
by Anna Claypoole Peale

Rebecca Gratz,
by Thomas Sully

Rachel Gratz,
by Edward Greene Malbone

Benjamin Gratz,
by Thomas Sully

Frances Gratz Etting,
by James Peale

Rebecca Gratz,
by Thomas Sully

Rebecca Gratz,
by William James Hubbard

Joseph Gratz,
by George P. A. Healy

Hyman Gratz,
artist unknown

Rebecca Gratz,
artist unknown

6

❧◦❧

Sentimental Language and
Social Power: 1840–1860

"Miss Aguilar's . . . works . . . took possession of our
minds and hearts."
REBECCA GRATZ, 1847[1]

Gratz approached her sixtieth birthday in a city far different from the town of cobblestone and dirt streets she had walked
as a child. Technological and population changes had transformed
both Philadelphia's landscape and the quality of life of its residents. More than half a million people now lived in the city.[2]
Gratz could recall a Philadelphia Jewish community of only three
hundred people and one synagogue, united under her family's
leadership; by 1840 nearly two thousand Jews sustained three separate congregations. The city's first skyscraper, the Jayne Building, owned by patent medicine manufacturer Dr. David Jayne,
appeared at Chestnut and Third Streets, near the site of Gratz's
childhood home. Three different private mail delivery companies
served the city in addition to postal services provided by the
government. The Pennsylvania Railroad offered passenger service
between Philadelphia and Harrisburg, and the Cunard Line soon
established a steamship route connecting Liverpool with the city's
port.[3] The telegraph linked New York and Philadelphia with Washington, D.C. These connections to distant places offered Philadelphians the benefits of modern communications, but diminished
the influence of old merchant families like the Gratzes.

In the 1840s, a women's culture was emerging in the United
States, largely on the strength of new printing technologies that

171

vastly increased the volume of pages printed, pages that often were written by, and marketed to, women. By 1848, the Harper brothers, publishers in New York City and Boston, could print twelve thousand pages in an hour, a rate "undreamt of two short decades before."[4] The revolutionized printing business dramatically increased the amount of reading material purchased by an expanding American population, many of whom had learned to read in Sunday schools. Periodicals expanded as well. In 1841, Sarah Josepha Hale moved *Godey's Ladies Book,* the country's most popular women's magazine, from Boston to Philadelphia. By 1850, *Godey's* subscription list claimed more than sixty thousand readers, and by 1860 more than a million.[5]

The publishing, technological, and financial revolution transformed writers' work habits. Older women writers like Catharine Beecher and Catherine Sedgwick usually depended on mentors and often had sought the patronage of clergymen. Younger women writers, like Harriet Beecher Stowe, could rely on their own assessments of life drawn from their experiences as women.[6]

For both generations of women, settings and characters reflected women's common focus on domestic concerns. However, younger fiction writers often depicted women solving plot conflicts by manipulating the other characters' emotions.[7] Although most popular writers used a serious moral tone, women's novels about domestic life were "purer in tone and content" than the more vivid moral sensationalism depicted by ministers, many religious tracts, and more secular male authors.[8]

Although the Harper brothers promised their readers that they would publish only items "such as are interesting, instructive, and moral," publishers interested in profits seldom critiqued the manuscripts of authors in the same manner as did the many clergymen who championed writers only a few years earlier. Not surprisingly, sentimental and romantic fiction by women sometimes expressed ideas and attitudes at odds with religious doctrines. The sentimental rhetoric of so much nineteenth-century fiction, full of homey imagery and piety, often voiced a feminism grounded in domesticity.[9]

After the 1830s and the enactment of universal white male suffrage, the deference formerly accorded high-status women eroded, leaving women like Gratz suddenly challenged to reclaim what they considered their rightful place in society.[10] Through sentimental fiction, women writers often voiced bitter hostility toward men, hostility toward the materialistic and individualistic values men were allowed to typify, or outright triumph over men and the values of the male sphere.[11] Perhaps these novelists were also voicing their turmoil in the face of new demands and conflicts within home life, which bore the brunt of the social stresses engendered when factory-based industrial labor replaced cottage industry. Wildly fluctuating economic booms and busts strained domestic economies. By imaginatively resolving dilemmas frustrating many different classes of women, women's fiction and sentimental literature found wide appeal.[12]

Although Gratz read voraciously and widely, often for the sheer joy and entertainment to be obtained, she had disdain for some authors' lack of "good principles." Although she thought Mary Shelley's *Last Man* "worth more than her other book," Gratz believed "her genius runs wild."[13] Nor did Gratz approve of Bulwer Lytton's work, admitting to her niece Miriam that "I do not care for brilliant talents unless they are used in a good cause." Gratz believed writers were obligated to consider the impact of their ideas. Some were "so apt to disguise vice under the shaping of fine sentiment or to make weakness interesting that [they are] apt to excuse themselves for little sins."[14] But neither Shelley nor Lytton addressed problems of domestic life in their writing, as did many new women writers in both England and America.

Gratz read the new sentimental fiction and, despite her reservations about unrestrained emotionality, found much of it useful. By the 1840s, sentimental fiction was one of the most popular forms of American writing, and one that Gratz used to justify her own charitable and educational work. By using the language of popular fiction to build support for Jewish charities, Gratz showed American Jewish women that the broad shift of cultural values that brought women into religious leadership and public activities, begun by Quakers in the late eighteenth century and carried on by evangelical women, included Jews.[15] Moreover, she demonstrated that by taking up these roles, Jewish women could promote and enrich Jewish life in America.

Since her youth, Gratz had used literature as a guide to life. In her hands, it framed both her understanding of the events around her and her emotional responses to them. Excerpts from her readings sparkled in her letters as she commented on historical events, daily life, and spiritual growth. Throughout her life, Gratz had added to the family's extensive library and shared many volumes of women's literature and popular histories with her friends, her brothers, and her relations.[16] She could not imagine an intelligent woman living without literature. After Maria Fenno Hoffman's stepdaughter married and moved to a new town in Ohio, where her husband would become the postmaster, Rebecca thought the girl a "poor soul" who was "shut out from every kind of literature—and craves it as mental food for which her soul craveth."[17]

Literature also shaped Gratz's attitude toward new immigrants. She swapped stories about them with her niece Miriam, who had hired a few as servants. "We sometimes meet with adventures as romantic as any recorded in tales," Rebecca wrote, "and characters in humble life that exhibit as fine feelings as those that adorn their pages."[18] The imaginative and intellectual appeal of immigrants' adventures drew her to them. By involving herself in the challenge and excitement of the new immigrants' lives, Gratz felt that she was participating in the grand historical drama of her age. Although she had often complained to friends about her brothers' tastes for adventure, the adventures of immigrants captured her imagination.

In her sixties, Gratz found ample time to read literature, correspond with distant family, and manage her organizations. In sixty years her family had been dramatically transformed, and her own domestic obligations now dwindled. Her interpersonal skills and impressions of the world had been forged in a childhood home crowded with siblings, servants, cousins, and parents. Traveling with siblings, she had visited relatives in Lancaster, Baltimore, and New York. Now Rebecca and her siblings were aging and younger relations were moving to distant places, some of which she would never see.

Gratz, like many other antebellum Americans, believed in the healthful benefits of human society,[19] but as she reached her sixtieth year she lived nearly alone. Rachel's children, now grown, communicated with her largely by mail. Rachel's younger daughter, Rebecca Moses, married Jonathan Nathan in 1840, and although she remained in Philadelphia, she occupied her time setting up her new household. In honor of the wedding, "Richea came from Baltimore looking quite well," Rebecca wrote to Maria Gist Gratz, "but, we are all growing old and bear the marks of it right visibly."[20] Rachel's son Horace, whom Gratz had raised since toddlerhood, remained single until after Gratz's death, but in the 1840s he often traveled. His brothers, Isaac and Simon, had moved to Mobile, Alabama, and St. Louis, Missouri. By the end of the decade, Rachel's daughter Sarah Moses married Jacob Henry Joseph and moved to Montreal, Canada.

Rebecca's brothers Hyman and Joseph, despite their age and local responsibilities, continued to travel on business, usually to Lexington, Kentucky, where they stayed for long periods with their brother Benjamin at his estate. More than ever, Gratz sought fulfillment in literature and in the organizations she had led for the last forty years.

Through those institutional associations she exercised considerable influence—as superintendent of the Hebrew Sunday School she led perhaps the largest Jewish institution in Philadelphia. Gratz keenly felt the criticisms often leveled at women who were called "benevolent ladies." In January 1840 she responded defensively to gossip about one such Charleston woman whom Miriam Moses Cohen described as one "whose zeal overstepped her judgment." Gratz retorted that "if [the woman's] character were better praised she would be too prominent in society to . . . attract . . . others, and the cause she serves would suffer." What appeared to Miriam to be a weakness in the woman appeared to Rebecca as another facet of the woman's ability to serve her cause—the woman's human frailties increased general support for her work. "Providence seems to use our weaknesses as well as our virtues to forward his wise purposes," Rebecca concluded, suggesting that her niece be less critical of both God and her elders.[21]

In June 1840, Gratz received a letter from Maria Edgeworth with the gift of a book written by Edgeworth and her father, *An Essay on Professional Education.* Despite her earlier dispute with Edgeworth about her favorable portrayal of intermarriage in *Harrington,* Gratz generally admired Edgeworth's work. "She . . . is the last of those illustrious women, who are so conspicuous for their genius . . . during the last half century," she wrote to Maria Gist Gratz. Rebecca admired Edgeworth as both a teacher and as a writer. "It is her highest praise that she has done so much to raise the character of her poor countrymen," she commented.[22]

Gratz's understanding of the international events of her own era also had been shaped by a lifetime of reading historical literature. These eighteenth- and nineteenth-century history books described either the march of progress, the hand of Providence, or the fulfillment of human nature. Whatever their choice of arguments, historians sought to edify and entertain. When Gratz learned about an international incident that horrified most Jewish Americans, she found the course of events "thrilling."

In 1840 the Ottoman government responded to accusations against Jews in Damascus with investigative techniques that included wholesale torture. The charge, that Jews used the blood of Christians to make Passover matzo (called the "blood libel"), insisted that Jews murdered Christians in order to carry out their rites.[23] The folkloric belief that Jews practiced secret rites that require the death of Christians underpinned many permutations of anti-Semitism in European history,[24] and Jews in America worried that anti-Jewish folklore transplanted from Europe might threaten Jewish freedoms in the United States.

Comprising less than one percent of the population, American Jews were wary. Historically, the blood libel was most prevalent in central and western Europe, the national origin of many nineteenth-century Americans. Jews still depended on the good wishes of more powerful allies, and American Jews believed that any link between the mythical Jew and the Jew next door would have to be eliminated.[25] The blood libel epitomized the twin dangers of ignorance and intolerance, and in an era that prided itself on its enlightened and universal values, the affair at Damascus was shocking.

When the Ottoman government sentenced seventy-two Jews to be hanged and put the entire Damascus Jewish community, nearly thirty thousand people, under suspicion, British and American ambassadors spoke out against the horrors. President Van Buren, the U.S. Secretary of State, and U.S. representatives in Egypt and Turkey all made it clear to the Ottoman government that the United States opposed its treatment of Turkey's Jews.[26] American Jews marveled that their government had spoken out to defend the accused before any of America's fifteen thousand Jews urged the government's action.

The Damascus incident challenged Gratz's belief that the age of Jewish persecution was passing, that American freedoms signaled a new age in both Jewish and human history. Following the American Revolution, the American popular press proclaimed that the age of enlightened freedom, perhaps "the beginning of a great deliverance," had begun.[27] To maintain her convictions, she looked at the effect the Damascus incident was having in

Philadelphia. She was pleased that it united local Jews at a time when differences in national origin and class, as well as "petty strife" divided them, prompting everyone to "act and pray for the oppressed." She believed that the actions of the American and British governments, as well as expressions of sympathy from local Christians, proved that anti-Semitism was waning.[28] Rebecca wrote enthusiastically to Maria Gist Gratz that "we are treading another passage in Jewish history as heart thrilling as any recorded since their dispersion."[29]

But to most other American Jews, the Damascus affair illustrated Jewish vulnerability. At gatherings of Jews in Philadelphia, Isaac Leeser began to argue that American Jews needed to unite to defend their coreligionists. In addition to raising funds to aid the threatened families overseas, Philadelphia's Jews discussed ways to take more direct action to defend Jews abroad. On August 27, 1840, they met at Mikveh Israel to organize a national protest, and although Jews held public meetings in several cities, they took no unified action. As Rebecca explained to her sister-in-law Maria, "What can be done . . . —the Jews have no representative powers, and can only vote in their individual capacities."[30] Leeser, despairing of the disunity, discussed the problems with Philadelphia's different Jewish congregations, and the next summer he issued a plan for national Jewish unity in ecclesiastic matters, a system of education, and a union of congregations. The city's three Jewish congregations—Mikveh Israel, Rodeph Shalom, and Beth Israel (founded in 1837)—signed the circular, which Leeser sent to Jewish congregations around the country, but to little avail.[31] Not until 1859, after several more anti-Semitic episodes abroad, did American Jews organize for Jewish defense.[32]

Unable to foresee those later crises, Gratz assured her sister-in-law that her optimistic interpretation of events in Damascus proved accurate. "Israel is still happy in the patriotism of her sons and more happy in the interest which all other nations accord to her in rejecting the oppression." She was especially pleased that Philadelphia's Jews were able to unite to some degree, if only for a brief time, in their action to aid the Damascus Jews. To Gratz, such behavior proved that Jews "feel and will act as become the chosen people." Reflecting on the import of the past months, she explained to Miriam, "This is quite a new age in our history and we should look well to improve the opportunities which 'the signs of the times' evidently point out."[33] She believed those signs indicated that Jews would eventually unite to aid coreligionists abroad and that such charity would carry with it a return to religion.

Finally, Gratz insisted that the whole affair indicated not a resurgence of anti-Semitism but its reverse. At least among Christians, Gratz insisted, anti-Semitism was diminishing. The actions by the American and British governments to defend Jews mirrored some of the sermons she had recently heard in Philadelphia churches. "The dispositions of the Christians would seem changed toward the Jews. I heard a Presbyterian clergyman preach in his own church, of the restoration of Israel—doubt that they would *ever* be converted, and prove from Isaiah that they would always be servants of the *one* true God—he brought in the gentiles . . . in as orthodox a manner as might have been preached in the synagogue . . . it was the most liberal discourse in favor of the ancient people [I] . . . ever heard."[34]

Changes in Judaism and Jewish Life

The dramatic events of 1840 were followed by a long and cold winter marked by the final closing of the Bank of the United States and a financial depression in Philadelphia. For Gratz, reading and other indoor activities warmed cold nights. Other Philadelphians faced greater hardships. The Music Fund Society mounted *The Magic Flute,* its first opera, to raise money for poor musicians.[35] During that icy March in Philadelphia, Gratz learned that the old Sephardic Jewish congregation in Charleston, South Carolina, had embraced Reform, brought an organ into their new synagogue, and renounced claims to Zion. Pressure to reform had been building in that congregation for some time. Almost twenty years earlier, a group had broken away to form a Jewish Reform congregation. When their efforts failed they returned to the congregation but remained reformists at heart.[36] By the 1840s, after the immigration of like-minded German Jews, they implemented their ideas.

An implacable foe of Reform, Gratz was distressed by the news. She told her niece Miriam that Charleston's Jews were "selling their birth-right for a mess of potage. Even the greatest enemies of the Jews never denied their claims on the country inherited from their fathers or doubted they would be restored to it." From Gratz's perspective, Charleston's Jews rejected the meaning of Scripture and the special relationship between God and Israel that it described. She was flabbergasted that Jews would take such a position and could only express her thoughts by a series of rhetorical questions. "Where is the [truth] of prophecy? Whence the fulfillment of promises? What is the hope of Israel? of what does the scattered people bear witness? Alas, we may . . . weep for the spiritual destruction of Jerusalem when her own children are content to sing the songs of Zion in a strange land and deny the words of God so often repeated by the prophets."[37] Three years later Gratz advised her niece Miriam, who had by then relocated with her husband to Savannah, Georgia, to warn Savannah's Jews to be wary when hiring a new minister, and to send for one from England instead of writing to New York for a new German immigrant. "Those who come . . . [to the United States] with reputations for learning often turn out to be innovators or persons who seek their own advantage as the first object," she explained.[38] American Jews rarely could authenticate the credentials carried by new immigrants, and Gratz suspected that German Jewish religious leaders encouraged their more troublesome clergy to emigrate.[39]

Charleston's Jews had embraced a religious movement that hoped to ease Jewish emancipation in Protestant countries by emphasizing Judaism's philosophy and ethics, trimming its rituals, and eliminating its national identification. The Reform movement grew increasingly popular as the nineteenth century progressed, and it remains an important force in American Judaism more than a century later. The new Savannah congregation, however, faced a more basic difficulty than any gripping Charleston's Jews—lack of funds. "Our synagogue will be shut up until we can afford to pay a [clergyman's] salary," Miriam complained to her aunt. Savannah's community of Jews was simply too small to hire a full-time hazan. "The gentleman who has been officiating has a family and declines reading any longer, being obliged to turn his attention to . . . business," Miriam explained. To raise the funds necessary to keep their synagogue open, the congregation sent a plea for donations to larger congregations along the eastern seaboard. Miriam sent one plea to Charleston through an acquaintance who "promises to go around herself to all the members of the congregation there." Miriam hoped Rebecca would help her contact Philadelphians. "I should like to have the same thing done in Philadelphia. What think you would be the best way of accomplishing it? Perhaps Mr. Hart being the President [of Mikveh Israel] would undertake it for us?" Justifying her plea for funds, Miriam added that her "congregation seems to be increasing in numbers constantly. . . . If we all set our shoulders to the wheel & call on our friends to assist us" the congregation should establish itself. It soon succeeded.[40]

More traditional Jews, like the members of Mikveh Israel, tried to stem the tide of Jewish religious reform and laxity among emancipated Jews by controlling Jewish domestic life through rules and regulations. In 1841, Mikveh Israel's officers tried to enforce standards of domestic piety long advocated by Judaism but which the congregation thus far had been unable to enforce in Philadelphia's tiny Jewish community. Simon Gratz, whose wife was a Christian, was too influential to be ousted by Mikveh Israel. Almost twenty years earlier, a proposal to deprive synagogue honors to anyone who married a non-Jew and did not raise their children as Jews had not passed. Away from Gratz influence, the same proposal succeeded across town at Rodeph Shalom.[41] But by 1844 the climate had so changed at Mikveh Israel that Louis Bomeisler, who had married a Gentile, encountered difficulties in getting Mikveh Israel to provide a formal conversion ceremony for his children.[42] Mikveh Israel and Rodeph Shalom struggled to control outmarriage by both sanction and outreach.[43] Their changed attitudes constituted a silent rebuke of the Gratz family and its intermarriages.

Before significant Jewish immigration in the 1830s, intermarriage was common, and many Jewish men, like Simon and Benjamin Gratz, married non-Jewish women, some of whom maintained Jewish households, raised their children as Jews, and lived as Jews without formal conversion. With numerous new immigrants from Europe, however, the Jewish population increased and standards became more conservative, and in 1841 a gentile woman in a Jewish family was denied burial in Mikveh Israel's cemetery. Irate, Rebecca Gratz wrote to the president of the synagogue, Lewis Allen, that his decision countermanded congregational precedent. Gratz urged Allen to check the congregation's register and learn that a black servant in a Jewish household, "living a religious life was allowed . . . burial in our ground," as was the wife of David Nones, who was not born a Jew but adopted Judaism. Perhaps overstating the case, she assured Allen that the recently deceased woman was "educated and reared in the observance of Jewish laws . . . kept the fasts and festivals, abstained from forbidden food . . . spent an innocent life in daily acts of devotion . . . and [was] an exemplary daughter of Israel." One hundred fifty years later, members of Mikveh Israel claimed that the woman was Mary Smith, Simon Gratz's wife.[44] However, it is more likely that the woman was his daughter Mary Gratz, who died the day before Gratz wrote to Allen. Mary Gratz, who never married, was no more than thirty-three at her death, and it is likely that Gratz would speak of a young, single woman as an "innocent." Gratz requested a ruling by the congregation's board of adjudication.

Despite Gratz's plea, Allen returned her letter to her with the remark that "no amount of presidents [*sic*] can make that right which is . . . wrong."[45] If the woman referred to in this interchange was indeed Simon's daughter, Gratz's letter is the only indication we have that Judaism was practiced in Simon's household and that his children had any knowledge of Judaism. If they did, it may explain why Louisa, his oldest child, formally converted to Judaism a few years later. Yet none of Simon's other children took that step; on the contrary, they embraced Christianity. Had Simon and his wife tried to raise their children in a blend of Judaism and Christianity, a blend that neither Jewish nor Christian congregations approved? Despite evidence suggesting that many intermarriages incorporated Judaism, the record concerning Simon Gratz's family is unclear.

In the 1840s, even Isaac Leeser began to feel the impact of the new attitude among some of the congregation's lay leadership. A bachelor, Leeser had long boarded in the home of a Christian woman who prepared his meals according to Jewish law. Some in Mikveh Israel thought Leeser's living arrangement unsuitable for their hazan. It was one of many disagreements Leeser would have with Mikveh Israel's leaders, and their difficulties culminated in Leeser's leaving the congregation in 1850.[46] Dismayed by the conflict, Gratz believed her congregation's opposition to Leeser's domestic arrangements refuted the principle on which many of her close friendships rested, that Christians and Jews could live together in both piety and peace.[47] At the same time, her own pragmatism and diplomacy, developed over long years of organizational leadership, recognized that Leeser was refusing to behave in a manner that would allow the conflict to be resolved.[48] Mikveh Israel's disputes reflected differences in religious standards that widened as the numbers of Jewish immigrants grew. Between 1840 and 1848, the number of Jews in America jumped from fifteen thousand to fifty thousand, and by the mid-1840s one fourth of all Jews in America lived in New York City, Philadelphia, and Baltimore.[49] New synagogue congregations reflected differences in worship styles of German and Polish Jews, and Jewish charitable societies also often reflected these divisions.

Charitable Responsibilities

Jews comprised only a small portion of the new immigrants to Philadelphia. Violent social conflicts erupted in Philadelphia as different socioeconomic, ethnic, racial, and religious groups blamed their frustrations on each other. In 1842, white factory workers in Moyamensing rioted against blacks.[50] In 1843, Irish weavers rioted in protest against factory conditions, provoking anti-Irish and anti-Catholic riots the following year. Fire companies often fought alongside neighborhood gangs.[51] In 1844, riots that began in the Kensington section spread to other areas through the summer, and a convent was burned. Because each section of the city had its own police, law enforcement agencies found it difficult to cooperate to put down the violence.[52]

As widespread poverty exacerbated Philadelphia's social conflicts, private charitable institutions carried almost the entire burden of caring for the poor, and women like Gratz who dedicated their lives to shouldering social burdens now carried serious social responsibilities. Despite her advancing age, Gratz continued her deep involvement in her organizations and often initiated unusual institutional projects. In 1842, for example, she asked the young female residents of the Philadelphia Orphan Asylum (POA) to create items that could be sold to raise funds for a new orphan asylum in Charleston, South Carolina.

Philadelphia's asylum accepted children from smaller southern towns unable to care for them. When Rebecca visited the POA one day, a young girl sent north by Miriam Cohen showed Gratz a bracelet she had plaited for Cohen. That bracelet was added to other items that Gratz sent south, including crocheted cushions and other "specimens of beautiful knitting."[53] Gratz's endorsement often proved decisive in providing aid to the needy. The following year, an orphaned teenage girl knocked on Gratz's door to beg help in getting her younger brother admitted to the POA. The girl supported them both with needlework, but had become "consumptive" and worried that she could no longer provide for her brother. She had been told that because her brother was lame the POA would not admit him, but was advised to call on Gratz before giving up. Gratz visited the girl and her brother in their home and, after confirming that they were "poor, industrious, meek, and uncomplaining," arranged for clothing, fuel, and food for the girl and a physician's letter for the boy, who then entered the POA.[54]

Despite her leadership abilities, Gratz preferred the job of secretary. Though officially only the secretary of the Female Hebrew Benevolent Society (FHBS), Gratz dominated the organization's handling of its cases. Her FHBS public report for 1845 included an eloquent plea for compassion for a woman well known to the community who had suffered a mental breakdown.[55] The society's sensitivity to emotionally disturbed women was unusual in that era, but reflected Gratz's intimate knowledge of emotional struggles in her family and her assessment of and concern for women's emotions.

The FHBS women deliberately sought out these cases. That year the society monitored two Jewish women in the Pennsylvania Hospital for the Insane. The FHBS sought to move a Jewish woman from a locked to a free ward, subsidized the board of her infant, and helped her find work after her release. The FHBS located another Jewish woman in the insane ward of an almshouse, where her husband had placed her before selling their possessions and moving with their two sons to Port-au-Prince. The FHBS met with the resident physician, secured a second opinion that the woman was "insane but not incurable," and moved her to a private room in the Pennsylvania Hospital for the Insane. Hoping to reunite the family, they obtained passage for her to join her husband five months later, but their hopes were misplaced. Soon after rejoining her husband, the woman's emotional state approached a "dangerous character," and she was readmitted to the Pennsylvania Hospital. The FHBS agreed to pay her board there for three months and formed a committee to follow her case. At the end of three months, although she no longer needed hospitalization, her husband's circumstances "did not admit of his providing for her." Abandoning all hope of reuniting the couple, the FHBS gave her a weekly stipend for the next three months, and finally provided a lump sum and donated furniture to help her set up house on her own.[56] These cases illustrate that though the FHBS hoped to strengthen families, its primary objective was to aid Jewish women and their children.

Yet the FHBS did provide the Jewish community a means by which to help families in crisis. Always hoping to keep distressed families intact, the FHBS sought to enable families to care for themselves. In 1846 a family of destitute German immigrants— husband, wife, and wife's sister—arrived in Philadelphia. The wife was about to give birth, but because she was ill and spoke no English she could not be admitted to the lying-in hospital. To resolve the problem, the FHBS paid the wife's sister to nurse her and feed the family.[57] Three years later, they encouraged a destitute widow to write to her relatives in England for aid, and made sure the letters were transmitted safely.[58] About the same time, a Jewish woman was discharged from the Pennsylvania Hospital for the Insane, but the society believed that her severe depression and her "great anxiety to return to her father render[ed] her incapable of earning a living." The members bought her a steerage passage to return to Europe and arranged for an "aged protector" for her through an acquaintance in New York.[59]

As these cases show, the FHBS preferred cases that required only temporary aid. A young woman with a broken arm received a weekly stipend until she recovered and could resume work. A Mrs. Lipman, whose shop was robbed during her illness, was given money to restock. Like other benevolent societies, the FHBS hoped this temporary aid would effect long-term change, and the society sometimes threatened to withhold funds if family members did not behave as the society wished. Mrs. Lipman was told she would receive nothing unless her daughter returned to the place the FHBS provided for her, probably an apprenticeship.[60] Another woman's family suffered "extreme penury," yet the society warned that without "radical change in their character they cannot continue on the list of pensioners."[61] By 1848, with immigration rising, the FHBS established a charity committee to take care of applications from strangers and dispense up to ten dollars without calling a meeting.[62]

As the guiding hand of the FHBS, Gratz made sure that it implemented her policies. The FHBS focused on destitute women, and told one woman who applied for a loan of fifty dollars with a deed of land as security that their services were not for her.[63] Similarly, the society refused to help a rabbi in Jerusalem who asked them for funds to help build a synagogue in the Holy Land.

Although the FHBS focused on helping Jewish women within Philadelphia, donations came from many other Jewish communities who counted on the FHBS to care for their own poor, including $3,000 from the estate of New Orleans magnate Judah Touro in 1854.[64]

Compounding the urgency of the crises faced by women in the cases outlined above, by 1843 Philadelphia's Christian Ladies Hebrew Mission Society was raising funds to hire professional missionaries to convert local Jews, especially targeting poor and needy Jewish women.[65] In 1830 women made up nearly 49 percent of the missionary force, and this percentage continued to rise steadily throughout the nineteenth century.[66] Gratz and the FHBS women strove to provide a Jewish source of aid to those Jews most often targeted by evangelists.

As new Jewish charitable societies emerged in the 1830s and 1840s, the FHBS solicited their aid in coordinating services to their pensioners. Especially active were the Ladies Sewing Societies, the Fuel Society, and several mutual aid societies run by Philadelphia's Jewish men. These organizations did not duplicate each other's work, but coordinated their special interests in caring for the poor. Often, members of the same families participated in all of these groups.

Gratz's leadership abilities and vision of Jewish unity gave Philadelphia's women rare opportunities for effectiveness and success. Only her independent Jewish women's organizations served the community as a whole. In New York, meetings of Jewish women's organizations were guided by synagogue clergy. When a minister's energies were drawn elsewhere, the organizations folded. In 1820 a Female Hebrew Benevolent Society was organized at Shearith Israel, the oldest synagogue in New York City, modeled closely on the Philadelphia group. Although it continued to exist until 1855, it identified so closely with its synagogue that it changed its name to the Female Hebrew Benevolent Society of Shearith Israel in 1854. During the 1840s, four more women's associations emerged in New York; after a few years, they either dispersed or lost their importance as larger groups took over their work. All limited themselves to their own congregations.[67]

Although she had been only four years old when Philadelphia's second synagogue, Rodeph Shalom, declared itself, Gratz firmly believed the city's Jews needed to be united, and she managed her organizations to promote unity. The FHBS promoted

Jewish domesticity along with the sort of civic activism that Gratz remembered from the Revolutionary era in her youth.[68] One means to unite an increasingly diverse Jewish population (more than half of Philadelphia's Jews were foreign-born in the 1840s) was for Gratz to address her secretary's reports to all American Jews, describing Jewish needs and duties in language that everyone could feel spoke to them personally. In the FHBS annual reports published in the *Occident,* Gratz explained that American Jews were "called on to teach [Jews from Europe] that they may . . . like other inhabitants of the soil, become . . . secure citizens." The FHBS improved Jewish women's lives by constructing a Jewish civic activism that both strengthened Jewish domesticity and Americanized recent immigrants.[69]

Jewish Women Writers

Gratz eagerly read new sentimental literature written by Jewish women in England, literature that Gratz thought promoted her own goals for Jewish women. She believed that for Judaism to thrive in Victorian culture, Jewish women must be educated in their faith and encouraged in religious activities. Bitterly, she remarked to Miriam that only the women of her family gathered to read the megillah, or story of Purim, in celebrating that holiday. Gratz took pride in the holiday—which memorializes Persian Jews' rescue from destruction by a Jewish woman, Queen Esther—her brothers ignored it. "The gentlemen take little interest in our female triumphs unless a favorite belle is the actress," she commented sardonically.[70] Leeser, however, eagerly published pious writings by Jewish women in his *Occident.*

Gratz and Isaac Leeser both believed that Victorian culture's emphasis on female piety invited Jewish women to deepen their commitment to Judaism. Yet the Christian arguments, symbols, and beliefs permeating most Victorian women's literature seemed to thwart their hopes. Jewish women in England faced a similar challenge, to defend themselves both as Jews to a Victorian Christian society and as pious women to the male leaders of the British Jewish community.[71]

Grace Aguilar was, by far, the most important of the new British Jewish women writers. In her few years (1816–1847) Aguilar wrote poems, fiction, and treatises on Judaism from a woman's perspective. As Michael Galchinsky has argued, the

debate over Jewish civil rights in England engendered an out-
pouring of popular fiction in which Jews were depicted as either
malleable for conversion (female) or intractably Judaic (male).
Aguilar's writings engaged this debate, arguing the spiritual dignity of Jews to Christians and that of Jewish women to the patriarchal leadership of London's Jewish community.[72] Gratz thought
Aguilar's *Women of Israel,* a commentary on women of the Hebrew
Bible, successfully "refuted the impression so much insisted on
that women were little considered for by the ancient people. . . .
Christians boast that the Gospel has done so much for women," Rebecca complained to her niece Miriam, "yet in the New Testament
I do not know a character so elevated as Deborah, or so lovely
and loving as Ruth."[73] In America, *Women* countered tracts like
The Dying Jewess, which claimed that because Judaism neglected
women's souls Jewish women longed to embrace Christianity but
were kept from it by their fathers.[74] Gratz thought *Women* was one
of Aguilar's best-written books and that it would "raise her reputation as an author and as an Israelite." Gratz obtained a copy from
Leeser and asked her niece Miriam Moses Cohen, whose husband
corresponded with Aguilar and distributed her books in the South,
to extend her "admiring regards." Through her close relationships
with both Leeser and her nephew Solomon Cohen, Gratz knew
that Aguilar and her mother depended on the money the volumes
raised. She thought that if printed cheaply, a volume for domestic
worship would be popular enough to "yield [Aguilar] some profit."[75]

Aguilar responded to Gratz's request with a volume called
Sabbath Thoughts. "Miss Aguilar stands at the head of the present
race of literary Jews," Gratz commented in 1847. "Her works took
possession of our minds and hearts raising them above the earth
and its cares and fixed them on the way that leads to Heaven."[76]

In 1842, after Aguilar's *Spirit of Judaism* reached America,
Miriam Moses Cohen told her aunt, "Miss Aguilar continues to
make converts. I have just heard of a young lady who has ban-
ished all forbidden things from her house who a few months since
thought very lightly of such matters and ascribes her change of
heart to . . . Miss A's arguments. Many of our Christian friends
have been . . . reading Miss A's book and our copies are continually
lent out—who think you has mine? I'm sure you'd never imagine—
Doctor Minis."[77]

Leeser reviewed and advertised Aguilar's book-length essays on Judaism and Jewish women in the *Occident.*[78] Aguilar's

work was eventually published in New York, Boston, Philadelphia, London, Leipzig, Prague, and Tel Aviv and reached far beyond the confines of Jewish communities. Indeed, she wrote some volumes specifically for gentile women readers.[79] Through her association with Leeser, Aguilar knew of Gratz and reported being "affected . . . most forcibly" when she received a letter from Gratz praising *The Spirit of Judaism.*[80]

Tragically, Aguilar died in 1847 at only thirty-one. Her mother, a widow, published her daughter's unfinished manuscripts and Gratz read them all. *The Mother's Recompense* was "full of pious thoughts, excellent morals, and interesting domestic incidents," she wrote, "but [with] faults . . . she would have corrected [had she lived to revise the book.]"[81] Later Gratz recommended *The Days of Bruce,* an early novel by Aguilar, to her sister-in-law Ann. "I have wept over it so plenteously, that . . . it must be good."[82]

The year that Aguilar died, Gratz wrote to her niece Miriam that the English "Misses Moss are very agreeable writers and we have some very fair authoresses on this side of the water." She urged Miriam and her husband to submit something to the *Occident.* "I wish . . . that you and Mr. C[ohen] would send . . . an essay, poem or tale. You used to exercise your fancy in compositions . . . [and] you may soon brush up the habit and put it to good account."[83]

Gratz promoted Aguilar's books because they defended Judaism's spirituality and its treatment of women in language that spoke clearly to both Protestant and Jewish women by using domestic metaphors and the standards for piety central to the emerging women's culture.[84] Work by other Jewish women appeared shortly after Aguilar's. Leeser's *Occident,* to which Gratz subscribed, provided an early and reliable forum for their work and became the first American forum for Jewish women writers. In the *Occident* Gratz read their work along with reviews by Leeser, Solomon Solis, and other leading men of her Jewish community.

New publishing opportunities like the *Occident* created the same revolution in Jewish literature that they did in general American literature.[85] Nineteenth-century Jewish women who continued and expanded an older tradition of women writing in the vernacular found a growing market, international distribution, and increasing outlets in Jewish periodicals.[86] Like Gratz, Leeser, who needed material to publish in the *Occident* every month, wanted to raise the level of Jewish knowledge among all American Jews, including women. In addition to works by Aguilar, he printed works by Hester Rothschild, Rebekah Hyneman, Rosa Emma Salaman, Marion Moss Hartog, Celia Moss Levetus, and others, along with reports of Jewish organizations from around the country, including those run by women. The first organizations to be so reported were run by Gratz. Although Gratz felt it improper for a "lady's" name to appear in print, Leeser insisted that such examples would encourage women around the country to take similar action. The *Occident* reached every major Jewish settlement in the country.[87]

The *Occident*'s images of American Jewish women provided its female readers with literary models with which to examine and reflect on their own changing lives as well as a forum where Jewish women confronted the evangelical assertion that only Christianity supported women's spirituality. Obituaries of notable Jewish women called them virtuous for fulfilling their duties to parents, husband, children, and God, as well as for acting charitably toward the poor. Reprints of annual reports from women's charitable societies encouraged women's philanthropy. Articles about women's role in Judaism commented on mixed seating in synagogues and female participation in choirs, both hot debates, and refuted charges of sexism in Judaism. Women's domestic piety and social responsibilities, touted in Victorian America, were endorsed as traditional Jewish duties. Many articles argued that divisions in religious duties by sex reflected limitations of the flesh only, and that no one should believe that Judaism thought women soulless.[88]

Like other nineteenth-century literature, Jewish women's literature strove to provide women with the means to control facets of their lives otherwise beyond their command.[89] Poems by Jewish women often referred to biblical women—especially Sarah, Rebecca, Rachel, and Leah—and encouraged Jewish women to refute the Christian biblical interpretations expounded by missionaries and the general press. These poems increased Jewish women's identification with biblical events while refuting the idea that God looked more favorably on Christians than on Jews. Meditations on God and Israel used images from the local or national environment or the daily life of the author. Short stories with domestic themes explored Jewish American family life and were often geared toward immigrant parents raising American-born children. Works by Englishwomen Marion Moss Hartog and

Celia Moss Levetus especially focused on communication problems that estranged parents and children, particularly over issues of courtship and marriage and between fathers and daughters.[90]

While Aguilar's impressive body of work claimed widespread attention, the Moss sisters produced shorter works that focused narrowly on domestic relations. Although their own father encouraged their work, they encountered a more ambivalent reception, if not outright hostility, from some of the leaders of London's Jewish community.[91] Both sisters produced short stories that dramatized the need for Jewish women to be educated in Jewish law and lore if Jewish families were to survive integration into Western society. In Marion Moss Hartog's "The Espousal: A Jewish Story," elder and younger sisters exchange places as bride to a young immigrant when he and the younger sister jokingly betroth themselves to each other. They are shocked when their families take them seriously. Hartog condemns the girl's father, aunt, and local gossips for harshly judging a girl who must, according to custom, be branded a divorcée. Hartog blames the immigrant's friend, a knowledgeable man who watched the transaction, for not stopping what was obviously a joke. The father's first reaction is to ban his daughter from his home, but the elder daughter intervenes on her sister's behalf. Hartog's story vividly demonstrates her belief that Jewish women must be taught Jewish customs to avoid the family tragedies that popular ideas of romance may engender.[92]

Hartog's story also countered some of the more offensive popular fictional depictions of Jews. She describes the heroine as a great beauty typifying the handsome features of her ancestors: olive skin, high brow, dark eyes, black hair, full lips, and a voluptuous figure, the standard for oriental beauty that influenced some of Thomas Sully's portraits of Gratz. The father in Hartog's tale is authoritarian, venting his anger at his wife, whose job is to raise children who did not shame him or his religion. But his concern for his own dignity provides the basis for his total honesty in business and good reputation among men. These points countered the caricatures of Jewish dishonesty, ugliness, and passivity that were found in the American press during these years as the rate of Jewish immigration rose.[93]

A story by Celia Moss paralleled Hartog's characterization of a division in parental responses to their children's actions. "The Two Pictures: A Sketch of Domestic Life" opens with a Jewish daughter converting to Christianity to marry a non-Jew. On learn-ing of the marriage, her father weeps and tells his wife, "She has forsaken us willingly, she is dead to us." He proceeds immediately to traditional mourning rites, ripping his own clothes and those of his wife and young child, and ordering them to sit on the ground. Her "name was mentioned no more in the dwelling of her father." Five years later, the mother learns from her sister that her daughter left Judaism because the mother's shallow faith had not earned her daughter's respect. To atone for her error, the mother devotes herself to charitable work. One day she discovers that a destitute woman and child whom she had been helping through an intermediary were in fact her estranged daughter and grandchild. The gentile husband had abandoned both his child and his dying wife. The mother brings the now repentant daughter home, reads Scripture to her, calls in a Jewish "preacher," and brings the girl back to Judaism. In the face of the mother's action, the father allows the daughter back into his home. The daughter dies, but the parents raise their grandchild together.[94]

In both of these brief dramas by the Moss sisters, the au-thors portray daughters whose ignorance of Judaism leads to personal and familial tragedies. Fathers reject their daughters until forced by female relations to relent, and mothers claim full responsibility for their children's failures. In Celia Moss's tale, the mother provides the sole route to reuniting a family torn apart by conflict between father and daughter. In both stories, Jewish daughters are more at ease in gentile society and more ignorant of Jewish tradition than their fathers realize, and the ensuing conflict creates the drama of the stories. Their fathers respond with an overwhelming sense of their own humiliation in the eyes of the Jewish community.[95] Both tales illustrate that Jewish women are in desperate need of an education in Judaism that they can impart to their children.

Aguilar and Marion Hartog also mined the Sephardic Jewish past for heroic themes in both poetry and fiction. Poetry and prose by these female authors also provided Gratz with more recent Jewish heroes than Deborah, Ruth, and Esther. Hartog's poetry series *Jewish Lyrics* extolled Jewish heroism. Her story "Milcah: A Case of the Spanish Jews of the Fifteenth Century" (1852) echoed a popular theme among Jewish writers, the heroism of the secret Jews of Isabella's Spain. Almost fifteen years earlier, Aguilar had popularized the topic with *The Vale of Cedars: or The Martyr.*[96]

Celia Moss's story "The King's Physician: A Tale of the Secret Jews of Spain" (1854) about an old, cruel aristocrat opposed by a religious, suffering servant, won readers in nineteenth-century America.[97]

In addition to providing satisfying depictions of Jewish women, heroic histories, provocative portrayals of Jewish family life, and philosophical discussions of Jewish spirituality, British Jewish women also wrote inspirational poetry. Leeser published many of these shorter items in the *Occident*. These poems illustrated an approach to spirituality similar to that which Gratz had long practiced, blending images drawn from English literature and popular women's fiction with Jewish principles and Bible stories. Rosa Emma Salaman and Grace Aguilar wrote poems heavy in female and nature imagery that echoed similar work by Christian women, lacking only references to Jesus or to events in the New Testament. In "Past, Present, and Future: A Sketch," Aguilar depicted a woman getting caught in the rain while visiting her mother's grave with her child. Rain, falling from heaven, links the grandmother's spirit to her child. "The cloud, Folding that spirit / melted into tears."[98] In Aguilar's "The Evergreen," she named evergreen trees an "emblem of God's omnific love / His never-changing care!"[99] In the language of romantic poetry, this was meant to refute the argument that Judaism had been superseded by Christianity. Her "Sabbath Thoughts" series echoed the popular idea that we will meet dead loved ones in angel form in heaven, and that heaven is therefore, in some way, a home.[100]

Rosa Emma Salaman's work, too, explored the theme of emotional ties to deceased loved ones. Salaman's poems appearing in the *Occident* echoed the hundreds of poems and short stories published in American and British women's magazines that depicted dead babies as angels. In these poems, mothers' spiritual ties to their dead infants increase their own spiritual power and enhance their ability to mediate between heaven and earth on their families' behalf.[101] In sentimental literature, this insistence that women have special ties to heaven through their dead infants eventually prompted some Christian denominations to insist on their own doctrinal and ecclesiastical authority. Salaman echoed part of this complex Christian idea of heaven popular among women, but her poems usually stopped short of insisting that women wielded more spiritual power than men. Nonetheless, in Salaman's "Angel and the Child" a dying infant tells its grief-stricken mother not to cry because the Angel of Death is "lovingly . . . clasping me," though the poor mother cannot see it. Like the popular poems on infant death in publications read by women, the child's innocence alone has brought it into heaven, "before one pang of earthly woe / has touched [its] sinless soul."[102]

By the 1850s one Jewish woman in Philadelphia was producing poetry and prose that reflected a fervent devotion to Judaism. The meek and humble servant of God was a favorite topic for Rebekah Gumperz Hyneman (1812–75). Hyneman, whose mother was not Jewish, converted to Judaism at her marriage to Benjamin Hyneman and remained a fervent Jew, living most of her life a widow. Her two sons died young, one of starvation in Andersonville prison during the Civil War. The work she did for the *Occident* explored biblical images that emphasized Jewish devotion to God despite hardships. She showed a real longing for Jerusalem and Jewish restoration to Zion.[103] Her "Address to the Soul" (1848) told Jews to accept misfortune and to "kiss the chastening rod" because each "earth wound" brought the soul "nearer to God."[104] Her series *Female Scriptural Characters* expressed her feelings about what it meant to be a Jewish woman through extrapolations on the lives of matriarchs mentioned in the Hebrew Bible. Here too, Hyneman's message was that no matter how unhappy a Jewish woman may be, regardless of her worries for her family's safety, she should remember her special place in God's interest and remain faithful and hopeful. "Rebekah" said that

> Deep, deep within each Jewish heart
> Are linked bright memories of the past;
> Memories that time can ne'er efface,
> Nor sorrow's blighting wing o'ercast.[105]

For Gratz, these Jewish women's fiction and poetry provided a framework for her charitable and educational work on behalf of American Jewish families. Moreover, these Jewish women authors argued that Jewish women must receive religious education and must educate their children. After working for more than twenty years to advance these same goals for Jewish women in America, Gratz finally could point to a wide variety of inspirational writings by Jewish women that supported her work. Although Gratz had attempted to solve problems of intermarriage, family conflict, and poverty among Jews in Philadelphia since the Female Hebrew

Benevolent Society was founded in 1819, the emergence of Jewish women's sentimental literature gave Gratz the encouragement and support she needed to continue her work as she approached old age.

7

Family Ties and Sectional Conflict: 1840–1850

"There is much more beauty in performing our duty than in any other accomplishment."
REBECCA GRATZ, 1845[1]

In her sixties, Gratz was well satisfied with the single life she had lived. She assured her new sister-in-law, Ann Gratz, that "no condition in . . . life [was] more destructive to happiness and morals than . . . an ill-advised marriage."[2] In these later years, Gratz often spoke about the need for judicious self-discipline in order to maintain harmony in interpersonal relationships. Since the 1830s, self-restraint, and impression management, detailed in myriad etiquette books, had become measures of respectability, and a family's status often was determined by the behavior and treatment of its women.[3] This popular philosophy, which Gratz embraced, formed a sharp contrast to the increasingly fractious discourse in the political sphere. Her admonition about poorly founded alliances echoed the nation's growing difficulties in maintaining unity and in governing new territories.

Forging Family Connections

In addition to her counsel about self-discipline, Gratz also embraced a philosophy of consolation. Despite her sister-in-law Maria's many years of religious devotion and study, she feared death, now that she had fallen seriously ill. Rebecca tried to soothe her with consoling letters. After Maria's death, Rebecca comforted her distraught brother, expressing her own gratitude to God that Maria's fears had abated and that she "breathed out her pure spirit calmly—and that her bodily sufferings were mitigated." Like many people trying to comfort others amid grief, Gratz encouraged her brother to believe that after a long illness death can be merciful, and she was able to turn his hopes to the future, promising him that he and Maria, along with their two deceased children, would be reunited in heaven. In comforting Benjamin, she also was comforted. "In a little while we shall be reunited, and . . . those who made our happiness here . . . will ever brighten the joys of the hereafter," she wrote.[4]

As Gratz lost the daily companionship of her family, she became increasingly aware of her continual dependence on God and grew even more deeply devout during her later years. One January day she tripped over a rocker in her room, bruised her face and arm, and sprained her neck. In a letter to Anna Maria Boswell Shelby, who joined the Gratz clan in July 1843 when she married Benjamin Gratz, Rebecca wrote that "the pain . . . has all passed away except the sense of divine goodness in preserving me from greater ill. . . . I hope I shall not appear presumptuous to you (as I know I should to many people) by believing that a kind providence is employed 'in all the good and ill that chequers life' . . . surely our heavenly Father extend[s] his Mercy over all he has created—and without his care, we cannot walk safely across our chamber—under it, may tempt the tempestuous ocean and tread the dreary forest."[5] The belief that God kept watch over her daily events provided Gratz with a sense of security that her mercurial family life now did not support.

But intimacy with God could not replace Gratz's need for her family. Until she herself could "meet Maria in Heaven," Rebecca desired a close correspondence with her new sister-in-law. By developing a close relationship with Benjamin's wife Gratz could better maintain her tie to Benjamin and his remaining children. She asked Ann to tell her about the details of their Lexington domestic life, just as she had done many years earlier with Maria Gist Gratz. She was delighted when Ann responded to her request, "at the very time my heart yearned for such information." But Ann's letters were small compensation for what she felt was Benjamin's neglect, and Rebecca could not resist tossing a little guilt his way via Ann. "I began to feel I was losing interest in my dear brother's regards, as he never addresses a line to me on any occasion, tho he knows how jealous I am lest long separation should rob me of any portion of his affection," Gratz wrote. Not wanting to offend her brother, however, she quickly retracted her remark: "But this idea is not harbored for a moment, he does not love to write and rather chooses that you should save him from the labor."[6] Her effort to prod Benjamin into writing more often did not succeed. The correspondence posed difficulties for Ann because, as she explained to Gratz, "being near sighted [I] am compelled to bend over the paper very much . . . [and am] unable to write more than a few lines at a time."[7] As Benjamin's children grew older, corresponding with Aunt Rebecca became a family responsibility.

Benjamin wrote to Rebecca to announce the birth of his new daughter in 1844 and to assure her that baby and mother were both doing well. Bernard traveled to Philadelphia to deliver the letter and to accompany Gratz back to Lexington so that she could meet Ann and her new niece. Others in Lexington were not doing so well; Benjamin's son Hyman Cecil was nursing a broken arm, and Cary was recovering from whooping cough.[8] Gratz enjoyed an extended visit with her Kentucky family. Almost a year later, Ann and Benjamin decided that the new baby would be named Miriam, after Benjamin's mother, the fourth grandchild to be so named. Rebecca approved Ann's selection. "My mother . . . was universally beloved in her generation and bore herself meekly through all the dangers and trials of her life. . . . I could not wish [those named for her] a better inheritance than that a portion of her spirit may descend upon them," she told Ann.[9]

Rebecca's friendship with Ann never attained the intimacy and mutual regard she had shared with Maria, perhaps because Gratz never abandoned the tone of older adviser that she first assumed with Ann. For Maria, Rebecca had couched information about Jewish holidays in religious discussions, whereas to Ann she sent more personal advice about good conduct. Echoing the focus on the emotions and conduct necessary to harmonious domesticity common in popular fiction, Gratz frequently advised her new sister-in-law on the attitudes and behaviors she deemed necessary for a happy household.

Almost two decades earlier Gratz had advised Benjamin's first wife, Maria, as she adjusted to Benjamin's decision to free his slaves, a decision Gratz applauded. Knowing that Maria held high standards for her own character, Rebecca pointed out that slavery limited the degree to which Maria could develop as a person.

Rather than arguing that slavery was brutal—Maria would have
retorted that she treated her slaves well—Rebecca explained that
slavery overindulged the slave mistress. "One of the curses of
slavery is the entire dependence the poor mistress is reduced to,"
she argued.[10]

Gratz now advised Ann on how to treat servants who were
free to leave. "There is no condition in life which does not require the exercise of our virtues to make us happy," she began,
universalizing the lesson about servants she was about to offer.
"Mutual forbearance is a necessary commodity . . . in every . . . domestic relation—it must exist between mistress and servants . . .
particularly where the latter are free to change whenever an offense is given," she explained.[11] Although Gratz opposed slavery,
she nonetheless believed in the class and social distinctions that
placed her among Philadelphia's elite. Moreover, she showed no
interest at all in the nascent women's rights movement. In Philadelphia and New York, except for a few individuals, even women
active in the antislavery cause seemed unconcerned with women's
rights.[12]

Reflecting her high regard for self-discipline, Gratz disliked
unbridled sentimentality in life and in literature. She believed
that both domestic and world peace could be achieved only when
individuals exercised self-discipline. She complained to Ann that
"female moralists sometimes laud candor as the . . . test of friendship—and care not how deeply they lacerate the feelings—and
poison the peace of families."[13] Although her relationship with
Ann was less intellectual than her friendship with Maria had
been, Rebecca delighted in Ann's anecdotes about her young nieces
and nephews. She explained to Ann that she took "great interest in young human beings and [tried] to find out what the future [adult] is to be by the early development of character and
disposition."[14]

At first Gratz did not discuss her charitable or educational
activities with Ann, instead telling her that she was growing
more "reclusive," relying on a few "kind friends and neighbors"
and the companionship of Julia Hoffman, who occasionally lived
with her.[15] Gratz seems to have deliberately misled Ann about
her work, perhaps to avoid intimidating her younger sister-in-
law. Though describing herself as a recluse, she was running
three organizations in addition to supervising and teaching in

the Hebrew Sunday School and seeking out English-language educational materials for teaching Judaism.

Ann inherited Maria's membership on the board of the Lexington Orphan Asylum, but soon revealed her own talents as the organization's treasurer. When Rebecca and Ann exchanged organizational records, Ann was amazed to see that the Philadelphia group achieved far more with less money than the Lexington women accomplished. Yet Ann was pleased overall. "Our Orphan Society [is] . . . in a prosperous condition. [As] I am the treasurer, I can say that funds are . . . more ample than usual notwithstanding some losses . . . in interest on money which we loaned to a house that failed," she wrote proudly to Gratz.[16]

Gratz's relationships with her nieces and nephews remained crucial to her. Shortly before her own visit to Lexington, she asked Ann and Benjamin to send their sons Hyman and Cary to Philadelphia for a visit, lest she "be entirely forgotten by the young folks."[17] Rebecca's sister Richea Hays wrote often to her from Baltimore, particularly when she could tell Gratz about women's religious activities. In May 1844, near the holiday of Shevuot (Feast of Weeks), Richea visited her daughter Rosa Marx in Richmond, Virginia. Rosa was working on a horticultural exhibit at Falls Plantation when "Emma Mordecai, Julia and Mr. and Mrs. Myers walked over . . . starting the festival with us. I was invited to spend the holy days with Rebecca Myers and attend synagogue but I declined," Richea told her sister. The women close to Gratz often discussed what she would think of the sermons and religious debates they heard.

Southern Attitudes

Rebecca's sister Richea assured Gratz that the younger generation of Jewish women in the South cared about Judaism. "Emma Mordecai (daughter of Hebraist Jacob Mordecai) is coming to spend a week with us [in Richmond]," Richea wrote to Rebecca. "[Emma] is a constant attendant at *shule* and at her Sunday school. She was much gratified with your remembrance and sends you her love." Rosa wrote her own note to Rebecca underneath her mother's text, assuring her aunt that she and her Jewish women friends had declined to attend a party because "it was the commencement of our holy days." To induce her niece to visit her, Gratz had written Rosa a bucolic account of life in Philadelphia.

Rosa did not visit, but thanked Gratz for her account of "dear old Philadelphia at peace and governed by the kindly impulses of charity and toleration," a description that surely did not fit a city wracked with ethnic violence, as Philadelphia then was, though it did echo Gratz's own life. Rosa also conveyed best wishes from Emma Mordecai and told Rebecca that both young women hoped to see her in Richmond one day.[18]

Richea's assurances about Emma Mordecai's dedication to Judaism consoled and surprised Gratz—two of Emma's older sisters had converted to Christianity, and Gratz had been saddened and appalled by their action. Commenting on their conversion to her niece Miriam Moses Cohen, Gratz insisted that their behavior would injure their characters as well as taint their father's memory. As those around her knew, Gratz believed that "we every day see the necessity of paying more attention to religious duties if we would not lose the dignity and honor of our national character."[19]

Of course, even Gratz proved unable to maintain constant self-discipline, and admitted to Ann that her own "nightly pillow [was] a reflector of each days deeds—and . . . often echoes back inconsiderate words and acts that I would recall or wish undone."[20] The entire nation seemed to be losing its capacity for self-control, she thought. Few other Americans could maintain pacifism in the face of the widening national disputes based on slavery and race. Gratz's own reactions to an attack on the newspaper office of Kentucky abolitionist Cassius M. Clay in August 1845 reveal the prejudices of people like Gratz—Union supporters who opposed slavery. Like most white Philadelphians, she also opposed abolitionists, who threatened Philadelphia's elite who were committed above all to keeping social order. Gratz argued that abolitionists would only increase white fears of black violence, and fear would push slaveholders to brutality: "I grieve for the poor blacks whose condition will be worsted [*sic*]—and their chains riveted, whereas, if let alone for a few years they would be likely to wear out in Kentucky." The fear of a slave uprising, common throughout the white South,[21] also crops up in a letter to Ann. "How do the [blacks] behave under this excitement? They must have a horror of any Abolitionist coming into the state," she wrote. Rebecca was concerned that the violence would divide white society, and asked Ann if the attack on Clay would not "raise up new troubles in your social circles?"[22] Clearly, peace at any cost was Gratz's goal.

When actress Fanny Kemble, whom Rebecca had befriended more than a decade earlier, married Georgia plantation owner Pierce Butler and visited Savannah, Rebecca wrote to her niece there asking her to receive the actress. Gratz had kept in touch with Kemble, worrying about the accounts of terrible conditions on Butler's Island and how Fanny would adjust to them. Fanny found slavery horrifying and her own role as planation mistress impossible. Nor was her marriage to Butler a happy one. Kemble was sickened by planation cruelty and viewed the rural conditions on Butler's Island as uncivilized and barbaric. She left Butler and returned to the stage and England where she could support herself financially. There she wrote a detailed account of the brutality of slavery on Butler's Island, although it was not published until 1863.[23] Kemble's book, *Journal of a Residence on a Georgia Plantation,* found a wide audience, and Gratz placed a copy in her own library.[24] Butler's vindictiveness during their divorce kept matters unsettled until 1849, and he did not allow her to see or communicate with their children. Gratz befriended Kemble and acted as intermediary between the children and their mother, conveying letters and messages to the daughters whom Kemble had left behind in Philadelphia.

To Gratz, Kemble's situation was not unlike those she had dealt with for forty years in organizations like the Female Association and the Female Hebrew Benevolent Society. Butler would not allow his daughters to visit Gratz, although he would allow her to convey letters between Kemble and the children. Kemble first reassured her "dear friend" Gratz that she was regaining her health after a "terrible overtension of the nerves" and then urged Rebecca to be useful to another woman at risk "as you must . . . all [to] whom you stretch forth your . . . hand." Primarily, however, Kemble wanted Gratz to understand that she was "in agony over loss" of her children.[25] Kemble had also developed a friendship with Sarah Moses, Rebecca's niece, and Sarah, only twenty-eight at the time, was shaken by the distressing course of Kemble's life.

The following winter, while visiting her sister Miriam Moses Cohen in Savannah, Sarah could not help linking domestic tensions with national unrest. From her sister's damp house she wrote her worries about the nation's future and its possible impact on Kemble's life. Like many antebellum Americans, Sarah worried first about what God would think of the way the country had conducted its political life: in compromises between slave and free states; in untenable rulings about new territories, allowing Indian treaties to be broken and Native Americans slaughtered; and entering into war with Mexico to gain its land.[26] "Nations as a rule are punished for their sins and if we should now be involved in warfare—I should look upon it as the result of the unhallowed system of politics that has been indulged in for the last few years," Sarah wrote to Gratz.[27]

Sarah's political sympathies echoed those of her aunt. Twelve years before Harriet Beecher Stowe's *Uncle Tom's Cabin* attacked slavery's devastation of black domesticity in 1852, Gratz described her sympathy for Native Americans in language that revealed her concern for their domestic lives. She empathized with their "private sufferings" at the hands of whites and expressed "horror and shame" at accounts of attacks on Indian villages and families as well as a fear and dread of Indians who "have so many wrongs to avenge."[28] Sentimental literature condemned politics ruled solely by economics, and in the North, political critiques increasingly voiced concern for violence to household and domestic life. Gratz and Stowe were not alone in their views.

Although Sarah and Rebecca linked their worries for the political future of the nation to worries about domestic tranquility among families, a theme that grew increasingly powerful in the North in the years leading up to Civil War, Sarah's sister Miriam never discussed politics with her northern aunt. Instead, Miriam described religious and familial activities and wrote about the natural beauty of the South. "March is mellow sunshine, yellow jasmine in bloom. You scarcely meet any one in the street without a sprig of it, even the horses are decorated with its bright flowers and the houses are perfumed with it," she wrote to Gratz. Miriam mentioned her love and concern for Gratz and talked about her father, Solomon Moses, whom she hoped would visit her for Passover. Miriam's family hosted a family celebration for Purim, which "chanced to fall on Mother C[ohen]'s birthday and we invited all her children and grandchildren to celebrate it with her which made quite a large party. She completed her 74th year on that day."[29]

Antebellum Jews, barely able to unite in their own defense, did not take a united stand on the issue of slavery. By 1848 Jews lived in all parts of the country, and their political views tended to reflect those of their region.[30] However, by carefully avoiding explosive issues and concentrating on other shared concerns, families and friends maintained ties to individuals they loved. Miriam, like Gratz, cared deeply about Judaism, and the two women usually commented on some religious matter in each letter. For Miriam, discussions about religion provided a continuing bond with her aunt, and Miriam rarely disagreed with Gratz or raised issues that might cause friction between them. Both women enjoyed essays by Reform rabbi Max Lilienthal, despite his advocacy of Reform Judaism. And like her aunt, Miriam noted works written by Jewish women. She "recognize[d] a piece of Emma Mordecai's in the last *Occident* which is quite well written," but she disliked Mordecai's schoolbook on Judaism.[31] Miriam's letters carefully maintained her bond with her aunt across a distance that increasingly carried differences in culture and political orientation.

Sarah's account of Jewish life in Savannah reveals differences in Jewish culture between northerners and southerners. Sarah reported to her aunt Rebecca that in the South, religious debates about tradition and Reform were being recast in the language of national conflict. One Friday evening Leeser visited the Cohen home, where "he had a long discussion . . . with the Levys— reform vs. anti-reform." Sarah, like Leeser and Gratz, opposed Reform, but felt inadequate to the debate that evening. "I wished for your aid," she wrote to Gratz. "The Southern Jews say that the Northern Jews will not believe that they can have any religion because they do not adhere to all the forms prescribed by the rabbis while the Southern Jews insist that the Northern and Conforming Jews lose all spirituality in blind adherence to what their fathers did before them." Sarah's frustrations were evident in her letter. "The discussion ended as it must do—by either party's remaining unconvinced," she concluded.[32] The discussion held little chance for resolution, embedded as it was in other, perhaps even more emotionally laden, controversies.

But Sarah assured Gratz that despite their interest in Reform, Miriam and her husband remained faithful Jews at home. "We kept Friday evening just as we do it at home . . . [and] I read my prayers quietly the next evening and thought of you." Sarah also admired Miriam for what she called her "well controlled nature." The more expressive and honest Sarah, soon to marry and move to Montreal, Canada, worried that she might never see her sister again. "How can I gain her well controlled nature?" she asked Gratz, "living in the present 'Heart within— God overhead'—with neither regrets for the past or fears for the future?" Sarah's comments reveal that she thought such self-control impossible to attain. She also worried about leaving Gratz alone in Philadelphia. "I can never bear to think of you without a female companion," Sarah wrote.[33]

Like her correspondence with Miriam, Rebecca's mail from her Lexington family often discussed the details of domestic life and the beauties of nature, topics that would cause little friction. When nephew Cary returned to Lexington from a boarding school in Philadelphia, Ann reported on their trip and the harsh treatment Cary's friend Jo received at the school. The boy was condemned to "three days of bread and water for not buying a knife approved by the master [of the school]." Benjamin and Ann would not send their son to Lexington's inferior schools, nor did they want to send the boys back to the same Philadelphia school where they had experienced such cruelty. They asked Gratz to investigate other good schools for boys in Philadelphia, which she did. "Jo speaks gratefully of your kindness to him," Ann wrote. At Gratz's urging, Ann took up Shakespeare "with renewed spirit" and found it "elevating and refining . . . thereby approximating us to our divine origin, perhaps as much as many of our clerical lecturers."[34] This was the sister-in-law Gratz hoped for, one who could appreciate the spiritual benefits of reading Shakespeare. Engaged in the details of each other's lives, Gratz and her Lexington family survived the worsening difficulties dividing other families across the nation.

Distant Bonds

Rebecca's lifelong efforts to develop close ties to her nieces and nephews and to Maria Fenno Hoffman's children were successful. When Benjamin's twenty-year-old son Hyman opened his first office, he wrote to Gratz that same day. "Not until today have I felt quite satisfied with my profession," he told his aunt. Hyman apologized to Gratz for not writing sooner but explained that he did not want to write until he could report success. He knew Gratz expected great things of him, and an earlier letter "would have discouraged you, in your hopes as much as I myself felt."[35] All her nieces and nephews felt Gratz's encouragement, but her approval was not easy to earn. They knew she expected them to set and attain high goals. Richea's son Isaac Hays, who provided medical services to Gratz's charities, was a staff physician at Wills

Eye Hospital and a founder of the American Medical Association. He was the first ophthalmologist in the United States to use cylindrical lenses to correct astigmatism, and invented a knife-needle for operating on cataracts.[36] His sister Sarah also adored her aunt. In 1847, just before a family reunion at the United States Hotel in Saratoga Springs, she boasted to Rebecca that her young daughter Laura said, "I hope aunt Becky will not be gone [from Saratoga Springs] before we get there—I want to see her so much." She went on, "All my children have a great affection for their aunt Becky and I encourage it as much as I can."[37] These close relationships were deeply important to Gratz.

Rebecca's closest ties were to Rachel's children, the nieces and nephews whom she had raised. In the spring of 1846, Rachel's son Horace wrote to Gratz about life in the military, complaining about hard labor, intense physical exertion, and few regular meals beyond breakfast and dinner. Homesick, Horace wrote, "You are the only mother I have ever known, and none would have shown more love, or anxious solicitude for the welfare of a child than you have always shown for me."[38] If Rachel's children thought of Gratz as their second mother, some of Maria Fenno Hoffman's children considered Gratz more family than friend. While stationed in central Pennsylvania, Horace arranged to stay for a time with George Hoffman, Maria Fenno Hoffman's son, and his family, where the two men discussed politics and history. George Hoffman was a leading literary figure of his day and had founded *The Knickerbocker Magazine* in 1833. His sister Julia worked as a governess when she was not visiting Gratz, though she found the work unspeakably dull. While Horace visited George, Julia was working at nearby Bear Gap, "vegetating as usual . . . Bear Gap offers . . . little . . . yet I look forward to some years here."[39] Julia spent as much time with Gratz as she could and thought of the Gratz household as a second home. After her brother Charles entered a mental hospital in Harrisburg, Pennsylvania, in 1849,[40] Julia grew closer to Gratz and lived with her during her later years.[41]

Rebecca's southern relations—Ann in Kentucky, like Miriam in Georgia—wrote to her about the beauties of nature and the details of their family life. Ann wrote proudly to Gratz of her extensive rose garden and regaled her with a detailed account of her gardening activities. "I engaged a gardener . . . to lay off below the flower garden two large semi-circles on each side of the main walk. In them are my roses planted—they are in full bloom, fifty varieties, some six feet high, growing on their sticks. I have twenty kinds of tea roses," Ann explained proudly. Her achievements earned her local fame. "One of my teas, Duke of Orleans, was exhibited in town as a curiosity and . . . [another rose] 'La Reine' . . . whose diameter was five inches . . . was pronounced by all as the largest and most wonderful rose ever seen of bright cherry hue," she wrote. Enthusiastically, Ann told Gratz about her fertilization techniques, which resulted in astonishing growth. Ann also boasted of the excellent memory possessed by her three-year-old daughter, Miriam, who could quote Shelley and identify each variety of her mother's flowers by name. She was also considered a musical genius.[42] Rebecca, who seldom gardened, based her admiration for Ann's horticultural activities on the flower symbolism she encountered in religious literature. "The pure and innocent and refined all love flowers," she wrote. "[Flowers] seem a creation of pure benevolence with which God has ornamented the earth . . . to gladden the heart of those who dwell in it."[43]

Few people could ever meet Gratz without learning about her religious beliefs, partly because she spent so much of her time in religious activities. Fanny Kemble, visiting Catherine Sedgwick in Lenox, Massachusetts, in the 1840s, met a Unitarian minister whom Gratz had met in Philadelphia twenty-eight years earlier. Kemble reported that the man "spoke enthusiastically of having met and known you . . . [you] heard him preach and he remembers your very first answer for speaking of the Jews as not holding the doctrine of the resurrection—he told me . . . how insulted he had been by what you had said to him on the subject."[44] Even Frank Blair, a non-Jewish Philadelphia businessman and later U.S. congressman who occasionally dined with Gratz's brothers, could not separate his impression of Gratz from her dedication to her religion, referring to her as "Queen of the Jews."[45] Far from avoiding the topic of religion with those who did not share her beliefs, Gratz made her faith so much a part of her identity that it was impossible to be her friend without addressing religious issues.

Gratz could turn almost any topic into an occasion to instruct others on religion or self-discipline, but deemed the lesson especially important in coping with tragedy. "I hardly know any state of peril that excludes hope," she wrote to Miriam Moses Cohen when one of her children fell ill.[46] And as the child's condition worsened and Miriam struggled to maintain hope, Gratz commented that "sorrow makes us all egotists and it is strange how our self love discovers itself in the desire we feel to find ourself thought of—and sympathized with—when we are smitten by some heavy calamity."[47] The same dependence on her Jewish faith that had long ago enabled Gratz to overcome her fears for her father and her revulsion to nursing had grown only deeper and more thoroughly a part of her personality by her sixties.

Although Gratz was undoubtedly one of the most influential Jewish women of the antebellum era, she believed that little could be accomplished in life without religious devotion. But Gratz did not endorse a passive dependence on God. She believed that a truly religious person would find spiritual instruction both in God's natural creation and in the inspired creations of people like Shakespeare and Grace Aguilar. For such a person, spiritual understanding should deepen and grow more sophisticated throughout life. Moreover, she believed that true spiritual growth ought not to remain a private matter but ought to lead one to charitable activities and to guiding others toward religious insight. Both of these attitudes are grounded in Judaism's teachings.

But Gratz drew these religious attitudes from American culture as well as from Judaism. By developing her own capacity for self-discipline and by lecturing others about its importance, Gratz displayed her own high status and enhanced that of her family. By embracing that popular definition of social respectability and making it her own, Gratz assuaged anxiety over status she may have felt she lost through her diminished family ties, her advancing age, her single life, or her family's reduced place in Philadelphia's Jewish community. By combining religious devotion with accepted standards of respectability, Gratz sought to control her world by the only means available to her. Religion and self-discipline empowered her to change the quality of life for herself and for many others—family, friends, and women in the organizations she led. She believed that self-discipline and religious devotion made her powerful. Not surprisingly, she believed America could grow powerful by behaving similarly.

8

Women in New Jewish Institutions: 1850–1860

"The memory of duties performed . . . consoles us for all our losses."[1]
REBECCA GRATZ, 1857

By 1850, immigration from Germany, Ireland, and England had boosted Philadelphia's population by 58 percent.[1] At the same time, Americans' commitment to national unity was dissolving. Across the nation, arguments about religious values, often linked to political turmoil, were growing shrill. Jews who hoped to maintain family and communal bonds across sectional and political differences were silent on important issues. Those writing to Gratz from the South carefully limited their correspondence to areas on which they might agree. Hoping that renewed piety would strengthen Jewish life, in 1850 Gratz wrote to Dr. Raphall, a popular Jewish clergyman in New York, "begging him to print his [sermons] for I think if we could collect a library of Sabbath reading books it would greatly tend to make the day more properly observed. Mr. Leeser's third volume contains some good discourses and his letters are excellent."[2] Both Gratz and Leeser believed that Jewish piety could enhance social harmony and strengthen bonds among American Jews.

Gratz, like Leeser, believed that for Judaism to thrive in the United States, Jewish education needed to improve substantially. Despite Leeser's efforts, in the 1850s nearly all Jewish scholarship and literature read by America's fifty thousand Jews was still

imported from Europe. Gratz and Leeser redoubled their efforts
to establish two new Jewish institutions, a day school and a foster
home. They sought to strengthen the religious, educational, and
charitable resources in a city increasingly marred by violence and
intolerance.

The Founding of the Jewish Foster Home

Although she supported Leeser's efforts to establish a day
school for Jewish children, Gratz believed that increasing numbers of poor Jewish families faced a special dilemma. Children in
these families either attended public school or were sent out to
work, obtaining almost no Jewish education. Families too poor
to care for their children were forced to send them to orphanages, which were thoroughly Christian environments. As the numbers of Jewish immigrants to America increased throughout the
nineteenth century, the Jewish community could no longer meet
the needs of poor families through private foster care for Jewish
children within more stable Jewish families. As early as 1848,
the Female Hebrew Benevolent Society (FHBS) began working to
establish a Jewish foster home in Philadelphia. Revealing the urgency they felt, their published annual reports began using more
direct language, addressing the audience as "you" the benefactor
and reader, and offering brief but heart-rending stories of the
effects of destitution on children along with inspiring accounts
of help provided by the FHBS.

Over the previous decade, Gratz and the FHBS women had
become convinced that Philadelphia needed a Jewish foster home.
Many elite antebellum Americans could imagine themselves reduced to poverty, and most claimed relations who were poor.[3]
The FHBS members included some of the most prominent Jewish names in Philadelphia, and their backing of a foster home
gave the institution its best chance for success. In the society's
1847 report Gratz explained that "every year the demands on
this institution . . . assume a more important character." Destitute
children needed a home that would give them an "early education,
industrious habits, and high moral and religious principles."[4]

Gratz never forgot the distress she felt when her father or
brothers were gone from home during extended business trips.
When Jewish immigration increased, she worried about the families of the many Jewish peddlers who traveled around the country.

She urged the community to make a "united effort" to provide for children whose parents "obtain a livelihood by journeying through the country." She promised that provision could be made "at small expense" and that the boys would be recommended to Jewish "mechanics or merchants as apprentices." All the FHBS needed would be a "suitable Jewish Matron and teacher . . . and . . . a Committee of Gentlemen" to raise funds. The women of the FHBS would do the rest.[5] FHBS member Matilda Cohen made the first donation, five dollars, which was saved in a special account until the home opened.[6]

In 1849, with support for a Jewish foster home growing, Leeser wanted to publish reports of the FHBS's early efforts at arranging foster care in the *Occident* and to include Gratz's name. Gratz's leadership of women's organizations had made her a public figure with a palpable effect on her community. Other women who chose serious benevolent society "careers" were likewise transformed.[7] Gratz resisted Leeser's plan to use her name because she "always disliked the ostentation of seeing Ladies names in print when the whole amount of their services are so very small" and quashed the plan. "The more quietly [people] go about doing good the better."[8]

The next year, Leeser and Gratz coordinated a plea for a Jewish foster home that was published in the *Occident.* Gratz's essay, which she signed "a Daughter in Israel," took up the first two pages of that month's issue. Appealing to readers' faith, she asked them to remember that their treatment of the poor would be discussed "at the judgment seat of . . . God" and that "good wishes alone will not avail . . . helpless children." She cautioned readers that their own children or grandchildren might one day be among the poor, and repeated her warning about God's judgment. Leeser followed her essay with his own four-page endorsement.[9]

The Jewish Foster Home (JFH) was to be administered according to the principles of "religious influence and maternal care," and discipline was to be tempered by "love, forbearance, and good judgment," Gratz wrote. She expected that pious rhetoric would solicit widespread support for her new institution. Both Gratz and the JFH records referred to the home's residents as a "family." True to Victorian ideals, the JFH women managers saw the home as a female responsibility, with the matron as its central figure. Women supervised and administered the home. Five men comprised the board of council, which gave financial and legal advice and supervised financial investments; the first members were Hyman Gratz, Abraham Hart, Sabato Morais, and men of the Moss and Newhouse families whose female relatives were managers.[10] The home's structure paralleled that of a large family in which the male providers were permanently away on business, while mother, siblings, and nearby female relatives ran the household and raised the children.[11]

Other New Institutions

Philadelphians supported many new sorts of educational institutions in this period of population and economic growth. In 1850, Jefferson Medical College graduated over 200 students and the University of Pennsylvania Medical School graduated 176. That year, a group of local physicians opened the country's first medical school for women, the Female Medical College. Despite their training, its graduates were denied clinical practice at local hospitals, and women doctors were barred from the Philadelphia County Medical Society, a practice that continued until late in the nineteenth century. The School of Design, which also trained women only, opened its doors in 1850 as well. The Christian Brothers, a Roman Catholic order, opened three schools in the city by 1853, employing female teachers. In 1851, Philadelphia's public schools employed 699 female teachers and only 82 male teachers.[12] This activity throughout Philadelphia opened doors for Jewish women to teach in public and private schools.

In 1851, Leeser opened the Hebrew Education Society (HES), a Jewish day school with a charter from the state of Pennsylvania, empowered to grant degrees. The first twenty-two pupils included both wealthy and poor, and no one knew who paid and who received their education for free. Leeser served as the school's first provost, and Michael M. Allen (a pupil of Leeser's who was preparing for the clergy) taught Hebrew. Evelyn Bomeisler, with several years' teaching experience in a Philadelphia public school, became the school's first English teacher. After six weeks, enrollment in the HES rose to sixty-seven students, with equal numbers of boys and girls, and two assistant teachers were hired. In 1854, New Orleans magnate Judah Touro died, leaving twenty thousand dollars to the HES. With these funds, the society purchased a building and renamed it Touro Hall. When the Hebrew Sunday School (HSS) moved into the HES building the next year, Touro Hall became the center for Jewish learning in Philadelphia. The HES soon boasted 170 pupils, added algebra and German to its curriculum, and hired a second principal to supervise its female teachers.[13]

While Philadelphia's Jewish women faced little opposition when teaching in secular or Sunday schools, Baltimore's Jewish women encountered resistance. There, Sarah N. Carvalho, a former teacher in Gratz's school, established a similar English-language school during the 1850s, but she met harsh criticism from the overwhelmingly German-speaking Jewish populace. Worse, her work was ridiculed and attacked by Rabbi David Einhorn, a powerful leader of Reform. Arguing that Carvalho's teachers knew neither Hebrew nor Judaism, he warned parents that their children would be "crippled by the *weibliche Theologie* [women's theology]." Isaac M. Wise, Einhorn's nemesis in Reform leadership, countered that a Sunday school education was better than none at all and that "the pious efforts of ladies should always meet with man's approbation and support." Isaac Leeser thought the school valuable despite its limitations. Einhorn, however, thought Leeser an ignoramus and was offended that the classes were not in German, the only language he thought proper for religious discourse. With Einhorn's opposition, the Baltimore school failed, and it was not until 1869, after the Civil War and after Einhorn left Baltimore, that women and men together joined in successfully launching an English-language Jewish school there.[14]

By the 1850s, Jewish Sunday schools provided women public roles in religious education in many communities. But in many cases, the success of these schools rested more on the efforts of dedicated leaders than on community support. Although Einhorn moved to a Philadelphia congregation, Keneseth Israel, in 1861, Gratz's twenty-three-year-old Hebrew Sunday School enjoyed secure support and his opposition did not threaten its existence.[15] In New York, by contrast, a Ladies Association for the General Instruction of Children of Jewish Persuasion sputtered briefly without strong leadership.[16] On the other side of the Appalachian Mountains, in Cleveland, Benjamin Peixotto established a Hebrew Sunday School with six teachers—two men and four women—at congregation Tifereth Israel after 1857. It was the first time women taught in Jewish religious schools there. The school was so dependent on Peixotto's leadership, however, that it closed when he left the congregation, even though it had a hundred students, and opened again when he rejoined Tifereth Israel in

1864. Peixotto's school taught Bible stories, a Jewish catechism, and rudimentary Hebrew.[17] Only in Charleston did a Jewish Sunday School meet with success similar to Philadelphia's. There, Penina Moise, an experienced teacher, poet, and author of the first American Jewish hymnal, took over the reins of the Jewish Sunday School from Sally Lopez in 1842. But the school was linked to one congregation, Beth Elohim, and therefore could never reach the size or influence on the city that Philadelphia's school achieved. Yet it was successful, and in 1845 Beth Elohim's school served fifty pupils in four classes.[18] One year before Moise took over the Charleston school, Richmond's Emma Mordecai initiated a religious school with the support of the Ladies Auxiliary of congregation Beth Shalome. Although Emma Mordecai served as the school's superintendent, and despite her family's reputation in both education and Jewish learning, other demands on the populace before and, especially, during the Civil War hampered the school's success. Mordecai herself left Richmond in 1864.[19]

The Growth of the Jewish Foster Home

Although Gratz and the FHBS began urging the founding of the Jewish Foster Home in the late 1840s, the actual establishment of the home coincided with a severe economic depression in Philadelphia and several personal losses in Gratz's own family. In 1852 her oldest sister, Frances Gratz Etting, died at age eighty-one. By 1853 Philadelphia had suffered an economic depression so severe that thousands of starving and homeless individuals were counted in the area bounded by 5th and 8th Streets and Lombard and Fitzwater, in south Philadelphia, alone.[20] By 1853 America's children's aid societies and asylums often sent poor children and orphans to homes in the Midwest, usually farm families who used child labor, providing further impetus for Jews to establish their own residence for orphans and destitute children.[21] But 1855, the year the JFH actually opened its doors, proved a year of deep sadness for Gratz as she mourned three nieces; Richea's daughters Elizabeth Rosa Hays Marx and Ellen Hays Etting died within a month of each other in October and November, and Frances's daughter Isabella died a month later, on December 24. Gratz's eighth decade was a tragic one.

Gratz hoped that the charitable activities the JFH offered its women managers would fire the religious dedication of younger

Jewish women. In 1855, Simon Gratz's daughter Louisa formally converted to Judaism, probably to join the board of the JFH.[22] Louisa also was a founder of the JFH, where she worked closely with her aunt. Before her conversion to Judaism, Louisa had been active in charities in the Christian community, also working in Sunday schools and with orphans.[23] Evelyn Bomeisler, a teacher in a public school and in the HES, whose mother was not a Jew, was secretary of the JFH and worked closely with Gratz in that capacity.[24] By offering Jewish women communal activities that paralleled those of non-Jewish women, Gratz's organizations eased the way for non-Jewish women to convert to Judaism.

Although Jewish women sometimes encountered opposition when they tried to establish religious schools, benevolent societies such as the JFH fulfilled basic needs and earned women praise. In enjoying public support for charitable societies, they shared a common experience with most women in the nineteenth century. Thus, having finally raised sufficient funds, the Jewish Foster Home, a nine-room house on North Eleventh Street in Philadelphia, opened on May 1, 1855, accepting five children, siblings in two families. For less than two hundred dollars per year, the building offered a good kitchen range and hot and cold water supplied to the bathroom. Members of the JFH's board of directors did much of the day-to-day work of the home, apart from that performed by the matron, a servant, and an occasional teacher. Simha Peixotto, a board member, taught Hebrew at the home. Like other foster homes, orphan asylums, and "homes for the friendless" around the country, the JFH, an institution with limited funds, depended on the personal commitment and labor of its female managers.[25]

The JFH was well organized.[26] The FHBS invested two thousand dollars from Judah Touro's three-thousand-dollar gift in city loans at 6 percent interest. The thirty managers divided themselves into managing committees focusing on specific tasks: purchasing, education, admission, clothing, and indenturing. Often, a single physician or dentist offered medical and dental services at a reduced rate.[27] Moreover, the JFH managers assured their donors that "every expenditure not in conformity with the most rigid economy has been avoided."[28]

The JFH printed its annual reports and circulated them among potential donors. The reports were designed to elicit donations. As noted in the account of the first annual meeting, held on February 12, 1856, at Mikveh Israel, the session opened with a prayer to God, "whose breath is love and whose voice is charity."[29] Although Charleston's Hebrew Orphan Society had been established in 1834, the Philadelphia home was, for its first five years, the only "institution for the exclusive protection of Jewish orphans and destitute children" in America.[30] Jewish tradition holds that the home is a sacred space for worship, and a good deal of Jewish ritual—certainly most of the rituals involving women—is designed to sanctify domestic life. The JFH tried to provide an entirely Jewish home environment, even arranging for boys to become bar mitzvah.[31] During its first year, in-kind donations included matzo and food for a Purim feast.[32]

Because it served Jews from throughout the country, the JFH received donations from as far away as Ohio, Texas, Alabama, Georgia, New York, South Carolina, Kentucky, England, and Canada, as well as from Philadelphia.[33] Until 1855, when Gratz and her friends opened their institution, American Jews used non-Jewish agencies or helped needy children by arranging adoptions or apprenticeships. Charleston and New York, two cities with a large Jewish population, both worked in this way, and New York did not open its Hebrew Orphan Asylum until 1867.[34] With increasing immigration, the need for a specifically Jewish foster home became evident. Children admitted into the JFH between 1855 and 1874 named Germany, Prussia, Poland, Bohemia, New York, Pennsylvania, and Georgia among the places of their birth.[35]

Despite the rhetoric used in early fund-raising pleas, the JFH records show that children of traveling peddlers were not the organization's first concern. The board acted most quickly in cases where a Jewish child was being raised by a Christian family or where an orphan had no relatives nearby.[36] Nineteenth-century Jewish women frequently bore more than five children, and stepparents occasionally sent children from the first marriage to live with neighbors or relatives or in foster homes. From 1855 to 1862 several widowers responded to the death of their wives by asking the home to take all of their children immediately because they felt unable to raise or care for them. The board rarely responded with the speed the fathers hoped for, and tried first to find a way for the children to stay with their parent. Admission procedures were formal and lengthy, requiring an interview with the admission committee and testimonials and letters from respectable, well-known individuals attesting to each applicant's need and good character.[37] Nonetheless, the children of widows and widowers were the majority of children admitted to the home. Indeed, the first children admitted were siblings of two families, three children of a widower, and two sons of a widow.[38]

But among widows, only the poorest, like a Mrs. Branus, who lost her job doing piecework at home because she refused to work on the Sabbath, were willing to put their children in the home. Once children were admitted, parents rarely saw them. Most orphan asylums minimized contact between children and parents on the assumption that the parents provided poor guidance, as well as to promote obedience and discipline among the residents. In the early years, parents could visit their children in the JFH from 9 A.M. to 5 P.M. on alternate Sundays. Day-long visits on alternate Sundays provided far more contact than that allowed in the nearby Baltimore Home of the Friendless, where one visit per month was standard.[39] By 1860 the JFH further restricted visiting hours to between 3 and 6 P.M. on the first Thursday of each month. Parents were warned against bringing any food or sweets to their children, and to give any gifts or items for their children only to the matron.[40]

The home restricted admission to children between four and eight years of age. Occasionally parents tried to send an older child in place of a younger one, as did Mrs. Blum, whose husband deserted her when he went west eight months before she applied to have two of her four children admitted. The managers agreed to take two children, but not the oldest, who was nine. When Mrs. Blum brought her eldest to the home instead of the younger child, the managers returned the child to her.[41] A few parents removed their children after just a few weeks, but most did not, and before 1875 the average length of time a child spent in the home was four and one-half years.

By 1860 parents were required to sign an agreement promising not to remove their children before six months had passed, to give two weeks' notice before doing so, not to bring sweets or food, and to agree to have the child apprenticed according to the discretion of the home's managers. Children were placed in apprenticeships only where they could observe Jewish Sabbath and holidays, boys to a mechanical trade and girls to housekeeping or dressmaking.[42] Parents were expected to pay a small amount toward the care of their child, usually twenty-five cents per week. Unlike the District of Columbia Orphan Asylum, the JFH did not require that parents leave their offspring until they reached maturity. Compared with other institutions, the JFH, which returned children to their parents when parents proved able to provide for them, displayed the FHBS goal of keeping families intact.[43]

The JFH managers hoped to ensure that children of poor Jews became industrious, pious, and capable, and the home's regimen followed that of other orphan asylums, especially the Philadelphia Orphan Asylum (POA). Both the POA and the JFH framed the children's days in prayer and maintained order and silence during meals and at night.[44] Still a board member of the POA, Gratz knew the routine well. At the JFH, the children rose at dawn, washed in tepid or cold water, met in the schoolroom for morning prayers, which included the Sh'ma, and then breakfasted on bread and milk. At midday they ate meat, vegetables, and one slice of bread, occasionally with soup and, on Sabbath, fruit or cold pudding. Dinner repeated breakfast's menu. Before meals, children washed and waited for the matron to recite a blessing; the matron recited a second blessing after each meal. Bedtime was at twilight, and the Sh'ma was recited again before bed. No lights were allowed to be left on during sleeping hours. School occupied six hours each day, and play was allowed only between breakfast and school and from supper to bedtime. Only the matron and teacher were allowed to punish any child. On the Sabbath eve, the matron read an appropriate prayer and the children sang a popular Hebrew hymn. Sabbath mornings, she led children in reciting selected portions of the morning service and in reading part of the Torah portion read that day in the synagogue.[45] Gratz hoped that by providing an orderly and safe environment for its children, the JFH would enable them to grow into educated, responsible, and religiously committed adults.

Although Gratz was a member of the board of managers of the home from its outset, she was not formally on its original executive board, though she did serve on several committees. At seventy-four, she was still superintendent of the HSS, her greatest love, and on the boards of the FHBS and POA. Nonetheless, people assumed that Gratz was in charge. In August 1855, when the matron resigned, she did so by sending a letter to Gratz.[46] The managers finally convinced Gratz to formally join the home's board, and in 1858 she became vice president. Her protégé was Evelyn Bomeisler, who served as the JFH secretary for nearly twenty years.[47] Gratz hoped to instill in younger women the same dedication that she counted on among her co-workers in the FHBS.[48]

The thirty women managers of the JFH divided themselves into seven visiting committees, and each committee visited the home five times in a two-week period. During the visits they checked the larder, the matron's accounts, the children's educational progress, and general cleanliness. They talked privately with the matron as well as with some of the children to make their assessments of the home's strengths and weaknesses. In 1855 the matron complained that parents visited their children too often and without notice, thereby destroying her authority. Children complained that the matron used physical punishment. The managers responded by posting the house rules prominently where matron, children, and visitors could see them, by severely limiting parental visiting hours, and by insisting that the matron stop hitting the children. Within a few weeks, the matron resigned and a new matron was sought.[49] Despite its difficulties, the home operated continuously from its founding and ultimately thrived, largely through the efforts of the women who comprised its board of managers. The home cared for 112 children from its opening in 1855 to its formal transfer to male administration in 1874.

The JFH board faced repeated problems in educating its children, primarily because it refused to use the city's public schools. Committed to keeping the children in a Jewish environment, the managers always looked for a matron who could teach. The first matron, Henrietta Brown, taught Hebrew, English, and German, but she soon quit the post. After a futile nationwide search for a matron with similar abilities, the board decided to send the older boys to Leeser's Hebrew Education Society. Girls' education posed the real problem, because the managers judged the distance from the home to the HES building too far for girls to walk twice each day. As the home's population grew, this dilemma worsened. In an effort to find larger accommodations, the home twice relocated northward in the next few years, moving further from the HES building. In 1860 an English teacher was hired and a special education committee formed, comprised of Gratz, her niece Louisa, Mrs. Henry Cohen, Mrs. Abraham Hart, and Evelyn Bomeisler. The teacher received only one hundred dollars per year plus car fare, and financial difficulties soon forced her dismissal.

Financial Problems

Each of Gratz's organizations shared a common management style, reflecting Gratz's own blend of Jewish traditionalism and American values. The FHBS regularly received a portion of the proceeds of the annual Hebrew Benevolent Ball, but fund-raising remained a constant problem. The FHBS regularly reprinted its constitution with an updated list of donors and subscribers and circulated the list among potential donors. Later, the JFH did the same with its annual reports. As an added incentive to donors, the JFH report described each in-kind donation it received: a sack of carrots, a dollar for a bar mitzvah treat, a length of fabric, books, and mattresses.[50]

The JFH's annual meetings were designed to raise funds from the Jewish community. At these public events, children of the home recited lessons to display their education and general profit from the institution. To counter the impression that Mikveh Israel financed the JFH and to encourage all segments of Philadelphia Jewry to donate, the annual meetings soon rotated among the congregations. The clergy of the host congregation addressed the assembly, and all Jewish clergymen were invited to attend. In 1859 the annual meeting was held at Rodeph Shalom, called the "German synagogue," in 1862 at Beth Israel, the "Polish synagogue," in 1863 at Beth El Emeth, Isaac Leeser's synagogue that year, in 1864 at Keneseth Israel, the Reform synagogue led by David Einhorn, and in 1865 at Benai Israel, the "Netherlander synagogue."[51] By rotating the annual meetings among congregations, the JFH women tried to counter the widening divisions in the Jewish community. In serving all Jews, the JFH hoped to strengthen their sense of community.

Despite the fund-raising efforts of both the women on the board and the men on the council, the greatest problem the Jewish Foster Home faced was a lack of financial support from the Jewish community. Although the list of donors regularly numbered between three and five hundred people, the average donations were so small—most often only two dollars—that the home could not pay expenses.[52] Most of the managers belonged to Mikveh Israel, the city's oldest congregation, and many people believed that the home was under its protection. However, most of Philadelphia's Jewish families depended on small shopkeeping, artisanry or factory work, and peddling and could offer little toward communal charity. The intellectuals among them—rabbis, teachers, and publishers—certainly were not of the financial elite. Perhaps Jewish Philadelphians' proximity to poverty increased their concern for institutions to serve the needy, but the actual funding of those institutions proved formidable.[53]

Women's Nature and American Jewish Theology

Late in her life, Gratz saw American Jewish religious leaders
endorse a blend of American and Jewish ideas similar to her
own. Noting the success of Jewish women like Gratz in American
Jewish Sunday schools and independent charitable institutions,
Jewish male religious leaders also took up the linked issues of
virtue, religion, and women's natures. In 1858, Leeser printed
a sermon about virtue that had been preached by New York's
Rev. Dr. Fischel, who remarked that religion, humanity, charity,
and hope "unite to free our souls from servitude [forged by our
passions]." Fischel re-created the Talmudic argument that the
"evil inclination" in each of us can be disciplined and pressed
into God's service by our inclination for good. But unlike Talmud,
Fischel did not address his remarks exclusively to men by using
masculine pronouns and cases, addressing the women only by
implication; he also spoke directly to the women among his congregation. His message to them was the century's popular, prag-
matic justification for enhancing women's religious obligations.
"The daughters of Judah," he said, "are not, like men, engrossed
day by day in the pursuit of gain, and cannot, therefore, plead
the excuse of that pernicious influence which constant application
to commerce necessarily brings with it." (The presumption that
men would have greater control of their passions because they
had greater exposure to religion's influence through daily prayer
and study obligations, as was the case in the rabbinic world, was
absent from Fischel's remarks.) Accordingly, antebellum women
must influence men toward religion and self-control. In this way,
Protestant women and Jewish women ultimately ended up with
the same religious duty. They were to be the models and teachers
of religious virtue in their families.[54]

Logically, women could only become men's religious models
if their souls were at least equally holy. The *Occident* had already
popularized this idea among American Jews though Solomon Solis's remarks on Grace Aguilar's *Women of Israel* in 1846. Solis
agreed that Aguilar had "proved from biblical evidence the truth
of her assumptions that Judaism taught spiritual equality between men and women, setting different obligations on them only
because of the demands of earthly life." Solis claimed that any
Jewish man who thought his wife "as soulless as is the brute" was
"degraded" and "blind." He urged men who were "so inconsistent"

as to believe that "those who gave them birth had no claim to the immortality which they consider their own by right of birth" to reread the Bible. Obituaries for Jewish women commonly mentioned that the departed "should enjoy eternal happiness" and that she was "prepared for heaven."[55]

Traditionalists like Gratz, Leeser, Fischel, and Solis used the popular arguments for women's moral virtue to strengthen traditional Jewish observance in America. To them, insisting that women were fully equal to men in their eternal soul did not imply that religious rites differentiated by gender ought to be changed. They argued for continuing the separations between men and women in the synagogue by using Jewish traditions that saw passions as antithetical to religious enlightenment, the same premise that increased women's moral and religious authority at home.[56]

Although Gratz has to be classified as primarily a benevolent society woman, she readily adapted mission society and Sunday school techniques in developing her Hebrew Sunday School. Whatever her organization, throughout her life she maintained a network of close associates, all of whom agreed on the need for both Jewish charity and Jewish education. Along with her attitudes typical of American benevolence, evident in her concern about each petitioner's worthiness, she remained committed to a vision of a new epoch in Jewish history, one marked by freedom and dignity.

Personal Tragedies

Gratz's closest family ties were with her unmarried brothers, with whom she lived throughout her life. But in 1856 her brothers' health began to fail. Joseph had a bad cold, and Hyman suffered an attack of gout. Jacob, who was already lame, died that December 25, and Hyman passed away a month later, on January 27, 1857. Rebecca wrote to Benjamin, "What can I say to comfort you? Alas, we are deeply afflicted. . . . Our brothers have escaped from pain and suffering and infirmities . . . and gone to rest from their labors." Sharing with her brother the good wishes and condolences she heard from friends in Philadelphia, she continued, "Everybody sympathizes in our grief and testif[ies] to the worth of the departed. We can only bow submissively under the stroke of . . . Almighty power."[57]

Despite her grief, Gratz resisted withdrawing from social contacts and both maintained her correspondence with friends and relations and attended the consecration of a new synagogue in Baltimore.[58] Typical of her lifelong approach to grief, soon after her brothers' deaths Gratz urged the founding of a Jews' soup house to aid the "many . . . beggars who claim brotherhood in Israel."[59] A soup house especially for Jews would offer foods prepared according to Judaism's dietary laws and would enable the poorest Jews to maintain those basic religious obligations. But as far as we know, no soup house emerged.

When her niece Miriam faced the death of a child and of her father in 1857, Gratz told her that "nothing in this troubled life brings us nearer to God than the taking away from us of those so loved and cherished." She knew that it was not easy to adjust to loss, and tried to find some way to comfort everyone. Hoping to assuage the guilt that sometimes occurs with grief, she told Miriam that "the memory of duties performed . . . consoles us for all our losses." Moreover, she wrote that such memories would reward Miriam, "for [her] painful winter's journey" to her father would soften the "hurting scene when God took . . . [him]."[60]

Benjamin, her youngest brother, sent money to Philadelphia for Gratz and their sister Richea, who was by then nearly blind.[61] Appreciative, Gratz told her brother, "We have never known a want which our brothers have not been prompt to supply."[62] A severe economic depression in 1857 hurt the Gratz family business, exacerbating the blow resulting from the brothers' deaths. Gratz admitted that she was completely ignorant about the family business, but remarked that in Philadelphia "many rich men have been shorn of their wealth and hundreds of poor men and women thrown out of employ."[63] Joseph's death followed in October 1858, and Gratz asked Leeser to run the mourner's service for Joseph at her home.[64] Richea died the next month, November 22. Only Benjamin and Rebecca were left.

In the course of mourning their siblings, Gratz and her brother rebuilt the close relationship they had shared in youth. "Your letters . . . are the day spring of my life and make me feel young again," she wrote to Benjamin, who worried about his aged sister now living alone in Philadelphia.[65] She assured him that her health was "very good for one of my age" and that she had "affectionate companions." Nephew Horace Moses and young friend Julia Hoffman were "very kind," but life was not as it was. Even Judaism could not provide her with the solace she needed. "Passover . . . formally [*sic*] so joyful is changed by the memories of the departed."[66] Yom Kippur, the Day of Atonement with its memorial service, better suited her mood. Gratz promised her sister-in-law Ann that she would remember her "in the house of prayer."[67]

When her old friend Washington Irving died in 1859, Gratz wrote to Benjamin that she was glad to see him "descended to the Tomb full of honors and glory." Nonetheless, she felt sad that so few of his early friends, especially Irving's close friend Joseph Gratz, were left to "give a heart offering to the general mourning."[68] Only one more calamity could deepen her grief, and that was about to happen. The Civil War plunged Gratz into despair for her country and into deep concern for her remaining family members, particularly her beloved niece, Savannah resident Miriam Moses Cohen.

9

Gratz's Last Years
and Legacy

"The crowning happiness of my days has been my
association with . . . my beloved companions [the
teachers and managers of the Sunday school] in the
duties we shared together. . . . [M]y last wish [is for]
the prosperity of the Jewish Sunday School."
REBECCA GRATZ, 1862

In her ninth decade, Gratz reluctantly reduced the time
she put into her organizations, limiting her concentration to her
remaining family, to the children of old friends, and to religious
worship. She slowly handed over leadership of her organizations to
younger women. By the time she retired from the Jewish Foster
Home in 1866 it was well organized, with standing committees
for admission, indenturing, education, clothing, and purchasing.
In June 1860 Gratz visited Savannah and was satisfied that her
niece Miriam was well cared for and enjoyed a happy marriage.
She wrote to her brother Benjamin that "Dear Miriam looks in full
health and is the picture of contentment—no one can be happier
in the domestic sense or more grateful to the Almighty giver of all
good than she is—truly Mr. Cohen repays her tenderness and our
great regard."[1]

Guiding Family and Community during National Conflict

Gratz outlived nearly all her friends and family, and in her
later years her closest associates were the children of late friends
and relations. In a letter to Ann, Gratz consoled herself with the
thought that "God permits us to hope for a reunion in another
world . . . [and] while I linger here . . . I [have] the love of [my

225

family and friends'] children."[2] Her beloved niece, Miriam Moses Cohen, remained an affectionate companion despite the distance that separated them. Gratz wrote to Miriam that she was "always sure of meeting your tender love and sympathy in all the cares and sorrows of my life . . . [because] in your young days your heart was schooled for the afterlife."[3] When Julia Hoffman died in April 1861, Gratz explained her grief to Benjamin: "Oh, My Dear Brother, the loss of her society is to me a trial to be borne by the conviction that her whole life was a preparation for a happy futurity, and her death the death of the righteous—her love and care of me could only be appreciated by those who witnessed it, and was continued to the last hour."[4] After Julia's death, Gratz thanked Solomon Cohen, Miriam's husband, for his condolences in an unusually garbled sentence that attests to her troubled emotions. "Your just appreciation of our beloved friend is very grateful to my feelings," she wrote. "I have indeed been sorely tried."[5]

Along with his condolences, Solomon Cohen also sent Gratz clippings from newspapers about events in Savannah that swept the Cohens along in the country's turmoil.[6] In 1861, Miriam had written despairingly to Gratz airing her foreboding that history would soon be writing the epitaph to the United States. "Here lies a people who in seeking the liberty of the negro, lost their own," she believed it would read.[7]

Miriam was outraged by the indictment of the southern way of life frequently found in the pages of newspapers, magazines, and fiction published in the North. She believed the attack on southern culture proved that "sickly sentimentality"—a phrase often used by southern polemicists to describe the antislavery movement in the North[8]—had enveloped "every class of [northern] society." Moreover, she believed that the cultural war against the South was part of a concerted effort to "incite the poor [and] uproot the foundations of . . . the Southern social system." She explained to her aunt that although southerners found the North's "system of white labor, with all its oppression and wrongs . . . abhorrent," they refrained from writing books and delivering sermons aimed at destroying the North's economic structure. In Cohen's view, that restraint on the part of southerners proved their moral superiority to northerners. Her position reiterated ideas widely echoed in southern newspapers and political speeches between 1840 and the end of the Civil War.[9] Despite her own Unionist political convictions, Gratz kept silent on politics when writing to Miriam.

Although Gratz found that her "heart was sick with every days account of wrongs and outrages," with Miriam's letters "before me I can look into [your] own loving heart."[10] Indeed, Gratz's "one great consolation" was that between herself and Miriam "there was no war in our own hearts."[11]

War placed Gratz in a state of "constant agitation," she explained to Benjamin's wife, Ann. Although a Unionist, Gratz detested the way the war tore apart families and friends. "Every day," she wrote, she heard of an "account of wrongs and outrages perpetrated by kindred on each other—of familiar friends becoming bitter foes."[12] The Non-Intercourse Law, passed in 1861, limited communication between North and South and interfered with her correspondence with Miriam, so Gratz asked individuals with special travel passes to convey letters for her. But travel across the Mason-Dixon Line was sharply curtailed, and six months sometimes passed between letters from her niece in Savannah. Gratz told her sister-in-law Ann that she didn't think it was fair for this law "to exist between us. . . . I had a rare treat of a letter from Miriam Cohen through a private opportunity. . . . [It is] sad when the natural flow of familiar intercourse is to be either stolen or only accidentally enjoyed."[13] She lamented not just for her own family, but for "our late happy country."[14] It seemed to Gratz that America's promise of a new era of peace and freedom might not be realized.

In August 1861, only five months after the start of the Civil War, Benjamin's son Cary, a soldier in the Union army, was killed in battle at Wilson's Creek. Gratz wrote to Cary's stepmother that the "outrages perpetrated by kindred on each other . . . [are] too appalling to be realized."[15] Gratz comforted Benjamin with the hope that he would be reunited with his son in another world.[16] But Union victories would not make Gratz happy. "I have so many dear [ones] scattered over the land," she explained to Ann. Gratz's nephew Charles E. Etting, who wrote to her during his training at West Point in 1861, fought in battles at Fredericksburg, Chancellorsville, and Gettysburg.[17] To Ann, she detailed her dilemma, as she watched those she loved, and who loved one other, arm themselves against each other. "I have been reading some loving letters from some so near to me in blood and affections whose arms are perhaps now raised against those hearts at which they have fed."[18] By the end of 1861, Gratz had "no faith in politicians" and thought only "Divine Providence" could convince national leaders that it was wrong to be "shedding Brothers blood in this unholy war."[19]

The following year she quit discussing politics with Confederate sympathizers, after Benjamin had admitted to her that he behaved similarly. Learning of the nascent women's movement and the outspoken political activities of younger women like Angelina Grimke, Lucretia Mott, and Elizabeth Cady Stanton, Gratz commented to Benjamin that, especially in "such time of trouble," it was "monstrous" for women to "step out of the sphere god designed [them] to fill."[20] After all, she told Ann, "There is much more beauty in performing our duty than in any other accomplishment."[21]

Once again, Gratz's organizations provided her with both companionship and gratification, offering a creative use of her talents and energies that enabled her to withstand losses and strains in her family life while avoiding the political tragedy that engulfed the nation. In 1860, when there were eight thousand Jews in Philadelphia, the Jewish Foster Home (JFH) annual reports no longer claimed to be the only American institution exclusively for the protection of Jewish children,[22] since a small number of similar institutions had emerged in Jewish areas around the country.[23] Nonetheless, the JFH continued to receive applications for Jewish children outside Philadelphia. In addition, the JFH board was pressed by the need to find a new matron, though they advertised in *New York Herald* as well as locally.[24] Many applicants were women whom Gratz considered "quite young . . . and of course . . . not . . . proper to undertake so responsible a duty."[25]

A new plan to provide the home with a more secure financial footing asked donors to promise contributions for three years, and despite its difficulties, the home thrived.[26] By 1860, when the home cared for twenty-four children, the annual report confidently claimed that the JFH "will always stand as a proud and glorious evidence of the kindness, love, and charity of the daughters of Israel."[27] Despite confident prose, financial crises were real. In 1863, on a motion from Louisa Gratz, the JFH board asked Louisa's brother Simon Gratz "to use his influence in [obtaining] an appropriation of three thousand dollars from the State Legislature."[28] But during the Civil War, Pennsylvania's funds were hardly more plentiful than private donations.

The financial constraints limited the home's educational resources. By 1862 the managers of the JFH found that the children were "very deficient" in arithmetic—that year's matron taught only reading, map reading, writing, and Scriptures. Hoping that improved discipline would lead to improved learning, Louisa Gratz wrote a list of rules for school management. Two years later, after Sabato Morais urged the managers to find a professional teacher, and after Gratz and Louisa provided the teacher's yearly wage, a search committee hired Juliet De La Motta on the condition that she become qualified to teach Hebrew as quickly as possible.[29]

As the children cared for by the JFH grew older, apprenticing loomed as the managers' next task. As early as 1857, they had decided to seek apprenticeships for twelve-year-olds and to inform parents of their children's placements afterward. Whenever possible, managers arranged mechanical trades for boys and indenturing as housekeepers for girls, although two sisters were apprenticed to the home to train them as teachers and matrons. Most indentures lasted five years. The first placements were informal agreements with men among the managers' own associates. Manager Matilda (Mrs. Henry) Cohen convinced her husband, a successful stationer and engraver, to take one boy. By 1863, however, the board had formally established a committee to arrange apprenticeships.[30] In both Europe and the United States, Jewish children were kept within the community by apprenticing them to other Jewish families.[31]

The women managers of Gratz's institutions developed administrative skills under her tutelage and often extended their commitments from Jewry to national needs, especially during the Civil War years. By the 1860s, many of those women embraced a variety of community responsibilities. In 1863, for example, Matilda Cohen was elected a delegate to the U.S. Sanitary Commission, which organized women around the country to supply bandages, clothing, and knitted goods for Union soldiers. More than 250 of Philadelphia's Jewish women joined the Ladies Hebrew Relief Association for Sick and Wounded Soldiers under Cohen's leadership. At the 1864 Sanitary Fair in Philadelphia, Cohen, Louisa Gratz, and other local Jewish women served on many committees.[32]

In her eighties, Gratz viewed her own birthdays "as solemn warnings . . . to prepare . . . for another state of being."[33] Niece Miriam urged Gratz to continue to find satisfaction in her organizational activities and to judge her life a success. Practicing the humility she thought God required of her, Gratz agreed only that she had been "given duties to perform" and that she had been "sustained by a merciful providence." Because she had been "allotted" more time than the biblical threescore and ten years, she would try to be thankful. It would be "ungrateful . . . to misreact at my destiny," she wrote.[34] Perhaps to console Gratz for her losses, and no doubt recognizing that her life was nearly over, the younger women of her organizations began to find occasions to tell Gratz of their great regard for her as a person and as a mentor. On Gratz's eighty-third birthday, sixty-one-year-old Louisa Hart wrote in ponderous prose of her "reverential affection and respect" for Gratz. "How shall we thank our God who grants to us living examples of truth and holiness to dwell in our midst?" Hart expounded. She begged Gratz to find room in her "fernery" for Hart's gift—a plant—and room in her heart for Hart herself.[35]

Miriam, fearing that Gratz would die while the Civil War still thwarted their communication, in 1864 managed to have a letter stamped "Flag of Truce." In it, Miriam wished her "Precious Aunt" birthday greetings, and then conveyed the sad news that her daughter Cecilia had died.[36] Soon afterward Gratz learned that her old friend Gertrude Meredith was near death. From the Sisters of Charity Hospital in St. Louis, Meredith wrote, "I shall never forget you, nor in life, nor in death. I shall pray for Israel's redemption."[37] Meredith's last letter to Gratz arrived with a note from a younger woman who explained that Meredith had died of heart failure, but had so praised Gratz that the young woman herself hoped to establish her own friendship with Gratz.[38]

As the war abated, Benjamin too made a special effort to visit his sister for her eighty-third birthday. Benjamin's wife allowed herself to hope that calm would soon return to Kentucky and that her family's welfare would be assured for the future. "Things are quiet, No Raids! I hope this fearful war is nearly over," Ann wrote. She thanked Gratz for gifts she sent west during the war, telling her that her daughter Miriam resembled Gratz. "God bless you dear sister from the heart of your loving sister Ann," she concluded gratefully.[39]

Gratz's more than sixty years of communal service were drawing to a close. On October 31, 1864, she wrote a letter to Louisa Hart in which she explained that she felt herself "unable to perform the duties of the Superintendent of the HSS" and asked that she be allowed to resign the position so that a younger member of the board of managers might be appointed. At eighty-three, Gratz felt she could no longer give the "attention necessary to insure the continued usefulness" of the HSS.[40] But it was with enormous reluctance that she stepped down. Only two years earlier, she had commented that "the crowning happiness of my days has been my association with my beloved companions [the teachers and managers of the HSS] in the duties we have shared together." Whatever she may have felt about her responsibilities as leader at the beginnings of the HSS, by the time she retired Gratz believed that its women managers "granted me the privilege of a leader" solely because she was the eldest. However, she did not consider herself their senior in abilities. "In all sincerity and truth," she wrote to them, "I disclaim any preeminence in the holy task so dear to us all—of leading our infant charges to the fountain of living waters." She asked that the women remember her as one whose "last wish was [for] the prosperity of the Jewish Sunday School."[41]

Because she shouldered less onerous responsibilities at the JFH, she stayed on its board another year. Gratz's final year there was 1865, when the JFH received five hundred dollars from the Pennsylvania State Legislature.[42] By then, the war was over, the Union had survived, and Gratz soon received reassuring letters from her family. Ann wrote to Gratz that life in Kentucky was returning to normal, and Kentuckians were returning from Canada and elsewhere. In Lexington, Transylvania College was flourishing.[43] With the smooth delivery of the mails restored, Sarah Gratz Moses Joseph wrote weekly from Montreal, assuring Gratz that "Your love, my darling aunt, is the treasure of my life—it warmed my orphan heart when God saw fit to remove my mother—and it has burnt steadily on without changes or diminution—and each year of my life I feel its influence."[44]

As if to illustrate Gratz's belief that respect for Judaism would grow in the United States, in 1866 both the University of Pennsylvania in Philadelphia and Columbia University in New York added to their curriculum courses in rabbinic literature taught by Jews.[45] These two cities were home to the largest Jewish populations in America. While the schools no doubt sought to draw students and financial support from the Jewish population, Gratz saw the move as a confirmation of her belief that the highest levels of American society would respect Judaism if Jews "reverence their religion."

In 1867, just two years before Gratz's death, the JFH administration printed a new constitution, which said that "the ladies
of several congregations" were in charge. After the success of
their earlier three-year donation plan, in 1867 the men on the
board of council directed a massive membership campaign asking
donors to promise contributions for five years. By increasing the
number of donors and participants to include Jews from all congregations, the council ensured the home's financial security until
1873.[46]

On August 27, 1869, Rebecca Gratz died, almost a year after
the death of Isaac Leeser, her compatriot and teacher. Rachel's
daughters, Rebecca, Miriam, and Sarah, were with her at the end.
Her will disbursed her estate, which totaled $38,855.48, mostly
in railroad stock and U.S. bonds, to her brother Benjamin and
her remaining nieces and nephews.[47] But her institutions, which
thrived long after her death, were her real legacy. After the Civil
War, Gratz's Jewish communal institutions grew even more important to American Jewish life than they had been before the war.
For the women who staffed these institutions, they confirmed the
hope that Jewish women could make a place for themselves and
for Judaism within American culture. By training younger Jewish
women in administering the agencies she founded, Gratz had
ensured that the Female Hebrew Benevolent Society, the Hebrew
Sunday School, and the Jewish Foster Home would continue to
flourish long after her death. In their work, these organizations
continued to provide Jewish women and children a way to be both
fully Jewish and fully American, and to resist the redoubled efforts
of evangelists.[48]

The Hebrew Sunday School: Growth after Gratz

Most benevolent organizations founded by antebellum
women were short-lived. Despite the fact that many nineteenth-
century schools, hospitals, and orphanages traced their origins
to women's benevolence, few women's organizations lasted more
than ten years. By contrast, Gratz's Jewish organizations—the
FHBS and the HSS—remained active for more than 150 years, and
the JFH thrived until it merged with later institutions for Jewish
children in Philadelphia. Gratz's understanding of the needs of
American Jews, along with her organizational abilities, ensured
her work's remarkable durability.

In 1870, a year after Gratz's death, the student population of the HSS dropped to 150 because of an epidemic and severe winter storms. But two years later, under the administration of Ellen Phillips, a branch opened at Twelfth and Chestnut Streets, south of Touro Hall, closer to another Jewish neighborhood. By December of that year, the society counted "nearly double the number we had when the division of the school was made, and every week we have new applicants for admission." Ten teachers and a librarian worked at the Twelfth Street school and sixteen teachers and a librarian at the Seventh Street site.[49] Teachers who saw pupils lacking warm clothing and who heard accounts of destitution and hardship often provided personal charity or referred the families to the FHBS or other charitable societies.

The Twelfth Street school soon proved the most innovative. Classes in trades—carpentry for boys and sewing for girls—were offered on Sunday afternoons. In 1873, under the direction of Rebecca Moss, a school for younger children opened there. This "Infant Class" soon proved so successful that another opened at the Seventh and Wood Streets school.[50] In 1880, the HSS women opened a Rebecca Gratz Sewing School, run by Gratz's niece Laura Mordecai, at Tenth and South Streets. By 1880 two more schools opened, one at Fifth and Parish Streets and one on Lake Street in Port Richmond, both new areas of Jewish immigrant settlement. When, in 1891, Touro Hall reopened northward at Tenth and Carpenter to accommodate eastern European immigrants settled there, the HSS offered classes there, too. By 1908 the HSS operated eight schools, and by 1943, twenty-two schools, all in the Philadelphia area, served over forty-five hundred students. The HSS remained the city's largest institution for Jewish education until after World War II, when private congregational schools flourished in suburban neighborhoods.[51]

Two Philadelphia rabbis had stepped in to advise the HSS faculty after Leeser's death in 1868. Sabato Morais, minister at Mikveh Israel after Leeser, probably was more actively involved in the school than any other minister in the city, and he always delivered the opening prayer at annual exams. In his eulogy for Gratz in 1869, Morais suggested that a special class designed to counter the arguments of Christian evangelists be set up to teach the "correct meaning of various Scriptural passages"—passages "on which the adherents of a creed antagonistic to [ours] strive to build their stronghold, to the ruin of our time-honored religious fabric." His conviction that the HSS served as a countermissionary force led to his forming a Bible class for graduates in 1873, with thirty to forty students. The American Sunday School Union also used the Bible as the text for their oldest students. In bringing parity to the religious knowledge of Jewish and Christian young people of the same age, Morais hoped to make sure that Jewish youths would not be left religiously defenseless among their Christian peers, some of whom were already experiencing conversion and learning to evangelize.[52] By 1878, Morais's Hebrew class was reading and translating eleven chapters of Genesis and six of Exodus. Some HSS students also worked with Jewish clergy during the week, probably in bar mitzvah preparation. Three years later, Morais offered Hebrew-language lessons at the HSS, as did the librarian, Mr. Weisenstein, and one of the superintendents, probably Simha Peixotto, who also taught Hebrew at the JFH. The next year the HSS teachers asked Morais to teach a special class for them, and he agreed.[53]

In 1874, Rev. George Jacobs, minister at Beth El Emeth, took an active interest in the school and produced a new catechism to replace Rachel Peixotto Pyke's *Scriptural Questions.* Jacobs became a regular figure at the annual exams, generally giving an address or offering the closing prayer. Fifty students worked with four teachers on "German Hebrew," called a "Sacred language" in the annual report. It is unclear whether this term described the dialect of Hebrew used in the German synagogues, not used by Morais, or if it was simply a fanciful rendering of Yiddish, a language generally considered a mix of Hebrew and German.[54]

Another HSS activity formalized after Gratz's death was, as the superintendent's report for 1878 said, "creat[ing] able teachers." HSS policy continued to emphasize the importance of establishing an emotional bond between faculty and students, and rewards included tales like *Hans Brinker,* given to Leah Goldsmith in 1885 for "punctual attendance and perfect recitations."[55] Through that bond, HSS faculty hoped to inspire graduating women to return as teachers and to motivate students to promote Jewish education as adults. Most notable of the latter was Cyrus Adler, later president of both Dropsie College of Hebrew and Cognate Language Studies and the Jewish Theological Seminary, and a guiding force for the Jewish Publication Society.[56]

Although there was some ambivalence about women teaching religion even among their supporters, it never was a significant threat to the HSS in Philadelphia. When George Jacobs was asked to teach the teacher's study group in 1877, he declined, unsure if it was proper. But by the 1880 annual exam, his address to the graduates asked the boys to continue their studies and encouraged the girls to "remember that upon them will mainly depend the preservation of our faith; for it is in the family circle, where woman exercises the highest influence, that religion can become an object of reverence."[57]

By the late 1870s, leadership training within the HSS was nearly programmatic, as former students became teachers and teachers became managers. In 1878 the teachers formed an adjunct unit, the Teachers Association. Both the society and the association worked to advance the Sunday school, but now their efforts were organized according to their specialties. Teachers focused more directly on classroom needs, while managers concentrated on fund-raising and allocation, book publishing, and overall governance. The managers of the Sunday school were the first source of substitute teachers, so they also knew the day-to-day condition in the classrooms. The Teachers Association made monthly reports to the managers, advising and requesting according to the needs they saw. Teachers and managers kept communication open and contact close.[58] Although by 1911 perhaps a third of the faculty members were men, women's education and leadership remained key priorities.[59]

During the latter part of the nineteenth century, the HSS sought to increase the Jewish content in the curriculum. In 1901, Rabbi Julius Greenstone, a graduate of New York's Jewish Theological Seminary, wrote a text for the HSS in which he noted that the HSS provided for "the religious education of more than three thousand pupils, most of whom [were] children of observant parents." Since 1881, increasing Jewish immigration to the United States from Russia and other countries of eastern Europe had been changing the face of American Jewish communities. Many in this group were traditionally observant Jews who maintained all the ritual details of a fully observant Jewish life. For children of these families, the faculty of the school "felt the need of a text-book that would treat all the laws and customs, as well as the principles of ethics and religion." In response, Greenstone "tried to cast light upon most of the religious practices of the home, and also on some of the ceremonies observed in the synagogue."[60] His text began with instructions for domestic celebrations such as the Sabbath and festivals. Consistent with traditional Ashkenazic observance, it insisted on abstention from "anything that requires physical exertion," travel, or business on the Sabbath, and on keeping two-day celebrations of the festivals. Brief discussions of fasts, festivals, benedictions, ritual objects and their use, dietary laws, and ethical duties were also included.[61]

Greenstone's book shows how far the school had come from the simple bibliocentric orthodoxy of its early classes, but it does not denote any change in intent or religious philosophy. The school's continuing goal was to provide an education in traditional Judaism for Jewish children with little time to spare. In 1916, the Society published a hymnal for the school's use. From 1880 through the 1950s, to further block access to Jewish youth by Christian missionaries, the HSS offered classes in English, stenography, bookkeeping, millinery, cigar making, plumbing, dressmaking, and telegraphy, where students obtained religious instruction in Judaism while learning a trade.[62] In 1986, almost 150 years after its founding, a still thriving Hebrew Sunday School merged with the Talmud Torah schools of Philadelphia, which offered Jewish children a more extensive religious education.

The struggle throughout the nineteenth century to find or create a trained faculty plagued not only the HSS but also the Hebrew Education Society and other institutions of Jewish education. No doubt influenced by his sister, Hyman Gratz entered into a deed of trust with the Pennsylvania Company for Insurance of Lives and Granting Annuities in 1856 that provided that income from his estate left after the death of his heirs would be used to establish a college for the education of Jews in Philadelphia. In 1893, after the death of Hyman Gratz's heirs, adopted son Robert Gratz and nephew Horace Moses, Hyman's estate transferred to Mikveh Israel. The trustees decided to design a curriculum especially for teachers in Jewish schools. Named Gratz College, it opened its doors with a catalog of Jewish history, literature, religion, and Hebrew-language study in 1897.[63] Today Gratz College continues to train religious schoolteachers and offers graduate degrees in Jewish studies.

The Jewish Foster Home: Later Growth

While the HSS grew steadily with a largely volunteer staff, for the more costly JFH, growth meant new financial burdens.

In 1874, with thirty-nine children in an overcrowded home, a financial crisis again struck the Jewish Foster Home. This time the administration of the home was formally handed over to the men of the council, under the direction of Abraham Hart, brother of Louisa B. Hart. The council renamed the institution the Jewish Foster Home and Orphan Asylum (JFH & OA) and placed women on an associate board, which supervised the children in the residence. Associate board members also sat on the five major committees. Men held the majority on all committees. JFH & OA meetings were open to both men and women, and women were able to speak and participate fully in meetings, but the officers were elected only from among the male managers.[64]

This transition was less dramatic than it first appears. Many of the same families still formed the core of the home's leadership. Isidore Binswanger, for example, who held the presidency of the home for many years, had begun as a member of the board of council while women of his family were members of the managing board. Nonetheless, with the transition to male leadership, the JFH & OA became more like the smaller men's mutual aid societies, which expected the women of their families to provide aid in sewing and other domestic matters to their beneficiaries. The home's internal supervision changed from matron leadership to governance by a married couple who served as superintendent and matron.

The new leaders of the home were more comfortable with a two-parent model of governance. Unlike the traveling male merchants of Gratz's own home, the new German leadership was composed largely of artisans, intellectuals, and small businessmen who had little experience with absent fathers. Moreover, they had emigrated from European Jewish communities led by a kahal, a male enterprise that coordinated charitable societies. In the kahal system, men's and women's responsibilities for charity were distinct but complementary, yet male leadership overall was the rule.

In soliciting funds, later publications of the JFH & OA often mentioned the "house of Israel," a traditional phrase that evoked dreams of peaceful, cooperative unity among Jews and, in the 1870s, echoed Lincoln's warnings about a house divided against itself. American political discussions about reconstruction of the South after the Civil War made men's involvement in local charities part of a new general discourse among American men about social welfare. The reports and constitutions of the JFH & OA implied that by contributing to their new family-style home with male leadership, American Jews would help poor children, the Jewish community, and America as a nation, as well as please God by performing their religious obligation of tzedakah.

The transfer to male administration kept the home financially secure.[65] In 1881 the JFH & OA moved to a bigger house on Mill Street in Germantown. The home flourished, and in 1929 it merged with the thirty-year-old Home for Hebrew Orphans, ultimately, in 1941, joining other Philadelphia Jewish family charities in the Association for Jewish Children.[66] Gratz's first Jewish organization, the FHBS, also continued to thrive and, in 1885, helped to organize the Young Women's Union, an agency designed to make the children of eastern European Jewish immigrants, more than a million of whom arrived in America between 1880 and 1924, into "good American citizens."[67]

Thirty-six years after Gratz's death, Philadelphia Jewish women founded a service to care for poor pregnant Jewish women and working girls, which they called the Rebecca Gratz Club. Five years later, by 1909, they had established the Rebecca Gratz House, a residence for these women, at 532 Spruce Street in Philadelphia.[68] By 1958 the Rebecca Gratz House had become a nonsectarian halfway house for young women with emotional problems, offering "opportunities for socialization and the warmth of a homelike atmosphere,"[69] and by 1964 it was run completely by a professional staff of social workers.[70]

Gratz was not forgotten by Philadelphia's Jews. Jewish women emigrating from Europe did not expect to lead men either in religion or in charity, yet Gratz's American domestic vision held women accountable for leadership. Through the FHBS, the HSS and the JFH, Gratz showed the newcomers that in America religious and communal leadership were women's duties.[71] Especially in the HSS, where many of Philadelphia's Jewish immigrants sent their daughters, Jewish girls learned from women who modeled new public roles for them. The school echoed popular sentiment when it taught its students to revere its founder, Gratz.

10

The Legend of
Rebecca Gratz

For more than 150 years, much of American Jewish interest in Rebecca Gratz hinged not on her public leadership, which was exemplary, but on a sentimentalized version of her life, what we might call the Gratz "legend." This legend, which began circulating as early as 1821, asserted that Gratz, out of devotion to her faith, refused to marry a gentile man, despite their mutual love, and instead remained single throughout her life, thereby serving as the inspiration for Sir Walter Scott's character Rebecca of York in his popular novel *Ivanhoe*. This legend has cloaked Gratz's life in sentimentality. An analysis of the popular versions of the Gratz legend can reveal how other Americans, Jews and non-Jews, men and women, used Gratz's story to assuage their fears and solve dilemmas posed by Jewish life in America.[1] Tracing Gratz's legend through its various forms and transformations requires placing it within the contexts of ideologies about women and Jews in America since the antebellum era.

The Gratz legend usually centers around Rebecca's self-denial and faithfulness to Judaism as a young woman. Like most legends, its details differ from telling to telling. One account identified Gratz's Christian lover as Henry Clay.[2] Another claimed that it was Washington Irving, who supposedly informed Scott

about Gratz after meeting her as she nursed Matilda Hoffman
at the girl's deathbed.[3] A third argued that Gratz's lover was
Samuel Ewing, the man cited in most versions of the legend, whom
Gratz refused to marry, claiming that she was too young, despite
being two years older than Ewing.[4] Many articles and essays, and
even a novel, have reported various versions of the Gratz legend
throughout the twentieth century.[5]

Gratz's unmarried life baffled those who most directly con-
formed to established Jewish traditions. Historically, Jewish law
discouraged delayed marriage, and Jewish rituals and customs
valorized marriage as "normal, exemplary, and sanctified." Judaism views lifelong celibacy as an aberration among women and
forbids it among men.[6] Although Gratz devoted her life to Jewish
community service and religious education, she did not fulfill what
most Jews, including some descendants of her own family, considered her first responsibility: to establish and nurture a Jewish
family. Because Gratz's real life did not conform to accepted standards, while nonetheless making her a respected and well-known
figure, her relatives and contemporaries may have originated the
legend out of circumstantial evidence and rumor.

The legend was already in circulation when the largest Jewish immigration to the United States began in 1881. Jews arriving
in the United States in the late nineteenth and early twentieth
centuries carried with them ideas of yichus. Among these immigrants, the observant Jews were more punctilious about their
religious life than most American Jews ever had been. When
these Jews heard the Gratz legend, they saw a woman acculturated to gentile society who had nonetheless dedicated her life
to Judaism. Even more confusing, she was a beautiful woman
with family yichus who had remained single. By the standards
of traditional society, she lost yichus by not marrying. In a society with marriage brokers, as in the European Jewish world,
she would have had to refuse suitors deliberately and repeatedly,
thereby throwing her parents' future security and her own religious virtue into question. Yet Gratz was reputed to have been a
dutiful and pious daughter; Gratz embodied the questions America posed to acculturating Jewish women. The legend offered these
women a way to make Gratz's life meaningful and understandable
to them.

By the time increasing numbers of religiously observant
Jews arrived in the United States in the late nineteenth century,

the legend already had begun to overshadow Gratz's actual accomplishments. The impressive facts of Gratz's community leadership were overlooked and the myth explaining her single life was printed in magazines, newspapers, books, and exhibition texts, told and retold to adults and children, in story and drama. Perhaps the Jewish men and women new to America found intimate questions about Jewish domesticity more interesting, and more urgent, than the histories of public institutions.

Throughout the nineteenth century, Americans faced new and confusing alternatives in lifestyles, and immigrants and other groups utilized a variety of languages, family styles, and religious perspectives to adapt to the changes. In the second half of the nineteenth century, women wanted to vote, to attend college, to be trained in the professions, and to have a choice about focusing their energies toward homemaking and family care.[7] By the last decades of the nineteenth century, between 40 and 60 percent of all college-educated women never married; among uneducated women, only 10 percent stayed single.[8] These changes ushered in new perspectives on the roles of men and women in American society.

The ideal of romantic marriage was espoused in stories in which romantic love triumphed over all problems—parental opposition, poverty, the potential groom's bad character, and religious differences. Moreover, in popular romantic literature and folklore, each woman "knew" that she had only one true love, and that she had to wait patiently for him to find her.[9] By contrast, in *Ivanhoe,* Scott's image of a virtuous woman refusing to marry the man she loved out of respect for her father's concern about the lover's religious differences illustrates a striking alternative to the concept of love found in popular literature. Jews acculturating into a society promoting romance-based marriage liked to believe that Scott's novel was partly based on the real life of an American Jewish woman, as the Gratz legend allowed them to reconcile their traditional views on domesticity with the new romantic ideology.

The Tale

The Gratz legend's circulation illustrates how individuals close to Gratz interpreted her life. The earliest record of the legend was written in a letter from Rachel Mordecai Lazarus to Maria Edgeworth, the British novelist and educator, in 1821. Lazarus told Edgeworth that Rebecca Gratz was the inspiration for Rebecca of York. Although Edgeworth knew Scott, she had not previously heard this account.[10] The story also circulated by word of mouth during Gratz's lifetime, making her something of a local celebrity. Members of Lazarus's family resented Gratz's fame for overshadowing that of Lazarus.[11]

Sabato Morais presented his own vision of Gratz at her funeral and expanded his eulogy of her at a speech to the Hebrew Sunday School Society shortly after her death. He described Gratz as a woman for whom reason and duty triumphed over emotion.[12] Working with Gratz regularly for most of her last years, Morais watched her struggle with grief and loneliness as nearly all of her family, and many of her friends, passed away. He believed the legend fit the pattern of her character.

In 1872, three years after Gratz's death, her niece Sarah Mordecai wrote *Recollections of My Aunt,* a brief and loving portrait of Gratz. "I was taught to consider her perfect," she wrote, hoping her book would teach younger relations to do likewise.[13] Mordecai claimed that the Ewing family believed that Gratz and Sam Ewing had continued to love each other all their lives, and she depicted the pair as star-crossed lovers. Ewing's granddaughter had commented that Gratz demonstrated her love during her visit to his coffin, on which she placed three roses and a miniature of herself. So romantic a gesture was quite out of character for Gratz, Ewing's granddaughter said, unless she still treasured her past love. Mordecai published a short version of her memoir of Gratz in the local press.[14]

Gratz's letters, however, suggest that her visit to Ewing's coffin was prompted by nostalgia for the lost friends of her youth, rather than undying romance. She had been friends with three Ewing siblings—Peggy, Amelia, and Samuel—all of whom died relatively young; thus the three roses. The miniature had been painted when Gratz was in her early twenties, when she was close to all three. Since none of her letters mention a special sadness at his death, we may conclude that friendship and not romance lay behind the symbolism of her visit to Ewing's coffin.[15]

The Gratz legend also seemed useful to Gratz's descendants who may have wanted to restore luster to their family's name after their influence had waned. In the *Century Magazine* of May 1882, an article by Gratz van Renssalaer titled "The Original of Rebecca in *Ivanhoe*" illustrated another sentimentalized version of Gratz's life. In the article, van Renssalaer repeated and embellished the earlier Gratz legend. Gratz had been chosen by Scott for her "gentle and benevolent spirit, instinctive refinement," and "innate purity," and because she inspired affection in everyone who knew her, he wrote. In a gesture toward biographical accuracy, van Renssalaer illustrated Gratz's "goodness and abilities" with a list of women's charitable societies that she had founded or led. According to van Renssalaer, Scott chose Gratz because she remained true to Judaism and refused to marry a non-Jewish man despite her deep love for him: "It is said that, when a young lady, Rebecca won the regard of a gentleman of character, position, and wealth whose passion was devotedly returned. . . . Her firmness in the strife between inclination and duty may be considered an index of the exalted character of the woman."[16]

Perhaps closer to van Renssalaer's real intention, the essay emphasized Gratz's close association with prestigious American non-Jews such as Henry Clay, Washington Irving, and James Paulding. Van Renssalaer presents the apparent circumstances of Scott's choice of Rebecca Gratz as the model for *Ivanhoe:* Irving actually visited Scott in 1817 while Ivanhoe was being formulated. But the supposed content of that historic conversation between Irving and Scott did not appear in print until the early twentieth century. According to these later accounts, discussed below, Irving sang Gratz's praises and so impressed Scott with his depiction of Gratz that Scott used Irving's description as the model for Rebecca, even using Gratz's real name. Scott supposedly sent Irving a copy of the book along with a note that asked, "How do you like your Rebecca? Does the Rebecca I have pictured compare well with the pattern given?"[17]

No one has ever found this note, though Scott's biographers have searched for it.[18] Nor do any letters between Gratz and Maria Fenno Hoffman mention any communication about Gratz between Irving and Scott. Irving was engaged to Maria Hoffman's stepdaughter Matilda until her early death. If Irving wrote neither to Gratz nor her brother Joseph, also his friend, about the rumored conversation, Gratz might have learned about it from Hoffman.

There is little to support the idea that an unfulfilled love affair was the pivotal experience of Gratz's life. Only one poem by Gratz, written on birch bark, declares her love for someone whom "the stern hand of religion" denied her. "Composure will be my mask of truth," she wrote, and with that mask she would get herself "a heart of ease." It was that "heart of ease," a refrain repeated four times, that was most precious to Gratz.[19] Though she had many "admirers," as she called them, none of her letters declare love or even a guarded desire to marry anyone. All we know is that she once remarked that James Paulding had the makings of an "agreeable domestic companion," that she preferred literary men to business men, and that many such men were friends she shared with her brother Joseph.[20]

And yet, despite the evocations, rumors, and denials, the legend has become an integral part of what many consider "real" knowledge about Gratz. In 1892 the *Philadelphia Times* ran an article titled "At Rebecca's Grave: The Burial Place of Miss Gratz the Original of Scott's Famous Heroine."[21] Four years later, the national monthly the *American Jewess* used the story to introduce Gratz in an article extolling her as the mother of American Jewish women's activities. In 1912, S. R. Crockett repeated it in his popular book "Originals of Scott."[22]

Perhaps the strongest endorsement of the legend appeared in the *Publications of the American Jewish Historical Society* in a 1914 essay by Joseph Jacobs titled "The Original of Scott's Rebecca." Jacobs concluded that despite the hearsay nature of the evidence, Gratz was indeed the model, and asserted that the "first scientific hypothesis [is] that any tradition has a basis in fact." Rebecca Gratz was more like Rebecca of *Ivanhoe* than other possibilities Jacobs considered. The grandnephew of Rebecca Franks claimed Franks for the model because her married life was spent near Scott's boyhood home. But, Jacobs argued, Franks had married her Christian suitor, and therefore could not have been Scott's model. Although Jacobs claimed that Scott himself wrote that his inspiration to use Jewish characters came from a friend's accounts of Jewish hardships in Germany, he insisted that the inspiration for Rebecca could not have come from Germany because nineteenth-century German Jewish women—he mentioned Dorothea Mendelssohn Schlegel and Rahel Levin Varnhagen— married Christian men. Although J. G. Lockhart, Scott's son-in-law and biographer, mentioned neither Gratz nor Washington Irving, Jacobs clung to the legend. He insisted that "a poet must draw from his experiences or the experiences of others."[23]

After Jacobs gave scholarly approval to the Gratz legend, other American Jews repeated it. An original play was written about it in the 1920s or 1930s, probably by teachers in a Jewish religious school, and another play about her, possibly written by a student at about the same time, won a prize from the National Council of Jewish Women. In 1935 Rollin Osterweiss mentioned it in his popular biography of Gratz. Two juvenile books repeated it, one in the 1950s and another in 1967. A rabbinic thesis about Gratz written in 1947 and a Ph.D. thesis in 1959 both offered the legend as a pleasant possibility with no substantial proof. The story became the foundation for an original opera about Gratz composed in 1976 and performed in 1976 and in 1995. E. Digby Baltzell repeated it in 1983 and a play about it was performed in Buffalo, New York in 1993.[24]

None of these accounts discussed Rebecca of York's significance in Scott's work and life. Scott's novels played on his own era's changing notions about nationhood, family, love, status, propriety and duty, ideals that were thrown into question in the age of revolution and the rise of bourgeois culture. Scott was confident that Rebecca of York, the novel's heroine of tragic virtue, would elicit sympathy in his audience. Moreover both Scott and his mother, Ann Rutherford, knew Lord and Lady Montague, Jewish members of the British nobility. Lord Montague's brother Charles, the fourth Duke of Buccleuch and Queensbury, was Scott's patron at this moment in his career. The Duke, whose daughters Scott described as "devoted," died in 1819.[25] His sympathetic depiction of Jewish filial devotion undoubtedly pleased the Montagues.

In Scott's England, neither Jews nor Catholics enjoyed civil rights equal to those of Protestants and the emancipation of religious minorities filled popular debates. Scott, a practicing Protestant, shared his mother's opinion that Catholicism was a "mean and depraved superstition," and that Cromwell was correct in inviting Jews to England. By making Rebecca a Jewish character, Scott spoke both for his own Protestant virtue—Rebecca embodied his values—and against medievalism, which to him meant Roman Catholicism, without arguing for general tolerance, which would have included Catholic emancipation.[26]

Scott's work also pleased Gratz. "I . . . felt a little extra pleasure from . . . Rebecca's being a Hebrew maiden," she wrote to Maria Fenno Hoffman. "I feel gratitude for his justification of the jewish character. . . . [O]ld Isaac's avarice is more the effect of persecution than natural baseness of mind. . . . It is worthy of

Scott at a period when persecution has re-commenced in Europe to hold up a picture of the superstition and cruelty in which it originated.[27]

American Society at the Turn of the Century

In 1882 debates raged among nativists, acculturationists, and traditionalists during this period of mass immigration. Nativists opposed the immigration of large, non-Protestant families. Acculturationists sought a model for Jewish integration into American society that retained Jewish identity. Traditionalists hoped to ensure the survival of the Jewish faith. This many-sided debate enlivened the popular press.

The issue of the *Century Magazine* that carried van Rens-salaer's article also featured other items on Jews and Jewish identity. In an editorial called "Jews and Jew-baiters," the writer commented that Russia's problems with its Jews stemmed from its own barbarism.[28] Commenting that it is "never safe to accept the account given of the downtrodden by the people who oppress them," Emma Lazarus, in "Russian Christianity versus Modern Judaism," refuted an earlier article by Mme. Ragozin that defended Russia's treatment toward its Jews. Ragozin had claimed that Jews were undermining the well-being of Russia by acting as a hostile state within a state, by usury, by selling foul meat and too much liquor to the peasantry, and by refusing to fight back when attacked. By detailing the reasons why these assertions were both absurd and false, Lazarus cooled American fears that Russian Jewish immigrants would be a detriment to American society, and, in fact, weaken it.[29] In Joaquin Miller's poem, "Jewess," an ode to the mysterious, sad beauty of Jewish women whose "black abundance of . . . hair / mourns thy people's mute despair," the final stanza reflects the popular idea that America had inherited Israel's role as God's favored nation. But America did not exclude Jews from God's favor; Jews had only to come to America to receive it.

> Then come where stars of freedom spill
> Their splendor, Jewess. In this land,
> The same broad hollow of God's hand
> That held you ever, outholds still.
> And whether you be right or nay,
> 'Tis God's, not Russia's, HERE to say.[30]

In this context, van Rensselaer's article on the civilized, faithful, charitable, romantic heroism of an upper-class Jewish woman, illustrating a Jew's contribution to America, valorized Rebecca Gratz. He omitted any mention of the specifically Jewish nature of the organizations Gratz founded, thereby emphasizing the possibility that Jews would be useful to the country as a whole and refuting slurs of clannishness. Extolling Gratz's refinement and acceptance by elite Gentiles in Philadelphia and New York also underlined the Jewish capacity to integrate into American society without changing it. Refuting the theories purporting that Jews would "dilute" the strength of America by intermarriage of Jews and Gentiles, van Rensselaer's version of the Gratz legend implied that, out of loyalty to their own faith, Jews who successfully acculturated would not want to marry Christians, and neither would Jews who wanted to retain old world traditions and customs. Van Rensselaer also implied that only the most genteel of new Jewish immigrants could ever be asked to marry into elite families, thereby "strengthening" the gene pool. Finally, van Rensselaer's account of Gratz suggested that Jewish immigrant women might not continue to bear children at a higher rate than the American elite; they too might become spinsters. All this would act as a brake on the forces of "degeneracy" that many nativists thought the country faced if it did not control immigration. The Gratz legend could comfort nativists, showing that Jewish adjustment to America would benefit the country. In attempting to soothe nativists' fears, however, van Rensselaer diminished Gratz's most powerful achievements by showcasing the legend only and extolling Gratz's virtues without revealing her strengths.

After the turn of the century American Jews had more complex reasons for retelling the legend of Rebecca Gratz. American culture was beginning to view unmarried women with suspicion. During Gratz's lifetime, America had accepted single women who nearly always lived within larger households. Between the Revolution and the Civil War "single blessedness" actually supported the cult of domesticity by reinforcing the idea that those who did marry did so for romance. Unmarried daughters contributed to family economies, often through wage labor. The cults of domesticity and single blessedness reinforced gender divisions of labor in service to the family.[31] According to historian Lee Chambers-Schiller, antebellum literature portrayed "old maids" as admirable

women if they lived domestic lives filled with piety and charity.[32] The antebellum way of thinking about single women was
illustrated by their economic and political treatment. A married
woman had no legal control over her earnings, and her legal
contracts could be voided by her husband. Single women began
working in factories, often saving money for marriage, whereas
a married woman's wages could legally be paid directly to her
husband. Women taking the more economically rewarding route
of owning a business, often an inn, were usually widows.[33]

It is not surprising, then, that antebellum single Jewish
women made striking contributions to Jewish domestic life. Rebecca Gratz, Louisa B. Hart, Ellen and Emily Phillips, Simha
Peixotto, and Penina Moise were all single women who were thoroughly integrated into American culture in an era when the single
life was seen as supportive of family life and not threatening to
the ideologies and economic structure supporting marriage.

By the end of the nineteenth century, however, America was
growing less comfortable with its single women—there were too
many of them, particularly talented and well-educated women,
who were often able to live independently.[34] The Civil War had
decimated the male population, women had taken up what were
formerly "men's jobs" only, and earned their own money. While
economic production moved to factories, ideas about domestic life
focused more and more on its role in providing emotional well-
being and stability to families. Accordingly, women waited for true
love to find them and propel them into marriage. Not finding it,
they put marriage off.[35]

Poor women who did not want to begin married life penniless
delayed marriage until they had worked for a few years. Many
single women joined labor unions. Middle- and upper-class women
went to college, often to a women's college, and entered professions, usually as teachers.[36] Married women bore fewer babies.
Educated women effected dramatic changes. In 1885, only 68 percent of married women who were college graduates bore children.[37]
Between 1890 and 1920, 60 percent of all high school graduates
were women. By 1910 women comprised over 30 percent of the
students enrolled in colleges, universities, and technical schools,
half of whom remained single.[38]

As millions of Catholic and Jewish immigrants from eastern
and southern Europe began arriving in the United States at the
turn of the century, America began to condemn celibacy among

Protestant women. Theodore Roosevelt told these women that they had a duty to bear many children because there were so many large Catholic families in the country. As science refuted religion's explanation of the facts of life, researchers and physicians used scientific arguments to condemn women's nondomestic activities, contending that educated women were overtaxing their brains and shrivelling their reproductive systems. Female celibacy became a disease that could be triggered by too much education and whose long-term effect could be insanity. Lamarckian ideas of inheritance and fears about national identity combined in the new field of sexology, which focused on what it considered abnormal adult sexual behavior and posited a causal link between childhood masturbation and celibacy, mental retardation, and insanity in adult life, all of which could be inherited. Homosexuality was linked to this "tainted stock" as was hermaphroditism, a condition in which a woman could have normal female genitalia but male personality attributes like independence, intelligence, ambition, and love for women. In 1901, Richard von Kraft-Ebing published *The Perverts,* in which he offered pseudo-scientific proof that sexual relationships other than heterosexual monogamy could be classed as diseases. By World War I, lesbianism, feminism, and spinsterhood were thoroughly linked. After World War I, Wilhelm Stekel published *Frigidity in Woman* in which he linked "race suicide," "class dilution," "sex deviance," "female careerism," and singlehood as the shared evils of modernity. He was sure that the "spiritual aristocracy of the race" was "dying out."[39]

These attitudes and ideas made friendships among women suspect and an unmarried adult often became the object of ridicule and abuse. In addition to other motives for marrying, women had to have husbands and children to legitimize their nondomestic activities and deflect suspicion of lesbianism, which was considered a form of insanity. Despite growing homophobia, women's networks, clubs, agencies, societies, and organizations continued to expand in scope, ambition, and effect. The National Council of Jewish Women was formed in 1893 after women delivered papers on the condition of American Jewish life at the Chicago World Congress of Religions.[40] In Philadelphia, the Jewish Maternity Association and Seaside Home maintained a nursing school, nursery, and mother's shelter in Philadelphia and a nursing home for mothers and children at the Jersey shore. It grew out of Ezrat Nashim, a group formed in the 1870s to help women through childbirth, and

was one of the few groups not part of the United Hebrew Charities,
a central governing agency for the city's Jewish charities run by
an all-male board.[41]

Gratz as a Model for Jewish Women

By the end of the nineteenth century, the Gratz legend was
used by Jewish women to legitimize their own nondomestic activities. For Gratz's life to be a model for Jewish women's activities, these public women needed to dispel any notion that
Gratz's life had improprieties. Further, women used Gratz's example to inspire female altruism and to teach self-sacrifice to
Jewish girls. As Minnie Louis explained in an 1895 article, altruism was both the essential nature of woman and the essence
of religion. Deeply influenced by Reform Judaism's emphasis on
ethics, Louis's primary religious values were renunciation, humility, loving-kindness, self-sacrifice, and devotion. Religious education, Louis claimed, moves women to action because the Bible
"unlock[s] the problem of Divinity . . . [which is centrally] ethics."
She argued that God wants all peoples to turn temples, synagogues, and churches into lecture halls, homes for the homeless,
schools, and hospitals.[42] In citing Gratz as an example of an altru-
istic, religious Jewish woman who should be extolled in religious
schools, Louis mined Gratz's life for traits that could add to her
usefulness as a model in evoking religion's highest ideals. A single
woman whose moral and mental capacity was tainted with suspi-
cions of lesbianism could not be used for so important a purpose.[43]
Minnie Louis's theology of female altruism picked up the legend
and spelled out an activist role for American Jewish women that
replaced traditional worship duties.

Indeed, Gratz was not the only notable unmarried Jewish
woman whose life was mined and sentimentalized for traits that
could inspire and instruct younger Jewish women. By the early
twentieth century, as the children of eastern European Jewish
immigrants adapted to American culture, models of accomplished
Jewish women who did not marry Gentiles became valuable cultural coin to those opposing intermarriage. Two weeks after
Louis's article, the *American Hebrew* published an essay by Annie
Josephine Levi titled "Intermarriage." With a format similar to
the *Saturday Evening Post,* the *American Hebrew* appealed to
an audience that was clearly on intimate terms with American

culture. That intimacy worried Levi. She brought British theologian Grace Aguilar into service against it. Aguilar's novels
were still popular, coming out in new editions through the 1920s,
almost eighty years after her death. Levi claimed that "amid
her many trials . . . Aguilar renounced her love for a Christian
for love of her faith. . . . It is but another gleam of light in the
halo that surrounds this noble Jewess."[44] In fact, Aguilar was
sickly all her short life and lived with her infirm mother until
her own untimely death at age thirty-one.[45] There never has been
any question of a non-Jewish lover, or any lover, but for Levi,
Aguilar epitomized the cultured Jewish woman who was also a
deeply faithful Jew. By mentioning Aguilar, whose books were
still popular, Levi also turned her readers' attention to Jewish
history. Aguilar, like Gratz, was faithful to what Louis and Levi
would have called traditional Judaism. Thus, individuals telling
the Gratz legend at this time found the basis for the argument
against intermarriage in historical tradition.

Legendary Logic

Structurally, the legend merges past and present, bringing
together two Rebeccas living in different eras but facing the same
dilemma: whether or not to marry a non-Jew. As a legend it enables
its interpreters to draw various meanings from its central logic.
Ivanhoe's setting in medieval England includes instances of Jewish oppression by the English. Even under such circumstances, the
fictional Rebecca does not leave her father and marry out when she
can. By calling up medieval history, the legend forms a cognitive
bridge to the entire Jewish past, including many instances of
martyrdom. This act of loyalty by a Jewish woman is, when seen
from a culture basing marriage on love, a kind of martyrdom, and
is valorized with all the aura of nobility that martyrdom carries.
It brings the weight of censure by all Jewish martyrs to bear
on each Jewish woman who marries a gentile man. At another
level, the legend about Rebecca Gratz of Philadelphia forms a
cognitive bridge to upper-class American Jews who were accepted
by elite gentile families. Such Jews were few indeed, especially
in Philadelphia. One historian remarked that in 1900, after elites
closed ranks against encroachment by immigrants, Jews had less
opportunity to move into local leadership in Philadelphia than in
any other town in America.[46] For Jewish women caught between

increasing American anti-Semitism and their own American identity, Gratz's rejection of a gentile man could be inspiring. Moreover,
the man was acceptable by Jewish cultural values that thought
wealth and literacy the most ideal combination, as well as by
the standards of romance-based marriage because he loved the
Rebecca of legend. There is nothing in the tale to make him unde-
sirable except for his religion. In rejecting her suitor, Rebecca loses
an almost perfect husband and subjects herself to ridicule as an old
maid. This too is martyrdom. Both the fictional Rebecca of *Ivanhoe*
and the legendary Rebecca of Philadelphia chose martyrdom for
the sake of Jewish loyalty.

The legend also stabilizes the traditional order of Jewish
families and subverts one threat of disorder. Rebecca of *Ivanhoe*
rejects her non-Jewish suitor because of her sense of duty to her
father and concern for her suitor's happiness. Rebecca Gratz rejects gentile suitors because of her commitment to Judaism. The
legend of Rebecca Gratz fuses these two tales into one and demonstrates the tension in the lives of American Jewish women—the
weight of Jewish history and the desire for American acceptance. A
route to an acceptable acculturation is thus laid out in the legend.
American Jewish women must take the responsibility for creating
Jewish families. This would make them modern American women,
different from the "low-class Hebrews" not yet Americanized and
different from premodern Jewish women subject to the arranged
marriage system. It modifies their Jewish identity by using American individualism and assumptions about women's inherently
religious nature to strengthen their commitment to Judaism.

Both Rebecca tales underline the message that love for a gentile man cannot be fulfilled and brings disappointment echoed in a
Yiddish proverb: "A bird and a fish can love one another, but where
will they build a home?"[47] The legend acknowledges the power
of love to draw people together to form marriages, but pushes
beyond that to question the quality of the home life that would
be created. It forms a brake on the unleashed values of romance-
based marriage. If women are able to negotiate their marriages
alone and without their fathers, then they must consider the
way the community feels about intermarriage. In the logic of the
legend, Gratz's spinsterhood implies the traditional response to
an intermarriage—the line of future generations has been cut. It
says that women who allow love for a Gentile to affect the gener-
ational continuity of Judaism will lose either the generations or

the man or both. This legendary logic imaginatively re-creates the ghetto wall, the most concrete form of Jewish disenfranchisement. In doing so, it questions the permanence of contemporary free-doms, calling up an earlier world in which familial responsibilities had top priority and sustained the entire Jewish community. In that world, romantic love was felt to be quixotic and fleeting and was not the foundation for interfamilial relationships. A Jewish woman would be wrong to allow romance to thwart the continuity of her family. The individualism that upholds the importance of romantic love is effectively trivialized as a foolish and foreign idea that allows personal desire to overrule the needs of family and community. The legend illustrates that a Jewish woman who allows love for a gentile man to keep her from her Jewish familial responsibilities will place herself at the edges of the community.

The real history of Gratz's life is seen then, in the context of the legend, as a model of usefulness and worth that atones for her not marrying. It promises that any American Jewish woman who felt the need to do so could earn the community's respect by joining a service organization and helping others who are less fortunate. If service could atone for so drastic a transgression as letting love for a Gentile keep one from forming a Jewish family, it might also clear the conscience of a woman who maintained a Jewish family but rejected traditional religious customs as she adjusted to America. By the 1930s, Conservative Judaism—a middle route between Orthodoxy and Reform—claimed the allegiance of many children of eastern European Jews, as did many secular philosophers.[48] Service to the community might also clear the consciences of the many Jewish women who bore few children, daughters of eastern European immigrants, women whom one sociologist has called the "most motivated and reliable users of birth control" in America since the earliest decades of the twentieth century.[49] Combined with Gratz's real achievements, the legend told such women that they could still be considered women of valor, and of virtue, as long as they were of service to their communities.

Echoes in American Culture

Rebecca Gratz's legend, like her life, was grounded in both American culture and in Judaism. Like most American women of her era, Gratz felt freest within female or familial environments. Like most upper-class women, she maintained lifelong relationships with an intergenerational network of kin and the families of friends, and relied on religion and religious institutions for much of her intellectual and social life. She heartily endorsed the community ethic inherent in the gender differentiation of spheres and the domestic utopianism enshrined in popular ideas about women. The community ethic emphasized the interdependence of separate places in society and was echoed by her experience of traditional Judaism. Her family's synagogue maintained the well-known gender differences in ritual obligations and synagogue leadership, along with masculine God-language.

There is no evidence that Gratz ever found this masculine leadership intimidating, frustrating, or alienating. On the contrary, patriarchy provided her with male company in her religious activities. The synagogue leaders were her father, uncle, and brothers, her lifelong sources of support, and men with whom she shared a strong and lively affection. Jewish religious language had taught her to consider God a merciful, caring, and just Father, and this was the language she continued to use all her life. Most likely, her competence and ease in creating new Jewish institutions grew out of her familiarity with the methods for successfully managing Philadelphia's Jews that she had learned from the Gratz men.

Cooperation among gender-differentiated antebellum Jewish organizations illustrated the strength of their shared understanding that separate spheres provided for an efficient community. Separate spheres were thus not ends in themselves but complementary structures. Interdependent obligations, epitomized by gender-differentiated religious obligations, made the dichotomy between the spheres as they were defined in American popular culture seem less severe in Jewish culture. Men's organizations like the United Hebrew Beneficent Society required their members to fulfill their religious obligations in Jewish life cycle rituals. Those men did not entirely hand domestic religion over to women.

But the individualism that was the basis of the "new epoch" of Jewish freedom, as Gratz called the last century, threatened Jewish life. This individualism was the basis of romance-based marriage, which broke the axis of the premodern Jewish society, the arranged marriage system, and made it impossible for the system to gain an effective foothold in America. Jewish marriage brokers who worked among immigrants in New York at the turn of the century complained that America's love affair with romance ruined their business; they either incorporated romantic images in their advertising or found another line of work.[50]

Many of Gratz's peers, leaders among Philadelphia's Jewish leaders, appear to have been ambivalent about both individualism and romance. Many, like Isaac Leeser, three of five Gratz brothers, Louisa B. Hart, Ellen and Emily Phillips, and Gratz herself, remained single, yet all of them tried to promote Jewish domesticity. For example, none of their charities required either their membership or their petitioners to attend synagogue, but many of these groups did require them to be married according to Jewish rites, to circumcise male children, and to maintain the Sabbath. With the feminization of American religion, a trend that emphasized both home worship and the ability of women to teach religion and to create a religious atmosphere, Gratz assumed the moral authority to establish her organizations.

In contrast to the older Jewish traditions, the roles Gratz developed for American Jewish women gave them duties to perform for the community that strengthened Jewish domesticity while weakening the traditional expectations that every woman would establish her own Jewish household through marriage. To women torn by the conflicting values of American romantic love and the Jewish tradition of viewing marriage as a duty to both God and her family, both Gratz and her legend offered an intermediate world of work that was respectable because it promoted domestic life. In the last decade of the twentieth century, when only 62 percent of Jewish women are married and 30 percent of married Jewish women married men not born to Jewish parents, the Gratz legend remains alive and popular.[51] As Jewish women and men compete and struggle within American culture, both Gratz's real work and her legend speak to the anxieties they still share.

Gratz's legend continues both to be meaningful and to cloud successive generations' understanding of her real life and accomplishments. Her values and attitudes toward philanthropy and domesticity blended Judaism with popular American ideas shared by gentile women of her class. Like other American benevolent women, Gratz wanted to aid the "worthy poor," especially poor children. She believed that she lived in a new epoch of Jewish history, one in which Jews were treated as equals. She believed that this new epoch demanded that Jews learn new attitudes of civic responsibility toward gentile nations. With many other Americans, Gratz shared the opinion that a proper home life would create good citizens, and she confidently directed her energies toward easing and Americanizing the domestic lives of poor Jews. Through the material aid of the Female Hebrew Benevolent Society, the spiritual aid of the Hebrew Sunday School and the familial care of the Jewish Foster Home, Gratz promoted an Americanized Jewish domesticity among Philadelphia's Jews. But Gratz, just like many Christian women, used a rhetoric based on domesticity to justify her own entry into public life, and her organizations promoting Jewish religious education and charitable services used institutional forms already proven successful by her Christian peers to advance Jewish life in America. As she watched antebellum Jewish men splinter Philadelphia Jewry with contrasting visions of Jewish life—visions foregrounding either European worship customs, rational philosophies, or national origins—Gratz formed broadly inclusive institutions sustained by American ideologies about women. By thus adapting Judaism to American conditions, Gratz invigorated Jewish life for generations to come.

NOTES

Abbreviations

AJA American Jewish Archives
AJHS American Jewish Historical Society
APS American Philosophical Society
CWWI *The Collected Works of Washington Irving,* vol. 1: *Letters, 1802–1823.* Ed. Ralph M. Aderman, Herbert L. Kleinfeld, and Jennifer S. Banks. Boston: Twayne, 1978–1982.
FA Female Association
FHBS Female Hebrew Benevolent Society
FL Free Library of Philadelphia
GCMG Gratz Collection, Department of Rare Books and Special Collections, McGill University Libraries
HSP Historical Society of Pennsylvania
HSS Hebrew Sunday School
JFH Jewish Foster Home
LCP Library Company of Philadelphia
MIA Mikveh Israel Archives
MMC Miscellaneous Manuscript Collection, Library of Congress
NMAJH National Museum of American Jewish History
PAJHS *Publications of the American Jewish Historical Society*
PJA-BIES Philadelphia Jewish Archives—Balch Institute of Ethnic Studies
RM Rosenbach Museum
SHC Southern History Collection
UHBS United Hebrew Beneficent Society
WW Edwin Wolf II and Maxwell Whiteman, *The History of the Jews of Philadelphia from Colonial Times to the Age of Jackson.* Philadelphia: Jewish Publication Society, 1957.

Introduction

1. For more on Rebecca Gratz see Dianne Ashton, "Souls Have No Sex: Philadelphia Jewish Women and the American Challenge," in M. Friedman, *When Philadelphia Was the Capital,* 34–57; Bodek, "Making Do," 143–62; Ann Braude, "The Jewish Woman's Encounter with American Culture," in Reuther and Keller, *Women and Religion in America,* 1:150–92; Mary M. Cohen, *An Old Philadelphia*

Cemetery: The Resting Place of Rebecca Gratz (Philadelphia: City History Society of Philadelphia, 1920); Osterweiss, *Rebecca Gratz;* Rosenbloom, "Rebecca Gratz and the Jewish Sunday School Movement"; Joseph Rosenbloom, "Some Conclusions about Rebecca Gratz," in *Essays in American Jewish History* (Cincinnati, Ohio: American Jewish Archives, 1958), 171–86; Wolf and Whiteman, *History of the Jews of Philadelphia;* Philipson, *Letters.*

2. Two of Gratz's siblings died in infancy, one long before Gratz's birth. She and nine siblings lived to adulthood. Brener, *The Jews of Lancaster,* 24.

3. Wolf, *Book Culture;* "Joseph Dennie," *Penn Monthly* 11 (1880): 722–25, APS.

4. Brener (*The Jews of Lancaster,* 25) concludes that Shinah Simon Schuyler's sister Belah did not communicate with her sister after her marriage to Nicholas Schuyler because Nicholas was a Gentile. However, Miriam Simon Gratz, Rebecca's mother and a sister of both Belah and Shinah Simon, did keep in touch with her sister and encouraged her children to do so also. Gratz's attitudes echoed those of her mother.

5. Fish, *Barnard and Michael Gratz,* 4.

6. WW, 47.

7. Ibid., 344.

8. Personal conversation, Prof. Monroe Moosenick, Transylvania University, December 2, 1994.

9. WW, 337.

10. Rosenbloom, "Some Conclusions about Rebecca Gratz," 171; Ashton, "Souls Have No Sex," 5–57.

11. WW, 36–64.

12. R.G. to Maria Fenno Hoffman, October 20, 1817, Rebecca Gratz Papers, P-9, AJHS.

13. R.G. to Maria Gist Gratz, 1824, ibid.

14. J. Matthews, *Toward a New Society,* 41; Scott, *Natural Allies,* 35–47.

15. WW, 343.

16. Because much of antebellum America's reading material was imported from England, the images in popular English fiction were familiar to American readers. Galchinsky, *Modern Jewish Woman Writer,* 50–61; Calisch, *The Jew in English Literature;* Modder, *The Jew in the Literature of England;* Appel, "Jews in American Caricature."

17. Stern, "Jewish Marriage and Intermarriage," 142–43; WW, 234–36.

18. R.G. to Miriam Moses Cohen, September 13, 1840, Rebecca Gratz Papers, Manuscript Collection no. 236, AJA.

19. J. Matthews, *Toward a New Society,* 123–24.

20. G. Matthews, *The Rise of Public Woman,* 92, 130–37.

21. Scott, *Natural Allies,* 35–47.

22. Douglas, *The Feminization of American Culture,* 94–123; Smith-Rosenberg, *Disorderly Conduct;* Auerbach, *Woman and the Demon,* 185–200; Nead, *Myths of Sexuality,* 12–38; D'Emilio and Freedman, *Intimate Matters,* 139–55.

23. Scott, *Natural Allies,* 74–75; G. Matthews, *The Rise of Public Woman;* Kuzmack, *Woman's Cause,* 14; Ryan, *The Empire of the Mother,* 77.

24. Butler, *Awash in a Sea of Faith,* 281–82; G. Matthews, *The Rise of Public Woman,* 41.

25. WW, 61.

26. R.G. to Maria Fenno Hoffman, March 9, 1818, Rebecca Gratz Papers, Manuscript Collection no. 236, AJA.

27. FHBS Constitution, 1819, LCP.

28. FHBS Minutes, 1819–1875, FHBS Collection, NMAJH.

29. National depressions hit between 1819 and 1823 and between 1837 and 1843. Two years after the founding of the Jewish Foster Home, depression hit again in 1857. McPherson, *Battle Cry of Freedom,* 10.

30. HSS Society Minutes, 1838–1864, PJA-BIES; HSS Society Minutes, 1870–1892, AJA.

31. Reznikoff and Engleman, *The Jews of Charleston,* 150; Emily Solis-Cohen, Jr., Archives, Folder: "Kupat Shel Sedakah: Ms. Final Copy," p. 36 of MS. Courtesy Helen Sax.

32. Sussman, *Isaac Leeser,* 43, 100–101.

33. JFH Minutes, 1855–1890, Association for Jewish Children Collection, box 1, PJA-BIES.

34. See the will of Hyman Gratz in Diane King, "A History of Gratz College, 1893–1928" (Ph.D. diss., Dropsie College, 1979), 380, Gratz College rare book room.

35. For example, see Diner, *A Time for Gathering;* N. Cohen, *Encounter with Emancipation;* Feldstein, *The Land That I Show You;* J. Feldman, *The Jewish Experience in Western Pennsylvania,* 3–118.

36. Hyman, *Gender and Assimilation;* for an examination of this process among Jews in Imperial Germany see Kaplan, *The Making of the Jewish Middle Class;* for discussions of American women and family status in the nineteenth century see Smith-Rosenberg, *Disorderly Conduct,* 79–90; D'Emilio and Freedman, *Intimate Matters,* 15–38, 171–220.

37. Jick, *The Americanization of the Synagogue;* Benny Kraut, "Reform Judaism and the Unitarian Challenge," in Sarna, *The American Jewish Experience,* 89–96; Meyer, *Response to Modernity,* 225–96; E. Feldman, *Dual Destinies,* 60–112; N. Cohen, *Encounter with Emancipation,* 159–210; Diner, *A Time for Gathering,* 116–26; Jack Wertheimer, ed., *The American Synagogue* (Cambridge: Harvard University Press, 1987), 37–110.

38. Modder, *The Jew in the Literature of England,* 53.

Chapter 1

1. Miriam Gratz to Barnard Gratz, September 26, 1790. Byars, *B. & M. Gratz,* 239.
2. Fish, "Role of Michael Gratz," 43–49.
3. Weigley, *Philadelphia,* 20.
4. For more on the Atlantic rim businesses see Faber, *A Time for Planting,* 1–50.
5. Theodore Thayer, "Town into City, 1746–1765," in Weigley, *Philadelphia,* 96–100.
6. Weigley, *Philadelphia,* 28–29.
7. WW, 32.
8. Harry M. Tinckom, "The Revolutionary City, 1765–1800," in Weigley, *Philadelphia,* 109–54.
9. Ibid., 100.
10. E. Feldman, *Dual Destinies,* 10, 11, 19.
11. WW, 33.
12. Thayer, "Town into City," 96–100.
13. Weigley, *Philadelphia,* 33–67; Faber, *A Time for Planting,* 27–50.
14. Thayer, "Town into City," 102.
15. Ibid., 73.
16. Ibid., 78.
17. Silesia was located in the northeastern section of eighteenth-century Germanic lands. WW, 36.
18. Byars, *B. & M. Gratz,* 11.
19. Ibid., 11–12; WW, 36–64.
20. Wolf and Whiteman call Michael a "rolling stone" (WW, 40).
21. Fish, *Barnard and Michael Gratz,* 12, 27.
22. Byars, *B. & M. Gratz,* 12.
23. M. A. Jones, *American Immigration,* 125–27; Kober, "Jewish Migration from Wurttemberg to the United States"; Brettell, "Is Ethnic Community Inevitable?"; Malkin, *The Journeys of David Toback;* Glenn, *Daughters of the Shtetl,* 52.
24. WW, 42; Jonas Bluch to Simon Gratz, 1801, Isaac Bluch to Hyman and Simon Gratz, 1821, Simon Gratz Collection, HSP.
25. WW, 36–40.
26. Margolis and Marx, *A History of the Jewish People,* 596–98; J. Katz, *Out of the Ghetto,* 162; Goldscheider and Zuckerman, *Transformation of the Jews,* 33–34.
27. H. Morais, *The Jews of Philadelphia,* 7–14; WW, 6–8; Feldstein, *The Land That I Show You,* 1–40.
28. Lavendar, "Arabic-Islamic and Spanish-Mediterranean Influences on 'The Jewish Mind'"; 25–35; Porter, "The Sephardi in America"; Feldstein, *The Land That I Show You,* 20–40.
29. Rosenbach, *The Jews of Philadelphia Prior to 1800,* 23.

30. Byars, *B. & M. Gratz,* 14–17.
31. Fish, *Barnard and Michael Gratz,* 23–67.
32. Baltzell, *Philadelphia Gentlemen,* 81; WW, 288.
33. Warner, *The Private City,* 11.
34. Brener, *The Jews of Lancaster,* 2–25.
35. Business ties among these Jewish merchants sometimes led to quasi-familial relationships. Another Jewish trader in what was then the Pennsylvania frontier was Aaron Levy, who owned 334 acres of fertile countryside in Penn's Valley, which he laid out as Aaronsburg in 1786, hoping that it would be named the capital of the new state. When it was not, the town withered and Levy moved back to Philadelphia in 1790, land-rich but cash-poor. In trade for taking care of Levy and his wife, Rachel, in their old age, Levy turned over almost all his land to Michael's oldest son, Simon Gratz. Simon later divided this land to form Gratz County (Brener, *The Jews of Lancaster,* 5).
36. WW, 125, 256.
37. J. Katz, *Tradition and Crisis;* Gittelman, *From Shtetl to Suburbia;* Meiselman, *Jewish Women and Jewish Law;* R. Biale, *Women and Jewish Law,* 10–43.
38. H. Morais, *The Jews of Philadelphia,* 269–70.
39. Byars, *B. & M. Gratz,* 10; Fish, "The Ancestral Heritage of the Gratz Family." These were Rabbi Jonathan Bluch of Crackow, Rabbi Jacob Koppel Bluch, and Rabbi Zevi (Henry) Hirsch Bluch.
40. Brener, *The Jews of Lancaster,* 23.
41. Fish, *Barnard and Michael Gratz,* 182.
42. WW, 58.
43. Fish, *Barnard and Michael Gratz,* 198.
44. In contrast to the northern European Jewish culture familiar to most Jews who came to America, the Sephardic religious legacy provided a Jewish "paradigm" for the accommodation of Jewish life to Western culture. One historian has argued that northern European Jews who hoped to change Jewish culture saw in the Sephardic legacy an authentic Judaism marked by "cultural openness, philosophic thinking, and an appreciation for the aesthetic." Schorsch, "The Myth of Sephardic Supremacy," 1.
45. N. Cohen, *Jews in Christian America,* 11–65.
46. Ibid., 22. For example, although most social clubs did not admit Jews, by the close of the Revolution, 25 percent of the members of the Sublime Lodge of Perfection, a Masonic lodge, were Jews. Fish, *Barnard and Michael Gratz,* 188.
47. WW, 57.
48. "The Gratz Brothers and the Revolutionary War," Gratz Family Papers, Collection no. 72, box 19, APS.
49. Fish, *Barnard and Michael Gratz,* 199.

50. WW, 259.
51. Fish, *Barnard and Michael Gratz,* 202–3.
52. Board of K.K. Mickve Israel to the President, Vice President, and Executive Council of Pennsylvania, Pennsylvania Archives, 1784, in Gratz Family Papers, Collection no. 72, box 11, APS.
53. Fish, *Barnard and Michael Gratz,* 209.
54. WW, 148.
55. N. Cohen, *Jews in Christian America,* 28.
56. WW, 148, 152.
57. Ibid., 114–245.
58. Ibid., 144.
59. In 1782, E. Flowers at Second and Front Streets boarded and educated young ladies in useful and ornamental needlework, reading, writing, arithmetic, grammar, and drawing, and, as the *Pennsylvania Packet* notes, with "strict attention paid to their health [and] morals" (*Pennsylvania Packet or the General Advertiser,* January 18, 1782, LCP). The education offered by E. Flowers was one that would enable a young woman to run a suitably charming drawing room. But women who owned shops and plantations, and women looking for situations as cooks, wet nurses, and companions, also placed ads in Philadelphia newspapers.
60. *Poulson's American Daily Advertiser,* February 16, 1819, LCP; Mary Beth Norton, "The Myth of the Golden Age," in *Women of America: A History,* ed. Carole Ruth Berkin and Mary Beth Norton (Boston: Houghton Mifflin, 1979), 46.
61. "On Female Authorship," *Ladies Magazine,* January 1793, 68, LCP.
62. Thomas Dilworth, *On the Education of Youth: An Essay Preface to the Schoolmaster's Assistant* (England, [1744?]), xiii; Mrs. Chapone, *Letters on the Improvement of the Mind: Addressed to a Young Lady* (Philadelphia, 1786), n.p.; J. Hamilton Moore, *The Young Gentlemen's and Lady's Monitor and English Teacher's Assistant* (New York: Hodge and Campbell, 1792), 134, all in Gratz Family Library Collection, NMAJH.
63. Moore, *Young Gentlemen's and Lady's Monitor,* preface.
64. Ibid., 135.
65. Written in 1794 and published in London, these volumes were given to Benjamin Gratz by Aaron Levy. *Genesis, Exodus, Leviticus, Numbers, Deuteronomy,* translated by David Levi from the version by Lion Soesmans (London, 1794), Gratz Family Books, box 1, MIA.
66. David Levi, *A Succinct Account of the Rites and Ceremonies of the Jews* (London, [1790?]), Gratz Family Prayer Books, box 1, MIA.
67. These were: *Form of Prayers for the Feast of Tabernacles According to the Custom of Spanish-Portuguese Jews* (London, 1794); *Form of Prayers for the Festivals of Passover and Pentecost According to the*

Custom of Spanish-Portuguese Jews (London, 1794); *Form of Prayer According to the Custom of Spanish-Portuguese Jews as Used in Their Synagogues and in Their Families* (London, 1795); *Form of Prayers for the Fast Days According to the Custom of Spanish-Portuguese Jews* (London, 1794), all translated by David Levi, Gratz Family Prayer Books, box 2, MIA.

68. Pierre Jean Grosley, *A Tour to London; or New Observations on England and Its Inhabitants,* translated from the French by Thomas Nugent (London, 1772); Louis Chambaud, *A Grammar of the French Tongue with a Prefatory Discourse Containing an Essay on the Proper Method for Teaching and Learning That Language,* 7th ed. (London: C. Bathurst, 1779), GCMG.

69. Marie Jean Antoine Nicolas Caritat, Marquis de Condorcet, *Outlines of an Historical View of the Progress of the Human Mind,* translated from the French (London, 1795); François de La Mothe Le Vayer, *Notitia historicorum selectorum, or Animadversions upon the Ancient and Famous Greek and Latin Historians* (Oxford, 1678), GCMG.

70. Napoleon I, Emperor of France, *Memoirs of the History of France during the Reign of Napoleon, Dictated by the Emperor at Saint Helena to the Generals Who Shared His Captivity; and Published from the Original Manuscripts Corrected by Himself,* 7 vols. (London, 1823), GCMG.

71. David Hume, *The History of England from the Invasion of Caesar to the Revolution in 1688,* vols. 1–5 (Philadelphia, 1795); *Milton's Paradise Lost with a Life of John Milton* (London, 1795); *Milton's Paradise Regained with a Complete Selection of His Miscellaneous Poems* (London, 1795); *The Poetical Works of Peter Pindar,* vol. 1 (Philadelphia, 1794); Manley Wood, *The Plays of William Shakespeare with Various Notes and Directions,* vols. 1–14 (London, 1806), all in Gratz Family Library Collection, NMAJH; R.G. to Maria Gist Gratz, October 12, 1833, excerpted in Philipson, *Letters,* 184.

72. Brener, *The Jews of Lancaster,* 24.

73. Sarah Mordecai, *Recollections of My Aunt* (Philadelphia, 1873).

74. Gordon, "The Young Ladies Academy," 68–91.

75. Rush, *Essays,* n.p., LCP.

76. Ibid.

77. *Rise and Progress,* preface, LCP.

78. R.G. to Miriam Moses Cohen, January 19, 1840, Rebecca Gratz Papers, Manuscript Collection no. 236, AJA.

79. T. Smith, "Feminism in Philadelphia," 252; Gordon, "The Young Ladies Academy"; John Swanick, *Thoughts on Education Addressed to the Visitors to the Young Ladies Academy in Philadelphia October 31, 1781* (Philadelphia: Dobson, 1787), LCP; *The Rise and*

Progress of the Young Ladies Academy (Philadelphia, 1794), LCP; Benjamin Rush, *Essays Literary, Moral and Philosophical* (Philadelphia, 1798), LCP.

80. Klein, *Jews in Lancaster,* 17.
81. For a discussion of these ideas, see Kerber, *Women of the Republic;* Linda Kerber, "A Constitutional Right to Be Treated Like American Ladies: Women and the Obligations of Citizenship," in *U.S. History as Women's History: New Feminist Essays,* ed. Linda K. Kerber, Alice Kessler-Harris, and Kathryn Kish Sklar (Chapel Hill: University of North Carolina Press, 1995), 24–27.
82. Saum, *The Popular Mood;* Feldstein, *The Land That I Show You.*
83. WW, 48–49. R.G. to Maria Fenno Hoffman, April 11, 1813, March 24, 1822, and to Miriam Moses Cohen, April 25, 1840, Rebecca Gratz Papers, Manuscript Collection no. 236, AJA.
84. WW, 141, 258.
85. Eleazer Lyon to Michael Gratz, ca. 1765, Michael Gratz Papers, Manuscript Collection, AJA.
86. David Levi, *Seder HaTefilot: Form of Prayer for the Fast Days According to the Custom of the Spanish-Portuguese Jews* (London, 5553 [1792]); Isaac Leeser updated Levi's work in 1837. Leeser, *Seder Sefati Tzadikim: Form of Prayers According to the Custom of the Spanish-Portuguese Jews* (Philadelphia, 5598 [1837]), MIA.
87. WW, 42.
88. H. Morais, *The Jews of Philadelphia,* 370; R.G. to Maria Fenno Hoffman, April 11, 1813, March 24, 1822, and to Miriam Moses Cohen November 4, [1837?], April 25, December 15, 1840, Rebecca Gratz Papers, P-9, AJHS. Gratz's uncle Barnard owned Levi's English-Hebrew prayer books for home worship, Sabbath, festivals, and holy days.
89. D'Emilio and Freedman, *Intimate Matters,* 42–52.
90. There is some disagreement over the identity of the two children who died in infancy. All agree that the first child born, Solomon, died at age four. However, Philipson (*Letters,* x) and Stern (*First American Jewish Families,* 42) claim that the second child, who died in infancy, was a son named Jonathan. Fish (*Barnard and Michael Gratz,* 181) argues that the second child was a daughter named Zipporah. Byars (*B. & M. Gratz,* 259) claims that three children died in childhood.
91. Degler, *At Odds,* 179–80.
92. Stern, *First American Jewish Families,* 43.
93. Stern, "Jewish Marriage and Intermarriage," 142–43; Marcus, *The American Jewish Woman, 1654–1980,* 270, says that Simon's family was shunned by the rest of the family and ignored by the Jewish community, but Louisa's behavior indicates that good relations were restored. Louisa converted to Judaism, indicating that family relationships remained cordial despite religious differences. R.G. to

Maria Gist Gratz, February 10, 1840, Rebecca Gratz Papers, Manuscript Collection no. 236, AJA. Although Judaism forbids intermarriage, antebellum American Jews differed in their attitudes about it. In the mid-1790s, in six Philadelphia families, husbands attended synagogue while their wives went to church. Miriam's sister Shinah, thirteen years her junior, married Dr. Nicholas Schuyler in 1782 in the Lutheran Trinity Church in Lancaster, and the couple later relocated to Troy, New York. Miriam remained close to her sister and encouraged her daughters to develop strong ties to their aunt, who had no children. WW, 224; Marcus, *On Love, Marriage, Children . . . and Death,* 21–23.

94. Brener, *The Jews of Lancaster,* 4, 5.
95. Ibid., 20.
96. Fish, *Barnard and Michael Gratz,* 155–78.
97. Bushman, *The Refinement of America,* 215–16.
98. Compare Miriam Simon Gratz letter in Marcus, *The American Jewish Woman,* with Miriam Gratz to R.G., June 8, 1797; Gratz Family Papers, Collection no. 72, box 16, APS.
99. Hench, "Letters of John Fenno"; Richard G. Miller, "The Federal City, 1783–1800," in Weigley, *Philadelphia,* 197–201.
100. Maria Fenno to R.G., June 21, 1795, Gratz Family Papers, Collection no. 72, box 16, APS.
101. Maria Fenno to R.G., 1795, ibid.
102. Maria Fenno to R.G., July 12, 1797, ibid.; R.G. to Richea Gratz, July 16, 1798, ibid., box 15.
103. Maria Fenno to R.G., July 12, 1797, ibid., box 16.
104. R.G. to Sarah Gratz, August 26, 1798, ibid., box 21.
105. R.G. to Rachel Gratz, July 26, 1798, ibid., box 15.
106. Hench, "Letters of John Fenno"; R.G. to Rachel Gratz, September 9, 1798, Gratz Family Papers, Collection no. 72, box 15, APS.
107. R.G. to Rachel Gratz, September 16, 1798, ibid.
108. Tuition receipt for the teaching of French, ibid., box 11.
109. R.G. to Rachel Gratz, December 30, 1798, ibid, box 15.
110. Maria Fenno to R.G., January 29, 1799, ibid., box 16.
111. R.G. to Sarah Gratz, July 18, 1800, ibid., box 20.
112. R.G. to Rachel Gratz, ca. 1799, ibid., box 9.

Chapter 2

1. Richardson, "Athens of America."
2. Frances Gratz Etting to Hyman Gratz, June 28, 1801, Etting Collection, HSP; Fish, *Barnard and Michael Gratz,* 175.
3. Gluckel of Hameln, *Memoirs of Gluckel of Hameln,* 154–56; Glenn, *Daughters of the Shtetl,* 9; Hundert, "Approaches," 22; Kaplan, *The Making of the Jewish Middle Class,* 25–66; Goldscheider and Zucker-

man, *Transformation of the Jews,* 100, report that "women . . . made up 15% of the labor force in the Pale"; Byars, *B. & M. Gratz,* 7–30.

4. Hoffman and Albert, *Women in the Age of the American Revolution,* 455.

5. Byars, *B. & M. Gratz,* 7–30; Feldstein, *The Land That I Show You,* 16, 27, 39–40, 90–91; WW, 181, 182, 339–54, 434–49.

6. Traditional Judaism assigns many religious responsibilities and rights by gender. Men are expected to lead religious activities both in the synagogue and at home. To perform those responsibilities, men's religious education, historically, far outdistanced that available to women. Synagogue voting rights, leadership, and even full participation were historically withheld from women. See Hyman, *Gender and Assimilation,* 48–59; R. Biale, *Women and Jewish Law,* 10–43.

7. Maria Fenno to R.G., February 1, 1800, Gratz Family Papers, Collection no. 72, box 16, APS.

8. Byars, *B. & M. Gratz,* 7–30.

9. Maria Fenno to R.G., June 8, 1801, Gratz Family Papers, Collection no. 72, box 16, APS.

10. Starr, *American Medicine,* 33–34.

11. A large family for their time, the Gratzes reflected the fertility trends of both European Jews and Americans. Comparable to many eastern European Jewish women, Lancaster-born Miriam Simon Gratz bore twelve children, far above the American national average (WW, 52; Hareven, "Modernization and Family History"; D. S. Smith, "Family Limitation"). From the eighteenth through nineteenth centuries, the eastern European Jewish population tripled (Hundert, "Approaches," 21; Baron, *Social and Religious History,* 15–23, 192–211; R. Biale, *Women and Jewish Law,* 46; Goldscheider and Zuckerman, *Transformation of the Jews,* 98). Population pressures there worsened the growing economic instability caused by industrialization in some Jewish towns and led to popular resistance to the kahal, the community network that, with rabbinic advice, supervised charitable, religious, and legal activities in Jewish communities (Hundert, "Approaches," 25). New ideologies in Jewish enlightenment and in mysticism, movements attractive to young people, thrived (R. Biale, *Women and Jewish Law,* 47–48). Not surprisingly, many young people also migrated from eastern Europe to more prosperous central Europe (Diner, *A Time for Gathering,* 1–30). In the 1830s and 1840s, Jewish women and men hoping to escape government-set limits on Jewish households emigrated from central Europe to the United States to marry (Glanz, *The Jewish Woman in America,* 2:9–11; Feldstein, *The Land That I Show You,* 41; N. Cohen, *Encounter with Emancipation,* 4–17). Brothers and sisters who had emigrated drew siblings after them, the oldest often emigrating first and the younger following

(Glanz, *The Jewish Woman in America,* 2:10). Three of Miriam Gratz's daughters—Richea, Rachel, and Fanny—followed her pattern, bearing ten, nine, and ten children, far above the declining American national average, which had dropped to seven births per woman by 1800 (D'Emilio and Freedman, *Intimate Matters,* 58).

12. R.G. to Sarah Gratz, July 28, 1800, Gratz Family Papers, Collection no. 72, box 21, APS.
13. R.G. to Sarah Gratz, July 18, 1800, Rebecca Gratz Papers, Manuscript Collection no. 236, AJA.
14. R.G. to Sarah Gratz, August 10, 1800, Gratz Family Papers, Collection no. 72, box 21, APS.
15. Miriam Gratz to Barnard Gratz, September 26, 1790, Byars, *B. & M. Gratz,* 239.
16. R.G. to Sarah Gratz, 1800, Gratz Family Papers, Collection no. 72, box 21, APS.
17. Maria Fenno to R.G., November 12, 15, 1800, ibid., box 16.
18. Sarah Gratz to R.G., November 16, 1800, ibid., box 15.
19. R.G. to Sarah Gratz, November 13, 1800, ibid., box 21.
20. R.G. to Sarah Gratz, November 17, 1800, ibid.
21. R.G. to Rachel Gratz, November 21, 1800, ibid., box 15.
22. Sarah Gratz to R.G., November 30, 1800, ibid.
23. R.G. to Rachel Gratz, November 19, 1800, ibid.
24. Sarah Gratz to R.G., November 30, 1800, ibid.
25. R.G. to Rachel Gratz, December 6, 1800, ibid.
26. Ibid.; Belenky, Clinchy, Goldberger, and Tarule, *Women's Ways of Knowing,* 131.
27. Cameron, *The Feminist Critique of Language,* 1–26; Hunter, "Hysteria, Psychoanalysis, and Feminism," 473–75.
28. R.G. to Rachel Gratz, December 6, 1800, Gratz Family Papers, Collection no. 72, box 15, APS.
29. Maria Fenno to R.G., December 12, 1800, ibid., box 16.
30. R.G. to Rachel Gratz, December 14, 1800, ibid., box 15.
31. R.G. to Rachel Gratz, December 16, 1800, ibid.
32. R.G. to Rachel Gratz, December 26, 1800, ibid., box 21.
33. R.G. to Maria Fenno, November 18, 1801, Rebecca Gratz Papers, P-9, AJHS; Starr, *American Medicine,* 32. Women commonly used manuals, the best-known of which was William Buchanan's *Domestic Medicine,* published in 1769 (Edinburgh) and 1771 (Philadelphia); this text went through thirty editions.
34. Rosenberg, *The Cholera Years.*
35. Warner, *The Private City,* 98–123.
36. R.G. to Maria Fenno Hoffman, October 31, 1809, October 25, 1820, March 23, 1821, Rebecca Gratz Papers, P-9, AJHS; Rosenberg, *The Cholera Years.*

37. Rosenberg, "The Therapeutic Revolution"; Starr, *American Medicine,* 32–44; Rosenberg and Smith-Rosenberg, "The Female Animal"; Shryock, *Medicine in America;* Benjamin Rush, "On the Causes of Death in Diseases That Are Not Incurable," and Nathaniel Chapman, "Remarks on the Chronic Fluxes of the Bowels," both in Breiger, *Medical America in the Nineteenth Century.*
38. WW, 352.
39. R.G. to Maria Fenno, March 24, 1801, Rebecca Gratz Papers, P-9, AJHS.
40. Maria Fenno to R.G., February 8, June 16, 1801, Gratz Family Papers, Collection no. 72, box 16, APS.
41. R.G. to Maria Fenno, June 28, 1801, Rebecca Gratz Papers, P-9, AJHS.
42. R.G. to Maria Fenno, July 23, 1802, ibid.
43. Sarah Gratz to R.G., August 19, 1802, Gratz Family Papers, Collection no. 72, box 15, APS.
44. Leonard Beerman, "An Analysis of the Life and Activity of the Foremost Jewess of the Nineteenth Century" (Ordination thesis, Hebrew Union College, 1947), 17–32.
45. Maria Fenno to R.G., June 22, 1801, Gratz Family Papers, Collection no. 72, box 16, APS.
46. Wolf and Whiteman list Richea as the sister who joined Rebecca and Miriam in contributing to the Female Association; however, the organization's records name Rachel (WW, 271; FA Constitution, 1801, LCP).
47. FA Constitution, LCP; FHBS Constitution, Small Collections, AJA.
48. FA Constitution, LCP.
49. Scott, *Natural Allies,* 26.
50. Hoffman and Albert, *Women in the Age of the American Revolution,* 452–53.
51. R.G. to Maria Fenno, June 21, 1801, Rebecca Gratz Papers, P-9, A2HS.
52. Richardson, "Athens of America," 226.
53. Glenn, *Daughters of the Shtetl,* 16–19; Kessler-Harris, *Out to Work,* 155–76.
54. Kessler-Harris, *Out to Work,* 24–25.
55. Lawrence, *Philadelphia Almshouses,* 9, FL.
56. Richardson, "Athens of America," 244.
57. Abramovitz, *Regulating the Lives of Women,* 157–58.
58. Lawrence, *Philadelphia Almshouses,* 8.
59. Abramovitz, *Regulating the Lives of Women,* 86–87; Lawrence, *Philadelphia Almshouses,* 10.
60. R.G. to Rachel Gratz, 1801, Gratz Family Papers, Collection no. 72, box 15, APS.
61. Wolf, *Book Culture,* 32.

62. Ibid.; "Joseph Dennie," *Penn Monthly* 11 (1880): 722–25, APS.

63. Michael Gratz and Joseph Simon paid thirty pounds sterling bond to their credit with Meredith. Stauffer Collection, folder S 90, HSP.

64. Joseph Dennie, ed., *Port Folio* 1 (1801), LCP.

65. "Journal of a Tour through Silesia," part 1, *Port Folio* 1 (1801): 1, LCP.

66. Joseph Dennie, "Morals," *Port Folio* 1 (1801): 37, 294, LCP.

67. "National Pride," *Port Folio* 2 (July–December 1809): 38, LCP.

68. *Port Folio* 1 (1801): 3, LCP. As a rule, Dennie never published authors' names. He himself used "Oliver Oldschool, Esq." and "Lay Preacher," among other pseudonyms.

69. Berlin, "Solomon Jackson's *The Jew*"; Haberman, "A Jewish View of the Idea of Progress."

70. Borden, *Jews, Turks, and Infidels;* Appel, "Jews in American Caricature"; Glanz, *The Jew in Early American Wit.*

71. R.G. to [?], 1802, Gratz Family Papers, Collection no. 72, box 19, APS.

72. Sam Ewing, August 1800, August 1802, ibid., box 11.

73. Margaret Ewing to R.G., July 6, [1802?], ibid., box 17.

74. R.G. to Maria Fenno, July 7, 1802, Rebecca Gratz Papers, MMC.

75. R.G. to Rachel Gratz, June 13, 1802, Gratz Family Papers, Collection no. 72, box 21, APS.

76. R.G. to Rachel Gratz, August 2, 1802, ibid.

77. R.G. to Rachel Gratz, May 26, 1803, ibid.

78. R.G. to Rachel Gratz, May 24, 1803, ibid., box 15.

79. R.G. to Rachel Gratz, May 26, 1803, ibid., box 21.

80. R.G. to Rachel Gratz, June 15, 1803, ibid., box 15.

81. Sam Ewing to R.G., June 21, 1803, ibid., box 9.

82. R.G. to Rachel Gratz, Baltimore, June 19, 1803, ibid., box 15; Wharton (*Lives of Eminent Philadelphians,* 357) describes Ewing as well known for his "kindness and . . . conversational powers." On Isaac D'Israeli see Galchinsky, *Modern Jewish Woman Writer,* 85.

83. R.G. to Rachel Gratz, July 18, 1803, Gratz Family Papers, Collection no. 72, box 15, APS.

84. R.G. to Rachel Gratz, June 15, 1803, ibid.

85. R.G. to Richea Gratz Hays, June 19, 1803, ibid.

86. R.G. to Richea Gratz Hays, July 18, 1803, ibid.

87. R.G. to Margaret Ewing, July 19, 1803, ibid., box 21.

88. R.G. to Margaret Ewing, September 19, 1803, ibid.

89. Brener, *The Jews of Lancaster,* 20–23. Given these facts of Simon's will, I cannot agree with the conclusion that Simon wrote Shinah out of his will because she married a non-Jew. Her inheritance was consistent with Simon's concern for his grandchildren. Also, it is evident that Simon's actual wealth was in dispute by the time of his death.

90. R.G. to Rachel Gratz, May 2, 1804, Gratz Family Papers, Collection no. 72, box 9, APS.

91. Brener, *The Jews of Lancaster,* 5.
92. Josiah Ogden Hoffman to R.G., October 5, 1804, Gratz Family Papers, Collection no. 72, box 15, APS.
93. Gertrude Gouverneur Meredith to William Meredith, September 30, 1805, Meredith Papers Correspondence, box 17, folder 11, HSP.
94. Gertrude Gouverneur Meredith to William Meredith, September 27, 1805, ibid.
95. R.G. to Gertrude Gouverneur Meredith, September 1805, ibid.; Gertrude Gouverneur Meredith to William Meredith, September 19, 1805, ibid.
96. D. S. Smith, "Family Limitation"; S. M. Evans, *Born for Liberty,* 76–96.
97. Mott, *American Magazines,* 243–48.
98. Mary Elizabeth Fenno to R.G., December 20, 1805, Henry Joseph Collection, box 238, AJA.
99. R.G. to Miriam Gratz, July 1805, Gratz Family Papers, Collection no. 72, box 9, APS.
100. Josiah Ogden Hoffman to R.G., December 11, 1805, ibid., box 15.
101. R.G. to Rachel Gratz, 1805, ibid.
102. Maria Fenno Hoffman to R.G., February 4, 1806, ibid.
103. Maria Fenno Hoffman to R.G., March 17, 1806, ibid.
104. R.G. to Sarah Gratz, May 21, [1806?], ibid., box 9.
105. R.G. to Sarah Gratz, July 8, 1806, July 10, 1806, ibid.
106. R.G. to Sarah Gratz, August 8, 1806, ibid.
107. R.G. to Kitty Etting, n.d., Rebecca Gratz Papers, Manuscript Collection no. 236, AJA.
108. R.G. to Maria Fenno Hoffman, February 9, n.d., Rebecca Gratz Papers, Manuscript Collection no. 236, AJA.
109. R.G. to Maria Fenno Hoffman, March 7, 1807, ibid.
110. Fern, *Mr. Sully.*
111. WW, 322–24.
112. Rebecca Gratz poems on birchbark, Gratz Family Papers, Collection no. 72, box 21, APS.
113. Many thanks to Rev. Dr. David Clowney for explaining the traditions of the Presbyterian Church. Their reading of 1 Corinthians 7:12–16 and 2 Corinthians 6:14–18 insisted on marriage between confessing Christians only.
114. R.G., "Lebanon Springs, 1806," Gratz Family Papers, Collection no. 72, box 21, APS. Many thanks to Prof. Sylvia Baer for this reading of the poem.
115. R.G., "As through the garden walk I stray'd . . . ," ibid.
116. "The Story of Reb Hanina, the Son-In-Law of Reb Judah the Hasid, and His Adventures in the Forest," in *Ma'aseh Book,* 341.
117. R.G. to Maria Fenno Hoffman, December 29, [1807?], Rebecca Gratz Papers, P-9, AJHS.

118. R.G. to Maria Fenno Hoffman, October 20, 1817, ibid.
119. For an account of their efforts, see Butler, *Awash in a Sea of Faith.*
120. Mrs. Edward Hoffman to John Francis Marion, February 11, 1985, Gratz Family Papers, Collection no. 72, box 19, APS.
121. Fern, *Mr. Sully.*
122. Gertrude Meredith to R.G., [1807?], Gratz Family Papers, Collection no. 72, box 15, APS.
123. Gertrude Meredith to R.G., September 6, 1807, Rebecca Gratz Papers, Manuscript Collection no. 236, AJA.
124. John Hall to R.G., May 9, 1807, Gratz Family Papers, Collection no. 72, box 15, APS.
125. John Hall to R.G., January 6, 1808, ibid.
126. John Hall to R.G., April 1808, ibid.
127. R.G. to Margaret Ewing, June 24, 1808, ibid., box 21.
128. R.G. to Rachel Gratz, June 24, 1808, ibid.
129. R.G. to Rachel Gratz, n.d., ibid.
130. R.G. to Margaret Ewing, August 8, [1808?], ibid.
131. Gertrude Meredith to Sarah Ewing Hall, February 17, 1808, Meredith Papers Correspondence, box 20, folder 2, HSP.
132. Sarah Gratz to R.G., May 21, 1808, Gratz Family Papers, Collection no. 72, box 9, APS.
133. Gertrude Meredith to R.G., 1808, Rebecca Gratz Papers, Manuscript Collection no. 236, AJA.
134. Caroline Ogden to R.G., November 20, 1808, Rebecca Gratz Papers, P-9, AJHS.
135. R.G. to Maria Fenno Hoffman, June 18, 1809, Rebecca Gratz Papers, Manuscript Collection no. 236, AJA.
136. R.G. to Maria Fenno Hoffman, April 14, 1808, Rebecca Gratz Papers, MMC.
137. Ann Hoffman to R.G., April 4, 1809, Gratz Family Papers, Collection no. 72, box 18, APS.
138. Ann Hoffman to R.G., May 2, 1809, ibid.
139. R.G. to J. Ogden and Maria Fenno Hoffman, April 28, 1809, Rebecca Gratz Papers, Manuscript Collection no. 236, AJA; Weissler, "The Traditional Piety of Ashkenazic Women"; Weissler, "Tkhinnes of the Matriarchs."
140. R.G. to Maria Fenno Hoffman, March 7, 1809, Rebecca Gratz Papers, MMC.
141. R.G. to Maria Fenno Hoffman, January 29, ca. 1812, February 24, 1815, October 20, 1817, Rebecca Gratz Papers, Manuscript Collection no. 236, AJA.
142. R.G. to Maria Fenno Hoffman, July 15, 1810, March 25, 1813, Rebecca Gratz Papers, MMC.
143. R.G. to Margaret Ewing, July 23, 1809, Gratz Family Papers, Collection no. 72, box 21, APS.

144. Chambers-Schiller, *Liberty: A Better Husband,* 10–28. The author refers specifically to Gratz on p. 15.

145. R.G. to Margaret Ewing, August 3, [1810?], Gratz Family Papers, Collection no. 72, box 21, APS.

146. Quoted in Ruth B. Sarner, "Rebecca Gratz, Address for Opening a Commemorative Exhibit," delivered at the HSP, December 9, 1969, FHBS Collection, folder 90.9.1, NMAJH.

147. Sarah Gratz to R.G., [1810?], Gratz Family Papers, Collection no. 72, box 15, APS.

148. R.G. to Joseph Gratz, August 26, 1810, Gratz Family Papers, RM.

149. R.G. to Maria Fenno Hoffman, October 28, 1812, Rebecca Gratz Papers, P-9, AJHS.

150. R.G. to Joseph Gratz, May 15, 1812, Gratz Family Letters, Correspondence File, AJA; R.G. to Maria Gist Gratz, August 10, 1841, Philipson, *Letters,* 292; R.G. to Joseph Gratz, March 2, 22, 31, April 14, May 11, 12, 27, 1810, Gratz Family Papers, RM.

151. Sarah Gratz to R.G., November 25, 1810, December 9, 1810, Gratz Family Papers, Collection no. 72, box 16, APS.

152. R.G. to Maria Fenno Hoffman, February 18, 1812, Rebecca Gratz Papers, P-9, AJHS.

153. Sarner, "Rebecca Gratz."

154. R.G. to Maria Fenno Hoffman, February 18, 1812, Rebecca Gratz Papers, P-9, AJHS.

155. Richardson, "Athens of America," 211.

156. Hyman Gratz to Sarah and Rebecca Gratz, Dripping Springs, Kentucky, August 31, 1812, and same to same, Glasgow, Kentucky, 1812, Gratz Family Papers, Collection no. 72, box 16, APS; Hyman Gratz to R.G., September 13, 1812, ibid., box 15.

157. R.G. to Maria Fenno Hoffman, March 15, 1812, Rebecca Gratz Papers, P-9, AJHS.

158. R.G. to Maria Fenno Hoffman, August 8, 18, 1812, March 25, 1813, ibid.

159. Sloe Hays to R.G., July 7, 1812, Gratz Family Papers, Collection no. 72, box 9, APS.

160. R.G. to Maria Fenno Hoffman, March 14, 1813, Rebecca Gratz Papers, MMC.

161. R.G. to Maria Fenno Hoffman, April 11, 1813, ibid.

162. D'Emilio and Freedman, *Intimate Matters,* 70.

163. Ibid., 86–88. Nineteenth-century anthropology also displayed these ideas; see Fee, "Sexual Politics."

164. D'Emilio and Freedman, *Intimate Matters,* 96.

165. M. Harris, "Touch, Sight, and Hearing."

166. Stern, *First American Jewish Families;* Hareven and Vinovskis, *Family and Population;* Wells, "Family Size and Fertility Control."
167. Sally L. Kitch, *Chaste Liberation: Celibacy and Female Cultural Status* (Urbana: University of Illinois Press, 1989), 74–90.
168. Berman, *Richmond's Jewry,* 102.
169. R.G. to Maria Fenno Hoffman, ca. 1812, Rebecca Gratz Papers, Manuscript Collection no. 236, AJA.
170. Douglas, *The Feminization of American Culture,* 78–80.
171. Rebecca Gratz letter, "Sothebys," June 26, 1895, p. 10, Gratz Family Papers, Collection no. 72, APS.
172. WW, 342.
173. Gertrude Meredith to R.G., June 15, 1813, Gratz Family Papers, Collection no. 72, box 15, APS; same to same, n.d., ibid.
174. R.G. to Maria Fenno Hoffman, March 25, 1813, Rebecca Gratz Papers, MMC.
175. Berkovits, *Not in Heaven,* 85–89.
176. Sered, *Women as Ritual Experts.* Note that the Musar movement in nineteenth-century Europe shifted Jewish practice significantly toward an emphasis on ethics for men and women alike; Goldberg, *Israel Salanter,* passim.
177. R.G. to Maria Fenno Hoffman, December 15, 1815, Rebecca Gratz Papers, P-9, AJHS.
178. Toll and Gillam, *Invisible Philadelphia,* 348.
179. R.G. to Maria Fenno Hoffman, ca. 1815, Rebecca Gratz Papers, Manuscript Collection no. 236, AJA.

Chapter 3

1. R.G. to Maria Fenno Hoffman, January 26, 1818, Rebecca Gratz Papers, P-9, AJHS.
2. R.G. to Maria Fenno Hoffman, February 14, 1817, Rebecca Gratz Papers, Manuscript Collection no. 236, AJA.
3. R.G. to Maria Fenno Hoffman, June 3, 1818, Rebecca Gratz Papers, P-9, AJHS.
4. R.G. to Maria Fenno Hoffman, January 26, 1818, Rebecca Gratz Papers, Manuscript Collection no. 236, AJA; same to same, 1817, ibid.
5. Richardson, "Athens of America."
6. Butler, *Awash in a Sea of Faith,* 67–95.
7. Saum, *The Popular Mood,* 224.
8. First Report of the Female Bible Society of Philadelphia (1815), LCP.
9. "By comparison, the overall United States population grew from about 4,000,000 in 1780 to 10,000,000 in 1820 and 31,000,000 in 1860"; Butler, *Awash in a Sea of Faith,* 270–71, 278–79.
10. Reuther and Keller, *Women and Religion in America,* vol. 1; Welter,

"She Hath Done What She Could"; Faith Rogow, "Step Right Up: The Attraction of Evangelicalism to Ante-Bellum Southern White Women," unpublished manuscript, 1984.

11. Reuther, *Religion and Sexism,* 242
12. Diner, *A Time for Gathering,* 56.
13. Ashton, "Souls Have No Sex," 36. Population statistics for Philadelphia are from Weigley, *Philadelphia,* 104–15. Population statistics for Jews in Philadelphia are from Whiteman, "Legacy of Isaac Leeser," 27, and Edwin Wolf II, "The German-Jewish Influence in Philadelphia's Jewish Charities," in M. Friedman, *Jewish Life in Philadelphia, 1830–1940,* 125.
14. Diner, *A Time for Gathering,* 177.
15. WW, 241–42.
16. Diner, *A Time for Gathering,* 86.
17. R.G. to Maria Fenno Hoffman, June 3, 1818, Rebecca Gratz Papers, Manuscript Collection no. 236, AJA.
18. R.G. to Maria Fenno Hoffman, March 9, 1818, ibid.
19. R.G. to Maria Fenno Hoffman, March 3, 1818, Gratz Family Papers, RM; S. I. Cohen, *Elements of the Jewish Faith,* translated from the Hebrew (Richmond, 1817; Philadelphia, 1823); Hyman Polock Rosenbach, "Notes on the First Settlement of Jews in Pennsylvania," *PAJHS* 5 (1897): 191–98.
20. Miller, "Women in the Vanguard," 312.
21. Moore, *Selling God,* 61.
22. Toll and Gillam, *Invisible Philadelphia,* 278
23. *Poulson's American Daily Advertiser,* January 21, 1819, LCP.
24. Ibid., January 1, 1819, LCP.
25. Ibid., January 22, 1819, LCP.
26. First Annual Report of the Philadelphia Orphan Asylum (1816), 17–18, "Pamphlets no. 992," APS.
27. R.G. to Maria Fenno Hoffman, n.d., Rebecca Gratz Papers, Manuscript Collection no. 236, AJA.
28. R.G. to Maria Gist Gratz, 1832, excerpted in Philipson, *Letters,* 133.
29. Jacob Gratz to R.G., Gratz Family Papers, Collection no. 72, box 16, APS.
30. R.G. to Maria Fenno Hoffman, December 13, 1817, Rebecca Gratz Papers, P-9, AJHS.
31. Joseph Gratz to R.G., July [1819?], July 31, 1819, Gratz Family Papers, Collection no. 72, box 16, APS.
32. Joseph Gratz to R.G., August 1819, ibid.
33. Joseph Gratz to R.G., August 26, 1819, ibid.
34. WW, 341.
35. Ibid.
36. Wainwright, "The Age of Nicholas Biddle," 282.

37. Richardson, "Athens of America," 249.
38. Bodek, "Making Do," 145, 147.
39. FHBS Constitution, LCP.
40. Glanz, *The Jewish Woman in America,* vol. 2; R.G. to Miriam Moses Cohen, January 24, 1843, Rebecca Gratz Papers, Manuscript Collection no. 236, AJA.
41. R. S. Friedman, "'Send Me My Husband.'"
42. Rebecca Gratz, *Female Hebrew Benevolent Society's Secretary's Report* (1858), Henry Joseph Collection, box 239, AJA.
43. Guardians of the Poor: Records 1822–1824, 4–5, HSP.
44. *Report of a Committee on the Subject of Pauperism* (New York, 1818), 9, APS. Although several causes for poverty were listed, charitable institutions were blamed for the "evils that flow from the expectations they necessarily excite." Mathew Carey, *Essays on the Public Charities of Philadelphia,* 4th ed. (Philadelphia, 1829), "Pamphlets no. 992," APS.
45. *Report of a Committee,* 14, APS.
46. Carey, *Essays,* 1–2.
47. William Ellery Channing, *A Sermon Delivered in Boston, September 18, 1818* (Boston, 1818), 8, "Pamphlets no. 992," APS.
48. Lawrence, *Philadelphia Almshouses,* 9.
49. Minute Book of the Junto for Congregation Mikveh Israel, April 18, 1824–February 14, 1881, MIA.
50. According to historian Ann Boylan ("Women in Groups"), antebellum women's organizations did not follow a linear development from small auxiliaries to independent, large public agencies. Instead, the groups were organized along distinct networks that often had little contact or communication with each other. While women's local mission societies usually began as small prayer meetings and grew into support systems for male-led church and national mission societies, benevolent societies began with public activities and independent administrations as early as 1800. Benevolent societies usually attracted women from merchant and clergy families and tried to "uplift" individuals among the "worthy poor." Moral reform societies focusing on the environmental causes of poverty appeared in the 1830s and drew their support from a more varied population of women. Finally, in the 1840s, when many states adopted the principle of universal white male suffrage, women's rights groups appeared. A crucial handful of women moved from leadership in the abolition movement to leadership in the fight for women's suffrage. As a rule, these different types of organizations existed as parallel sets of societies with little in common. Boylan concludes that antebellum women's social activism is best explained by personal class and religious experiences of the women involved.

51. FHBS Constitution 1820, LCP. D. S. Smith, "Family Limitation," 119–36; Scott, *Natural Allies,* 11–37.
52. Ginzberg, *Women and the Work of Benevolence,* 53.
53. Di Leonardo, "The Female World of Cards and Holidays."
54. FHBS Constitution, LCP. Phillips's granddaughter Ellen Phillips bequeathed over $100,000 to numerous Philadelphia Jewish and municipal philanthropies when she died in 1891. Will of Ellen Phillips, Ellen Phillips Papers, HSP.
55. Byars, *B. & M. Gratz,* 35–55; Bodek, "Making Do," 142.
56. Scott, *Natural Allies,* 13.
57. Ginzberg, *Women and the Work of Benevolence,* 215.
58. FHBS Constitution, 1819, AJA.
59. FHBS, Board Minutes, 1814–1875, FHBS Collection, NMAJH.
60. FHBS Constitution, AJA.
61. Welter, "The Feminization of American Religion."
62. Scott, *Natural Allies,* 15.
63. Welter, "She Hath Done What She Could"; WW, 78.
64. Diner, *A Time for Gathering,* 163.
65. H. Morais, *The Jews of Philadelphia,* 432; WW, 180, 202, 293–99.
66. R.G. to Maria Fenno Hoffman, October 20, 1817, to Miriam Moses Cohen, November 14, 1837, and to Maria Fenno Hoffman, October 31, 1819, all in Rebecca Gratz Papers, Manuscript Collection no. 236, AJA.
67. R.G. to Maria Gist Gratz, 1820, Rebecca Gratz Papers, P-9, AJHS.
68. R.G. to Maria Gist Gratz, 1819, Philipson, *Letters,* 21.
69. R.G. to Maria Gist Gratz, 1820, ibid., 27.
70. R.G. to Maria Gist Gratz, February 23, 1840, Rebecca Gratz Papers, P-9, AJHS.
71. Butler, *Awash in a Sea of Faith,* 97.
72. *Poulson's American Daily Advertiser,* December 1838, LCP.
73. R.G. to Maria Fenno Hoffman, 1817, Rebecca Gratz Papers, P-9, AJHS.
74. Hall's *Port Folio* pseudonym was Constantia. R.G. to Maria Fenno Hoffman, ca. 1817, Miriam Gratz Moses Cohen Papers and Books, Collection no. 2639, SHC.
75. Douglas, *The Feminization of American Culture,* 99.
76. Butler, *Awash in a Sea of Faith,* 278.
77. R.G. to Maria Gist Gratz, April 4, 1820, Rebecca Gratz Papers, Manuscript Collection no. 236, AJA.
78. R.G. to Maria Gist Gratz, May 10, 1820, ibid.
79. MacDonald, *The Education of the Heart,* 28.
80. R.G. to Maria Edgeworth, n.d., ca. 1822, APS, box 9.
81. Gratz also wrote to her old friend Maria Fenno Hoffman about *Harrington* and her concerns about its message. Gratz understood that

"religious tolerance . . . [is] the message [Edgeworth] would inculcate," but she disliked Edgeworth's plot. "I think however a more
interesting and natural story might have been produced in making
the characters of Jew and Christian associate and assimilate in all
the respective charities of social life without bringing the passions
into contact. I believe it is impossible to reconcile a matrimonial
engagement between persons of so different a creed without requiring
one or the other to yield. In all instances we have heard of in real life
this has been the case & where a family of children are to be brought
up it appears necessary that parents should agree." R.G. to Maria
Fenno Hoffman, October 20, 1817, Rebecca Gratz Papers, Manuscript
Collection no. 236, AJA.

82. Ellen Hays to R.G., August 7, 1821, Gratz Family Papers, Collection
no. 71, box 16, APS.
83. Scott, *Natural Allies,* 19.
84. Carey, *Essays.*
85. WW, 326.
86. Jacob Gratz to R.G., 1821, Gratz Family Papers, Collection no. 72,
APS, box 16.
87. WW, 97.
88. S[arah] Hall to R.G., ca. 1821, Gratz Family Papers, APS, Collection
no. 72, box 16.
89. Ginzberg, *Women and the Work of Benevolence,* 36–45.
90. R.G. to Maria Fenno Hoffman, n.d., Gratz Family Papers, Collection
no. 72, box 16, APS.
91. R.G. to Maria Gist Gratz, May 4, 1828, Rebecca Gratz Papers, P-9,
AJHS.
92. Richardson, "Athens of America," 208–56.
93. R.G. to Maria Fenno Hoffman, March 2, 1822, Rebecca Gratz Papers,
Manuscript Collection no. 236, AJA.
94. Eighth Annual Report of the Philadelphia Orphan Asylum, 1822,
Pamphlet no. 922, APS.
95. R.G. to Maria Fenno Hoffman, April 6, 1823, Rebecca Gratz Papers,
Manuscript Collection no. 236, AJA.
96. R.G. to Maria Fenno Hoffman, n.d., ibid.
97. "Obituary of Rachel Gratz Moses by Mrs. Gertrude Meredith," Gratz
Family Papers, Collection no. 72, box 17, APS.
98. Toll and Gillam, *Invisible Philadelphia,* 348. They comment that
after Gratz's resignation the organization's minutes became perfunc-
tory.
99. R.G. to Maria Fenno Hoffman, ca. 1815, Rebecca Gratz Papers, Manuscript Collection no. 236, AJA.
100. R.G. to Maria Gist Gratz, 1824, Rebecca Gratz Papers, P-9, AJHS.
101. WW, 343–44.

102. Richardson, "Athens of America," 249; WW, 361.
103. Gertrude G. Meredith to William Meredith, January 21, 1825, Meredith Papers Correspondence, box 34, folder 2, HSP.
104. Quoted in WW, 362.
105. WW, 367–68.
106. Richardson, "Athens of America," 208–56.
107. Wainwright, "The Age of Nicholas Biddle"; Weigley, *Philadelphia,* 267–69.
108. Wainwright, "The Age of Nicholas Biddle," 301.
109. United Hebrew Beneficent Society, Annual Reports, 1822, 1825, 1841, UHBS Collection, PJA-BIES.
110. Diner, *A Time for Gathering,* 46–47.
111. WW, 242.
112. Ibid., 240.
113. Sara Hale, "Sketches of an American Character," *The Ladies Magazine* (1828): 202, LC.
114. Douglas, *Feminization;* Welter, "The Feminization of American Religion," 83–102; Houghton, *The Victorian Frame of Mind;* Auerbach, *Woman and the Demon;* Stansell, *City of Women,* 68–75, 7; Bell, *Crusade in the City.*
115. On women's piety as a mark of middle-class status in Europe see Hyman, *Gender and Assimilation,* 28; on a more activist version of that phenomenon in America see Reuther and Keller, *Women and Religion in America,* Vol. 1: The Nineteenth Century; McDannell, *The Christian Home in Victorian America.*
116. Douglas, *Terrible Honesty.*
117. Bloch, "American Feminine Ideals in Transition," 2.
118. Sarah Hale, "Sketches of an American Character: The Village Schoolmistress," *The Ladies Magazine* (1828): 202, LC.
119. See for example Sarah Hale, "A Review of *Religion at Home* by Mrs. William Providence," *The Ladies Magazine* 2, no. 9 (1828): 436–37, LC.
120. G. Matthews, *The Rise of Public Woman,* 72–73; Jane Tompkins, "Sentimental Power: *Uncle Tom's Cabin* and the Politics of Literary History," *Glyph* 8 (1981): 79–102; G. Brown, "Getting into the Kitchen with Dinah," 503–23.
121. WW, 344, 345.
122. R.G. to Maria Fenno Hoffman, February 19, 1826, Rebecca Gratz Papers, Manuscript Collection no. 236, AJA.
123. Sarner, "Rebecca Gratz," 6.
124. R.G. to Maria Gist Gratz, 1826, Rebecca Gratz Papers, Manuscript Collection no. 236, AJA.

Chapter 4

1. R.G. to Maria Gist Gratz, 1832, Rebecca Gratz Papers, P-9, AJHS.
2. Wainwright, "The Age of Nicholas Biddle," 267.
3. Diner, *A Time for Gathering*, 91.
4. Wainwright, "The Age of Nicholas Biddle," 281.
5. Ibid., 291.
6. R.G. to Miriam Moses Cohen, May 20, 1838, Rebecca Gratz Papers, Manuscript Collection no. 236, AJA.
7. Davis and Haller, *The Peoples of Philadelphia*, 74; Baltzell, *Puritan Boston and Quaker Philadelphia*, 179–82.
8. Wainwright, "The Age of Nicholas Biddle," 295.
9. Butler, *Awash in a Sea of Faith*, 281–82; Boylan, *Sunday School*.
10. M. Katz, *In the Shadow of the Poorhouse*, 63.
11. Ashton, "Souls Have No Sex," 42; Carey (*Essays*) listed thirty-three private charitable societies, but his count was not exhaustive.
12. Whiteman, "Legacy of Isaac Leeser," 27.
13. Sloe Hays to R.G., February 19, 1829, Rebecca Gratz Papers, Manuscript Collection no. 236, AJA; same to same, n.d., ibid.
14. Whiteman, "Legacy of Isaac Leeser," 27.
15. Ashton, "Souls Have No Sex," 46; Sussman, "Isaac Leeser and the Philadelphia Pattern."
16. Stern, "Jewish Marriage and Intermarriage," 142–43; Rosenwaike, *On the Edge of Greatness*, 54.
17. Goode, "The Theoretical Importance of Love," 2nd ed.
18. D'Emilio and Freedman, *Intimate Matters*, 42, 43.
19. Nancy Cott, cited in ibid., 45.
20. R.G. to Maria Gist Gratz, January 14, 1830, Rebecca Gratz Papers, P-9, AJHS.
21. Kelley, "Woman Alone."
22. Sloe Hays to R.G., January 17, 1826, Gratz Family Papers, Collection no. 72, box 15, APS.
23. "Catherine Sedgwick," *Dictionary of American Biography*.
24. Catherine Sedgwick to R.G., January 16, 1830, Gratz Family Papers, Collection no. 72, box 9, APS.
25. Fern, *Mr. Sully*, 24.
26. R.G. to Maria Gist Gratz, April 18, 1832, Rebecca Gratz Papers, P-9, AJHS.
27. R.G. to Maria Gist Gratz, January 31, 1832, ibid.
28. R.G. to Benjamin Gratz, June 19, 1831, Philipson, *Letters*, 126. "Uncle Ben and Aunt Maria . . . exhibited such a picture of rational and perfect happiness that you have elevated [the girls'] ideal of married life"; R.G. to Maria Gist Gratz, June 26, 1831, ibid., 128.
29. R.G. to Maria Gist Gratz, July 31, 1831, ibid., 127.

30. R.G. to Maria Gist Gratz, June 19, 1831, Gratz Family Papers, Collection no. 72, box 18, APS. This letter contradicts traditions that Gratz nursed Maria Fenno Hoffman on her deathbed. See for example an essay written by Gratz's niece, Sarah Anne Hays (later Sarah Hays [Mrs. Alfred] Mordecai), daughter of Richea Gratz Hays. That essay is found in FHBS Collection, folder 90.9.1, NMAJH. While it is possible that Gratz tended Hoffman at some point in her life, she did not do so at her death.

31. R.G. to Maria Gist Gratz, August 19, 1831, Gratz Family Papers, Collection no. 72, box 18, APS.

32. R.G. to Maria Gist Gratz, July 31, 1831, Philipson, *Letters,* 127.

33. R.G. to Maria Gist Gratz, July 28, 1833, Philipson, *Letters,* 177.

34. Wainwright, "The Age of Nicholas Biddle," 291.

35. Abramovitz, *Regulating the Lives of Women,* 75–101.

36. M. Katz, *In the Shadow of the Poorhouse,* 60.

37. For example, see McDannell, *The Christian Home in Victorian America,* passim.

38. R.G. to Maria Gist Gratz, [December] 1831, Philipson, *Letters,* 133.

39. Wainwright, "The Age of Nicholas Biddle," 291.

40. R.G. to Maria Gist Gratz, January 12, 1832, Philipson, *Letters,* 136.

41. Many thanks to Prof. Anne M. Boylan for this information.

42. M. Katz, *In the Shadow of the Poorhouse,* 63.

43. Carey, *Essays.* For more on the ASSU see Boylan, *Sunday School.*

44. McDannell, *The Christian Home in Victorian America;* Boylan, *Sunday School.*

45. Odendahl, *Charity Begins at Home,* 100–117.

46. R.G. to Maria Gist Gratz, April 18, 1832, Rebecca Gratz Papers, P-9, AJHS.

47. R.G. to Maria Gist Gratz, 1820, ibid.

48. R.G. to Maria Gist Gratz, October 12, 1832, ibid.

49. R.G. to Maria Gist Gratz, November 20, 1832, Philipson, *Letters,* 162.

50. R.G. to Maria Gist Gratz, February 16, 1832, Rebecca Gratz Papers, P-9, AJHS.

51. R.G. to Maria Gist Gratz, January 12, 1832, Gratz Family Papers, Collection no. 72, box 18, APS.

52. Sarah Anne Hays reported that for some years Julia Hoffman lived for half of each year with Rebecca Gratz and half with her brother George. Sarah Anne Hays, *Recollections of My Aunt,* FHBS Collection, folder 90.9.1, NMAJH.

53. R.G. to Maria Gist Gratz, January 6, 1834, Philipson, *Letters,* 190; R.G. to Miriam Moses Cohen, January 10, 1838, Rebecca Gratz Papers, Manuscript Collection no. 236, AJA.

54. R.G. to Maria Gist Gratz, December 18, 1832, and 1834, Philipson, *Letters,* 164, 216.

55. Idelsohn, *Jewish Liturgy,* 245, 292.
56. Fishbane, "Action and Non-Action."
57. R.G. to Maria Gist Gratz, June 29, 1834, December 16, 1838, Philipson, *Letters,* 199, 257.
58. R.G. to Maria Gist Gratz, April 18, 1832, Rebecca Gratz Papers, P-9, AJHS.
59. Douglas, *The Feminization of American Culture,* 70–71.
60. R.G. to Maria Gist Gratz, December 27, 1834, Rebecca Gratz Papers, P-9, AJHS. Martineau's autobiography, published posthumously, created a stir in more traditionally religious Christian circles. In it she admitted that she was not devout and had stopped praying when only in her twenties. Reviewers sometimes remarked that she was "deficient in spiritual gifts." F. T. W., "Miss Martineau," *Penn Monthly* 11 (1880): 888–94.
61. Wainwright, "The Age of Nicholas Biddle," 291.
62. R.G. to Maria Gist Gratz, December 18, 1832, Rebecca Gratz Papers, P-9, AJHS.
63. Fern, *Mr. Sully,* 24.
64. R.G. to Maria Gist Gratz, 1832, Philipson, *Letters,* 145.
65. R.G. to Maria Gist Gratz, October 12, 1832, ibid., 160.
66. R.G. to Maria Gist Gratz, January 31, 1832, Rebecca Gratz Papers, P-9, AJHS.
67. Hanft, "Mordecai's Female Academy."
68. R.G. to Maria Gist Gratz, January 31, 1832, Philipson, *Letters,* 142.
69. R.G. to Maria Gist Gratz, January 31, 1832, Rebecca Gratz Papers, P-9, AJHS.
70. R.G. to Benjamin Gratz, February 27, 1835, Philipson, *Letters,* 73.
71. R.G. to Miriam Moses Cohen, n.d., Manuscript Collection no. 236, AJA; Gotthold Solomon, *Twelve Sermons,* Gratz Family Library Collection, NMAJH.
72. R.G. to Maria Gist Gratz, 1834, Rebecca Gratz Papers, P-9, AJHS.
73. R.G. to Maria Gist Gratz, January 6, 1834, Philipson, *Letters,* 190.
74. R.G. to Maria Gist Gratz, October 12, 1834, ibid., 210.
75. R.G. to Maria Gist Gratz, July 21, 1834, Rebecca Gratz Papers, P-9, AJHS.
76. R.G. to Maria Gist Gratz, August 9, 1831, ibid.
77. R.G. to Miriam Moses Cohen, January 19, 1840, Rebecca Gratz Papers, Manuscript Collection no. 236, AJA; Aime Martin, *Woman's Influence and Woman's Mission* (Philadelphia: Willis P. Hazard, 1854).
78. R.G. to Maria Gist Gratz, July 30, 1832, Philipson, *Letters,* 206–7.
79. R.G. to Maria Fenno Hoffman, December 15, 1815, Rebecca Gratz Papers, Manuscript Collection no. 236, AJA.
80. R.G. to Maria Fenno Hoffman, ca. 1812, ibid.

81. R.G. to Maria Gist Gratz, June 20, 1834, Rebecca Gratz Papers, P-9, AJHS; also in Philipson, *Letters,* 203.
82. R.G. to Miriam Moses Cohen, May 2, 1838, Miriam Gratz Moses Cohen Papers and Books, Collection no. 2639, SHC.
83. R.G. to Miriam Moses Cohen, November 4, [1836?], Rebecca Gratz Papers, Manuscript Collection no. 236, AJA.
84. R.G. to Maria Gist Gratz, 1835, Rebecca Gratz Papers, P-9, AJHS; Wainwright, "The Age of Nicholas Biddle," 264.
85. Joseph Gratz to R.G., 1837, Gratz Family Papers, Collection no. 72, box 15, APS.
86. R.G. to Maria Gist Gratz, August 27, 1837, Rebecca Gratz Papers, P-9, AJHS.
87. R.G. to Maria Gist Gratz, February 6, 1837, Philipson, *Letters,* 230.
88. R.G. to Maria Gist Gratz, February 19, 1837, ibid., 233; see also R.G. to Maria Gist Gratz, September 21, 1833 (p. 181), October 21, 1833 (p. 185), November 5, 1837 (p. 245), R.G. to Benjamin Gratz, March 7, 1819 (p. 17).
89. R.G. to Maria Gist Gratz, November 5, 1837, ibid., 115.
90. Davis and Haller, *The Peoples of Philadelphia,* 51.
91. WW, 344.
92. Wainwright, "The Age of Nicholas Biddle," 280.
93. Davis and Haller, *The Peoples of Philadelphia,* 60.
94. Wainwright, "The Age of Nicholas Biddle," 293.
95. Diner, *A Time for Gathering,* 43, 76.
96. Ibid., 84; also see Jewish Foster Home and Orphan Asylum, Minutes, 1878–1892, Jewish Foster Home and Orphan Asylum Collection, PJA-BIES.
97. Diner, *A Time for Gathering,* 82.
98. Todes, "History," 4–7.
99. Wainwright, "The Age of Nicholas Biddle," 296.
100. R.G. to Miriam Moses Cohen, January 10, 1838, Rebecca Gratz Papers, P-9, AJHS.
101. Lydia Maria Child, *The Mother's Book* (Boston: Carter, Hendee, and Babcock, 1831); Sklar, *Catherine Beecher;* Catherine Beecher, *An Essay on the Education of Female Teachers* (1835).
102. "Report," FHBS, 1835, Gratz Family Papers, Collection no. 72, box 17, APS.
103. Todes, "History," 11.
104. R.G. to Miriam Moses Cohen, May 20, 1838, Rebecca Gratz Papers, P-9, AJHS.
105. Ledger, Kaal Kadosh Mickve Israel, 1810–1850, MIA; Minutes of the HSS Society, AJA; "Brief History of the Hebrew Sunday School Society," box 4, folder 18, MS 6, p. 1, PJA-BIES. Although her name appears as "Simma" in the records of Mikveh Israel, in the records of

the HSS Society and the Jewish Foster Home she appears as "Simha." Because Simha eventually became a Hebrew teacher at the Jewish Foster Home and for Jewish students in Philadelphia, it is likely that she preferred the Hebrew pronunciation implied in the latter spelling.

106. Ledger, Kaal Kadosh Mickve Israel, 1826, MIA; Minutes of the HSS Society, 1838 to 1875, AJA; "Brief History of the Hebrew Sunday School Society," box 4, folder 18, MS 6, p. 2, PJA-BIES.
107. R.G. to Miriam Moses Cohen, March 4, 1840, Rebecca Gratz Papers, P-9, AJHS.
108. R.G. to Maria Gist Gratz, December 16, 1838, ibid.
109. R.G. to Maria Gist Gratz, December 31, 1831, Rebecca Gratz Papers, Manuscript Collection no. 236, AJA, and in Philipson, *Letters,* 131.
110. Isaac Leeser, *Occident* 4 (1846): 60; Todes, "History," 71.
111. David de Sola Pool, *An Old Faith in a New World* (New York: Columbia University Press, 1955), 363–64.
112. Reznikoff and Engleman, *The Jews of Charleston,* 150.
113. R.G. to Miriam Moses Cohen, May 20, 1838, Rebecca Gratz Papers, Manuscript collection no. 236, AJA.
114. Wainwright, "The Age of Nicholas Biddle," 301.

Chapter 5

1. Geffen, "Industrial Development," 307–14.
2. Isaac Leeser, "Progress of Persecution in Pennsylvania," *Occident* 13 (1855): 496–505, FL.
3. Boylan, "Presbyterians and Sunday Schools"; Boylan, *Sunday School,* passim; Lynn and Wright, *The Big Little School.*
4. Minutes of the HSS Society: 1838–1879, AJA.
5. Leeser, *Occident* 9 (1851), quoted in Todes, "History," 5.
6. Todes, "History," 9.
7. Ibid., 8; Sussman, *Isaac Leeser,* 23–24.
8. King, "Jewish Education in Philadelphia," 241; Lewis Allen wrote to Gratz: "The building back of the synagogue is being finished. . . . I have the pleasure of offering the Sunday School one or two rooms for the accommodation of the school." Gratz replied: "I will confer with the teachers . . . and inform Mr. Allen whether we can accept his kind offer." Lewis Allen to R.G., October 11, 1841, her note inserted, Gratz Family Papers, Collection no. 72, box 15, APS.
9. In a letter to Grace Nathan (October 23, 1842, Rebecca Gratz Papers, Manuscript Collection no. 236, AJA), Gratz wrote that classes had moved into the synagogue, but this was only a temporary measure. Rosenbloom, "Rebecca Gratz and the Jewish Sunday School Movement"; Minutes of the HSS Society, 1838–1875, AJA; "Brief History

of the Hebrew Sunday School Society," box 4, folder 18, MS 6, p. 2, PJA-BIES.

10. King, "Jewish Education in Philadelphia," 241.

11. Jick, *The Americanization of the Synagogue;* S. Morais, *Address* (1869), 7, AJA; Meyer, *Response to Modernity,* 225–55.

12. R.G. to Miriam Moses Cohen, April 12, 1843, Rebecca Gratz Papers, Manuscript Collection no. 236, AJA; Minutes of the HSS Society, 1838–1879, AJA.

13. A translation of the opening line of the Sh'ma is: "Hear oh Israel, the Lord our God, the Lord is One." The assertion of God's unity was considered Judaism's creed.

14. Bahya Ibn Pakuda, *Duties of the Heart;* Hesther Rothschild, trans., *Preires d'un Coeur Israelite,* revised by Isaac Leeser (Philadelphia, 1864); Idelsohn, *Jewish Liturgy;* Gershom Sholem, *Major Trends in Modern Jewish Mysticism* (New York: Schocken Press, 1961); Douglas, *The Feminization of American Culture,* 143–310; Porterfield, *Feminine Spirituality in America,* 51–82; Smith-Rosenberg, *Disorderly Conduct,* 129–63.

15. David Levi, "Grace after Meat," *Form of Prayers,* 169, MIA.

16. "Monday Morning," "Wednesday Morning," "Morning Prayer Thursday," Gratz Family Papers, Collection no. 72, box 9, APS.

17. Sussman, "Another Look at Isaac Leeser"; Rosenbloom, "Rebecca Gratz and the Jewish Sunday School Movement"; Barnett Elzas, "Leaves from My Historical Scrapbook," *The Sunday News* (Charleston, South Carolina), February 16, 1908, Rebecca Gratz Papers, Biographies File, AJA; Simma Peixotto, *Elementary Introduction to the Hebrew Scriptures for the Use of Hebrew Children* (Philadelphia, [1839?]), HSS Society Collection, PJA-BIES; Whiteman, "Legacy of Isaac Leeser," 41–42. By 1838 the ASSU had moved away from its early authoritarian style that focused on memorizing Bible passages and discipline. Sunday schools had become a children's arm of the revival movement, and children began to experience conversion. The goals of the schools changed from keeping the children from sin to actually preparing them for their conversions. Corporal punishment was dropped, Bible lessons were organized logically around central ideas, and teachers explained acceptable interpretations to the students. Students were rewarded for good work with colored tickets that could be accumulated and put toward the purchase of a Sunday school book or tract. Once the ASSU made these changes, Gratz could borrow some of the materials and style with only minor modifications. (A book like *Union Questions,* which was designed to precipitate conversion by posing unanswered questions that forced students to focus on their sins and on their need to repent, was not borrowed.)

Boylan, "Changing Evangelical Views"; Lynn and Wright, *The Big Little School,* 10–17.

18. Prayer Card, 1942, HSS Society Collection, PJA-BIES; Joshua Block, "Rosa Mordecai's Recollection of the First Hebrew Sunday School," *PAJHS* 42 (1953): 397–406; Todes, "History," 56.

19. Minutes of the HSS, PJA-BIES.

20. Minutes of the HSS, AJA; R.G. to Miriam Moses Cohen, March 4, 1840, Rebecca Gratz Papers, P-9, AJHS.

21. E. Feldman, *Dual Destinies,* 58–78; N. Cohen, *Encounter with Emancipation,* 66, 75, 79–80.

22. Diner, *A Time for Gathering,* 167.

23. Isaac Leeser, *Discourses, Argumentative and Devotional on the Subject of the Jewish Religion* (Philadelphia, 5601 [1841]), 215–33; Isaac M. Wise, *Occident* 1 (1843): 113–20, 409–14; *Occident* 2 (1844): 280–81; *Occident* 4 (1846): 65; *Occident* 15 (1857): 120–25, quoted in N. Cohen, *Encounter with Emancipation,* 67.

24. Blau and Baron, "Local Courts and Sabbath Laws," 21–25; Whiteman, "Legacy of Isaac Leeser"; Minutes of the HSS Society, 1838–1874, AJA.

25. Leeser, "Progress of Civil and Religious Liberty," *Occident* 13 (1855): 496–505.

26. Leeser, *Occident* 4 (1846): 511.

27. Leeser, *Occident* 6 (1848): 299.

28. Leeser, *Occident* 6 (1848): 413–15.

29. Leeser, *Occident* 4 (1846): 563.

30. Leeser, *Occident* 16 (1858): 269–85; *Occident* 8 (1850): 93–97; *Occident* 8 (1851): 54, 51; *Occident* 13 (1856): 226–27, 543–77.

31. *Occident* 15 (1858): 231.

32. Sussman, "Another Look at Isaac Leeser," 159–90; Leeser, *Occident* 11 (1853): 285–87.

33. For one account of the demise of Victorian culture, see Douglas, *Terrible Honesty,* passim.

34. "Superintendent's Report," May 1864, Minutes of the HSS Society, AJA.

35. Todes, "History," 12.

36. Prayer Card, ca. 1942, HSS Society Collection, PJA-BIES.

37. Mrs. (Rachel Peixotto) Pyke, *Scriptural Questions for the Use of Sunday Schools for the Instruction of Israelites* (Philadelphia, reprint 1854), HSS Society Collection, PJA-BIES.

38. Simha Peixotto, *Elementary Introduction to the Scriptures for the Use of Hebrew Children* (Philadelphia, [1839?]), 7, HSS Society Collection, PJA-BIES.

39. Meyer, *Origins of the Modern Jew,* 54.

40. Isaac Leeser, *Catechism for Younger Children* (Philadelphia, 1839),

1, HSS Society Collection, PJA-BIES; Sobel, "Legitimation and Antisemitism"; Sarna, "The American Jewish Response to Nineteenth-Century Christian Missions."

41. Todes, "History," 55.
42. "Monday Morning," Wednesday Morning," "Morning Prayer Thursday," Gratz Family Papers, Collection no. 72, box 9, APS.
43. Jacob Petuchowski, "Manuals and Catechisms of the Jewish Religion in the Early Period of Emancipation," in Altmann, *Studies in Nineteenth-Century Jewish Intellectual History,* 47–64.
44. Todes, "History," 12.
45. Ibid.
46. Grace Aguilar, *The Spirit of Judaism* (Philadelphia: C. Sherman and Co., 1842), 60–61; Schorsch, "The Myth of Sephardic Supremacy," 47–66.
47. Aguilar, *Spirit of Judaism.* See Leeser's notes in introduction (n.p.) and throughout text. Aguilar, *The Jewish Faith* (London: R. Goombridge and Sons, 1846).
48. R.G. to Miriam Moses Cohen, November 8, 1847, Rebecca Gratz Papers, Manuscript Collection no. 236, AJA; *Hanucah Entertainment of the Grace Aguilar Sunday School of the Hebrew Sunday School Society of Philadelphia,* Sunday, December 25, 1910, and *Purim Entertainment of the Grace Aguilar Sunday School of the Hebrew Sunday School Society of Philadelphia,* Sunday, March 19, 1911, both in HSS Society Collection, PJA-BIES.
49. Aguilar, *Spirit of Judaism,* author's introduction, n.p.
50. Schorsch, "The Myth of Sephardic Supremacy," 7. Moreover, Spanish-Portuguese Jews in Hamburg and Amsterdam were known for their efficient Jewish educational system, and Jews of this heritage were very influential in Aguilar's community. Bermant, *The Cousinhood,* 10–30.
51. Aguilar, *Spirit of Judaism,* 54.
52. Philip Weinberger, "The Social and Religious Thought of Grace Aguilar" (Ph.D. diss., New York University, 1970), 2–10.
53. Aguilar, *Spirit of Judaism,* editor's footnote, 54.
54. Ibid., 56.
55. Ibid., 52.
56. Ibid., 66, 67.
57. Ibid., 60–61.
58. Ibid., 72, 77.
59. Ibid., author's introduction, n.p.
60. Ibid., 80.
61. Isaac Leeser, "How to Educate Jewish Girls" (1835), in Marcus, *The American Jewish Woman: Documents,* 130.
62. Thanks to Prof. Jonathan Sarna for this information.

63. Goldman, "The Ambivalence of Reform Judaism"; Meyer, *Origins of the Modern Jew,* 379–80.

64. Meyer, *Origins of the Modern Jew,* 237; Samuel Pike, *A Compendious Hebrew Lexicon Adapted to the English Language* (1801), HSS Society Collection, PJA-BIES.

65. Charles G. Addison, *Damascus and Palmyra: A Journey to the East with Sketches and Prospects of Syria under Ibrahim Pasha* (Philadelphia: Carey and Hart, 1838); *Seder Tefillah: The Order of Prayer for Divine Service,* revised by Dr. Leo Merzbacher of Temple Emanu El (New York, 1855); *Torah Moshe: The Law of Moses: A Catechism of the Jewish Religion,* revised by Abraham Pereira Mendes, 3rd ed. (London, 1870); *Thoughts Suggested by Bible Texts Addressed to My Children* (Philadelphia: Hebrew Sunday School Society, 1860), all in PJA-BIES.

66. Minutes of the HSS Society, 1860–1880, AJA.

67. See, for example, "Little Nellie's Catechism," *Hebrew Sunday School Visitor,* January 1874, vol. 1, no. 1, pp. 2, 7; vol. 1, no. 3, pp. 10–11, HSSS Collection, AJA; Baym, *Woman's Fiction.*

68. For a discussion of how this Victorian ideology affected Catholic and Protestant American families see McDannell, *The Christian Home in Victorian America,* passim.

69. *The Parent and Teachers Assistant: or Thirteen Lessons Conveying to Unformed Minds the First Ideas of God and His Attributes . . . by an American Jewess* (Philadelphia: C. Sherman Printer, 5605 [1845]), 10–12, MIA. Abraham Karp points out that the first edition of this volume identified the author as a young woman. Gratz was sixty-four in 1845. He suggests that the author was Simha Peixotto. Maxwell Whiteman suggested Emma Mordecai as the author. Personal conversations, Abraham Karp and Maxwell Whiteman.

70. Ibid., 14, 31–33, 35.

71. Kaplan, "Tradition and Transition"; R.G. to Miriam Moses Cohen, n.d., ca. 1840, Rebecca Gratz Papers, P-9, AJHS.

72. D'Emilio and Freedman, *Intimate Matters,* 85–108.

73. Minutes of the HSS Society, 1860–1880, AJA.

Chapter 6

1. R.G. to Miriam Moses Cohen, February 2, 1847, Gratz Family Papers, Manuscript Collection no. 236, AJA.

2. Geffen, "Industrial Development," 317.

3. Ibid., 312, 316, 323.

4. Douglas, *The Feminization of American Culture,* 96.

5. Geffen, "Industrial Development," 333.

6. Ibid., 96–104.

7. Ibid., 102–23.

8. Moore, *Selling God,* 25–26, 37.

9. Quoted in ibid., 34; S. M. Evans, *Born for Liberty,* 95–96.
10. Geffen, "Industrial Development," 125.
11. For discussions of literature voicing these sentiments, see Cowie, "The Vogue of the Domestic Novel," 420; Helen Waite Papashvily, *All the Happy Endings: A Study of the Domestic Novel in America, the Women Who Wrote It, the Women Who Read It, in the Nineteenth Century* (New York: Harper and Bros., 1956); Garrison, "Immoral Fiction"; Douglas, *The Feminization of American Culture;* Baym, *Woman's Fiction,* passim.
12. Tompkins, "Sentimental Power," 4.
13. R.G. to Maria Gist Gratz, February 28, 1834, Rebecca Gratz Papers, Manuscript Collection no. 236, AJA.
14. R.G. to Miriam Moses Cohen, 1838, Rebecca Gratz Papers, Manuscript Collection no. 236, AJA.
15. G. Matthews, *The Rise of Public Woman,* 93–96.
16. R.G. to Maria Gist Gratz, 1834, 1840, Philipson, *Letters,* 215, 272.
17. R.G. to Miriam Moses Cohen, January 19, 1840, Rebecca Gratz Papers, Manuscript Collection no. 236, AJA.
18. R.G. to Miriam Moses Cohen, January 24, 1843, ibid.
19. Saum, *The Popular Mood,* 195.
20. R.G. to Maria Gist Gratz, January 15, 1840, Philipson, *Letters,* 270.
21. R.G. to Miriam Moses Cohen, January 19, 1840, Rebecca Gratz Papers, Manuscript Collection no. 236, AJA.
22. R.G. to Maria Gist Gratz, June 17, 1840, Philipson, *Letters,* 279.
23. A Catholic priest and his servant had disappeared, and Damascus Jews had been accused of killing the men, draining their blood to use in the baking of Passover matzo, and then hacking the bodies to pieces. N. Cohen, *Encounter with Emancipation,* 212–15.
24. The first documented case of Jews tried and executed for blood libel occurred in England in 1148. Executions spread through France, Germany, England, Bohemia, and Castile through the sixteenth century and were especially common in Germany. The idea that Christian blood was a component of matzo is an inversion of the idea that Jesus' blood and body are somehow part of the substance of communion wafers, flat crackers nearly identical to matzo. Hsia, *The Myth of Ritual Murder,* 1–5.
25. Sarna, "The Mythical Jew and the Jew Next Door."
26. N. Cohen, *Encounter with Emancipation,* 214.
27. R.G. to Miriam Moses Cohen, September 13, 1840, January 24, 1843, Rebecca Gratz Papers, Manuscript Collection no. 236, AJA.
28. Quoted in Feldstein, *The Land That I Show You,* 90.
29. Quoted in N. Cohen, *Encounter with Emancipation,* 213.
30. R.G. to Maria Gist Gratz, August 27, 1840, Philipson, *Letters,* 282.
31. Whiteman, "Legacy of Isaac Leeser," 31.

32. Diner, *A Time for Gathering,* 155.
33. R.G. to Miriam Moses Cohen, September 13, 1840, Rebecca Gratz Papers, Manuscript Collection no. 236, AJA.
34. Ibid.
35. Geffen, "Industrial Development," 307, 342.
36. Feldstein, *The Land That I Show You,* 71–72.
37. R.G. to Miriam Moses Cohen, March 29, 1841, Rebecca Gratz Papers, Manuscript Collection no. 236, AJA.
38. R.G. to Miriam Moses Cohen, November 1, 1846, ibid.
39. Sarna, *People Walk on Their Heads,* 8–9; Diner, *A Time for Gathering,* 3.
40. Miriam Moses Cohen to R.G., August 21, 1842, Gratz Family Papers, Collection no. 72, box 15, APS.
41. WW, 241. They report that at Rodeph Shalom, special exception was made for Aaron Dropsie.
42. Ibid., 452n.
43. Ibid., 240; Simon Gratz, Will, No. 131, Book XIII, 598, Register of Wills, County of Philadelphia; Louisa Gratz, Obituary, Simon Gratz Collection, HSP; WW, 452n.
44. Mrs. Florence Finkel, March 1991, personal conversation with the author, Mikveh Israel Archives, Philadelphia.
45. R.G. to Lewis Allen, May 31, 1841, Correspondence File, MIA. Allen's response to Gratz is written on her letter to him.
46. Sussman, "Isaac Leeser and the Philadelphia Pattern," 29.
47. R.G. to Miriam Moses Cohen, March 29, 1841, Rebecca Gratz Papers, Manuscript Collection no. 236, AJA.
48. R.G. to Miriam Moses Cohen, n.d., ibid.
49. Diner, *A Time for Gathering,* 54–57, 94.
50. Geffen, "Industrial Development," 353.
51. Dennis J. Clark, "The Philadelphia Irish: Persistent Presence," in Davis and Haller, *Peoples of Philadelphia,* 135–54; Bruce Laurie, "Fire Companies and Gangs in Southwark: The 1840s," in ibid., 71–88; Feldberg, *The Philadelphia Riots of 1844.* Also see Feldberg's *Turbulent Era.*
52. Geffen, "Industrial Development," 356.
53. R.G. to Miriam Moses Cohen, December 12, 1842, Rebecca Gratz Papers, Manuscript Collection no. 236, AJA.
54. "Female Hebrew Benevolent Society Annual Report," *Occident* 10 (1852): 445; R.G. to Miriam Moses Cohen, January 24, 1843, Rebecca Gratz Papers, Manuscript Collection no. 236, AJA.
55. FHBS Board Minutes, 1845 Report, FHBS Collection, NMAJH.
56. FHBS Board Minutes, January 7, 1846, ibid.
57. FHBS Board Minutes, October 7, 1846, ibid.
58. FHBS Annual Report, 1849, ibid.

59. FHBS Board Minutes, March 1, 1848, ibid.
60. FHBS Board Minutes, April 1, 1848, ibid.
61. FHBS Board Minutes, January 6, 1847, ibid.
62. FHBS Board Minutes, November 10, 1848, ibid.
63. FHBS Board Minutes, June 21, 1848, ibid.
64. FHBS Board Minutes, 1854 Report, ibid.
65. A. J. Brown, *One Hundred Years,* 1:68–70.
66. Welter, "She Hath Done What She Could," 119.
67. Grinstein, *The Rise of the Jewish Community,* 152–56.
68. "Female Hebrew Benevolent Society Annual Report," *Occident* 4 (1846): 441; R.G. to Miriam Moses Cohen, December 12, 1842, Rebecca Gratz Papers, P-9, AJHS.
69. "Female Hebrew Benevolent Society Annual Report," *Occident* 4 (1846): 441; R.G. to Miriam Moses Cohen December 12, 1842, Rebecca Gratz Papers, P-9, AJHS.
70. R.G. to Miriam Moses Cohen, [1838?], Rebecca Gratz Papers, Manuscript Collection no. 236, AJA.
71. Galchinsky, *Modern Jewish Woman Writer,* 31. Indeed, a new emphasis on women's importance in religious education has marked Jewish assimilation throughout the western world. Hyman, *Gender and Assimilation,* 47–48. See also Dianne Ashton, "The Feminization of Jewish Education," *Transformations* 5, no. 2 (Fall 1992): 15–22.
72. Galchinsky, *Modern Jewish Woman Writer,* 135–56.
73. R.G. to Miriam Moses Cohen January 31, 1845, Rebecca Gratz Papers, Manuscript Collection no. 236, AJA; Aguilar, *The Women of Israel* (London, 1845).
74. *The Dying Jewess,* AJA, Small Collections. Reprinted from an article in *The Ladies Literary Cabinet* 4 (6 October 1821): 173–74. For more on discussions about conversions in nineteenth-century literature see Diner, *A Time for Gathering,* 175–80; Harap, *Image of the Jew,* 74–77, 135–38, 145–88.
75. R.G. to Miriam Moses Cohen, June 3, 1845, Rebecca Gratz Papers, Manuscript Collection no. 236, AJA.
76. R.G. to Miriam Moses Cohen February 2, 1847, ibid.; Aguilar, *Sabbath Thoughts and Sacred Communings* (London, 1847).
77. Miriam Moses Cohen to R.G., August 21, 1842, Gratz Family Papers, Manuscript Collection no. 72, box 15, APS. Aguilar's work was first distributed in the United States by a Miss Palache, who ran a boarding school in New York and was the agent for the London-based *Cheap Jewish Library,* edited by Charlotte Montefiore. Although Gratz liked Aguilar's prose better than her poetry, she was pleased that the British Jewish journal, *The Voice of Jacob,* credited Aguilar with a "brilliant reputation for poetry." Galchinsky, *Modern Jewish Woman*

Writer, 139; R.G. to Miriam Moses Cohen, December 12, 1843, Rebecca Gratz Papers, Manuscript Collection no. 236, AJA; Aguilar, *Spirit of Judaism.*

78. S. Solis, "Remarks on Miss Aguilar's *Women of Israel,*" *Occident* 4 (1846): 81.

79. Mrs. Shroeder to R.G., July 20, 1847, Gratz Family Papers, Collection no. 72, box 15, APS.

80. Grace Aguilar to R.G., August 14, 1842, ibid., box 9.

81. R.G. to Miriam Moses Cohen, March 14, 1850, Rebecca Gratz Papers, Manuscript Collection no. 236, AJA; Aguilar, *The Mother's Recompense* (London: R. E. King, 1850?).

82. R.G. to Ann Gratz, August 13, 1852, Philipson, *Letters,* 387.

83. R.G. to Miriam Moses Cohen, February 2, 1847, Rebecca Gratz Papers P-9, AJHS.

84. Galchinsky, *Modern Jewish Woman Writer,* 135–56. See also Ashton, "Grace Aguilar and the Matriarchal Theme," 79–93; and Ashton, "Grace Aguilar and the Popular Response to Evangelists," 22.

85. The physical means of book production available to the Jews of Europe before the early nineteenth century were meager and usually controlled by a coalition of wealthy men and rabbinic scholars. Because women had no formal Jewish education, they could not be considered credible authors of books on Jewish matters. Nonetheless, a few Jewish women did successfully publish devotional materials for women, usually in Yiddish. Weissler, "Tkhinnes of the Matriarchs," 51–53; and Weissler, "The Traditional Piety of Ashkenazic Women."

86. By 1850, Isaac M. Wise also published Jewish women's writings in his national English-language periodical *The Israelite,* also called *The American Israelite,* and in his German-language magazine for women, *Die Deborah.* It is likely that Gratz read Wise's English-language periodicals.

87. Leeser also published fiction by Jewish women in his pamphlet series *The Jewish Miscellany.* Sussman, *Isaac Leeser,* 42–43.

88. Solis, "Remarks on Miss Aguilar's *Women of Israel,*" 81.

89. Thomas, *Dreams of Authority,* 5–15.

90. For more on the significance of the father-daughter relationship in these works see Galchinsky, *Modern Jewish Woman Writer,* 102. Much of popular Jewish literature since then has explored family tensions, often revolving around the issue of free marital choice, after the collapse of the arranged marriage system. Gittelman, *From Shtetl to Suburbia;* Sholem Aleichem, *Tevye's Daughters,* 2nd printing (New York: Crown Publishers, 1949).

91. Galchinsky, *Modern Jewish Woman Writer,* 105–34.

92. Marion Hartog, "The Espousal: A Jewish Story," *Occident* 2 (1844): 567–74.
93. Appel, "Jews in American Caricature"; Glanz, *The Jew in Early American Wit,* 110–20.
94. Celia Moss, "The Two Pictures: A Sketch of Domestic Life," *Occident* 4 (1846): 435–37.
95. These early stories fit thematically with those of Sholem Aleichem (Rabinovitch, 1859–1916) and I. L. Peretz (1852–1915). While super-seding Gratz's generation, these two giants of the first generation of Yiddish writers focused on family dynamics and examined issues of filial duty, propriety, and social change. In Aleichem's well-known *Tevye* stories, for example, the drama centers around problems be-tween Tevye and his daughters. The Moss and Hartog stories reflect the same issues appearing in the 1840s among American Jewish families who adjust to emancipation and modernization in America and England and who write in English. No Yiddish-language culture existed in America before the Civil War. These tales in the *Occident* were, however, domestic lessons for American Jews to ponder. Gittel-man, *From Shtetl to Suburbia.*
96. *National Union Catalog, Pre 1956,* Imprints vol. 1, 354.
97. Marion Hartog, "Jewish Lyrics" *Occident* 4 (1846): 125; "Jewish Lyrics No. 3," *Occident* 4 (1846): 278, and others; Hartog, "Milcah: A Case of the Spanish Jews of the Fifteenth Century," *Occident* 9 (1852); Mrs. Levetus (Celia Moss), "The King's Physician: A Tale of the Secret Jews of Spain," *Occident* 12 (1854); Grace Aguilar, *The Vale of Cedars: or The Martyr* (London, 1843).
98. Grace Aguilar, "Past, Present, and Future: A Sketch," *Occident* 3 (1845): 184–85.
99. Grace Aguilar, "Communings with Nature No. 6: The Evergreen," *Occident* 4 (1846): 79.
100. McDannell and Lang, *Heaven,* 221–45.
101. When a woman died, she was said to be gathered to her babies into a "golden circle" composed of her dead children and God. Interestingly, husbands often were not depicted in this circle with God's presence. Indeed, men were said to be gathered to their fathers at death. Even in heaven, the separation of spheres for men and women continued, but God joined the women's circle. Ibid., 221–45.
102. Rosa Emma Salaman, "The Angel and the Child," *Occident* 13 (1855): 36–38.
103. Lichtenstein, *Writing Their Nations,* 10.
104. Rebekah Hyneman, "An Address to the Soul," *Occident* 6 (1848): 594.
105. Rebekah Hyneman, "Female Scriptural Characters: Rebekah," *Occident* 4 (1846): 241.

Chapter 7

1. R.G. to Ann Gratz, January 28, 1845, Philipson, *Letters,* 312.
2. R.G. to Ann Gratz, May 27, 1842, Manuscript Collection no. 236, AJA. Ann Maria Boswell Shelby Gratz's name is sometimes spelled "Anna" in historical accounts. Gratz's letters, however, uniformly refer to her as "Ann" and to her daughter as "Anna." I follow Gratz's usage.
3. Kasson, *Rudeness and Civility;* Butsch, "Bowery B'Hoys and Matinee Ladies."
4. R.G. to Benjamin Gratz, November 19, 1841, Philipson, *Letters,* 297.
5. R.G. to Ann Boswell Shelby Gratz, January 29, 1844, ibid., 299.
6. R.G. to Ann Gratz, March 24, 1844, ibid., *Letters,* 301.
7. Ann Gratz to R.G., March 14, 1844, Gratz Family Papers, Collection no. 72, box 16, APS.
8. Benjamin Gratz to R.G., April 30, 1844, ibid.
9. R.G. to Ann Gratz, December 8, 1845, Philipson, *Letters,* 322.
10. R.G. to Maria Gist Gratz, November 11, 1820, ibid., 39.
11. R.G. to Ann Gratz, December 28, 1844, ibid., 309.
12. Scott, *Natural Allies,* 49.
13. R.G. to Ann Gratz, November 24, 1845, Rebecca Gratz Papers, P-9, AJHS.
14. R.G. to Ann Gratz, January 28, 1845, ibid.
15. Ibid.
16. Ann Gratz to R.G., April 2, 1844, Gratz Family Papers, Collection no. 72, box 16, APS.
17. R.G. to Ann Gratz, March 24, 1844, Philipson, *Letters,* 301.
18. Richea Gratz Hays to R.G., May 27, 1844, Gratz Family Papers, Collection no. 72, box 16, APS.
19. R.G. to Miriam Moses Cohen, November 4, [1840s?], Rebecca Gratz Papers, Manuscript Collection no. 236, AJA.
20. R.G. to Ann Gratz, November 24, 1845, Philipson, *Letters,* 319.
21. Morison, *History of the American People,* 2:261, 263–64, 277.
22. R.G. to Ann Gratz, August 31, 1845, Philipson, *Letters,* 317.
23. Frances Anne Kemble, *Journal of a Residence on a Georgia Plantation, 1838–1839* (London: Roberts and Green, 1863).
24. Johnson, *American Actress,* 92–107.
25. Fanny Kemble to R.G., October, 11, 1845, Gratz Family Papers, Collection no. 72, box 15, APS: "Oh dear Rebecca I believe having found my child once more . . . my child seems really fond and my heart is filled with joy." Fanny was permitted to write to Sarah, so their separation was mitigated. See also Fanny Kemble to R.G., March 14, n.d., ibid.
26. Morison, *History of the American People,* 2:133–35, 137, 214, 138–39, 261–64, 273–82.

27. Sarah Gratz Moses to R.G., February 1846, Gratz Family Papers, Collection no. 72, box 16, APS.
28. R.G. to Miriam Moses Cohen, May 20, 1838, Miriam Moses Cohen Papers and Books, Collection no. 2639, SHC.
29. Miriam Moses Cohen to R.G., March 22, 1846, Gratz Family Papers, Collection no. 72, box 16, APS.
30. Korn, *American Jewry and the Civil War;* Richard Tedlow, "Judah P. Benjamin," in *Turn to the South,* ed. Kaganoff and Urofsky, 44–54; E. Evans, *Judah P. Benjamin.*
31. This book may be the *Thirteen Lessons* discussed earlier. Miriam Moses Cohen to R.G., March 22, 1846, Gratz Family Papers, Collection no. 72, box 16, APS.
32. Sarah Gratz Moses to R.G., April 1846, ibid.
33. Ibid.
34. Ann Gratz to R.G., April 2, 1846, ibid.
35. Hyman Gratz to R.G., May 7, 1846, ibid.
36. WW, 328, 327.
37. Sarah Hays Mordecai to R.G., August 5, 1847, Gratz Family Papers, Collection no. 72, box 15, APS.
38. Horace Moses to R.G., April 5, 1846, ibid., box 15.
39. Julia Hoffman to R.G., July 8, 1846, ibid., box 11.
40. John Francis Marion Notes, ibid., box 21.
41. "I hope the cool breezes or sparkling water are giving you the strength which you are so much in want of at this season of the year. Just got your letter from Saratoga, please visit here. I am well tho . . . not more than half as strong as formerly. I become fatigued soon especially in driving and am as prudent as possible in all things—in some [ways] I am in the same state as I was when I saw you but do not suffer as much from flushes and heat and blood in my head so I believe my constitution is gradually settling down to its new ways. But of course warm days I am not as comfortable as I have been in days gone by. . . . [L]ove to Fanny [Etting?] I imagine the operation she had was similar to the one I have yet to undergo." Julia Hoffman to R.G., August 12, 1847, ibid., box 15.
42. Ann Gratz to R.G., June 23, 1847, ibid.
43. R.G. to Ann Gratz, July 22, 1847, Philipson, *Letters,* 341.
44. Fanny Kemble to R.G., January 11, n.d., Gratz Family Papers, Collection no. 72, box 15, APS.
45. Frank Blair to R.G., November 13, 1842, ibid., box 11; Hyman Gratz to R.G., August 2, 1847, ibid., box 15.
46. R.G. to Miriam Moses Cohen, October 3, 1847, Rebecca Gratz Papers, Manuscript Collection no. 236, AJA.
47. R.G. to Miriam Moses Cohen, August 2, 1846, ibid.

Chapter 8

1. Geffen, "Industrial Development," 309.
2. R.G. to Miriam Moses Cohen, January 23, 1850, Rebecca Gratz Papers, Manuscript Collection no. 236, AJA.
3. Scott, *Natural Allies,* 35.
4. FHBS Board Minutes, 1847 Report, FHBS Collection, NMAJH.
5. Ibid.
6. FHBS Records, 1848, NMAJH.
7. Scott, *Natural Allies,* 27.
8. R.G. to Isaac Leeser, November 9, 1849, Rebecca Gratz Papers, Manuscript Collection no. 236, AJA.
9. "A Foster Home," *Occident* 8 (1850): 1.
10. JFH Annual Report, 1856–57, Association for Jewish Children Collection, series 1, box 1, folder 4, PJA-BIES.
11. JFH Constitution, 1855, ibid., folder 3.
12. Geffen, "Industrial Development," 321, 335, 341.
13. Todes, "History," 45, 63, 64–69, 70, 72.
14. Fein, *The Making of an American Jewish Community,* 123.
15. Meyer, *Response to Modernity,* 251.
16. Grinstein, *The Rise of the Jewish Community,* 152.
17. Gartner, *History of the Jews of Cleveland,* 51–56.
18. Reznikoff and Engleman, *The Jews of Charleston,* 150.
19. Berman, *Richmond's Jewry,* 56.
20. Geffen, "Industrial Development," 335.
21. Abramovitz, *Regulating the Lives of Women.*
22. Conversion Certificate of Louisa Gratz, 1855, signed by Sabato Morais and witnessed by Abraham Finzi, MIA.
23. Louisa Gratz, obituary, Simon Gratz Collection, HSP.
24. JFH Minute Book, 1855–1875, Association for Jewish Children Collection, series 1, box 1, folder 3, PJA-BIES.
25. Scott, *Natural Allies,* 25, 179.
26. Ibid., 21.
27. JFH Annual Report, 1856, Association for Jewish Children Collection, series 1, box 1, folder 4, PJA-BIES.
28. JFH Annual Report, 1857, ibid.
29. JFH Annual Report, 1856, ibid.
30. J. C. Levy, President, *An Address Delivered in Charleston, South Carolina, November 5, 1834,* "Pamphlets no. 992," APS.
31. For example, in 1858 the JFH board asked the president of the German synagogue if a young resident who had been taught to read "German Hebrew" could be allowed to read his bar mitzvah service there. JFH Board Minutes, April 13, 1858, Association for Jewish Children Collection, series 1, box 3, folder 1, PJA-BIES. Simha Peixotto also taught Hebrew and prepared boys living in the home for bar mitzvah.

32. JFH Annual Report, 1856, ibid., box 1, folder 4.

33. JFH Annual Reports, 1856 through 1867, ibid., folder 1.

34. Grinstein, *The Rise of the Jewish Community,* 155–60.

35. JFH Roll Book of Children in the Home, 1855–1874, Association for Jewish Children Collection, series 1, box 3, folder 11, PJA-BIES.

36. JFH Board Minutes, ibid., folder 4.

37. JFH Board Minutes, 1856, ibid., folder 1.

38. Register of Children, JFH, May 1, 1855, ibid., box 4, folder 1.

39. Rothman, *Discovery of the Asylum,* 223.

40. "Rules for the Regulation of the Home," Association for Jewish Children Collection, series 1, box 1, folder 4, PJA-BIES.

41. JFH Society Board Minutes, February 10, 1858, ibid., box 3, folder 1.

42. JFH Matron's Every and Account Book, 1876–1888, ibid., box 4, folder 2.

43. Rothman, *Discovery of the Asylum,* 221.

44. Ibid., 228; First Annual Report of the Philadelphia Orphan Society, 1816, Philadelphia, "Pamphlets no. 992," APS.

45. "Rules for the Regulation of the Home," published with the JFH Constitution, 1855, Association for Jewish Children Collection, series 1, box 1, folder 4, PJA-BIES.

46. JFH Board Minutes, August 1855, ibid., folder 1.

47. JFH Annual Report, 1858, ibid.

48. When longtime FHBS and JFH member Rachel Pesoa died in 1857, she was memorialized in the JFH minutes: "In her ascent heavenward may her mantle of charity have fallen on a successor, who will emulate her virtues and follow in the long-trodden path of her charities." JFH Second Annual Report, 1857, Association for Jewish Children Collection, ibid., series 1.

49. JFH Board Minutes, 1855–1856, Association for Jewish Children Collection, ibid., box 1, folder 4.

50. JFH Annual Reports, 1856 to 1873, ibid.

51. JFH Board Minutes, 1856 to 1865, Association for Jewish Children Collection, series 1, box 3, folder 1, PJA-BIES.

52. JFH Annual Reports, 1856 to 1873, Association for Jewish Children Collection, series 1, box 1, folder 4, PJA-BIES.

53. Whiteman, "The Philadelphia Group," 163–78.

54. Cott, "Passionlessness"; "The Poor, the Rich, and the Handsome on the Day of Judgment," in *Ma'aseh Book,* 107–10; on the Yetzer ha-ra: Gen. 6:5, 8:21, Deut. 6:5, Siphrei Deut. 32, Kiddushin, 30b; Fischel, "Religious Liberty" *Occident* 16 (1858): 21.

55. Solomon Solis, "Remarks on Miss Aguilar's *Women of Israel,*" *Occident* 4 (1846): 23, 81, and *Occident* 13 (1855): 142–43.

56. B., "Ladies Singing in Synagogue," *Occident* 13 (1855): 37.

57. R.G. to Benjamin Gratz, February 1, 1859, Philipson, *Letters,* 405.

58. R.G. to Julia Hoffman, R.G. to Mary Elizabeth Fenno Verplank, n.d., Gratz Family Papers, Collection no. 72, box 19, APS.
59. FHBS Annual Report, Secretary's Report, 1858, Henry Joseph Collection, box 239, AJA.
60. R.G. to Miriam Moses Cohen, December 29, n.d., Rebecca Gratz Papers, Manuscript Collection no. 236, AJA.
61. "My Sister's want of sight makes her dependent, but she has an intelligent cheerful girl who is attentive and acceptable to her who with whose services Sister is content—we spend part of every day together." R.G. to Ann Gratz, December 23, 1857, Philipson, *Letters*, 407.
62. R.G. to Benjamin Gratz, March 25, 1856, Rebecca Gratz Papers, P-9, AJHS.
63. R.G. to Ann Gratz, December 3, 1857, ibid. On the economic depression of 1857 see McPherson, *Battle Cry of Freedom*, 189–98.
64. Horace Moses to Isaac Leeser, October 25, n.d., courtesy Lance Sussman.
65. R.G. to Benjamin Gratz, June 6, 1862, Rebecca Gratz Papers, P-9, AJHS.
66. R.G. to Benjamin Gratz, April 17, 1859, ibid.
67. R.G. to Ann Gratz, September 12, 1861, ibid.
68. R.G. to Benjamin Gratz, December 21, 1859, ibid.

Chapter 9

1. R.G. to Benjamin Gratz, June 24, 1860, Rebecca Gratz Papers, Manuscript Collection no. 236, AJA.
2. R.G. to Ann Gratz, August 23, 1861, Philipson, *Letters*, 425.
3. R.G. to Miriam Moses Cohen, January 26, n.d., Rebecca Gratz Papers, Manuscript Collection no. 236, AJA.
4. R.G. to Benjamin Gratz, May 8, 1861, Philipson, *Letters*, 421.
5. R.G. to Solomon Cohen, May 22, 1861, Rebecca Gratz Papers, Manuscript Collection no. 236, AJA.
6. Mrs. James T. Dent, Clipping, Gratz Family Papers, Collection no. 72, box 11, APS.
7. Miriam Moses Cohen to R.G., January 1861, ibid., box. 9.
8. Quoted in McPherson, *Battle Cry of Freedom*, 103.
9. Miriam Moses Cohen to R.G., January 1861, Gratz Family Papers, Collection no. 72, box 9, APS. For more on the sectional political ideas voiced in the South between 1840 and the Civil War see McPherson, *Battle Cry of Freedom*, 78–117.
10. R.G. to Miriam Moses Cohen, August 8, 1862, Gratz Family Papers, Collection no. 72, box 11, APS.
11. R.G. to Miriam Moses Cohen, n.d., ibid.
12. R.G. to Ann Gratz, August 23, 1861, Philipson, *Letters*, xxiii.

13. R.G. to Ann Gratz, June 8, 1861, Rebecca Gratz Papers, P-9, AJHS.
14. R.G. to Ann Gratz, August 23, 1861, Philipson, *Letters,* xxiii.
15. R.G. to Ann Gratz, August 23, 1861, ibid., xxii. In the same letter Gratz also wrote that Cary would "rise in angel's form to whisper peace memorials of all his virtues and loveliness—his pure heart and innocent life, his brave qualities, the noble heart as tender and as full of filial love—all perfected and immortal—will in future be to [Benjamin] his very son, his beloved Cary."
16. R.G. to Ann Gratz, August 23, 1861, ibid., 425.
17. John W. Jordan, *Colonial and Revolutionary Families of Pennsylvania,* vol. 3 (Baltimore: Genealogical Publishing Co., 1978), 1243–45.
18. R.G. to Ann Gratz, September 12, 1861, Philipson, *Letters,* 426.
19. R.G. to Ann Gratz, October 30, 1861, Rebecca Gratz Papers, P-9, AJHS.
20. R.G. to Benjamin Gratz, June 6, 1862, Rebecca Gratz Papers, Manuscript Collection no. 236, AJA.
21. R.G. to Ann Gratz, September 12, 1861, Philipson, *Letters,* 427.
22. JFH Annual Report, 1860, Association for Jewish Children Collection, series 1, PJA-BIES.
23. Reena Sigman Friedman, "Founders, Teachers, Mothers, and Wards: Women in American Jewish Orphanages," unpublished manuscript (1995), 5.
24. R.G. to Miriam Moses Cohen, February 16, 1860, Rebecca Gratz Papers, Manuscript Collection no. 236, AJA.
25. R.G. to Miriam Moses Cohen, February 29, 1860, ibid.
26. Miriam Moses Cohen's husband, Solomon Cohen, added his own donation to the funds collected. R.G. to Miriam Moses Cohen, February 16, 1860, ibid.
27. R.G. to Miriam Moses Cohen, February 29, 1860, ibid.; JFH Annual Report, 1860, Association for Jewish Children Collection, series 1, PJA-BIES.
28. JFH Board Minutes, November 10, 1863, Association for Jewish Children Collection, series 1, box 3, folder 1, PJA-BIES.
29. JFH Board Minutes, 1860–1864, ibid., box 1, folder 1.
30. JFH Board Minutes, September 8, 1857, to October 13, 1863, ibid.
31. Glenn, *Daughters of the Shtetl,* 16–20.
32. H. Morais, *The Jews of Philadelphia,* 319.
33. R.G. to Miriam Moses Cohen, March 14, [1863?], Rebecca Gratz Papers, Manuscript Collection no. 236, AJA.
34. R.G. to Miriam Moses Cohen, January 26, [1865?], ibid.
35. Louisa B. Hart to R.G., March 4, 1864, Gratz Family Papers, Collection no. 72, box 9, APS.
36. Miriam Moses Cohen to R.G., February 18, 1864, ibid.
37. Gertrude Meredith to R.G., [1864?], ibid.

38. Julia Chouteau to R.G., January 2, [1864?], ibid.
39. Ann Gratz to R.G., February 20, 1864, ibid.
40. R.G. to Louisa B. Hart, October 31, 1864, box 11, ibid.
41. R.G. to The Teachers and Pupils of the Jewish Sunday School, March 4, 1862, ibid.
42. JFH Minutes, Association for Jewish Children Collection, series 1, PJA-BIES.
43. Ann Gratz to R.G., November 9, 1865, Gratz Family Papers, Collection no. 72, box 9, APS.
44. Sarah Moses Joseph to R.G., December 27, 1865, ibid.
45. Diner, *A Time for Gathering*, 167.
46. S. N. Fleischman, *A History of the Jewish Foster Home and Orphan Asylum* (Philadelphia, 1905), 80–90.
47. Estate of R.G., 1869, Gratz Family Papers, Collection no. 72, box 17, APS.
48. Evangelism did not abate after the war. In the second half of the nineteenth century, more Christian women were involved in missionary work than in all areas of social reform and women's rights movements combined (Reuther, *Religion and Sexism*, 242). By 1876, Presbyterians, who had organized the Ladies Jewish Mission Society under their foreign missions board, moved evangelism of American Jews to their home missions board, which organized churches nationwide. A. J. Brown, *One Hundred Years*, 1:68–70.
49. Minutes of the HSS Society, 1838–1875, AJA.
50. Todes, "History," 57.
51. King, "Jewish Education in Philadelphia," 235–52.
52. S. Morais, *Address* (1869), 7, AJA; Minutes of the HSS Society, [1869?], AJA; Sobel, "Legitimation and Antisemitism"; Boylan, "Changing Evangelical Views."
53. Minutes of the HSS Society, 1878–1882, AJA.
54. Minutes of the HSS Society, 1874, AJA.
55. Minutes of the HSS Society, 1878, AJA; Mary Mapes Dodge, *Hans Brinker, or The Silver Skates* (New York: Scribners, 1879), inscribed: "Punctual Attendance and Perfect Recitations to Leah Goldsmith 1885," HSS Society Collection, PJA-BIES.
56. "Superintendent's Report," Minutes of the HSS Society, 1878, AJA; Sarna, *JPS: The Americanization of Jewish Culture*, passim; Murray Friedman, "The Making of a National Jewish Community," in M. Friedman, *Jewish Life in Philadelphia, 1830–1940*, 1–25.
57. George Jacobs, "Address," Minutes of the HSS Society, 1877–1880, AJA.
58. Bodek, "Making Do," 143–62; Smith-Rosenberg, "The Female World of Love and Ritual," 1–30; Minutes of the HSS Society, 1840–1880, AJA.

59. *Purim Entertainment,* Grace Aguilar School of the Hebrew Sunday School Society, 1911, HSS Society Collection, PJA-BIES.
60. Julius Greenstone, *The Religion of Israel: A Book for Use in Religious Schools and the Home* (Philadelphia: Hebrew Sunday School Society, 1901), preface, n.p., HSS Society Collection, PJA-BIES; Nathan Glazer, *American Judaism* (Chicago: University of Chicago Press, 1972), 75–120; Feldstein, *The Land That I Show You,* 185–96; Robert Tabak, "Orthodox Judaism in Transition," in M. Friedman, *Jewish Life in Philadelphia, 1830–1940,* 48–63.
61. Greenstone's text also presented central beliefs about God, revelation, reward and punishment, the soul, and the messiah. The final section, titled "Sources of the Jewish Religion," looked at five books of Moses, early and later prophets, hagiography, apocryphal writings, and Talmud. The appendix offered a list of benedictions and a Hebrew calendar.
62. "Brief History of the Hebrew Sunday School Society," box 4, folder 18, MS 6, p. 4, PJA-BIES.
63. King, "Jewish Education in Philadelphia," 245–47.
64. Jewish Foster Home and Orphan Asylum Constitution, 1874, Association for Jewish Children Collection, series 1, box 1, folder 5, PJA-BIES.
65. Fleischman, *History of the Jewish Foster Home and Orphan Asylum,* 90.
66. "History," Association for Jewish Children Collection, 1855–1974, Inventory, PJA-BIES.
67. *History of the Young Women's Union* (Philadelphia, 1910), 3, Association for Jewish Children Collection, series 3, PJA-BIES.
68. Rebecca Gratz Club Minutes, Rebecca Gratz Club Records, PJA-BIES.
69. *Rebecca Gratz Club Newsletter,* January 1964, Rebecca Gratz Club Records, PJA-BIES.
70. Rebecca Gratz Club Records, PJA-BIES.
71. Kaplan, "Tradition and Transition," 3–35; Kaplan, "Priestess and Hausfrau: Women and Tradition in the German-Jewish Family," in *The Jewish Family,* ed. Cohen and Hyman, 62–82.

Chapter 10

1. As Gerda Lerner explains, sentimentality often has obscured women's knowledge of their past. Lerner, *The Creation of Feminist Consciousness,* 21–46.
2. "Obituary of Horace Moses," 1878, Gratz Family Papers, Collection no. 72, box 11, APS. Gratz knew Henry Clay through her sister-in-law, Maria Gist Gratz, Clay's niece.
3. Homer F. Barnes, *Charles Fenno Hoffman* (New York: Columbia

University Press, 1930) 59; the account was repeated the following year in *Dictionary of American Biography,* ed. Allen Johnson and Dumas Malone (New York: Scribner, 1931), 7:439. We have seen that Gratz was in Philadelphia at the time of Matilda's death in New York.

4. Elisabeth Ellicott Poe, "Half-Forgotten Romances of American History," *Washington Post,* March 2, 1936, Gratz Family Papers, Collection no. 72, box 19, APS.

5. These are: Hannah R. London, "Portraits of Rebecca Gratz by Thomas Sully," 98 *Antiques* (n.d.): 115–17; Mac Davis, *Jews at a Glance* (New York: Hebrew Publishing Company, 1956), 57; Harry Smirnoff, *Jewish Notables in America, 1776–1865* (N.p., 1956), 172–75; Mrs. Sol Brody, "In Philadelphia Were Sown the Seeds of American Jewish Philanthropy," *Jewish Exponent,* November 9, 1962, 27; "Gratz Family Placed Liberty above Success," *Philadelphia Inquirer,* October 25, 1967; Joseph X. Dever, "The Life, Times and Legend of Rebecca Gratz," *Evening Bulletin,* December 11, 1969; Ruth B. Sarner, "Remembering a Distinguished Lady," *Jewish Exponent,* October 24, 1969; Tina Levitan, *Jews in American Life* (New York: Hebrew Publishing Company, 1969), 46–48; Biskin, *Pattern for a Heroine;* "Rebecca Gratz," *National Cyclopedia of American Biography,* vol. 10 (1967), University Microfilms International reprint; Belva Plain, *Crescent City* (New York: Dell Publications, 1984), 72, 110; all Gratz Family Papers, Collection no. 72, box 19, APS.

6. Fishman, *A Breath of Life,* 18–19.

7. These changes are described in Smith-Rosenberg, *Visions of Gender;* Chambers-Schiller, *Liberty: A Better Husband;* Stansell, *City of Women;* Auerbach, *Woman and the Demon;* Nead, *Myths of Sexuality Representations of Women in Victorian Britain.*

8. Kessler-Harris, *Out to Work,* 3–20.

9. McDannell and Lang, *Heaven,* 228–275. Note such children's stories as "Cinderella" and "Sleeping Beauty."

10. MacDonald, *The Education of the Heart,* 28.

11. Berman, *Richmond's Jewry,* 57.

12. S. Morais, *Address.*

13. Sarah Mordecai, *Recollections of My Aunt* (Philadelphia, 1872; 1893 reissue by Rosa Mordecai), PJA-BIES.

14. Mrs. Alfred Mordecai, "Memoir of Rebecca Gratz Written by Her Niece Mrs. Alfred Mordecai," AJA, microfilm no. 3438.

15. R.G. to Maria Fenno Hoffman, July 28, 1808, February 26, 1809, March 2, 1812, and to Harriet Fenno, September 24, 1800, all Rebecca Gratz Papers, P-9, AJHS.

16. Gratz van Rensslaer, "The Original of Rebecca in Ivanhoe," *Century* (May 1882): 679–82.

17. Joseph Jacobs, "The Original of Scott's Rebecca," *PAJHS* no. 22

(1914): 53–59; Frank Willing Leach, "Old Philadelphia Families," *North American,* December 1, 1912, 109, HSP.

18. Personal correspondence, Dr. Iain G. Brown, Assistant Keeper, Manuscripts Division, National Library of Scotland, March 1, 1994.

19. "World! World! What are thou to me," Lebanon Springs, 1806, and "Complain no more deluded youth," Gratz Family Papers, Collection no. 72, box 21, APS.

20. R.G. to Maria Fenno Hoffman, October 20, 1817, Rebecca Gratz Papers, P-9, AJHS; R.G. to Sloe Hays, 1798, Gratz Family Papers, RM; Mordecai, *Recollections of My Aunt;* Byars, *B. & M. Gratz.* Even in 1990, unmarried women reported being more serene than married women. See Fishman, *A Breath of Life,* 25.

21. Leslie Gilliam, "At Rebecca's Grave: The Burial Place of Miss Rebecca Gratz the Original of Scott's Famous Heroine," *Philadelphia Times,* July 23, 1892, RM.

22. Bee Dee, "An American Jewess," *American Jewess* 2, no. 11 (1896): 38–39, Klau Library Periodicals Center, Hebrew Union College, Cincinnati, Ohio; J. R. Crockett, *Originals of Scott* (London, 1912), 42.

23. Jacobs, "The Original of Scott's Rebecca," 78; Lockhart, *Life of Sir Walter Scott;* Arendt, *Rahel Varnhagen.*

24. Beatrice T. Mantel, "Rebecca Gratz," publication of the National Council of Jewish Women, New York, ca. 1920s, and "The Fairy Godmother," both courtesy of Dr. Faith Rogow; Osterweiss, *Rebecca Gratz,* 10, 37–39; Margretta Lawler, *Childhood,* referred to in letter to Dr. Alvin D. Rubin from Margretta Lawler, Correspondence file, AJA; Biskin, *Pattern for a Heroine;* Leonard Beerman, "An Analysis of the Life and Activity of the Foremost Jewess of the Nineteenth Century" (Ordination thesis, Hebrew Union College, 1947); Joseph Rosenbloom, "And She Had Compassion: The Life and Times of Rebecca Gratz" (Ph.D. diss., Hebrew Union College, 1959); synopsis for an opera depicting the life of Rebecca Gratz, written by David Bamberger (Cleveland, Ohio, 1976), Biographies File, AJA; E. Digby Baltzell, "The Jewish Communities of Philadelphia and Boston: A Tale of Two Cities," in M. Friedman, *Jewish Life in Philadelphia, 1830–1940,* 290–313; Patricia Donovan, "Deluded: A Big Story, But Not This Big," review of "The Gratz Delusion" written by Rebecca Ritchie, *Buffalo News,* Friday, June 4, 1993, "Gusto," 23.

25. Walter Scott to Lord Montague, November 12, 1818, and May 6, 1819. H. J. C. Grierson, *The Letters of Sir Walter Scott 1819–1821* (London: Constable and Co., 1934). Scott wrote, regarding the Duke: "I never thought it was possible that a man could have loved another so much where the distance of rank was so great" (377–78).

26. Lockhart, *Life of Sir Walter Scott,* 6:78; Aguilar, *Spirit of Judaism,* introduction.

27. R.G. to Maria Fenno Hoffman, n.d., Rebecca Gratz Papers, P-9, AJHS.
28. "Jews and Jew-Baiters," editorial, *Century Magazine* (May 1882): 149.
29. Emma Lazarus, "Russian Christianity versus Modern Judaism," *Century Magazine* (May 1882): 48–56.
30. Joaquin Miller, "Jewess," *Century Magazine* (May 1882): 149.
31. Chambers-Schiller, *Liberty: A Better Husband,* 35–48; Cott, "Passionlessness"; Degler, *At Odds,* 384.
32. Chambers-Schiller, *Liberty: A Better Husband,* 24–27.
33. Degler, *At Odds,* 368.
34. Chambers-Schiller, *Liberty: A Better Husband,* 204.
35. Ibid., 38.
36. Kessler-Harris, *Out to Work,* 195; Chambers-Schiller, *Liberty: A Better Husband,* 195; Degler, *At Odds,* 379–81.
37. Chambers-Schiller, *Liberty: A Better Husband,* 194.
38. Ibid., 191.
39. Ibid., 194, 199, 200; Smith-Rosenberg, *Disorderly Conduct,* 245–97; Jeffreys, *The Spinster and Her Enemies,* 110–12.
40. For discussion of these activities see Sue Ellen Elwell, "Education Programs of the National Council for Jewish Women, 1895–1918" (Ph.D. diss., Indiana University, 1982); Rogow, *Gone to Another Meeting;* Golumb, "The 1893 Congress of Jewish Women."
41. Bodek, "Making Do," 152–62.
42. Minnie Louis, "The Influence of Women in Bringing Religious Conviction to Bear upon Daily Life," *American Hebrew* 57, no. 8 (1895): 183–86.
43. Minnie Louis, "Religious Schools," *American Hebrew* 59, no. 3 (1896): 73–76.
44. Annie Josephine Levi, "Intermarriage," *American Hebrew* 59, no. 3 (1896): 56–58.
45. Philip Weinberger, "The Social and Religious Thought of Grace Aguilar" (Ph.D. diss., New York University, 1970), 78–85.
46. Lukacs, *Philadelphia Patricians and Philistines,* 19, quoted in M. Friedman, *Philadelphia Jewish Life,* 4.
47. I am grateful to my grandmother, the late Tillie Kaminker Keller, for this proverb and many others.
48. Eli Soren, *A Time for Building: The Third Migration* (Baltimore: Johns Hopkins University Press, 1992), 174–90.
49. Fishman, *A Breath of Life,* 107.
50. Joselit, *The Wonders of America,* 15–17.
51. Fishman, *A Breath of Life,* 24, 272n. 17.

Selected Bibliography

The following is intended to serve as a general guide to works useful in understanding Rebecca Gratz, women, and Jews in nineteenth-century America. It is not an exhaustive listing of materials used in this study. Other citations can be found in the Notes.

Archival Collections

American Jewish Archives, Cincinnati, Ohio
    Biographies File
    Correspondence File
    Rebecca Gratz Papers, Manuscript Collection no. 236
    Michael Gratz Papers
    Hebrew Sunday School Society Collection
    Henry Joseph Collection
    Small Collections

American Jewish Historical Society, Waltham, Mass.
    Rebecca Gratz Papers, P-9

American Philosophical Society, Philadelphia, Pa.
    Gratz Family Papers, Collection no. 72

Historical Society of Pennsylvania, Philadelphia, Pa.
    Etting Collection
    Simon Gratz Collection
    Meredith Papers Correspondence
    Guardians of the Poor Collection
    Ellen Phillips Papers
    Stauffer Collection

Library of Congress, Washington, D.C.
    Miscellaneous Manuscript Collection

McGill University Libraries, Montreal, Quebec, Canada
    Gratz Collection, Department of Rare Books and Special Collections

Mikveh Israel Archives, Philadelphia, Pa.
    Correspondence File
    Gratz Family Books

Gratz Family Prayer Books

National Museum of American Jewish History
Female Hebrew Benevolent Society Collection
Gratz Family Library Collection

Philadelphia Jewish Archives—Balch Institute of Ethnic Studies, Philadelphia, Pa.
Association for Jewish Children Collection
Hebrew Sunday School Society Collection
Jewish Foster Home and Orphan Asylum Collection
Rebecca Gratz Club Records
United Hebrew Beneficent Society Records

Rosenbach Museum, Philadelphia, Pa.
Gratz Family Papers

Southern History Collection, University of North Carolina, Chapel Hill
Miriam Gratz Moses Cohen Papers and Books, Collection no. 2639

Secondary Sources

Abramovitz, Mimi. *Regulating the Lives of Women: Social Welfare Policy from Colonial Times to the Present.* Boston: South End Press, 1988.

Aderman, Ralph M., Herbert L. Kleinfield, and Jennifer S. Banks, eds. *The Collected Works of Washington Irving.* Volume 1. Boston: Twayne, 1978–83.

Altmann, Alexander, ed. *Studies in Nineteenth-Century Jewish Intellectual History.* Cambridge: Harvard University Press, 1964.

Appel, John J. "Jews in American Caricature, 1820–1914." *American Jewish Historical Quarterly* 71, no. 1 (1981): 103–33.

Ashton, Dianne. "Grace Aguilar and the Female Response to Evangelists." *Jewish Folklore and Ethnology Review* 12, nos. 1–2 (1990): 22.

———. "Grace Aguilar and the Matriarchal Theme in Jewish Women's Spirituality." In *Active Voices: Women in Jewish Culture,* ed. Maurie Sacks, 79–93. Urbana: University of Illinois Press, 1995.

Arendt, Hannah. *Rahel Varnhagen: The Life of a Jewish Woman.* New York: Harcourt, Brace, Jovanovich, 1974.

Auerbach, Nina. *Woman and the Demon: The Life of a Victorian Myth.* Cambridge: Harvard University Press, 1982.

Baltzell, E. Digby. *Philadelphia Gentlemen: The Making of a National Upper Class.* New York: Transaction Books, 1989.

———. *Puritan Boston and Quaker Philadelphia.* Boston: Beacon Press, 1979.

Baron, Salo. *A Social and Religious History of the Jews.* Philadelphia: Jewish Publication Society, 1976.

Bartelt, Pearl. "Women and Judaism." In *God, Sex, and the Social Project,* ed. James H. Grace, 65–78. Lewiston, New York: Edwin Mellen Press, 1978.

Baum, Charlotte, Paula Hyman, and Sonya Michel. *The Jewish Woman in America.* New York: Plume Books, 1975.

Baym, Nina. *Woman's Fiction: A Guide to Novels by and about Women in America, 1820–1870.* Ithaca: Cornell University Press, 1978; 2nd ed., Urbana: University of Illinois Press, 1993.

Belenky, Mary Field, Blythe McVicker Clinchy, Nancy Rule Goldberger, and Jill Mattuck Tarule. *Women's Ways of Knowing.* New York: Basic Books, 1986.

Bell, Marion. *Crusade in the City: Revivalism in Nineteenth-Century Philadelphia.* Lewisburg, Pa.: Bucknell University Press, 1977.

Berg, Barbara. *The Remembered Gate: Origins of American Feminism: The Woman and the City, 1800–1860.* New York: Oxford University Press, 1978.

Berkovits, Eliezer. *Not in Heaven: The Nature and Function of Halakha.* New York: KTAV, 1983.

Berlin, George. "Solomon Jackson's *The Jew:* An Early American Jewish Response to the Missionaries." *American Jewish Historical Quarterly* 71, no. 1 (1981): 10–28.

Berman, Myron. *Richmond's Jewry, 1769–1976.* Charlottesville: University Press of Virginia, 1979.

Bermant, Chaim. *The Cousinhood: The Anglo-Jewish Gentry.* London: Eyre Spottiswoode, 1971.

Biale, David. "The Jewish Family in the Eastern European Jewish Enlightenment." In *The Jewish Family: Myths and Reality,* ed. Steven M. Cohen and Paula E. Hyman, 45–61. New York: Holmes and Meier, 1986.

Biale, Rachel. *Women and Jewish Law.* New York: Schocken, 1984.

Biskin, Miriam. *Pattern for a Heroine: Life Story of Rebecca Gratz.* New York: Union of American Hebrew Congregations, 1967.

Blau, Joseph, and Salo Baron, eds. "Local Courts and Sabbath Laws, 1793–1833." In *The Jews of the United States, 1790–1840,* 21–25. New York: Columbia University Press, 1963.

Blauvelt, Martha Tomhave. "Women and Revivalism." In *Women and Religion in America,* vol. 1: *The Nineteenth Century,* ed. Rosemary Radford Reuther and Rosemary Keller, 1–45. New York: Harper and Row, 1981.

Bloch, Ruth. "American Feminine Ideals in Transition: The Rise of the Moral Mother, 1785–1815." *Feminist Studies* 4 (1978): 101–26.

Bodek, Evelyn. "Making Do: Jewish Women and Philanthropy." In *Jewish Life in Philadelphia, 1830–1940,* ed. Murray Friedman, 143–62. Philadelphia: ISHI Press, 1983.

Borden, Michael. *Jews, Turks, and Infidels.* Chapel Hill: University of North Carolina, 1984.

Boylan, Anne M. "Presbyterians and Sunday Schools in Philadelphia, 1800–1824." *Journal of Presbyterian History* 58, no. 4 (1980): 299–310.

———. *Sunday School: The Formation of an American Institution.* New Haven: Yale University Press, 1988.

———. "Sunday Schools and Changing Evangelical Views of Children in the 1820s." *Church History* 48, no. 3 (1979): 320–34.

———. "Women in Groups: An Analysis of Women's Benevolent Organizations in New York and Boston, 1797–1840." *Journal of American History* 71, no. 3 (1984): 497–524.

Breiger, Gert, ed. *Medical America in the Nineteenth Century.* Baltimore: Johns Hopkins University Press, 1972.

Brener, David. *The Jews of Lancaster, Pennsylvania: A Story with Two Beginnings.* Lancaster, Pa.: Lancaster County Historical Society, 1979.

Brigham, Clarence. *History and Bibliography of American Newspapers, 1690–1820.* 2 volumes. Worcester, Mass.: American Antiquarian Society, 1947.

Brown, Arthur Judson. *One Hundred Years: History of Foreign Missions.* 2 volumes. London: Fleming H. Revell and Co. 1936.

Brown, Gilliam. "Getting into the Kitchen with Dinah: Domestic Politics in *Uncle Tom's Cabin.*" *American Quarterly* 36, no. 4 (1985): 503–23.

Bushman, Richard L. *The Refinement of America: Persons, Houses, Cities.* New York: Knopf, 1992.

Butler, Jon. *Awash in a Sea of Faith: Christianizing the American People.* Cambridge: Harvard University Press, 1990.

Butsch, Richard. "Bowery B'Hoys and Matinee Ladies: The Re-Gendering of Nineteenth Century Theater Audiences." *American Quarterly* 46, no. 3 (1994): 374–405.

Byars, William V. *B. & M. Gratz: Merchants in Philadelphia.* Jefferson City, Mo.: Hugh G. Steffans, 1916.

Calcott, George. *History in the United States, 1800–1860: Its Practice and Purpose.* Baltimore: Johns Hopkins University Press, 1970.

Calisch, Edward. *The Jew in English Literature as Author and as Subject.* New York: Bell, 1909.

Cameron, Debra, ed. *The Feminist Critique of Language: A Reader.* London: Routledge, 1990.

Chambers-Schiller, Lee. *Liberty: A Better Husband: Single Women in America: The Generations of 1780–1840.* New Haven: Yale University Press, 1984.

Chernow, Ron. *The Warburgs.* New York: Vintage Books, 1994.

Christ, Carol. "Victorian Masculinity and the Angel in the House." In *A Widening Sphere: Changing Roles of Victorian Women,* ed. Martha Vicinus, 146–63. Bloomington: Indiana University Press, 1977.

Coale, Ainsley J., and Melvin Zelnik. *New Estimates of Fertility and Population in the United States.* Princeton: Princeton University Press, 1963.

Cohen, Naomi W. *Encounter with Emancipation: The German Jews in the United States, 1830–1914.* Philadelphia: Jewish Publication Society, 1984.

———. *Jews in Christian America: The Pursuit of Religious Equality.* New York: Oxford University Press, 1992.

Cohen, Robert. "The Demography of the Jews in Early America." In *Modern Jewish Fertility,* ed. Paul Ritterband, 12–25. Leiden: Brill, 1981.

Cohen, Steven M., and Paula E. Hyman, eds. *The Jewish Family: Myths and Reality.* New York: Holmes and Meier, 1986.

Cott, Nancy. "Passionlessness: An Interpretation of Victorian Sexual Ideology, 1790–1850." *Signs* 4, no. 2 (1978): 219–36.

Cowie, Alexander. "The Vogue of the Domestic Novel, 1850–1870." *South Atlanta Quarterly* 41 (October 1942).

Davis, Allen, and Mark Haller, eds. *The Peoples of Philadelphia: A History of Ethnic Groups and Lower-Class Life, 1790–1940.* Philadelphia: Temple University Press, 1973.

Degler, Carl. *At Odds: Women and the Family in America from the Revolution to the Present.* New York: Oxford University Press, 1980.

D'Emilio, John, and Estelle B. Freedman. *Intimate Matters: A History of Sexuality in America.* New York: Harper and Row, 1988.

Di Leonardo, Micaela. "The Female World of Cards and Holidays: Women, Families, and the Work of Kinship." *Signs* (1987): 440–53.

Diner, Hasia. *A Time for Gathering: The Second Migration, 1820–1880.* Baltimore: Johns Hopkins University Press, 1992.

Douglas, Ann. *The Feminization of American Culture.* New York: Avon, 1977.

———. *Terrible Honesty: Mongrel Manhattan in the 1920s.* New York: Farrar, Straus, and Giroux, 1995.

Evans, Eli. *Judah P. Benjamin: The Jewish Confederate.* New York: Free Press, 1988.

Evans, Sara M. *Born For Liberty: A History of Women in America.* New York: Free Press, 1989.

Faber, Eli. *A Time for Planting: The First Migration, 1654–1820.* Baltimore: Johns Hopkins University Press, 1992.

Fee, Elizabeth. "The Sexual Politics of Victorian Social Anthropology." *Feminist Studies* 1, nos. 3–4 (1973): 23–39.

Fein, Isaac M. *The Making of an American Jewish Community: A History of Baltimore Jewry from 1773–1920.* Philadelphia: Jewish Publication Society, 1971.

Feldberg, Michael. *The Philadelphia Riots of 1844: A Study of Ethnic Conflict.* Westport, Conn.: Greenwood Press, 1975

———. *Turbulent Era: Riot and Disorder in Jacksonian America.* New York: Oxford University Press, 1980.

Feldman, Egal. *Dual Destinies: The Jewish Encounter with Protestant America.* Urbana: University of Illinois Press, 1990.

Feldman, Jacob. *The Jewish Experience in Western Pennsylvania, 1755– 1945.* Pittsburgh: Historical Society of Western Pennsylvania, 1986.

Feldstein, Stanley. *The Land That I Show You.* New York: Anchor, 1979.

Fern, Alan. *Mr. Sully: Portrait Painter.* Exhibition catalog, National Portrait Gallery, Smithsonian Institution, 1983.

Fish, Sidney M. "The Ancestral Heritage of the Gratz Family." In *Gratz College Anniversary Volume,* ed. Isidore David Passow and Samuel Tobias Lachs, 47–62. Philadelphia, 1971.

———. *Barnard and Michael Gratz: Their Lives and Times.* New York: University Press of America, 1994.

———. "The Role of Michael Gratz in Blockade Running and Privateering." In *Community and Culture: Essays in Honor of the Ninetieth Anniversary of the Founding of Gratz College.* Philadelphia: Seth Press, 1987.

Fishbane, Michael. "Action and Non-Action in Jewish Spirituality." *Judaism* 33, no. 3 (1984): 318–29.

Fishman, Sylvia Barak. *A Breath of Life: Feminism in the American Jewish Community.* New York: Free Press, 1993.

Fout, John, ed. *German Women in the Nineteenth Century: A Social History.* New York: Holmes and Meier, 1984.

Freedman, Estelle. "Separatism as Strategy: Female Institution Building and American Feminism, 1870–1930." *Feminist Studies* 5, no. 3 (1979): 512–27.

Friedman, Murray, ed. *Jewish Life in Philadelphia, 1830–1940.* Philadelphia: ISHI Press, 1983.

———. *Philadelphia Jewish Life: 1940–1985.* Ardmore, Pa.: Seth Press, 1986.

———. *When Philadelphia Was the Capital of Jewish America.* Cranbury, N.J.: Associated University Presses, 1992.

Friedman, Reena Sigman. " 'Send Me My Husband Who Is in New York City': Husband Desertion in the American Jewish Immigrant Community, 1900–1926." *Jewish Social Studies* 44 (Winter 1982): 1–8.

Galchinsky, Michael. *The Origin of the Modern Jewish Woman Writer: Romance and Reform in Victorian England.* Detroit: Wayne State University Press, 1996.

Garrison, Dee. "Immoral Fiction in the Late Victorian Library." *American Quarterly* 28 (Spring 1976): 71–89.

Gartner, Lloyd P. *History of the Jews of Cleveland.* New York: Jewish Theological Seminary, 1978.

Geffen, Elizabeth M. "Industrial Development and Social Crisis, 1841–1854." In *Philadelphia: A Three Hundred Year History,* ed. Russell Weigley, 307–62. New York: Norton, 1982.

Ginzberg, Lori D. *Women and the Work of Benevolence: Morality, Politics, and Class in the Nineteenth-Century United States.* New Haven: Yale University Press, 1990.

Gittelman, Sol. *From Shtetl to Suburbia: The Jewish Family in Jewish Literary Imagination.* Boston: Beacon Press, 1978.

Glanz, Rudolph. *The Jew in Early American Wit and Graphic Humor.* New York: KTAV, 1973.

———. *The Jewish Woman in America: Two Immigrant Generations.* 2 volumes. New York: KTAV, 1976.

Glenn, Susan. *Daughters of the Shtetl: Life and Labor in the Immigrant Generation.* Ithaca: Cornell University Press, 1990.

Gluckel of Hameln. *The Memoirs of Gluckel of Hameln.* Trans. Marvin Lowenthal. New York: Schocken, 1977.

Goldberg, Hillel. *Israel Salanter: Text, Structure, Idea: The Ethics and Theology of an Early Psychologist of the Unconscious.* New York: KTAV, 1982.

Goldman, Karla. "The Ambivalence of Reform Judaism: Kaufmann Kohler and the Ideal Jewish Woman." *American Jewish Historical Quarterly* 79, no. 4 (1990): 477–99.

Goldscheider, Calvin, and Alan Zuckerman. *The Transformation of the Jews.* Chicago: University of Chicago Press, 1984.

Golumb, Deborah. "The 1893 Congress of Jewish Women: Evolution or Revolution in American Jewish History?" *Publications of the American Jewish Historical Society* 70 (1981): 52–67.

Goode, William. "The Theoretical Importance of Love." In *The Family: Its Structures and Functions,* 2nd edition. Ed. Rose Coser, 143–56. New York: St. Martin's Press, 1974.

Gordon, Ann D. "The Young Ladies Academy of Philadelphia." In *Women of America: A History,* ed. Carol Berkin and Mary Beth Norton, 68–92. Boston: Houghton Mifflin, 1979.

Gottleib, Lynn. "The Secret Jew: An Oral Tradition of Women." In *On Being A Jewish Feminist,* ed. Susannah Heschel, 273–77. New York: Schocken, 1983.

Grinstein, Hyman. *The Rise of the Jewish Community of New York, 1654–1860.* Philadelphia: Jewish Publication Society, 1947.

Grose, Peter. *Israel in the Mind of America.* New York: Schocken, 1984.

Haberman, Jacob. "A Jewish View of the Idea of Progress." *Journal of Jewish Studies* 35, no. 1 (1984): 57–70.

Hanft, Sheldon. "Mordecai's Female Academy." *American Jewish History* 79, no. 1 (1989): 72–93.

Harap, Louis. *The Image of the Jew in American Literature: From Early Republic to Mass Migration.* Philadelphia: Jewish Publication Society, 1974.

Hareven, Tamara K. "Modernization and Family History: Perspectives on Social Change." *Signs* 2, no. 1 (1976): 190–206.

Hareven, Tamara K., and Maris A. Vinovskis. *Family and Population in Nineteenth-Century America.* Princeton: Princeton University Press, 1978.

Harris, Barbara. *Beyond Her Sphere: Women and the Professions in American History.* Westport, Conn.: Greenwood Press, 1978.

Harris, Monford. "Touch, Sight and Hearing in Jewish Sexuality." *Judaism* 131, no. 33 (1984): 346–52.

Hedrick, Joan D. *Harriet Beecher Stowe: A Life.* New York: Oxford University Press, 1994.

Hench, John, ed. "Letters of John Fenno and John Ward Fenno, 1779–1800." *American Antiquarian Society Proceedings* 89 (1979): 299–308.

Henry, Sondra, and Emily Taitz. *Written Out of History: Our Jewish Foremothers.* New York: Biblio Press, 1983.

Hershberg, Theodore, ed. *Work, Space, and Family Life in Nineteenth-Century Philadelphia.* Philadelphia: University of Pennsylvania Press, 1983.

Himmelfarb, Harold. "Patterns of Assimilation-Identification among American Jews." *Ethnicity* 6 (1976): 249–67.

Hoffman, Ronald, and Peter J. Albert, eds. *Women in the Age of the American Revolution.* Charlottesville: University Press of Virginia, 1989.

Houghton, Walter. *The Victorian Frame of Mind: 1830–1870.* New Haven: Yale University Press, 1957.

Hsia, R. Po-Chia. *The Myth of Ritual Murder: Jews and Magic in Reformation Germany.* New Haven: Yale University Press, 1988.

Hudson, Winthrop. *Religion in America.* 2nd ed. New York: Scribner, 1973.

Hundert, Gershon David. "Approaches to the History of the Jewish Family in Early Modern Poland-Lithuania." In *The Jewish Family: Myths and Reality,* ed. Steven M. Cohen and Paula E. Hyman, 17–28. New York: Holmes and Meier, 1986.

Hunter, Dianne. "Hysteria, Psychoanalysis, and Feminism: The Case of Anna O." *Feminist Studies* 9, no. 3 (1983): 465–88.

Hyman, Paula E. *Gender and Assimilation in Modern Jewish History.* Seattle: University of Washington Press, 1995.

Idelsohn, A. Z. *Jewish Liturgy and Its Development.* New York: Schocken Books, 1975.

Jeffries, Sheila. *The Spinster and Her Enemies.* Boston: Pandora Press, 1985.

Jick, Leon. *The Americanization of the Synagogue.* Waltham, Mass.: Brandeis University Press, 1976.

Johnson, Claudia. *American Actress: Perspectives on the Nineteenth Century.* Chicago: Nelson Hall Press, 1984.

Jones, Charles. "Knickerbocker Santa Claus." *New York Historical Society Quarterly* 38, no. 4 (1954): 357–83.

Jones, Deborah. "Gossip: Notes on Women's Oral Culture." In *The Feminist Critique of Language: A Reader,* ed. Deborah Cameron, 242–50. London: Routledge, 1990.

Jones, Madwyn Allen. *American Immigration.* Chicago: University of Chicago Press, 1960.

Joselit, Jenna Weissman. *The Wonders of America: Reinventing Jewish Culture, 1880–1950.* New York: Hill and Wang, 1994.

Kaganoff, Nathan M., and Melvin I. Urofsky, eds. *Turn to the South: Essays on Southern Jewry.* Charlottesville: American Jewish Historical Society, 1979.

Kaplan, Marion. *The Making of the Jewish Middle Class.* New York: Oxford University Press, 1991.

———. "Tradition and Transition: The Acculturation, Assimilation, and Integration of Jews in Imperial Germany: A Gender Analysis." *Leo Baeck Institute Yearbook* 27 (1982): 3–35.

Karp, Abraham. *The Jewish Experience in America,* part 3: *The Emerging Community,* 1–27. Waltham, Mass.: American Jewish Historical Society, 1969.

Kasson, John. *Rudeness and Civility: Manners in Nineteenth-Century America.* New York: Hill and Wang, 1990.

Katz, Jacob. *Out of the Ghetto.* New York: Schocken, 1978.

———. *Tradition and Crisis.* New York: Schocken, 1961.

———, ed. *The Role of Religion in Modern Jewish History.* Cambridge: Harvard University Press, 1975.

Katz, Michael. *In the Shadow of the Poorhouse.* New York: Basic Books, 1986.

Kelley, Mary. "The Sentimentalists: Promise and Betrayal in the Home." *Signs* 4 (1979): 434–46.

———. "Woman Alone: Catherine Maria Sedgwick's Spinsterhood in Nineteenth-Century America." *New England Quarterly* 51, no. 2 (1978): 209–25.

Kerber, Linda. *Women of the Republic: Intellect and Ideology in Revolutionary America.* Chapel Hill: University of North Carolina Press, 1980.

Kessler-Harris, Alice. *Out to Work: A History of Wage-Earning Women in the United States.* New York: Oxford University Press, 1982.

King, Diane E. "Jewish Education in Philadelphia." In *Jewish Life in Philadelphia, 1830–1940,* ed. Murray Friedman, 235–52. Philadelphia: ISHI Press, 1983.

Kitsch, Sally. *Chaste Liberation: Celibacy and Female Cultural Status.* Urbana: University of Illinois Press, 1989.

Klein, Frederick Shriver. *A History of the Jews in Lancaster.* Lancaster, Pa.: Lancaster Historical Society, 1955.

Kober, Adolf. "Jewish Migration from Wurttemberg to the United States, 1848–1855." In *The Jewish Experience in America* volume 3, ed. Abraham Karp, 1–27. Waltham, Mass.: American Jewish Historical Society, 1969.

Korn, Bertram W. *American Jewry and the Civil War.* Cleveland: World Publishing Co., 1961.

———. *Eventful Years and Experiences: Studies in Nineteenth-Century American Jewish History.* American Jewish Archives, 1954.

Kuzmack, Linda Gordon. *Woman's Cause: The Jewish Woman's Movement in England and the United States, 1881–1933.* Columbus: Ohio State University Press, 1990.

Lamm, Maurice. *The Jewish Way in Love and Marriage*. New York: Harper and Row, 1980.

Landes, David. "Bleichroders and Rothschilds: The Problem of Continuity in the Family Firm." In *The Family in History,* ed. Charles Rosenberg, 95–115. Philadelphia: University of Pennsylvania Press, 1975.

Laquer, Thomas. *Religion and Respectability: Sunday Schools and Working-Class Culture, 1780–1850*. New Haven: Yale University Press, 1976.

Lavendar, Abraham D. "Arabic-Islamic and Spanish-Mediterranean Influences on 'The Jewish Mind': A Comparison to European-Christian Influence." *Journal of Ethnic Studies* 8 (1981): 25–35.

Lawrence, Charles. *History of the Philadelphia Almshouses and Hospitals from the Beginning of the Eighteenth Century to the End of the Nineteenth Century*. Philadelphia, 1905.

Lerner, Gerda. *The Creation of Feminist Consciousness: From the Middle Ages to the Eighteenth Century*. New York: Oxford University Press, 1993.

Levi-Strauss, Claude. *The Savage Mind*. Chicago: University of Chicago Press, 1966.

Lichtenstein, Diane. *Writing Their Nations: The Traditions of Nineteenth-Century American Jewish Women Writers*. Bloomington: Indiana University Press, 1992.

Lockhart, J. G. *Life of Sir Walter Scott*. 1902. Reprint, New York: AMS Press, 1983.

Lukacs, John. *Philadelphia Patricians and Philistines, 1900–1950*. New York: Farrar, Straus, Giroux, 1981.

Lynn, Robert, and Elliott Wright. *The Big Little School: Sunday Child of American Protestantism*. New York: Harper and Row, 1971.

Ma'aseh Book. Trans. Theodore Gaster. Philadelphia: Jewish Publication Society, 1981.

Malkin, Carole. *The Journeys of David Toback*. New York: Schocken, 1981.

Marcus, Jacob Rader. *The American Jewish Woman, 1654–1980*. Detroit: Wayne State University Press, 1981.

———. *The American Jewish Woman: Documents*. Detroit: Wayne State University Press, 1981.

———. *The Colonial American Jew*. Detroit: Wayne State University Press, 1976.

———, ed. *On Love, Marriage, Children, . . . and Death Too: Intimate Glimpses into the Lives of American Jews in a Bygone Era as Told in Their Own Words*. Philadelphia: Jewish Publication Society, 1965.

Margolis, Max L., and Abraham Marx. *A History of the Jewish People*. New York: Athenaeum, 1975.

Matthews, Glenna. *The Rise of Public Woman: Woman's Power and Woman's Place in the United States, 1630–1970.* New York: Oxford University Press, 1992.

Matthews, Jean. *Toward a New Society: American Culture and Society, 1800–1830.* Boston: Twayne, 1991.

McDannell, Colleen. *The Christian Home in Victorian America.* Bloomington: Indiana University Press, 1986.

McDannell, Colleen, and Bernhard Lang. *Heaven: A History.* New Haven: Yale University Press, 1988.

MacDonald, Edgar, ed. *The Education of the Heart: Correspondence of Rachel Mordecai Lazarus and Maria Edgeworth.* Chapel Hill: University of North Carolina Press, 1977.

McPherson, James. *Battle Cry of Freedom: The Civil War Era.* New York: Ballantine, 1988.

Meiselman, Moshe. *Jewish Women and Jewish Law.* New York: KTAV, 1978.

Meyer, Michael. *Origins of the Modern Jew.* Detroit: Wayne State University Press, 1967.

———. *Response to Modernity: A History of the Reform Movement in Judaism.* New York: Oxford University Press, 1988.

Miller, Page Putnam. "Women in the Vanguard of the Sunday School Movement." *Journal of Presbyterian History* 58, no. 4 (1980): 311–25.

Mithun, Jacqueline. "The Role of the Family in Acculturation and Assimilation in America: A Psychocultural Dimension." In *Culture, Ethnicity, and Identity: Current Issues in Research,* ed. William C. McCreedy, 209–21. Academic Press, 1983.

Modder, Frank Montagu. *The Jew in the Literature of England: To the End of the Nineteenth Century.* New York: Meridian Books, 1960.

Moore, R. Laurence. *Selling God: American Religion in the Marketplace of Ideas.* New York: Oxford University Press, 1994.

Morais, Henry Samuel. *The Jews of Philadelphia.* Philadelphia: Levytype, 1894.

Morais, Samuel. *Address to the Hebrew Sunday School on the Life and Character of Miss Rebecca Gratz.* Philadelphia: Collins, 1869.

Morison, Samuel Eliot. *The Oxford History of the American People.* 3 volumes. New York: Signet, 1972.

Mott, Frank Luther. *A History of American Magazines, 1741–1850.* Cambridge: Harvard University Press, 1938.

Nead, Lynda. *Myths of Sexuality: Representations of Women in Victorian Britain.* London: Basil Blackwood, 1988.

Neusner, Jacob. *Scriptures of the Oral Torah.* New York: Harper and Row, 1987.

Odendahl, Theresa. *Charity Begins at Home: Generosity and Self-Interest among the Philanthropic Elite.* New York: Basic Books, 1990.

Osterweiss, Roland. *Rebecca Gratz: A Study in Charm.* New York: Putnam, 1935.

Papishvily, Helen Waite. *All the Happy Endings: A Study of the Domestic Novel in America, the Women Who Wrote It, the Women Who Read It, in the Nineteenth Century.* New York: Harper and Brothers, 1956.

Philipson, David, ed. *The Letters of Rebecca Gratz.* Philadelphia: Jewish Publication Society, 1929.

Porter, Jack Nusan. "The Sephardi in America." In *The Sociology of American Jews: A Critical Anthology,* 2nd edition, 35–43. New York: University Press of America, 1980.

Porterfield, Amanda. *Feminine Spirituality in America: From Sarah Edward to Martha Graham.* Philadelphia: Temple University Press, 1980.

Reardon, B. M. G. *Religious Thought in the Nineteenth Century.* London: Cambridge University Press, 1966.

Reuther, Rosemary Radford, and Rosemary Keller, eds. *Women and Religion in America,* vol. 1: *The Nineteenth Century.* New York: Harper and Row, 1981.

Reznikoff, Charles, and Uriah Z. Engleman. *The Jews of Charleston.* Philadelphia: Jewish Publication Society, 1950.

Richardson, Edgar P. "The Athens of America, 1800–1825." In *Philadelphia: A Three Hundred Year History,* ed. Russell Weigley, 208–57. New York: Norton, 1982.

Rogow, Faith. *Gone to Another Meeting: The National Council of Jewish Women, 1893–1993.* Tuscaloosa: Alabama University Press, 1994.

Rosenbach, Hyman Polock. *The Jews of Philadelphia Prior to 1800.* Philadelphia, 1887.

Rosenberg, Charles. *The Cholera Years.* Chicago: University of Chicago Press, 1974.

———. "The Therapeutic Revolution: Medicine, Meaning, and Social Change in Nineteenth Century America." In *The Therapeutic Revolution,* ed. Morris Vogel and Charles Rosenberg, 3–26. Philadelphia: University of Pennsylvania Press, 1979.

Rosenberg, Charles, and Carroll Smith-Rosenberg. "The Female Animal: Medicine and Biological Views of Woman and Her Role in Nineteenth-Century America." *Journal of American History* 60 (1973): 332–56.

Rosenbloom, Joseph. "Rebecca Gratz and the Jewish Sunday School Movement in Philadelphia." *Publications of the American Jewish Historical Society* 47, no. 2 (1958): 71–75.

Rosenwaike, Ira. *On the Edge of Greatness: A Portrait of American Jewry in the Early National Period.* Cincinnati: American Jewish Archives, 1985.

Rothman, David. *The Discovery of the Asylum: Social Order and Disorder in the New Republic.* New York: Little, Brown, 1990.

Royce, Anya Peterson. *Ethnic Identity: Strategies of Diversity.* Bloomington: Indiana University Press, 1982.

Ryan, Mary P. *The Empire of the Mother: American Writing about Domesticity, 1830–1860.* New York: Harrington Park Press, 1985.

Sarna, Jonathan D. "The American Jewish Response to Nineteenth-Century Christian Missions." *Journal of American History* 68 (1981): 35–51.

———. "From Immigrants to Ethnics: Toward a New Theory of Ethnicization." *Ethnicity* 5 (1978): 370–78.

———. "The American Jewish Response to Nineteenth-Century Christian Missions." *Journal of American History* 68, no. 1 (June 1981): 35–51.

———. *Jacksonian Jew: The Two Worlds of Mordecai Manuel Noah.* New York: Holmes and Meier, 1981.

———. *JPS: The Americanization of Jewish Culture, 1888–1988.* Philadelphia: Jewish Publication Society, 1989.

———. "The Mythical Jew and the Jew Next Door." In *Anti-Semitism in America,* ed. David A. Gerber, 57–78. Bloomington: Indiana University Press, 1987.

———, ed. *The American Jewish Experience.* New York: Holmes and Meier, 1986.

———, ed. *People Walk on Their Heads.* New York: Holmes and Meier, 1981.

Saum, Lewis. *The Popular Mood of Pre–Civil War America.* Westport, Conn.: Greenwood Press, 1980.

Schorsch, Ismar. "The Myth of Sephardic Supremacy." *Leo Baeck Institute Yearbook* 34 (1989): 47–66.

Scott, Anne Firor. *Natural Allies: Women's Associations in American History.* Chicago: University of Illinois Press, 1991.

Sered, Susan Starr. *Women as Ritual Experts: The Religious Lives of Elderly Jewish Women in Jerusalem.* New York: Oxford University Press, 1992.

Shryock, Richard Harrison. *Medicine in America: Historical Essays.* Baltimore: Johns Hopkins University Press, 1966.

Singerman, Robert. "The American Jewish Press, 1823–1983: A Bibliographic Survey of Research and Studies." *American Jewish Historical Quarterly* 73 (1984): 4–27.

Sizer, Sandra. "Politics and Apolitical Religion: The Great Urban Revivals of Late Nineteenth Century." *Church History* 48, no. 1 (1979): 81–99.

Sklar, Katherine Kish. *Catherine Beecher: A Study in American Domesticity.* New York: Norton, 1973.

Smith, Daniel Scott. "Family Limitation, Sexual Control, and Domestic Feminism in Victorian America." In *Clio's Consciousness Raised,* ed. Mary Hartman and Lois Banner, 119–36. New York: Harper, 1974.

Smith, Thelma. "Feminism in Philadelphia, 1790–1850." *Pennsylvania Magazine of History and Biography* 68 (1944): 250–60.

Smith-Rosenberg, Carroll. *Disorderly Conduct: Visions of Gender in Victorian America.* New York: Knopf, 1985.

———. "The Female World of Love and Ritual: Relations between Women in Nineteenth-Century America." *Signs* 1, no. 1 (1975): 1–30.

Sobel, B. Z. "Legitimation and Antisemitism as Factors in the Functioning of a Hebrew-Christian Mission." *Jewish Social Studies* 23, no. 3 (1961): 170–86.

Sproat, John. *The Best Men: Liberal Reformers in the Gilded Age.* Chicago: University of Chicago Press, 1982.

Stansell, Christine. *City of Women: Sex and Class in New York City, 1789–1860.* Urbana: University of Illinois Press, 1987.

Starr, Paul. *The Social Transformation of American Medicine.* New York: Basic Books, 1982.

Stern, Malcolm. *First American Jewish Families: Six Hundred Genealogies.* Detroit: American Jewish Archives/American Jewish Historical Society, 1978.

———. "Jewish Marriage and Intermarriage in the Federal Period (1776–1840)." *American Jewish Archives* 19, no. 2 (1967): 140–43.

Sussman, Lance. "Another Look at Isaac Leeser and the First Jewish Translation of the Bible in the United States." *Modern Judaism* 5, no. 2 (1985): 159–90.

———. *Isaac Leeser and the Making of American Judaism.* Detroit: Wayne State University Press, 1995.

———. "Isaac Leeser and the Philadelphia Pattern." In *Jewish Life in Philadelphia, 1830–1940,* ed. Murray Friedman, 22–34. Philadelphia: ISHI Press, 1983.

Todes, David Uriah. "The History of Jewish Education in Philadelphia, 1782–1873: From the Erection of the First Synagogue to the Closing of Maimonides College." Ph.D. thesis, Dropsie College for Hebrew and Cognate Learning, 1952.

Toll, Jean Barth, and Mildred S. Gillam. *Invisible Philadelphia: Community through Voluntary Associations.* Philadelphia: Atwater Kent Museum, 1995.

Tompkins, Jane. "Sentimental Power: *Uncle Tom's Cabin* and the Politics of Literary History." *Glyph* 8 (1981): 79–102.

Umansky, Ellen M. *Lily Montague and the Advancement of Liberal Judaism: From Vision to Vocation.* Lewiston, New York: Edwin Mellen Press, 1983.

Wainwright, Nicholas B. "The Age of Nicholas Biddle." In *Philadelphia: A Three Hundred Year History,* ed. Russell Weigley, 258–306. New York: Norton, 1982.

Warner, Sam Bass, Jr. *The Private City: Philadelphia in Three Periods of Its Growth.* Philadelphia: University of Pennsylvania Press, 1968.

Webber, Jonathan. "Between Law and Custom: Women's Experience of Judaism." In *Women's Religious Experience: Cross Cultural Perspectives,* ed. Pat Holden, 143–62. London: Croom Helm, 1983.

Weigley, Russell, ed. *Philadelphia: A Three Hundred Year History.* New York: Norton, 1982.

Weissler, Chava. "Tkhinnes of the Matriarchs." In *Four Centuries of Jewish Women's Spirituality,* ed. Ellen M. Umansky and Dianne Ashton, 51–55. Boston: Beacon Press, 1992.

———. "The Traditional Piety of Ashkenazic Women." In *Jewish Spirituality from the Sixteenth-Century Revival to the Present,* ed. Arthur Green, 245–82. New York: Crossroads Press, 1989.

Wells, Robert V. "Family Size and Fertility Control in Eighteenth-Century America: A Study of Quaker Families." *Population Studies* 25, no. 1 (1971): 73–82.

Welter, Barbara. "The Feminization of American Religion: 1800–1860." In *Dimity Convictions: The American Woman in the Nineteenth Century,* ed. Welter, 83–102. Athens: Ohio University Press, 1976.

———. "She Hath Done What She Could: Protestant Women's Missionary Careers in Nineteenth-Century America." In *Women in American Religion,* ed. Janet Wilson James, 111–25. Philadelphia: University of Pennsylvania Press, 1980.

Wharton, Thomas I. *The Lives of Eminent Philadelphians.* Philadelphia: Simpson, 1859.

Whiteman, Maxwell. "The Legacy of Isaac Leeser." In *Jewish Life in Philadelphia, 1830–1940,* ed. Murray Friedman, 26–47. Philadelphia: ISHI Press, 1983.

———. "The Philadelphia Group." In *Jewish Life in Philadelphia, 1830–1940,* ed. Murray Friedman, 163–78. Philadelphia: ISHI Press, 1983.

Wilson, George. *Stephen Girard: The Life and Times of America's First Tycoon.* Conshohocken, Pa.: Combined Press, 1995.

Wolf, Edwin, II. *The Book Culture of a Colonial American City: Philadelphia Books, Bookmen, and Booksellers.* New York: Oxford University Press, 1988.

Wolf, Edwin, II, and Maxwell Whiteman. *The History of the Jews of Philadelphia from Colonial Times to the Age of Jackson.* Philadelphia: Jewish Publication Society, 1957.

Young, Crawford. *The Politics of Cultural Pluralism.* Madison: University of Wisconsin Press, 1976.

Zatlin, Linda. *The Nineteenth-Century Anglo-Jewish Novel.* Boston: Twayne, 1981.

INDEX

BOOKS IN THE AMERICAN JEWISH CIVILIZATION SERIES

DATE DUE		
DEC 1 4 200		